DESCRIPTIVE
ITALIAN GRAMMAR

CORNELL ROMANCE STUDIES: VOLUME II

DESCRIPTIVE ITALIAN GRAMMAR

By ROBERT A. HALL Jr.

Associate Professor of Linguistics
Cornell University

PUBLISHED BY

CORNELL UNIVERSITY PRESS AND
LINGUISTIC SOCIETY OF AMERICA

ITHACA, NEW YORK * 1948

Copyright 1948 by Cornell University

Cornell University Press

London: Geoffrey Cumberlege

Oxford University Press

PRINTED IN THE UNITED STATES OF AMERICA BY
THE WAVERLY PRESS, INC., BALTIMORE, MARYLAND

The publication of this volume has been aided by a
grant from the American Council of Learned Societies

To HILDA NORMAN BARNARD

TABLE OF CONTENTS

0. INTRODUCTION

0.0. PURPOSE AND SCOPE. The purpose of this book is to give a description of present-day standard Italian, using the techniques of analysis and description developed by modern linguistics. The language described is that of everyday conversation and non-belletristic prose of the first half of the twentieth century; literary and archaic features are discussed only incidentally and with no attempt at completeness. The chief source of examples, outside of everyday speech, has been Collodi's Avventure di Pinocchio, a book notable for its easy, natural, colloquial style.

It is hoped to supplement this work at a later date by an Italian Lexicon, which will list all the morphemes of Italian with cross-references to the grammar, and which will thus serve, in a way, as an index to this book.

0.01. DESCRIPTIVE LINGUISTICS, as applied to any given language, has as its basic aim the description of the structure of that language, as spoken at a given point of time. By its nature, it treats of writing ('the written language') and of historical development of language only incidentally.

The essential aspects under which linguistic structure is to be analyzed are 1) PHONOLOGY, or the study of sounds; 2) MORPHOLOGY, or the study of minimum forms; and 3) SYNTAX, or the study of combinations of minimum forms in utterances. Phonological analysis is based first of all on the description and classification of speech-sounds as such, in the study of PHONETICS, and then upon the determination of significant classes of speech-sounds or PHONEMES, in the study of PHONEMICS. Morphological analysis studies meaningful combinations of phonemes, or LINGUISTIC FORMS, and establishes the classes of minimum forms (MORPHEMES) and their relations to each other in INFLECTION and DERIVATION. Syntactic analysis treats of the patterns in which forms of various form-classes are combined in utterances (PHRASES, CLAUSES) and analyzes these patterns of combination into their constituent elements.

For each of the stages of descriptive linguistics, special terminology and symbolism are current. To describe and represent the sounds of a language, special symbols (PHONETIC symbols) are used, which stand in a one-to-one relation with the sounds represented; for representing the phonemes of a language, PHONEMIC symbols, likewise in a one-to-one relation to the phonemes for which they stand, are used. The use of phonetic and phonemic transcription permits of accurate and unambiguous reference to sounds and phonemes (usually more complete and economical than the corresponding conventional spelling would afford), and in this respect is comparable to the use of clearly and consistently defined symbols in mathematics or chemistry. Phonemic transcription affords the simplest and clearest symbolization of the significant features of sound of a language, and hence is the best base on which to build up further description of morphology and syntax, much as chemical formulae are built with symbols for elements, valency, etc.

In this description of Italian linguistic structure, full use is made of current terminology and symbolism. For a fuller description of typographical conventions and special signs, see §§0.22 and 1.6; for brief definitions of phonetic and phonemic symbols and of technical terms, see the Glossary of Technical Terms (pp. 224–228).

0.1. THE ITALIAN LANGUAGE is spoken, in Italy, in most of the area included within the current political boundaries (1947), the chief non-Italian linguistic areas being those of Provençal in Piedmont, of German in the Tyrol, and of Albanian and Greek in Southern Italy. Outside of Italy there are, in Europe, areas of Italian speech in Venezia Giulia, the Canton Ticino of Switzerland, Corsica, and southern France; and there are substantial groups of emigrants among whom Italian (mostly dialectal) is spoken in North and South America, especially in the United States, Brazil and Argentina. The approximate number of speakers of Italian is given as 43,700,000.[1]

0.11. THE ITALIAN DIALECTS fall into two main groups: North Italian and Central-South Italian. These two areas are separated by a large bundle of isoglosses running roughly east and west from the vicinity of La Spezia on the Tyrrhenian to Rimini on the Adriatic. Among the North Italian dialects, the major divisions are:

1. Piedmontese, spoken in Piedmont.
2. Lombard, spoken in Lombardy and the Canton Ticino.
3. Ligurian, spoken in Liguria and along the Tyrrhenian coast to the transitional zone of Lunigiana in the vicinity of La Spezia.
4. Venetian, spoken in the Tre Venezie, and including the dialects of the mainland and that of the city of Venice.
5. Emilian, spoken in Emilia and Romagna.

The Central Italian dialects include:

6. Marchigiano, spoken in the Marche.
7. Tuscan, spoken in Tuscany and on adjacent islands in the Tyrrhenian, including Corsica.
8. Umbrian, spoken in Umbria.
9. The dialects of Lazio and of the city of Rome. The two last-mentioned groups form a zone of transition between the dialects of Central Italy and those of Southern Italy, along a very wide and flaring bundle of isoglosses whose main axis extends north and south from Rome near the Tyrrhenian to Ancona on the Adriatic.

The South Italian dialects include:

10. Campanian and Neapolitan, spoken in Naples and surrounding territory.
11. Abruzzese, spoken in the Abruzzi.
12. Apulian, spoken in Apulia.
13. The dialects of the Basilicata and Lucania.
14. Calabrian, spoken in Calabria.
15. Sicilian, spoken in Sicily.

0.12. STANDARD ITALIAN is based, in its historical origin and its phonological and morphological correspondences, on archaic (thirteenth and fourteenth century) Tuscan, more specifically Florentine, with a considerable admixture of

[1] World Almanac 347 (New York, 1947).

non-Tuscan features and not showing certain features of the modern Tuscan vernacular. Among the most markedly Tuscan characteristics of Standard Italian are:

1. Diphthongization of Proto-Romance /e o/ in stressed free syllables, without umlauting effect of final vowels such as is found in North and South Italian dialects: e.g. It. buóno *good* < PRom. *bónu; It. piéde *foot* <PRom. *péde.

2. The development, before vowel, of It. unstressed /i/ < PRom. /ri/: e.g. It. áia *threshing floor* < PRom. *ária; It. kuóio *leather* < PRom. kóriu; It. ⁺áio *-arian, worker in or connected with* . . . < PRom. ⁺áriu.

3. The use of the 1. pl. suffix -iámo in Present A (traditionally known as the 'present indicative') of all conjugations, replacing archaic and dialectal -ámo (Conjugation I) -émo (Conj. III and most of IV) -ímo (Conj. II) < PRom. *-ámus -éʌmus -íʌmus: e.g. kantiámo *we sing*:dial. kantámo < PRom. *kantámus; prɛndiámo *we take*:dial. prɛndémo < PRom. *preʌndéʌmus; dɔrmiámo *we sleep*:dial. dɔrmímo < PRom. *dormíʌmus.

At present, regional varieties of Standard Italian are forming themselves, with a certain reflection of the phonemic structure of the local dialects: for instance, North Italians (in whose local dialects no double consonants occur), although observing the phonemic distinction between single and double consonants, often omit the doubling of word-initial consonants following the final vowel of certain preceding elements (/ˣ/; §1.622); Romans, in whose local dialect many words have double consonants following the stress where the corresponding word in Tuscan has a single consonant, often carry this pronunciation over into Standard Italian, e.g. tɛrríbbile *terrible*:Tuscan tɛrríbile; róbba *stuff*:Tuscan róba.

0.13. CHARACTERISTICS. In comparison with 'Standard Average European',[2] Standard Italian has a fairly simple phonology, with seven vowel and twenty consonant phonemes, three levels of significant stress, and four main phrasal pitch-contours. Alternations of phonemes in inflection and derivation are not frequent, and are rather scattered in their distribution; only a few are frequent enough to require special symbolization (§1.6).

Italian inflection shows four main form-classes: substantives, pronouns, verbs, and indeclinables. Substantives are further divided into adjectives and nouns; pronouns, into personal, demonstrative, interrogative, relative and indefinite; and indeclinables, by virtue of their syntactic functions, into adverbs and introductory elements: prepositions, connectives, coordinators and subordinators. The grammatical categories of Italian inflection are: number (singular and plural), present in all inflected forms; gender (feminine and masculine, i.e. non-feminine) in substantives and pronouns; case (nominative, oblique, dative and prepositional) in pronouns; person (1., 2., 3.) in personal pronouns and verbs; and tense (present, past, timeless ['subjunctive'] and imperative) in verbs. Substantive inflection is simple, with few irregularities; pronoun inflection is complicated and idiosyncratic, but not extensive; and verb inflection is fairly complicated and quite extensive. The normal Italian verb is

[2] Cf. Benjamin Lee Whorf, in Language Culture and Personality 78 ff. (Menasha, 1941).

built on a root, from which three stems are derived; on each stem are built two or more finite tenses (each, except in the imperative, consisting of six forms, distinguishing three persons and two numbers) and one or more non-finite forms. There are four main conjugations of verbs, characterized by different stem-vowels: /a/, /i/, /e/ and zero; and a number of verb roots show irregularities in the formation of one or more of the three stems.

Derivation of inflected forms in Italian is accomplished by affixation (suffixation and prefixation) and compounding. Italian derivation is relatively regular, at least in comparison with the extreme irregularity of derivation in English or French; even so, it is quite complex, with a number of irregularities in the bases from which forms are derived, and in pre-suffixal elements. The number of prefixes and suffixes is large, and their distribution both widespread and scattered. Some derivational affixes occur only in one or two forms, others may be added to almost any base, necessitating far greater space devoted to their enumeration and exemplification than is customary in descriptive or historical grammars. Compounding is not widespread, and is limited to certain types, only a few of which are productive. The sources of Italian vocabulary and derivation are further increased by the widespread practice of borrowing from Latin almost at will, with a minimum of adaptation (cf. Appendix, Chapter 8, The Treatment of Latin Loan-Words in Italian).

Syntax is, in general, similar to that of other West European languages. Phrases composed of two or more morphemes occur taking the place of single inflectional elements, and single free morphemes and phrases are combined into utterances. The favorite type of utterance, or major clause, is that containing a verbal form as the center of the predicate, which may or may not be accompanied by a subject further specifying the agent beyond the indication of person and number given by the verbal form. Other types of utterance (minor clauses), particularly individual free morphemes and non-verbal phrases, occur frequently, particularly in conversation.

0.2. ANALYSIS AND PRESENTATION.

0.21. DESCRIPTIVE TECHNIQUE is that of a purely synchronic, analytical grammar. Historical considerations have been taken into account but sparingly, and only where they could cast light on otherwise doubtful points of analysis. Every attempt has been made to describe Italian in terms of its own inherent linguistic structure, not that of Latin, English or any other language. All Italian forms are cited exclusively in phonemic transcription; Italian conventional orthography is used only in occasional obiter dicta and in the Appendix, Chapter 6 (Italian Orthography).

The sequence of divisions in the grammar follows the order of increasing complexity in the material described, with three major subdivisions: Sounds, Forms, Utterances. In the first part are described the sounds of Italian and their patterning, in terms of significant units of sound or PHONEMES. In the second are described the minimum linguistic forms of the language and their partial similarities to each other, in terms of the classes into which the forms fall (form-classes or INFLECTION) and of the processes by which forms of each class are derived from those of others (DERIVATION). In the third part are described the groupings into which linguistic forms are combined, first the smaller combinations (PHRASES) which take the place of single forms and then the larger combinations (CLAUSES) into which phrases are joined and which are the normal units of utterance in ordinary speech.

0.22. TERMINOLOGY AND TYPOGRAPHICAL CONVENTIONS. The terminology used is that of present-day linguistic analysis, particularly as developed in Bloomfield, Language (New York, 1933). Wherever possible, traditional terms such as 'feminine' and 'masculine' have been retained, if necessary with some re-definition; on the other hand, misleading traditional terms such as 'subjunctive' or 'mood' have been discarded wherever it seemed desirable to do so.

Typographical style is, in general, that prescribed in Bulletin 14.3–9 (1941) of the Linguistic Society of America; but Italian and Latin linguistic forms are cited in roman type, and English glosses or Italian conventional spelling in italics. When two glosses (Italian orthography and English meaning) are given in succession, the first is in italics and the second in roman type enclosed in quotation marks; for examples, see chapter 6. Phonetic transcriptions are given in IPA (International Phonetic Alphabet) characters, enclosed in square brackets; phonemic transcriptions are normally not enclosed, but are placed between slant lines wherever necessary for clarity.

Abbreviations are those customary in grammatical discussion. The following signs are used with special meanings:

< 'replacing' (descriptively) or 'developing from' (historically).

> 'replaced by' (descriptively) or 'developing into' (historically).

~ 'alternating with'.

: not preceded or followed by space, 'related to' or 'derived from'.

- (hyphen) indicates syllable division in phonetic transcription (enclosed in square brackets); in phonemic transcription, it indicates that the form it precedes or follows is inflectionally bound (§2.02).

⁺ indicates that the form it precedes or follows is derivationally bound.

⌒ indicates that the form it precedes or follows is clausally bound.

The meaning of special symbols for alternations of phonemes is explained in §1.6.

0.3. ACKNOWLEDGMENTS are due to the following:

1. Informants, who served as subjects of observation, here listed with their place of origin in Italy: Giorgio Ausenda (Milan); Mrs. Anna Maria Cady (Naples); Mrs. Bianca Maria Calabresi (Bologna); Mrs. Pierina Castiglione (Florence); Vincenzo Cióffari (Calitri); Giacomo Francesco Mormile (Piedimonte d'Alife); Renato Poggioli (Florence); Mrs. Renata Poggioli-Nordio (Venice); and Mrs. Luciana Sacerdote (Turin), in addition to many other Italians whose speech I had the opportunity of observing to a greater or lesser extent in Italy (1930, 1933–4, 1939) and in the United States.

2. Critics who have discussed points of analysis, either during the process of analysis and formulation or after the publication of resultant articles whose substance has been re-worked and included in this book: especially Professors Bernard Bloch, Leonard Bloomfield, Charles F. Hockett and Henry R. Kahane.

3. The editors of Italica and Language, for permission to use the substance of articles which originally appeared in those journals.[3]

4. My predecessors in the field of Italian descriptive grammar, from Bembo to Migliorini; and especially to R. Fornaciari's Grammatica della Lingua Italiana and B. Migliorini's La Lingua Nazionale, from which a number of examples have been used by permission of the author. The material in Cappuccini-Migliorini, Vocabolario della Lingua Italiana (Torino, 1945), has been worked through from beginning to end for the analysis of derivation in Chapter 3.

5. D. C. Heath and Co., for permission to use material from and give references to their edition of Le Avventure di Pinocchio (edited by Prof. Emilio Goggio; Boston, 1932).

6. The American Council of Learned Societies, for a generous grant-in-aid in support of the publication of this work, and Professor J Milton Cowan and the Standing Committee on Research of the Linguistic Society of America, and Professors Morris G. Bishop and Thomas G. Bergin, for their kind assistance in furthering its publication.

[3] 'Italian Phonemes and Orthography', Italica 21.70–80 (1944); 'Italian Inflection', Language 20.11–20 (1944).

PART I. SOUNDS

CHAPTER I. PHONOLOGY

1.1. THE PHONEMES of Italian are of four types: LINEAR phonemes, all of whose components are of one-phoneme length; phonemes of JUNCTURE, whose components extend over more than one phoneme; phonemes of STRESS, whose domain is a single syllable; and phonemes of PITCH-CONTOUR, whose domain is a sequence of syllables.

1.11. LINEAR PHONEMES are twenty-seven in number, and include:

1.111. VOWELS. In these, the determining features are: 1) VERTICAL tongue-position, with contrast between a) high, b) close-mid, c) open-mid, and d) low; and 2) HORIZONTAL position, with contrast between a) front (unrounded) and b) back (rounded). These contrasting features are combined in seven vowel phonemes. Table Ia shows, in a two-dimensional diagram, the vowel phonemes of Italian; contrast in height of tongue-position is shown in vertical columns, and that between front and back position in horizontal planes. The low vowel /a/ is indifferent as to front or back tongue-position.

Of the individual vowel phonemes, /i/ and /u/ have as positional variants or allophones the following:

1. Homorganic semi-consonant ([j] and [w] respectively, unstressed before vowels: iéri *yesterday* ['jɛ:-ri]; kiáma *he calls* ['kja:-ma]; buóno *good* ['bwɔ:-no].

2. Homorganic semi-vowel ([i̯] and [u̯] respectively), unstressed after vowels: fái *thou dost* ['fai̯]; káusa *cause* ['kau̯-sa], ['kau̯-za].

3. Full vowel ([i] and [u] respectively), stressed and unstressed elsewhere: finíre *to finish* [fi-'ni:-re]; uníto *united* [u-'ni:-to]; bútto *I throw* ['but-to]; múlo *mule* ['mu:-lo].

The other vowels have, as their unique allophones, the full vowel sounds, stressed and unstressed:

/e/: séta *silk* ['se:-ta]; métte *he puts* ['met-te].

/ɛ/: béne *well* ['bɛ:-ne]; sétte *seven* ['sɛt-te]; servíre *to serve* [sɛr-'vi:-re].

/a/: kása *house* ['ka:-sa]; mátto *crazy* ['mat-to].

/ɔ/: buóno *good* ['bwɔ:-no]; kótto *cooked* ['kɔt-to]; dormíre *to sleep* [dɔr-'mi:-re].

/o/: kóme *how* ['ko:-me]; prodótto *product* [pro-'dot-to].

The vowel /ø/ occurs in the minor-clause form pø' ['pø] *pooh!*.

1.112. CONSONANTS have as their determining features: 1) POSITION of articulation; 2) MANNER of articulation; and 3) VOICING. In the position of articulation, contrast exists between: a) labial (in stops and nasals) or labio-dental (in fricatives); b) apical-dental; c) dorsal-velar (in stops) or frontal-palatal (in other manners of articulation). Contrasting manners of articulation are: a) plosive; b) fricative (in labio-dental position) or assibilate (in dental and palatal positions); c) nasal; d) sibilant; e) lateral; and f) trill. In voicing, there is contrast between a) voiced and b) unvoiced phonemes. These features are combined in the twenty consonant phonemes shown schematically in Table Ib. In the three dimensions of this diagram, contrasts of manner of ar-

7

ticulation are shown in vertical columns; those of position, in horizontal planes from left to right; and those of voicing, in horizontal planes from foreground to background. Labial or labio-dental articulation is found only in plosives, fricatives and nasals; palatal or velar articulation, in all manners of articulation except trills. Contrast in voicing is present only in plosives, fricatives and assibilates.

Phonetically, all unvoiced sounds are fortis, all voiced sounds lenis. Plosives are unaspirated.

TABLE I(a)
ITALIAN VOWEL PHONEMES

	Front		Back
High	i		u
High-Mid	e		o
Low-Mid	ε		ɔ
Low		a	

TABLE I(b)
ITALIAN CONSONANT PHONEMES

	Labial and Labio-Dental	Dental	Palatal and Velar
Plosive	p	t	k
	b	d	g
Fricative or Assibilate	f	c	č
	v	ʑ	ǧ
Nasal	m	n	ɲ
Sibilant		s	š
Lateral		l	ʎ
Trill		r	

Under the individual consonant phonemes are subsumed the following allophones:

1. Plosives: /p b t d/ have as their only allophones the unvoiced and voiced plosive sounds [p] [b] [t] [d] respectively: pépe *pepper* ['pe:-pe]; káppa *cape* ['kap-pa]; bábbo *father* ['bab-bo]; tútto *all* ['tut-to]; káde *falls* ['ka:-de]; kádde *fell* ['kad-de]. /k g/ are pre-velar [k̓] [ĝ] before front vowels, medio-velar [k] [g] elsewhere: kéto *quiet* ['k̓e:-to]; kása *house* ['ka:-sa]; girlánda *garland* [ĝir-'lanⁿ-da]; góla *throat* ['go:-la].[1]

2. Fricatives and Assibilates: /f v/ have [f] [v] as their unique allophones: fátto *done* ['fat-to]; báffi *moustache* ['baf-fi]; vánno *they go* ['van-no]; dóve *where* ['do:-ve]. /c ʑ/ are [tˢ] [dᶻ], i.e. [t] and [d] with sibilant release: cío *uncle* ['tˢi:-o];

---

[1] In Tuscany, the unvoiced stop phonemes have unvoiced fricatives as allophones when single in intervocalic position: kápo *head* ['ka:-ɸo]; dáto *given* ['da:-θo]; lakása *the house* [la-'χa:-sa], [la-'ha:-sa].

grácie *thanks* ['gra:-tˢje]; mécco *overripe* ['met-tˢo]; ʒélo *zeal* ['dᶻɛ:-lo]; méʒʒo *half* ['mɛd-dᶻo]. /č ǧ/ are [tˢ] [dᶾ], i.e. palatal occlusives with sibilant release: čínkue *five* ['tˢiŋᵛ-kwe]; káčo *cheese* ['ka:-tˢo]; káččo *I chase* ['kat-tˢo]; ǧénte *people* ['dᶾɛnⁿ-te]; áǧo *ease* ['a:-dᶾo]; máǧǧo *May* ['mad-dᶾo].[2]

3. Nasals: /m ɲ/ have the voiced nasal continuants [m] and [ɲ], respectively, as their only allophones: máno *hand* ['ma:-no]; mámma ['mam-ma] *mother*; ɲókki *gnocchi* ['ɲɔk-ǩi]; báɲɲo *bath* ['baɲ-ɲo]. /n/ has the following allophones:

a. [ɱ] (labio-dental nasal) before /f v/: infátti *in fact* [im-'fat-ti]; invásione *invasion* [iɱ-va-'zjo:-ne].

b. [ŋ] (velar nasal) before /k g/: báŋka *bank* ['baŋᵛ-ka]; ráŋgo rank ['raŋᵛ-go].

c. [n] elsewhere: nónno *grandfather* ['nɔn-no]; dénte *tooth* ['dɛnⁿ-te]; dénso *dense* ['dɛnⁿ-so]; guánča *cheek* ['gwanⁿ-tˢa].

4. Sibilants: /š/ has the palatal unvoiced sibilant [š] as its only allophone: šáme *swarm* ['ša:-me]; lášša *leaves* ['laš-ša]. /s/ has the following allophones:

a. [z] before voiced consonants: sdéɲɲo *disdain* ['zdeɲ-ɲo]; ásma *asthma* ['azᶻ-ma].

b. [s] in word-initial position except before voiced consonants, and in medial position except before voiced consonants or intervocalically sóno *I am* ['so:-no]; stánko *tired* ['staŋᵛ-ko]; kásto *chaste* ['kasˢ-to]; kássa *chest* ['kas-sa]; pólso *wrist* ['pol-so].

c. [s] and [z] in free alternation (regional[3]) in intervocalic position: kása *house* ['ka:-sa], ['ka:-za]; sposáre *to marry* [spo-'sa:-re], [spo-'za:-re].

5. Laterals: /l/ and /ʎ/ each have the voiced dental and palatal laterals [l] and [ʎ], respectively, as their only allophones: mále *badly* ['ma:-le]; ǧállo *yellow* ['dᶾal-lo]; káldo *hot* ['kalˡ-do]; fíʎʎo *son* ['fiʎ-ʎo].

6. Trill: /r/ has [r] (voiced dental flap or trill[4]) as its normal single allophone: rósso *red* ['ros-so]; káro *dear* ['ka:-ro]; kárro *car* ['kar-ro]; kárta *paper* ['karʳ-ta].

The sounds [j] and [w] are allophones of /i/ and /u/ respectively (cf. §1.111).

[2] In Central Italy, the occlusive element in these phonemes is not present and the palatal sibilant element is pronounced alone, but with lenis articulation, when they occur single in intervocalic position: káčo *cheese* ['ka:-ṣo]; áǧo *ease* ['a-ẓo]. Speakers from other parts of Italy often hear and imitate Central Italian [ṣ] as a fortis palatal sibilant [š]: ['ka:-šo].

The extensive and often acrimonious debate as to the PHONETIC nature of the assibilates, whether they be single or compound consonant sounds, does not affect their phonemic interpretation, which can only be as unitary phonemes.

[3] As there is no case of minimal contrast between [s] and [z], these two sounds must be grouped together under the same phoneme, and varying according to regions: [s] in Southern Italy (['ka:-sa], [spo-'sa:-re]); [z] in Northern Italy (['ka:-za], [spo-'za:-re]); and both, in different words (but often varying from one speaker or one district to another) in Central Italy: (['ka:-sa], but [spo-'za:-re]). For those North Italian speakers who do not have double consonant clusters in standard Italian (§1.222.2), [z] comes to be in contrast with [s] and hence to be a distinct phoneme: káza *house* ['ka-za] vs. kása *chest* ['ka-sa]; cf. Migliorini, Pronunzia fiorentina o pronunzia romana 69–70.

[4] Other types of articulation occur in some speakers' usage, e.g. retroflex apical flap or trill, uvular spirant or trill, etc.; the latter is primarily an urban phenomenon, usually considered a Gallicism.

All consonants occur in geminate clusters, which are phonetically long consonants, with 'hold' 1½ to 2 times as long as is normal for a single consonant; after a stressed vowel, the 'hold' is longer than elsewhere.[5] The consonants /š ʎ ɲ/ occur only double in the interior of a word.[6]

1.2. THE SYLLABLE comprises one or more phonemes, uttered normally on a single chest-impulse. The center, or highest point of sonority, of a syllable is normally a vowel, diphthong or triphthong (as defined in §1.21); in a few minor-clause forms, the center of the syllable is a consonant, e.g. /s/ in pśt *pst!*. In the following discussion, V = any vowel; V̂ = any stressed vowel; C = any consonant.

1.21. OCCURRENCE OF VOWELS in the syllable is as follows:

1.211. MONOPHTHONGS: V̂ or V: eočéniko *Eocenic* [e-o-'tˢɛ:-ni-ko].

1.212. DIPHTHONGS, consisting of one V or V̂ and the other V, unstressed, /i/ or /u/:

1. VV̂: biánko *white* ['bjaŋᵖ-ko].
2. V̂V: pói *then* ['pɔi].
3. VV: stipéndio *stipend* [sti-'penⁿ-djo]. If both unstressed vowels are of the same quality (usually /ii/) they normally fuse into a single long, unstressed vowel sound: stipéndii *stipends* [sti-'penⁿ-di:].

Under other conditions than those described in the three preceding paragraphs, V + V form two separate syllables, phonetically and phonemically: pío *pious* ['pi:-o]; dúe *two* ['du:-e]; čenčaiuólo *ragman* [tˢɛnⁿ-tˢai̯-'wɔ:-lo].

1.213. TRIPHTHONGS: VV̂V, the unstressed V being /i/ or /u/: buói *oxen* ['bwɔi̯]; miéi *mine* ['mjɛi̯].

1.22. OCCURRENCE OF CONSONANTS is as follows:

1.221. SYLLABLE-INITIAL, i.e. preceding the center of the syllable:

1. C: any consonant: šáme *swarm* ['ša:-me]; ʎi- *to him* [ʎi]; ɲókki *gnocchi* ['ɲɔk-ki].
2. CC:

a. /s/ + any stop, fricative, or /m n ǧ l/ (only in word-initial position): spavénto *fright* [spa-'venⁿ-to]; sǧeláre *to unfreeze* [zdᶻɛ-'la:-re]; slítta *sled* ['zlit-ta].

b. Plosive or /f/ + /r/: prímo *first* ['pri:-mo]; frána *landslide* ['fra:-na].

c. Plosive or /f/ or /v/ + /l/: plátano *plane-tree* ['pla:-ta-no].

d. /p/ + /n/:[7] pneumátiko *pneumatic* [pneu-'ma:-ti-ko].

---

[5] For statistical data on long consonants in Italian, cf. Josselyn, Etude sur la phonétique italienne, ch. X, and Metz. Ein experimentell-phonetischer Beitrag zur Untersuchung der italienischen Konsonantengemination.

[6] Panconcelli-Calzia (Italiano 11) states that /c/ and /ʒ/ are also 'per loro natura lunghe'; but this is certainly not so, in view of such words as grátie *thank you* ['gra:-tˢ je], in which the [tˢ] is short and the stressed vowel is long, the normal situation with a stressed vowel before a short consonant. But even if /š ʎ ɲ/ occur only long in the interior of a word, that is no reason for regarding them as functionally single, as does Porru (TCLP 8.207) in order to follow a pre-established pattern.

[7] These combinations occur only in learned words. In popular pronunciation, a group consisting of stop + stop or nasal, or of nasal + nasal, is replaced by the double consonant of the order of the second stop or nasal in the cluster: thus pragmátiko is replaced by prammátiko, etc.

e. /m/ + /n/:[7] mnɛmóniko *mnemonic* [mnɛ-'mɔ:-ni-ko].

f. /t/ + /m/:[7] tmési *tmesis* ['tme:-si].

g. /p/ + /s/:[7] psɛudo- *pseudo-* ['psɛu̯-do].

3. CCC (only in word initial position): /s/ +:

a. plosive or /f/ + /r/: spreǧáre *to despise* [spre-'dˣa:-re]; sdraiáre *to stretch out* [zdra-'ja:-re]; sfruttáre *to exploit* [sfrut-'ta:-re].

b. /p/ or /k/ + /l/:[7] sklerósi *sclerosis* [skle-'rɔ:-si].

1.222. SYLLABLE-FINAL, i.e. following the center of the syllable:

1. Before disjuncture [§1.42], any plosive, nasal, fricative, or dental sibilant, lateral or trill. Consonants in word-final position occur, however, only in loan-words, except for /m n l r/ in poetry or oratorical speech with apocopation of final vowel (§1.612): andiám *let us go!* (instead of andiámo).

2. Before close juncture (§1.41), only before another consonant or consonants in the following syllable. Any consonant phoneme may occur before the same consonant beginning the next syllable, i.e. in a geminate cluster: fíʎʎo *son* ['fiʎ-ʎo]; lášša *leaves* ['laš-ša]; bátte *beats* ['bat-te]; etc. The following consonants also occur in syllable-final position:

a. /r/ before:

i. all single consonants: sárto *tailor* ['sarʳ-to]; perʎ(i)uómini *for the men* [per-ʎ(i)-'wɔ-mi-ni].

ii. /kr tr/:[7] artralǧía *pain in the joints* [ar-tral-'dˣi:-a].

b. /l/ before:

i. all single consonants except /ɲ ʎ/: kálca *stocking* ['kalˡ-tˢa]; ilrispétto *the respect* [il-ris-'pɛt-to].

ii. /fr/[7] and /tr/: áltro *other* ['alˡ-tro].

c. /m/ before:

i. labial plosive: kámpo *field* ['kamᵐ-po].

ii. labial plosive + /r/ or /l/: ómbra *shade* ['omᵐ-bra].

d. /n/ before:

i. all consonants except laterals, nasals or labial stops: tónfo *thud* ['toŋ-fo]; ǧénte *people* ['dˣɛnⁿ-te]; ánci *nay rather* ['anⁿ-tˢi]; ánke *also* ['aŋᵑ-ke].

ii. non-labial plosive or labio-dental fricative + /r/: kánkro *crab* ['kaŋᵑ-kro].

e. /s/ before:

i. any plosive, labial nasal, fricative, /ǧ/ or /l/: časkúno *each one* [tˢasˢ-'ku:-no]; pásta *paste* ['pasˢ-ta].

ii. unvoiced plosive + /r/: áspro *harsh* ['asˢ-pro].

iii. /p k f/ + /l/: esplosívo *explosive* [es-plo-'si:-vo].

f. /b/ before /n/ or /d/:[7] abdikáre *to abdicate* [ab-di-'ka:-re].

g. /t/ before /n/ or /l/:[7] atlánte *atlas* [at-'lanⁿ-te].

h. /d/ before /m/:[7] kádmio *cadmium* ['kad-mjo].

j. /k/ before /m/ /n/ or /s/:[7] tékniko *technical* ['tɛk-ni-ko]; uksɔričída *uxoricide* [uk-sɔ-ri-'tˢi:-da]; eks⁺ *ex-* [eks].

k. /g/ before /m/:[7] pragmátiko *pragmatic* [prag-'ma:-ti-ko].

1.3. PHONEMES OF STRESS have a single syllable as their domain, and will be indicated in phonemic notation by accent marks written over the letter symbolizing the center of the syllable (§1.2).   There are four significant levels of stress in Italian:

1. Weak, symbolized by the absence of any accent mark: andiámočɛne *let's go away!* [an-'dja:-mo-tˢɛ-ne].

2. Intermediate, symbol /ˋ/. This type of stress occurs only in compounds, where it takes the place of full stress on the first member of the compound: pòrtabagáʎʎi *luggage-carrier, porter* [ˌpɔrʳ-ta-ba-'gaʎ-ʎi].

3. Full, symbol /ˊ/: dóve *where* ['do:-ve]; čittá *city* [tˢit-'ta].

4. Emphatic, characterized by more forceful expulsion of breath from the lungs than in full stress, and by raising of pitch: symbol /ˮ/: vvĭle *VILE!* [ˮvvi:-le].

1.4. Juncture is of two main types: close juncture and 'open' juncture or disjuncture.

1.41. Close Juncture is the absence of any interruption between linear phonemes: symbol, absence of space between linear symbols. Certain phonemic replacements and allophonic variations are here classed as concomitant phenomena of close juncture:

1.411. Phonemic Replacements conditioned by close juncture are:

1. /e o/ > /ɛ ɔ/, respectively, when unstressed and preceding nasals, laterals, or trills:[8] ména *he leads*, but mɛnáre *to* lead; kóme *how*, but kɔmúnkue *however*.

2. /ɛ ɔ/ > /e o/, respectively, when unstressed and not preceding nasals, laterals, or trills: sɛ́tte *seven*, but settimána *week*; umpɔ́ko *a little*, but umpokíno *a little bit* (dim.).

3. Unstressed /i/ preceding another vowel > 0 after /č ǧ š ɲ ʎ/, the last three of which are then automatically doubled in intervocalic position (cf. subsection 9, below):[9] -iámo 1. pl. Present A ending (§§2.341.2, 2.35.4) > -ámo after such a consonant, e.g. manǧ- *eat* + -iámo > manǧámo *we eat*.

4. Before /sC/ or /š/, and especially after a consonant, 0 > /i/ (optionally): e.g. stória or istória *history*; inˌ *in* + spírito *spirit* > in(i)spírito *in spirit*; perˌ *through* + šagúra *misfortune* > pɛrišagúra *unfortunately*.

5. Automatic assimilation:

a. Before a plosive or nasal consonant, a non-homorganic nasal is replaced by the corresponding homorganic nasal, normally /n/ > /m/ before /p b m/: e.g. unˌ *a* + pátto *pact* > umpátto *a pact*.

b. Before /r/, /č l n/ are assimilated, i.e. replaced by /r/: e.g. pón- *put* + /re/ Stem B formant + zero ending > pórre *to put*.

---

[8] Cf. the discussion of the mid vowels in unstressed syllables by E. B. Davis, 'Italian *e*'s and *o*'s', Italica 14.117–125 (1937), and G. L. Trager's comment in a letter to Davis, printed in Italica 16.145 (1939). Davis finds that the occurrence of close and open vowels is determined solely by position, so that in unstressed syllables, open and close /e/ and /o/ are in complementary distribution; due to this 'neutralization', most discussions of the point deny the occurrence of /ɛ ɔ/ in unstressed syllables.

[9] This replacement is not made by some speakers, especially South Italian, in imitation of the *ci gi* of standard orthography (§6.2.1.a, b.i), e.g. manǧiámo *we eat*, spelled *mangiamo*; čiéko *blind*, spelled *cieco* (cf. Cappuccini-Migliorini, Vocabolario della Lingua Italiana 299 [Torino, 1945], 'La forma *cèco*, che fedelmente rispecchia la pronunzia comune [emphasis ours], non attecchisce').

6. Concomitantly with emphatic stress (§1.3.4), any consonant is optionally doubled at the beginning of the word; this is the only instance in which double consonants occur in word-initial position: béstia *beast*, but bbéstia *BEAST!*.

7. Before another consonant except /r/, or after another consonant, a double consonant > single consonant, and before another consonant, /n/ + dental plosive > /n/ alone (with further replacement if called for according to §1.411.5): béll- *beautiful* > bɛl-, e.g. in umbélǧóvane *a handsome youth*; kantɛrést- *would sing* (Past B) + -te 2. pl. personal ending > kantɛréste; sant- *holy, Saint* > sán₁, e.g. in sántommáso *St. Thomas*, sámmárko *St. Mark*; grand- *great* > gran-, e.g. in granvirtúˣ *great virtue*.

8. Before /č/, /t/ > 0: e.g. fant- *boy* + ⁺čúll- diminutive suffix > fančúll-.

9. Between two vowels, /ʎ ɲ š/ are automatically doubled: e.g. vɔʎ- *wish* + -(i)ámo 1. pl. Present A ending > (hypothetical) vɔʎámo (subsection 3, above) > vɔʎʎámo *we wish*.

10. The combinations /s/ + /č/ and /s/ + /š/ both > /šš/ (simplified to /š/ when not in intervocalic position, subsection 7 above and §1.221): e.g. dis⁺ *dis-* + ⁺čérn- *perceive* > diššérn- *discern*; s⁺ privative prefix + čɛrvéll- *brain* > šervéll- *remove, rack the brain*; dis⁺ *dis-* + šénd- *go down* > diššénd- *descend*.

11. Before plosive or /s/, /ʎ/ > /l/: e.g. tóʎʎ- *take* + -se- 'strong' Past C formant > tól-se-; kóʎʎ- *gather* + -t- Non-Finite C formant > kól-t-; likewise, /ɲ/ > /n/ before /t s/: e.g. spéɲɲ- *extinguish* + -se- 'strong' Past C formant > spén-se-.

1.412. ALLOPHONIC VARIATIONS determined by close juncture include:

1. In vowels:

a. Lengthening (to 1½–2½ morae) when stressed in free syllables, in close juncture with a following syllable (i.e. not in word-final position):[10] káro *dear* ['ka:-ro], vs. kárro *car* ['kar-ro]; fáto *fate* ['fa:-to], vs. fátto *done* ['fat-to]. This lengthening is often not made by North Italian speakers.

b. Optional slight nasality before or after a nasal consonant:[11] baróne *baron* [ba-'ro:-ne], [ba-'rõ:-ne].

2. In consonants: sibilants, nasals, laterals and trills are slightly lengthened in syllable-final position before another consonant: básta *it is enough* ['basˢ-ta]; skálco *barefoot* ['skalˡ-tˢo]; kánto *I sing* ['kanⁿ-to]; sárto *tailor* ['sarʳ-to].

1.42. DISJUNCTURE is the separation of linear phonemes, e.g. by hesitation, interruption of the breath stream, change of pitch contour, or complete pause. Pause disjuncture is symbolized by /⌗/; other disjuncture is symbolized by space between linear symbols. Disjuncture does not normally occur in the interior of a pitch-phrase in rapid conversation; but it on occasion serves to separate individual elements for emphasis or clarity, as in deliberate speech or when explaining to someone who does not understand (e.g. a foreigner): mɛnevádo *I'm going away* in normal speech, but /me ne vádo/ in deliberate speech.

[10] Cf. the statistics on the relation between consonant length and the length of a preceding stressed vowel, in Josselyn, Etude sur la phonétique italienne, ch. X.

[11] Cf. Josselyn, ch. IX; Panconcelli-Calzia, De la nasalité en italien.

1.5. PITCH-CONTOURS[12] extend over a succession of syllables; the domain of a given pitch-contour will be termed a PITCH-PHRASE. A significant pitch-contour in Italian consists of a succession of relative pitches on the stressed syllables of the pitch-phrase. The pitch of the unstressed syllables is phonemically non-significant. Unstressed non-final syllables are normally lower in pitch than preceding or following stressed syllables, but follow the general rise or fall of the contour in which they are involved. Unstressed final syllables are higher than the preceding stressed syllable in rising contours; in falling or rising-falling contours, they are indifferently higher or lower.

1.51. RISING contours are of two types:

1. Non-Final, in which the pitch rises gradually on successive stressed syllables:[13] - - ‾ ‾. This is the normal pitch-contour for non-final phrases in an utterance. Symbol zero, together with space indicating disjuncture (§1.42): míofíʎʎoǧovánni ɛandátoannápɔli *my son John has gone to Naples.*

2. Final, in which the pitch rises on successive stressed syllables, with a sharp rise on the last stressed syllable: - - ‾ ‾. This is the normal intonation in the last pitch-phrase of questions not introduced by an interrogative element. Symbol /?/: tɔrnáteakkása? *Are you returning home?.*

1.52. RISING-FALLING contour involves gradual rise of pitch on successive stressed syllables up to and including the next to the last; on the last stressed syllable, the pitch falls abruptly to a point as low as or lower than the beginning: - - - ‾ ‾ ‥. This is the normal intonation in final phrases of non-interrogative utterances. Symbol /./: sónovɛnúta kɔndúekɔmpáɲɲe. *I came with two companions.*

1.53. FALLING contour involves fall of pitch on successive stressed syllables: ‾ - - - ‥. This is the normal intonation in utterances introduced by an interrogative element. Symbol /¿/: kékkɔ́savɔlétɛ́ *What do you want?.* In some (especially South Italian) speakers' usage, this contour is replaced by:

1.54. FALLING-RISING contour, in which the pitch falls on successive stressed syllables as far as the next to the last, and then rises sharply on the last: ‾ ‾ - - ‾. Symbol /!/: dóveséiandáto! *Where did you go?.*

1.55. PITCH-DISPLACEMENT accompanies emphatic stress (§1.3.4), with the highest pitch of the phrase passing onto the syllable thus stressed: máddǒveséiandátoɛ́ *But WHERE did you go?,* with contour - ‾ - ‥.

1.56. SEQUENCES OF PITCH-CONTOURS. In a succession of rising pitch-contours, each successive pitch-contour begins on a slightly higher pitch than did the previous pitch-contour, for the first two or three pitch-phrases. In longer utterances, the succession of pitch-contours rises to a high point toward the middle of the utterance, after which each rising contour begins on a slightly lower pitch than did the preceding one. The high point of pitch in a longer utterance will be marked by /,/: ilpóvɛruómo ɛ́bbeúnamalattía, pɛrkúipɛrdétte túttiisuóikapélli. *The poor man had a disease in which he lost all his hair.*

In a succession of falling pitch-contours, each successive pitch-contour begins

---

[12] Cf. C. E. Parmenter and S. N. Treviño, 'Italian intonation', Italica 7.80–84 (1930).

[13] In the diagrams in these sections, hyphens represent the relative pitch of STRESSED syllables.

on a slightly lower pitch than did the previous one: kékkósé kwélgrándedifíčo addéstraɛ́ *What is that large building to the right?*.

1.6. ALTERNATIONS OF PHONEMES in related forms, which are widespread enough to be profitably enumerated and symbolized in advance of the discussion of the forms themselves, are discussed here. Other alternations will be enumerated under the individual forms in which they occur.

1.61. VOWEL ALTERNATIONS.

1.611. DIPHTHONGIZATION is replacement of a front mid vowel by /ié/ and of a back mid vowel by /uó/, respectively, as in tɛn- *hold* vs. tiéne *he holds*; mɔr- *die* vs. muóre *he dies*. Symbols /ɛ/ and /ɔ/, respectively, e.g. in tɛn- *hold* and mɔr- *die*.

1.612. APOCOPATION is the replacement by 0, in phrasal combinations, of a word-final vowel (usually /e/, sometimes other vowels) before a consonant: e.g. vedére *to see* + či, *us* > vedérči *to see us*. No symbol.

1.613. ELISION is the replacement by 0 of a vowel before a following vowel: e.g. partíre *depart* (Stem B) + tense-sign -re- and personal ending -ai (2. sg.) > partirái *you will depart*. Symbol ⊗.

1.62. CONSONANT ALTERNATIONS.

1.621. PALATALIZATION is replacement of a dental by a palatal consonant, and occurs as follows:

1. /k/ > /č/ and /g/ > /ǧ/ before a front vowel:

a. Before /i/ of the m. pl. ending (§2.122) and in derivation: e.g. mónako *monk* ~ mónači *monks*; amíko *friendly* (m.sg.) ~ amíči *friendly* (m. pl.). Symbols /K G/ respectively: mónaK- *monk*, amíK- *friendly*.

b. Before /i e ɛ/ (but not in endings of ⁺0- I/Reg/W [§3.116.2.a]); and before thematic vowel /u/ of Non-Finite C in verb forms (§2.322.III): e.g. léggo *I read* ~ léǧǧi *you read* (2.sg.), léǧǧe *he reads*. Symbols /K G/ respectively. When /K/ follows /s/ and comes to stand in the positions just mentioned, the resultant /s/ + /č/ > /šš/ (§1.411.10): e.g. kɔnósK- *know* + /e/ > kɔnóšše *he knows*; kɔnósK- + -ut- Non-Finite C ending > kɔnoššút- *known*.

2. /l/ > /ʎ/ before /i/ m. ending in certain forms, e.g. élla *she* vs. éʎʎi *he*. Symbol /L/: éLL- 3. person pron. stem.

3. /t/ and /d/ > /c/ and /ʒ/ respectively (but not after /s/) in certain forms, as in arrogánte *arrogant* vs. arrogánca *arrogance*.

When considered as part of a morpheme, palatalization will be symbolized by △, e.g. arrogánt- + ⁺△a > arrogánca.

1.622. DOUBLING OF CONSONANTS.

1. After certain forms which end in a vowel before /✳/ or before a vowel, a single initial consonant or /Cr Cl/ of any element following in the same pitch-phrase is doubled,[14] as in the examples in Table II. Before any other following consonant cluster, vowel, or pause, the vowel is short and no other change takes place. Symbol /ˣ/: thus, the forms in the first column of Table II will

[14] For a summary of the discussions of this point, with bibliographical references, and a listing of the words which normally are followed by doubling of an initial consonant, cf. H. L. Norman, Italica 14.58–62 (1937). This type of doubling in sentence-sandhi is often not made by North Italian speakers.

be transcribed a$^x_1$ *to*; da$^x_1$ *from*; vá^x *goes*; dá^x *give*; kuí^x *here*; lačittá^x *the city*; kantá^x- *sing*, Stem C.

2. Before certain endings, the final consonant of a root is doubled: e.g. kád-*fall* + /e/ > kádde- 'strong' Finite C stem (§2.333.2.d). Symbol ⅔: thus, kád- +-⅔e- > kád-de-.

1.623. ASSIMILATION, i.e. replacement of a double cluster of dissimilar consonants by a geminate cluster of the second consonant, as in diK- *say* + stem-formant /s/ of Stem C > dis-se- 'strong' form of Stem C. Symbol □: thus, diK- + -□se- > dís-se-.

TABLE II

DOUBLING OF CONSONANTS IN PHRASAL SANDHI

Isolated Forms		Form in Sandhi
a$_1$ *to*	kása *house*	akkása *home(wards)*
	lakása *the house*	allakása *to the house*
	rivedérči *to see ourselves*	arrivedérči *au revoir*
da$_1$ *from*	mé *me*	dammé *from me, by myself*
	kápo *head*	dakkápo *from the beginning*
	véro *true*	davvéro *in truth*
vá *goes*	béne *well*	vabbéne *all right*
	présto *quickly*	vapprésto *he goes fast*
dá *give*	mi *to me*	dámmi *give me*
	lo *it*	dállo *give it*
kuí *here*	vičíno *near*	kuívvičíno *nearby*
lačittá *the city*	dɛlvatikáno *of the Vatican*	lačittáddɛlvatikáno *Vatican City*
kantá- *sing* (Stem C)	-mo 1. pl. personal ending	kantámmo *we sang*

1.624. LOSS OF FINAL ELEMENTS.

1. The final consonant of a morpheme > 0: e.g. rád- *shave* ~ rá-se- 'strong' form of Stem C. Symbol ↓: thus, rád- + ↓ > rá-.

2. The vowel or diphthong of the final syllable and all that follows it in the syllable > 0: e.g. sap- *know* ~ s-ɔ́^{x} *I know*; av- *have* ~ ɔ́^{x} *I have*. Symbol ↓↓: thus, sap- + ↓↓ > s-; av- + ↓↓ > 0.

1.625. OTHER CONSONANT ALTERNATIONS include:

1. /t/ > /s/ before $^+$i- stem-vowel or formant: e.g. ɛrétiko *heretic* ~ ɛresía *heresy*; osmótiko *osmotic* ~ osmósi *osmosis*; asfíttiko *asphyctic* ~ asfissía *asphyxia*. Symbol /T/: thus, ɛreT$^+$ *heret- heres-*; osmoT$^+$ *osmot- osmos-*; asfiTT$^+$ *asphyct-*.

2. /r/ before vowels or $^+$0- I/Reg/W ~ /s/ before consonants: e.g. funéreo *funereal* ~ funésto *disastrous*; mɔ́dɛr- *to moderate* ~ modésto *modest*. Symbol /R/: thus, funɛR$^+$, modɛR$^+$.

1.63. RECESSIVE STRESS, in word-formation, to whatever syllable precedes the phonemes cited, is symbolized by /'/ written alone before the form: e.g. e⁺ *out* + ⁺'dit- *given* > édit- *published*. Unless otherwise stated, recessive stress is accompanied by opening of a mid vowel, as in the example given. When /'/ is written before a form cited as a free form (e.g. 'mɛtro *meter*), the form cited has recessive stress in compounds (such as tɛrmómetro *thermometer*) and stress on the first syllable when not compounded (métro *meter*).

PART II. FORMS
CHAPTER II. INFLECTION

The forms of Italian show two layers of variation: INFLECTION and DERIVATION. Inflected forms ('words') fall into a number of form-classes or 'parts of speech' formed by affixation, with some concomitant non-automatic root-modification; derived forms, each of which falls into one of the classes of inflected forms, are formed by affixation and by compounding. Inflected forms are of three types: minimum free forms, phrasally bound forms, and clausally bound forms.[1]

2.0. CATEGORIES OF INFLECTION AND FORM-CLASSES.

2.01. CATEGORIES OF INFLECTION are the following:

1. Gender: feminine and 'masculine' (i.e. not exclusively feminine).[2] Where the linguistic form involved has sex-reference, the grammatical gender and the sex-reference normally, but not always, coincide: e.g. dónna *woman* f.; uómo *man* m.; but guárdia *guard*, always f.

2. Number: singular (referring to one of the items concerned) and plural ('more than one'), e.g. távɔla *table* sg.; távɔle *tables* pl.

3. Case:

   a. Nominative, used as subject in clauses (§5.12); e.g. ío *I*.

   b. Prepositional, used after prepositions: e.g. kúi *whom* in pɛrkúi *for whom*.

   c. Accusative, used as direct object of verbs (§4.133.1.b) and (in free forms) after prepositions; e.g. mé^x *me*; permé^x *for me*.

   d. Oblique, indicating possessor or indirect object: e.g. kúi *of whom, to whom*.

   e. Dative, indicating indirect object: ʎi, *to him*, le, *to her*.

4. Animation: animate (referring to living beings) and inanimate (referring to non-living things).

5. Person: first (person speaking), second (person spoken to), and third (all others). The 2.sg. is used by mature speakers only in speaking to those with whom the speaker is not on a basis of social respect or distance (e.g. it is used to friends of the same sex, a fiancé[e] or spouse, parents, children, animals). For those to whom social respect is shown, the 2. pl. is used in Southern Italy, and the third person sg. and pl. are used in Central and Northern Italy (from Rome north) with the 3. sg. subject pronoun élla or léi (lit. *she*; §2.21) and the 3. pl. subject pronoun lóro (lit. *they*); this use of the 2. pl. or 3. sg. and pl. in the meaning *you* will be referred to as the FORMAL mode of address.

---

[1] For these terms, cf. 'A Note on Bound Forms', Journal of English and Germanic Philology 45.450 (1946).

[2] The gender-categories are, of course, two immense classes of forms determined by the occurrence of morpheme-alternants in syntactic concordance. As such, they might just as well be termed 'Class A' and 'Class B', or any other convenient labels; but in the Romance languages, the gender-classes and their sex-reference (if any) are close enough to warrant retention of the traditional terms.

6. Tense: past (referring specifically to past time), 'non-past' or present (not referring specifically to past time), timeless (not referring to time) and imperative (giving a command). A TENSE is here defined as a set of forms having the same time-reference and differing from each other only in regard to the person and number of the actor.

2.02. FORM-CLASSES are:

1. Substantives, showing variations in gender and number: e.g. dónna *woman* f.sg., dónne *women* f.pl.; bósko *forest* m.sg., bóski *forests* m.pl.; buóno *good* m.sg., buóni m.pl., buóna f.sg., buóne f.pl.

2. Pronouns, which substitute for substantives and which show variations in number, case, animation and (in the third person) in gender; e.g. ío *I*; mé^x *me*; kí *who?* ké^x *what?*.

3. Verbs, showing variations in person, number, and tense: e.g. kantiámo *we sing*; kantavámo *we used to sing*; kantávano *they used to sing*. Verbal forms which are inflected for person and number are termed FINITE forms; those not so inflected, NON-FINITE forms.

4. 'Indeclinables', which do not have variations in any of the categories of inflection, with the sub-classes:

   a. Prepositions, certain of which have alternate forms determined either phonologically (e.g. ad *to* before a vowel ∼ a^x before a consonant) or morphologically (e.g. dɛ^x *of* before a form of the definite article ∼ d[i] elsewhere).

   b. Adverbs (e.g. béne *well*);

   c. Connectives (e.g. nón, *not*; ma^x, *but*);

   d. Conjunctions (e.g. ke^x *that*);

   e. Minor Clause forms (e.g. ái *ow!*).

Of the above form-classes, prepositions, connectives, and certain pronouns and adverbs are phrasally bound, and conjunctions are clausally bound; the others are minimum free forms.

All free, phrasally bound and clausally bound forms consist of inflectionally bound elements, which will be indicated by the symbol /-/ placed before or after them: thus, the personal ending -mo; the root uóm- *man*.

Forms of all classes except verbs have the structure: Root + Stem-Vowel (abbreviated SV): thus, líbro *book* = root líbr- + SV -o. For the structure of verb-forms, cf. §2.31.

2.1. SUBSTANTIVES show the following variations and have sub-classes established according to the relations of their forms in gender and number:

2.11. GENDER-RELATION. The gender-morpheme (masculine, feminine) is always morphologically zero, i.e. is determined by concordance of forms in larger combinations (phrases, clauses).

2.111. ADJECTIVES have both genders. They fall into two sub-classes:

1. Common adjectives (abbreviated adj.), on which may be formed adverbial compounds in ⁺ménte -*ly* (§3.225.2.a.ii) and/or adjectives in ⁺íssimo *very* . . . : e.g. brávo *brave* ∼ bràvaménte *bravely*; mólto *much* ∼ moltíssimo *very much*.

2. Numerals (abbreviated num.), which do not have corresponding adverbs in ⁺ménte -*ly* or adjectives in ⁺íssimo *very* . . . , but which are like adjectives in

other respects and which have special derivational features: e.g. vénti *twenty*, on which is formed ventésimo *twentieth*.

The definite article (based on the stem L- *the*, cf. §2.123) is morphologically an adjective, with certain special syntactical characteristics (§4.111.5.b.iv).

2.112. Nouns are of masculine or feminine gender, e.g. matíta *pencil* f.; búko *hole* m.; fónte *fountain* m.; análisi *analysis* f. Some nouns are of both genders: e.g. artísta *artist* mf.[3] The gender of nouns is determined lexically, i.e. must be stated separately for each noun.

2.12. Number-Relation is indicated by the choice of stem-vowel in the singular and the replacement thereof by a different stem-vowel or the addition of a suffix in the plural.

2.121. Singular. There are six possible stem-vowels, of which each substantive has one in each gender in the singular:

I. /a/; e.g. fɛríta *wound* f.; nuóva *new* f.; idióta *idiot(ic)* f. or m.; tɛlegrámma *telegram* m.; bóia *executioner* m.

II. /o/; e.g. dɛlítto *crime* m.; nuóvo *new* m.; máno *hand* f.; bráččo *arm* m.; áuto *auto* f;. ámbo *both f.* or m.; kuáttro *4* num.

III. /e/; e.g. mónte *mountain* m.; léǧǧe *law* f.; fórte *strong* mf.; mílle *1000* num.; spéče *species* f.

IV. /i/; e.g. bríndisi *toast* m.; análisi *analysis* f; pári *equal* f. or m.

V./u/; e.g. sóddu *Soddu*; ǧennarǧéntu *Gennargentu*; dómu *Sardinian house*.[4]

VI. 0, after consonant or /ˣ/; e.g. lápis *pencil* m.; trám *tramcar* m.; čittáˣ *city* f.;. álbum *album* m.; piúˣ *more* f. or m.

2.122. Plural, which is indicated by the substitution of a given stem-vowel for that of the singular (in one instance with concomitant change of gender) or by the addition of a phoneme.[5] The possible changes are:

a. SV > /e/; e.g. fɛríte *wounds*; nuóve *new* f.; idióte *idiot(ic)* f. This substitution occurs only with f. nouns and adjectives having SV no. I, i.e. /a/.

b. SV > /i/; e.g. tɛlegrámmi *telegrams*; dɛlítti *crimes*; máni *hands*; mónti *mountains*; léǧǧi *laws*.

c. SV > /a/, with change of gender from m to f in nouns; bráčča *arms* f.pl.; míla *thousands* (: mílle *thousand* sg.). Nouns with plural formation of this type (all belonging to singular type II) usually have also a plural of type b, with masculine gender and figurative or transferred meaning: e.g. bráčči *arms* (e.g. of the sea).

d. 0, i.e. no change in SV: e.g. bóia *executioner*; áuto *auto*; spéče *species*; bríndisi *toasts*; análisi *analyses*; lápis *pencils*; trám *tramcars*; čittáˣ *cities*; ámbo *both* f. or m.; pára *equal* f. or m.; and all numerals above un- *one* num/I–II, but not including mílle *1000* num/IIIc: e.g. dúe *two*; treˣ *three*; kwáttro *four*; diéči *ten*; etc. This is the only plural formation for nouns with singular of type IV and for almost all those of type VI; furthermore, it occurs with all nouns used

---

[3] Distinguished from adjectives by not having the derivational features of the latter, especially adverbs in ⁺ménte *-ly*.

[4] This stem-vowel occurs only in loan-words from Sardinian and Sicilian.

[5] The words chosen as examples are those given in §2.121.a for the singular.

as family names (e.g. imalavóʎʎa *the Malavoglias*) and with many types of compounds (e.g. ipɔ̀rtabagáʎʎi *the luggage-carriers, porters*).

e. Addition of /s/, only in a few Sardinian words and foreign loans: dómus *Sardinian houses*; álbums *albums*.

TABLE III(a)
SINGULAR AND PLURAL FORMATIONS
A: NOUNS

Plural Formation:	a (SV > e)	b (SV > i)	c (SV > a)	d (0)	e (−s)
Singular Formation: I (SV/a/)	fɛríta -e	tɛlegrámma -i		bóia	
II (SV/o/)		dɛlítto -i	bráččo -a	áuto	
III (SV/e/)		mónte -i	mílle míla	spéče	
IV (SV/i/)				análisi	
V (SV/u/)					dómu -s
VI (SV 0)				lápis	álbum -s

TABLE III(b)
B: ADJECTIVES

Plural Formation:	a (SV > e)	b (SV > i)	c (SV > a)	d (0)
Singular Formation: I (SV/a/ fm.)	idióta -e (f.)	idióta -i (m.)		
I–II (SV/a/ f., /o/ m.)	nuóva -e (f.)	nuóvo -i (m.)		
II (SV/o/ fm.)				ámbo, kuáttro
III (SV/e/ fm.)		fórte -i	mílle míla	čínkue
IV (SV/i/ fm.)				pári
VI (SV 0 fm.)				piú[x], tré[x]

The existing combinations of these singular and plural formations are shown in Tables IIIa (for nouns) and IIIb (for adjectives). When substantives are cited,[6] their subclass in the case of adjectives (adj; num) or their gender in the

[6] Either in full form or in root form.

case of nouns (m; f; mf) will be given after the linguistic form and its gloss, and after a solidus (/), their singular and plural formations: thus, fɛríta *wound* f/Ia; nuóv- *new* adj/I–II.

2.123. ALTERNATIONS IN ROOTS, concomitant with the addition of the singular and/or plural suffixes, are:

1. In stressed vowel of root:

a. /ɛ́/ > /i/ before m.sg. ending -o in dɛ́- *god* mf/I–II: dío.

b. Replacement of high vowel by /iɛ uɔ/, respectively, takes place before m.pl. ending -i in mí- *my*, tú- *thy*, and sú- *his hers its*, all adj/I–II, and in bu-*ox* m/IIIb: miéi, tuói, suói, buói.

2. in final consonant:

a. /L/ occurs in the following adjectives of I–II: bɛ́LL- *beautiful*, kuéLL-*that*, and L- *the*.   The resultant m.pl. forms bɛ́ʎʎi, kuéʎʎi and ʎi are used before 'impure' consonant or consonant cluster:[7] e.g. kuéʎʎistudénti *those students*; ʎispɛ́kkii *the mirrors*.   The archaic form li, *the* (m.pl.) is used only in dates (e.g. litréǧǧennáio *January 3*) as an alternant to il, *the* m.sg. (cf. §4.111.3.b.iii).

b. Loss of final consonants of root, before m.pl. -i, in the adjectives mentioned in the preceding paragraph; the resultant forms béi, kuéi, i are used before 'pure' consonant or cluster: e.g. ibéilíbri *the fine books*; kuéimónti *those mountains*.

c. Double consonant > single, in míll- *1000* adj/IIIc before pl. -a: míla *thousands*.

3. A syllable is added:

a. /in/ in uóm- *man* m/IIIb > uómin- before pl. -i: uómini *men*.

b. /ɔr/ in témp- *season* (Catholic religious occasion) m/IIc before pl. -a: témpɔra *seasons*.

4. SV 0 occurs in certain adjectives, in certain forms and positions:

a. With automatic phonemic alternations wherever required (cf. §1.6), in the following:

i. In m. or f.sg. before vowel, in L- *the*: e.g. luómo *the man*; lánitra *the duck*; ʎinnočénti *the innocents*.

ii. In m.sg. before vowel or pure consonant, and in f.sg. before vowel, in the following adjectives of I–II: bɛ́LL- *beautiful*; buón- *good*; kuéLL- *that*; un- *one, a, an*; (optionally) altr- *other*; and (before proper names) sant- *Saint*; and in grand- *large* adj/IIIb.   Thus: umbɛ́lluómo *a handsome man*; buónǧórno *good day*; sánǧovánni *St. John*; sántágata *St. Agatha*; unáltramíka or unáltra-amíka *another friend* (f.).

b. With replacement of /L/ by /il/, in L- *the* in m.sg. before a pure consonant or cluster (except after dɛ˟- *of*, kɔ˟- *with*, pɛ˟- *for*, cf. §2.41.1.b): e.g. ilristɔránte *the restaurant*; iltréno *the train*.   The regular form lo, *the* m.sg. is used before impure consonant or cluster: e.g. lospɛ́kkio *the mirror*; locío *the uncle*; and in the set phrases lopiú˟ *the more* and lɔméno *the less*.

[7] Here defined as /c ʐ ɲ ps š sC/; all other consonants and clusters are 'pure'. The phoneme /h/ in foreign words is sometimes treated as 'pure', sometimes 'impure': /lohégɛl/ or /ilhégɛl/ *Hegel*.

2.2. PRONOUNS are of the following types: personal, demonstrative, relative, interrogative and indefinite.

2.21. PERSONAL PRONOUNS.

1. Free forms are built on the roots í- and m- 1.sg.; nó- 1.pl.; t- 2.sg.; vó- 2.pl.; éLL- and l- 3.; s- 3. reflexive. These combine with the endings -o -a -i and -ú nom.sg., -i nom. and acc.pl., -é^x acc.sg., -ui acc.sg.m., -éi acc.sg.f., and -óro nom.- acc.-obl.pl., to form the set of pronouns shown in Table IV.[8]

2. Phrasally bound forms are built on the roots m- 1.sg.; č- 1.pl.; t- 2.sg.; v- 2.pl.; l- and ʎ- 3.sg. and pl.; s- 3.refl. These roots combine in 1., 2., and 3. refl. with the ending -ɛ (before following /ne/ pronominal adverb [§2.4] or

TABLE IV

PERSONAL PRONOUNS

	Free		Bound	
	Nominative	Accusative-Prepositional	Accusative	Dative
1. sg.	ío	mé^x	mi	
2. sg.	tú^x	té^x	ti	
3. refl.	—	sé^x	si	
3. sg. { m.	éʎʎi	lúi	lo	ʎi
3. sg. { f.	élla	léi	la	le
1. pl.	nói		či	
2. pl.	vói		vi	
3. pl. { m.	lóro[9]		li	—
3. pl. { f.			le	—

3.sg. or pl. pronominal forms) ∼ -i elsewhere, forming pronouns with accusative and dative meaning. In 3.sg. and pl., l- with the endings of adjective declension I–II (§2.122, table III) forms accusative pronouns, m. and f.; special dative bound pronouns are formed on ʎ- m. and l- f., with the endings -i and -e respectively. Cf. Table IV for paradigmatic listing of the pronouns thus formed. The 3.sg. feminine pronouns élla and léi (free), la₁ (bound direct object) and le₁ (bound indirect object) and 3.pl. lóro are used in the meaning *you* in formal address (§2.01.5); for their agreement, cf. §4.02.

2.22. DEMONSTRATIVE PRONOUNS are built on the roots č- *that*; kɔl- *that* ('ille'); kost- *that* ('iste'); kuéLL- *that* and kuést- *this*. All except the form built on č- refer only to persons. These bases combine with the suffixes -ó^x (abstract[10]) nom.-acc.; -i m.sg. nom.; -úi m.sg. nom.-obl.; -éi f.sg. nom.-obl.; and -óro pl. nom.-acc., to give the forms shown in Table V.

[8] The 3.pl. nom. forms éʎʎino *they* (m.) and éllɛno *they* (f.), formed with substantive plural endings plus the verbal plural suffix /no/ (§2.35.6.b), are archaic or sub-standard.

[9] Also oblique case.

[10] I.e. referring to some feature of the linguistic or practical context, but not to a specific linguistic antecedent.

2.23. INTERROGATIVE PRONOUNS are built on the root k- *what?*, with the endings -í^x animate nom.-acc. and -é^x inanimate nom.-acc., forming kí^x *who? whom?* and ké^x *what?*.

2.24. RELATIVE PRONOUNS are built on the root k- *that*, with the endings -e^x nom.-acc. and -úi obl. and prepositional, forming ke^x *who, whom, which*; kúi *whom* (after prep.), *whose, to whom*.

2.25. INDEFINITE PRONOUNS are built on the root altr- *other*, with the endings -i m.sg. nom. and -úi m.sg. obl. and prepositional: áltri *someone else*; altrúi *someone else* (after prep.), *someone else's, to someone else*.

2.3. VERBS are inflected for person, number, and tense (cf. §2.01.2, 5, 6). The imperative tense has only 1., 2.pl. and 2.sg. forms, except in the defective verb ékko *here is (are), there is (are)*, which has only the one imperative form, non-contrastive as to person and number; the other tenses have six forms each (three persons in two numbers). Forms showing distinction of person and num-

TABLE V
DEMONSTRATIVE PRONOUNS

	Sg.		Pl.
	m.	f.	
Nom.-Acc.	kɔlúi	kɔléi	kɔlóro
	kostúi	kostéi	kostóro

čó *that*

Nom.	{ kuéʎʎi *that man*
	{ kuésti *this man*

ber are FINITE forms; in addition to these, each normal verb has four NON-FINITE forms, which are derivationally bound forms serving as bases for further derivation, two being built on Stem A and one each on Stems B and C of the verb (cf. §2.32).

2.31. STRUCTURE OF VERB FORMS. Each finite form has the structure: Stem + Tense-Sign + Personal Ending, the last-mentioned indicating person and number. In non-finite forms, the element following the stem will be equated with the tense-sign of finite forms; by definition, non-finite forms have no personal ending.

2.32. ROOT AND STEMS. The ROOT of each verb will be defined as that sequence of phonemes preceding -ándo or -éndo of the gerund (§3.117.6.b). Thus: kánt- *sing*:kantándo *singing*; skrív- *write*:skrivéndo *writing*; párt- *depart*:part-éndo *departing*. When the root is cited alone, the syllable on which the root is stressed will be indicated, except in the case of roots which never bear the stress.

On the root of a verb are formed three stems, here termed A, B, and C; each stem is formed on the root by the addition of a THEMATIC VOWEL (abbreviated TV) and a STEM-SUFFIX. On Stem A are built four tenses and two non-finite forms; on Stems B and C, two tenses and one non-finite form each. The resultant tenses and non-finite forms are listed in Table VI, with their traditional names in parentheses.

Of these forms, the Past refers exclusively to past time, punctual in Past C and non-punctual (durative, repetitive, etc.) in Past A and Past B. The Present refers to time not limited exclusively to the Past; the Timeless does not have time-significance; and the Imperative gives a command. Forms built on Stem A refer in general to real conditions; on Stem B, to hypothetical conditions; on Stem C, to past reality in Past C, and, in constructions where its use is significant, to unreal conditions or implying an emotional overtone in Timeless C.

2.321. RHYZOTONIC AND ARHYZOTONIC FORMS. The stress in each verb form occurs in one of three places, defined morphologically: on the last syllable of the root, on the first syllable following the root, or the second syllable following the root. *also pennlt of root, e.g., prédico, verifico.*

TABLE VI
VERB STEMS AND TENSES

Stem A ('Present Stem')	Stem B ('Future Stem')	Stem C ('Preterite Stem')
Present A ('Present')	Present B ('Future')	
Past A ('Imperfect')	Past B ('Conditional')	
Timeless A ('Present Subjunctive')		Past C ('Preterite')
		Timeless C ('Past Subjunctive')
Imperative		
Non-Finite[1] A ('Gerund')	Non-Finite B ('Infinitive')	Non-Finite C ('Past Participle')
Non-Finite[2] A ('Present Participle')		

1. A verb form in which the stress falls on the last syllable of the root is termed RHYZOTONIC. This type of stress occurs in:

a. Present and Timeless A, 1.-3. sg. and 3.pl., and Imper 2.sg. of all verbs: e.g. kánto *I sing*; kánti *you sing*; kánta *he sings*; kántano *they sing*; kánti *(that) I, you, he sing*; kántino *(that) they sing*; kánta *sing!*, all on the root kánt- *sing*.

b. Present, Timeless and Imperative A 1., 2.pl. of ɛss- *be*: siámo *we are*, *(that) we be, let's be!*; siéte *you are*; siáte *(that) you be, be!*.

c. Present A and Imperative 2.pl. of dá- *give* and stá- *stand*: dáte *you give*, *give!*; státe *you stand, stand!*.

d. Past A, 1.-3.sg. and 3.pl., and all finite forms built on Stem C, of dá- *give*, stá- *stand* and éss- *be*: e.g. dáva *he used to give*; stávano *they used to stand*; éra *he used to be*; státo *stood, been*.

e. Non-Finite B of verbs of class IIIb (§2.324): e.g. léǧǧere *to read*; léǧǧ- *read*.

f. Past C, 1.-3.sg. and 3.pl., and Non-Finite C, of 'strong' verbs (§2.324), with TV (§2.322) > 0: e.g. tínse *he dyed*, tínto *dyed*:tínG- *dye*.

2. All other verb forms are ARHYZOTONIC, i.e. not stressed on the root. In arhyzotonic forms, stress falls:

a. On the second syllable following the root in Past A, 1.-2.pl. and in all of the finite forms built on Stem B, except where TV is 0 (cf. §2.33): e.g. kantavámo *we used to sing*, kantɛrémo *we shall sing*:kánt- *sing*; but davámo *we used to give*, darémo *we shall give*:dá- *give*.

b. Elsewhere, on the first syllable following the root: e.g. kantávano *they used to sing*:kánt- *sing*; finíre *to finish*:fin- *finish*; fačémmo *we did*:fáč- *do*; vɛndéssimo *(that) we sold:* vénd- *sell*.

2.322. THEMATIC VOWELS. There are four main classes or CONJUGATIONS of verbs, established by the thematic vowel used in the formation of the three stems. The four conjugations have normally:

I. /ɛ/ in Present and Past B: e.g. kantɛró[x] *I shall sing*, kantɛrébbɛro *they would sing*:kánt- *sing*.

/a/ elsewhere; e.g. kantáte *you sing*; kantáre *to sing*; kantássimo *(that) we sang*.

II. /i/ throughout: e.g. sentíte *you hear*, sɛntíre *to hear*, sɛntiró[x] *I shall hear*, sɛntíssimo *(that) we heard*:sént- *hear*. But vɛn- *come* and tɛn- *hold* have TV /u/ in Non-Finite C: vɛnút-, tɛnút   *tɛn ɩs IIIa !*

III. /u/ in Non-Finite C: e.g. vɛndút- *sold*:vénd- *sell*.

/e/ elsewhere, e.g. vɛndéte *you sell*; véndɛre *to sell*; vɛndɛrébbɛro *they would sell*; vɛndéssimo *(that) we sold*.

IV. 0 in Stem B and Non-Finite C, e.g. pórre *to put*, pɔrró[x] *I shall put*, pɔst- *put*:pón- *put*.

0 elsewhere in dá- *give* and stá- *stand*: e.g. dáte *you give*; státe *you stand*.

/e/ elsewhere in other verbs of IV: e.g. pɔnéte *you put*; pɔnéssimo *(that) we put*.

2.323. STEM-SUFFIXES are:

1. In Stem A: 0, as in kánta *he sings*; partí-te *you depart*; vɛndé-va *he used to sell*.

2. In Stem B:

a. /re/in Past B 1. and 3.sg. and 3.pl.: e.g. kantɛ-ré-bbe *he would sing*; parti-ré-i *I would depart*; vɛndɛ-ré-bbɛro *they would sell*.

b. /re/ elsewhere: e.g. kantá-re *to sing*; parti-ré-mo *we shall depart*.

3. In Stem C:

a. /[x]/ in:

i. Timeless C of all verbs; e.g. kantá-sse *(that) he sang*; partíssi-mo *(that) we departed*; vɛndé-sse *(that) he sold*.

ii. Past C 3.sg. of 'weak' verbs (§2.324) and of ɛss- *be*: e.g. kantó[x] *he sang*; partí[x] *he departed*; fú[x] *he was*.

iii. Past C 1. and 3.sg. and 3.pl. of the alternate forms of verbs of IIIb (§2.324) before the tense-sign /te/ (§2.342): e.g. vɛndétte *he sold*; vɛndéttɛro *they sold*.

b. 0 elsewhere; e.g. kantá-i *I sang*; partí-rono *they departed*; vɛndú-t- *sold*.

2.324. CLASSIFICATION OF VERBS. Verbs are to be classified by their thematic vowels (§2.322), and by the relation of Stems A and C to the root. Under conjugation III, there are two sub-classes:

IIIa, in which Non-Finite B is arhyzotonic: e.g. kadére *to fall*.

IIIb, in which Non-Finite B is rhyzotonic: e.g. léǧǧɛre *to read*.

Verbs in which Stem A is equal to the root (unchanged) throughout will be termed REGULAR (abbreviated Reg); those in which the root has special alternants in one or more forms built on Stem A will be termed IRREGULAR (Irr). Those in which the irregularity consists of the addition of /ísK/ to the root in rhyzotonic forms (§2.331.1.d) will be marked with the sign ísK instead of Irr. But verbs whose only irregularity consists of having one of the alternations of phonemes discussed and symbolized in §1.6 (mostly /K G/) will be marked Reg.

Verbs in which there is irregularity in the root or TV in the formation of Stem B will be marked by the letter x after the conjugation number.

Verbs in which Stem C has the normal thematic vowel of its conjugation throughout, and in which the root appears unchanged throughout, will be termed WEAK (W). Those having variant forms of root or TV in Past or Timeless C will be termed STRONG[1] (S[1]); those having a variant form of root or TV in Non-Finite C, STRONG[2] (S[2]).

By these criteria a verb may be classified: as belonging to Conjugations I, II, IIIa, IIIb or IV, with or without x in each of these; as regular, irregular or -ísK-; as W, S[1], S[2] or S[1, 2]. A few sample listings follow:

kánt- *sing* I/Reg/W	fin- *finish* II/ísK/W	mɔv- *move* IIIb/Reg/S[1, 2]
and- *go* Ix/Irr/W	tém- *fear* IIIa/Reg/W	pón- *put* IV/Irr/S[1, 2]
sént- *feel, hear* II/Reg/W	vénd- *sell* IIIb/Reg/W	da- *give* IV/Irr/S[1]
ápr- *open* II/Reg/S[1, 2]	bév- *drink* IIIbx/Reg/S[1]	

In the following will be discussed: the relation of stems to root, together with irregularities in thematic vowels (§2.33); tense-signs (§2.34); and personal endings (§2.35).

2.33. RELATION OF STEMS TO ROOT. In most verbs, the root remains unchanged in all three stems; but in some, the root appears in a variant form in one or more of the stems, or a substitute thematic vowel appears in the formation of the stem. The specific variations which thus occur are listed here according to the forms (classified by stem, tense, person, and number) in which they occur. The classification of each verb (§2.324) is given the first time the verb is mentioned, but not thereafter.

2.331. STEM A.

1. In rhyzotonic forms:

a. /u/ > /ɔ/ in ud- *hear* II/W: ɔ́do *I hear*, ɔ́di *you hear*, ɔ́de *he hears*; ɔdono *they hear*; ɔ́da (*that*) *I, you, he, hear*; ɔ́dano (*that*) *they hear*; ɔ́di *hear!*.

b. /u/ > /ε/ in usK- *go out* II/W: έsko *I go out*, έšši *you go out*, έšše *he goes out*, etc.

c. /o/ > /e/, with further optional replacement of /v/ by /bb/ before a back vowel, in dov- *owe* IIIax/W: dévo (débbo) *I owe*, dévi *you owe*, déve *he owes*; dévɔno (débbɔno) *they owe*; déva (débba) (*that*) *I, you, he owe*, etc.

d. /ísK/ is added to the root in a number of verbs of II/W, e.g. in fin- *finish*: finísko *I finish*; finíšši *you finish*; finíšše *he finishes*; etc.

2. In Present and Timeless A:

a. Before a back vowel:

i. Alone:

A. /g/ is added to the root:

1. With no further change, in:

dɔl- *hurt* IIIax/S¹ (optional, alternating with /l/ > /ʎʎ/)
kóʎʎ- *gather* IIIb/S¹˒²
⁺mán- *remain* IIIax/S¹˒²
pón- *put* IV/S¹˒²
sál- *go up* II/W
šéʎʎ- *choose* IIIb/S¹˒²

šóʎʎ- *undo* IIIb/S¹˒²
tɛn- *hold* IIIax/S¹
tóʎʎ- *take* IIIb (x)/S¹˒²
tráˣ- *draw* IV/S¹
vál- *be worth* IIIax/S¹˒²
⁺véll- *pull off* IIIb/S¹˒²
vɛn- *come* IIx/S¹

E.g.: póngo *I put*; póngɔno *they put*; pónga (*that*) *I, you, he put*; póngano (*that*)
they put; tólgo *I take*; trággo *I draw*; etc.

       ii. Preceded by □, optionally in: kiéd- *ask* IIIb/S¹˒²; sɛd- *sit*
IIIa/W; and véd- *see* IIIax/S¹˒². Thus: siéde (séggo) *I sit*; siédɔno (séggɔno)
they sit; siéda (ségga) (*that*) *I, you, he sit*; siédano (séggano) (*that*) *they sit*;
and likewise kiédo or kiéggo *I ask*; etc.

       B. /ɲɲ/ > /ng/ in spéɲɲ- spéɲɲ- *extinguish* IIIb/S¹˒²: spéngo *I*
extinguish; etc.

    ii. And also before /iá/:

       A. /l/ > /ʎʎ/ in: dɔl- *hurt* (optional, alternating with addition of
/g/); sɔl- *be wont* IIIb/S²; vɔl- *wish* IIIax/S¹. Thus: vóʎʎo *I wish*; vóʎʎɔno
they wish; vóʎʎa (*that*) *I, you, he wish*; vóʎʎano (*that*) *they wish*; and likewise
dóʎʎo *I hurt*, etc.; sóʎʎo *I am wont*, etc.

       B. /t/ > /ss/ in pɔt- *be able, can* IIIax/W: pósso *I can*; póssɔno *they*
can; póssa (*that*) *I, you, he can*; póssano (*that*) *they can*.

       c. /r/ > /i/ (optional before /iá/) in: mɔr- *die* II(x)/S¹˒²; par-
appear IIIax/S¹˒²; ⁺par- *appear* II/S¹˒²-W. Thus: muóio *I die*; mɔriámo
(moiámo) *we die*; muóiɔno *they die*; muóia (*that*) *I, he, she die*; muóiano (*that*)
they die; and likewise páio *I appear*, etc.

       b. In 1.pl., /v/ > /bb/ in dov- *owe*: dobbiámo *we owe*.

       c. In Pres. A. 1.sg. and in rhyzotonic forms of Timeless A, /an/ >
/va/ in and- *go* I(x)/W: vádo *I go*; váda (*that*) *I, he, she go*; vádano (*that*) *they*
go.

       d. In Pres. A 1.sg. (except in sáp- *know*), 1.pl. and 3.pl. (except in fáč-
do and sáp- *know*), and in Timeless A throughout: ʒ is added (i.e. the final
consonant is doubled) in: fáč- *do* IV/S¹; ǧáč- *lie* IIIa/S¹; nɔč- *harm* IIIb/S¹;
piáč- *please* IIIa/S¹; sáp- *know* IIIa/S¹; táč- *be silent* IIIa/S¹. Thus: fáččo *I*
do; faččámo *we do*; fáčča (*that*) *I, you, he do*; faččamo (*that*) *we do*; faččáte (*that*)
you do; fáččano (*that*) *they do*.

   3. In Present A:
     a. In rhyzotonic forms, TV > 0 and the following further changes take
place:
       i. The root has ↓↓, before the tense-sign /⊗aˣ/ (§2.341.1.a) and personal
endings (§2.35) in: da- *give* IV/S¹; av- *have* IIIax/S¹n; fác- *do*;[11] sap- *know*

---

[11] The l.sg. forms fɔˣ *I do* and vɔˣ *I go* (beside fáččo *I do* and vádo *I go*, §2.331.2.c, d) are
poetical or non-standard.

IIIax/S¹; sta- *stand* IV/S¹. Thus: dɔ́ˣ *I give*; dái *you give*; dáˣ *he gives*; dánno *they give*; ɔ́ˣ *I have*; ái *you have*; áˣ *he has*; ánno *they have*; and likewise fɔ́ˣ *I do*, etc.; sɔ́ˣ *I know*, etc.; stɔ́ˣ *I stand*, etc.

ii. /and/ > /v/, before the tense-sign /⊗aˣ/ and personal endings: vɔ́ˣ *I go*;[11] vái *you go*; váˣ *he goes*; vánno *they go*.

b. In 1.sg., /ɛss/ > /son/ in éss- *be* IIIbx/S¹: sóno *I am*.

c. In 2.sg.:

i. /ɛss/ > /sɛ/ in ɛss- *be*: séi *you are*.

ii. The root has ↓ in pɔt- *be able, can*: puói *you can*.

d. In 3.sg., /ss/ and /t/ > /ˣ/ in éss- *be* and pɔt- *be able*: έˣ *he is*; puɔ́ˣ *he can*.

e. In 1.pl., /ɛss/ > /s/ in éss- *be*: siámo *we are*.

f. In 2.pl., /ɛss/ > /siɛ/ in éss- *be*: siéte *you are*.

g. In 3.pl., /ɛss/ > /so/ in éss- *be*: sóno *they are*.

4. In Present A 2.pl. and Imper. 2.sg. and pl., TV is 0 and the root has ↓, in díK- *say* IV/S¹, ² and fáč- *do*: díte (*you*) *say*; díˣ *say!*; fáte (*you*) *do*; fáˣ *do!*.

5. In Past A, TV > /a/ and /ss/ > /r/ in éss- *be*: éra-, in éro *I was*, éri *you were*, éra *he was*, ɛravámo *we were*, ɛraváte *you were*, érano *they were*.

6. In Timeless A, /a/ > /i/ in da- *give* and sta- *stand*: día (*that*) *I, you, he give*; diámo (*that*) *we give*; diáte (*that*) *you give*; díano (*that*) *they give*; and likewise stía (*that*) *I, you, he stand*, etc.

7. In Timeless A and Imperative:

a. /ɛss/ > /si/ in éss- *be*: sía (*that*) *I, you, he be*, etc.; síi *be!*; siámo *let's be!*; siáte *be!*.

b. /v/ > /bbi/ in av- *have*: ábbia (*that*) *I, you, he have*, etc.; ábbi *have!*; abbiámo *let's have*; abbiáte *have!*.

8. In Imperative 2.sg., vad- (:and-) *go* has ↓: váˣ *go!*.

2.332. STEM B.

1. In finite forms:

a. /ɛss/ > /sa/ in ɛss- *be*: sarɔ́ˣ *I shall be*, etc.

b. TV > 0, preceded by:

i. □, in bév- *drink* IIIb (x) /Reg/S¹ (optional, beside regularly formed Stem B bever-) and dɔl- *hurt*: bɛrrɔ́ˣ *I shall drink*, etc.; dɔrrɔ́ˣ *I shall hurt*, etc.

ii. No further non-automatic change in the root, in:

and- *go* (opt.)	pár- *appear* IIIa[12]	vál- *be worth*
kád- *fall* IIIax/Reg/S¹	pɔt- *be able, can*	véd- *see*[13] IIIa/Reg/S¹, ²
dóv- *owe*	sáp- *know*	vɛn- *come*
⁺mán- *remain*	tɛn- *hold*	vív- *live*[14] IIIb/Reg/S¹, ²
mɔr- *die* (opt.)	tóʎʎ- *take* (opt.)	vɔl- *wish*

---

[12] But not in ⁺par- *appear* II.

[13] Not in the derivatives prevéd- *foresee*; provvéd- *provide*; stravvéd- *see too much*; travvéd- *see imperfectly, see double*; optional in avvéd- *perceive* (refl.)

[14] Not in the derivatives kɔnvív- *live with*: sopravvív- *survive*.

2. In Non-Finite B:

a. Optionally, TV is 0 and the root has ↓ in bév- *drink*: bére *to drink*, beside the (rare) regularly formed bévere.

b. The root has ↓ in díK- *say* and fáč- *do*: díre *to say*, fáre *to do*.

2.333. Stem C.

1. In finite forms:

a. All forms are based on a variant root, with:

i. /a/ > /e/ in da- *give* and sta- *stand*: e.g. désti *you gave*; démmo *we gave*; stéssi (*that*) *I stood*; etc.

ii. /ɛss/ > /fo/ in éss- *be*: e.g. fósti *you were* (2.sg.); fóste *you were* (2.pl.); fóssi (*that*) *I were*; etc.

b. In Past C 1.pl. and regularly rhyzotonic forms: /o/ > /u/ in fú- (:éss-) *be*: fúmmo *we were*; fúi *I was*; fú* *he was*; fúrɔno *they were*.

2. In rhyzotonic forms of Past C and/or Non-Finite C, as specified in each instance, in the following strong verbs (all of IIIb/Reg unless otherwise specified or previously mentioned) the root has:

a. Alternation of phonemes alone, as follows:

i. /a/ > /e/ in Past C before TS /e/, in fáč- *do*: féč-e-.

ii. /e/ > /i/ in Past C before TS /e/, in véd- *see*: víd-e-.

iii. /e/ > /ɛˣ/ in Past C before TS /te/, in dé- (:da-) *give* (optional, alternating with /e/ > /iɛ́/, cf. subsection iv) and sté- (:stá-) *stand*: dét-te-; stét-te-.

iv. /e/ > /iɛ/ in Past C before TS /de/, in de- (:da-) *give* (optional, cf. subsection iii): diɛ́-de-.

v. /ɛ/ > /u/ in Past C before TS /se/ and in Non-Finite C before TS /s/, in ⁺péll- *-pel*: e.g., for espéll- *expel*, espúl-se-, espúl-s-.

vi. /i/ > /ɛ/ in Non-Finite C before TS /t/ in ⁺im- *-eem*: e.g., for redím- *redeem*, redén-t-.

vii. /ed/ > /is/ in Non-Finite C before TS /t/ in véd- *see*: vís-t-.

viii. /r/ > /ɛr/ in Past C before TS /se/ and in Non-Finite C before TS /t/ in the four verbs of II/Reg ápr- *open*, kópr- (kɔpr-) *cover*, óffr- *offer* and sóffr- *suffer*: apér-se-, kopér-se-, offér-se-, soffér-se-; apér-t-, kopér-t-, offér-t-, soffér-t-.

ix. Final C or /sK/ > /kk/ in Past C before TS /ue/, in násK- *come into being*, nɔč- *harm* and the three verbs of IIIa/Irr ǧáč- *lie*, piáč- *please*, and táč- *be silent*: nákk-ue-, nókk-ue-, ǧákk-ue-, piákk-ue-, tákk-ue-.

x. Final C or /nd/ > /s/ in Non-Finite C before TS /t/, in kiéd- *ask*; ⁺mán- *remain* IIIa/Irr; naskónd- *hide*; pón- *put*; and rispónd- *answer* (with optional /o/ > /ɔ/ in the last two): kiés-t-, ⁺más-t-, naskós-t-, pós-t- (pɔ́s-t-), rispós-t- (rispɔ́s-t-).

b. ↓, preceded by:

i. No other change:

A. In Past C before TS /se/ and Non-Finite C before TS /s/, in:

árd- *burn*

assíd- *seat*

+ číd- *-cide, -cise*

divíd- *divide*

esplód- *explode*

intríd- *knead*

intrúd- *intrude*

kiúd- *close*

+ klúd- *-clude*

kórr- *run*

léd- *injure*

+ lid- *-lide*

+ lud- *-lude*

+ mɛrG- *-merge*

mórd- *bite*

pérd- *lose*

rád- *shave*

ród- *gnaw*

sparG- *scatter*

+ spérG- *-sperse*

+ suád- *-suade*

šénd- *descend*

térG- *wipe*

+ túnd- *-tude*

+ vád- *-vade*

Thus: ár-se-, assí-se-, uččí-se- *killed*, etc.; ár-s-, assí-s-, uččí-s-, etc.

B. In Past C before TS /se/ and Non-Finite C before TS /t/, in:

akkórG- *notice*

attínG- *draw*

činG- *gird*

fínG- *feign*

fránG- *break*

fúnG- *serve as*

ǧúnG- *join, arrive*

indúlG- *indulge*

kóʎʎ- *gather*

múnG- *milk*

piánG- *weep*

pínG- *paint*

pórG- pórG- *offer*

púnG- *prick*

sórG- *rise*

spénG spénG- *extinguish*

strínG- *press*

šéʎʎ- *choose* IIIb/Irr

šóʎʎ- *undo* IIIb/Irr

tínG- *dye*

+ tíngu- *-tinguish*

tóʎʎ- *take* IIIb/Irr

tórK- *twist*

únG- *smear*

+ véll- *pull off* IIIb/Irr

vínK- *conquer*

vólG- *turn*

c. In Past C before TS /se/:

I. The verbs listed in §2.333.1.a.x: kié-s-, +má-s-, naskó-s-, pó-s-, rispó-s-.

II. The following: érG- *raise*, +fúlG- *shine*: ér-s-, +fúl-s-.

D. In Non-Finite C before TS /t/, in nasK- *come into being*: ná-t-.

ii. /ɛ/ > /e/, in Past C before TS /se/ and Non-Finite C before TS /s/, in aččénd- *light*, +fénd- *-fend*, +pénd- *-pend*,[15] prénd- *take*, rénd- *give back*, ténd- *stretch*: aččé-se-, +fé-se-, +pé-se-, pré-se-, ré-se-, té-se-; aččé-s-, +fé-s-, +pé-s-, pré-s-, ré-s-, té-s-.

iii. /o/ > /u/ in Past C before TS /se/ and Non-Finite C before TS /s/, in fónd- *melt*: fú-se-, fú-s-.

c. □, preceded by:
   i. No other change:
   A. In Past C before TS /se/ and in Non-Finite C before TS /s/, in:

+ čéd- *cede*[16]

flétt- *bend*

+ kɔt- *shake*

métt- *put*

mɔv- *move*

+ nétt- *-nect*

šínd- *split*

---

[15] In the derivatives appénd- *append*; dipénd- *depend*; propénd- *propend*; sospénd- *suspend*; spénd- *spend*; vilipénd- *vilipend*; but not in the simplex pénd- *hang*.

[16] In the derivatives končéd- *concede*; suččéd- *succede*.

B. In Past C before TS /se/ and in Non-Finite C before TS /t/, in:

fíGG- *fix*	kɔč- *cook*	skrív- *write*
+ flíGG- *-flict*	léGG- *read*	strúGG- *melt*
fríGG- *fry*	protéGG- *protect*	vív- *live*
fránG- *break*	réGG- *rule*	

Thus: fís-se-, +flís-se-, frís-se-, kós-se-, etc.; fít-t-, +flít-t-, frít-t-, kót-t-, etc.

    C. In Past C before TS /se/ in díK- *say* IV/Irr and +dúK- *-duce*, *-duct*: dís-se-, +dús-se-.

    D. In Past C before TS /be/, in kɔnósK- *know* and krésK- *grow*: konób-be-, kréb-be-.

    E. In Non-Finite C before TS /t/, in fáč- *make* and rómp- *break*: fát-t-, rót-t-.

    ii. /i/ > /e/, in Non-Finite C before TS /t/, in strínG- *press*: strét-t-.

    iii. /i/ > /ɛ/:

    A. In Past C before TS /se/ and in Non-Finite C before TS /s/, in +prím- *-press*: +prés-se-, +prés-s-.

    B. In Past C before TS /se/ and in Non-Finite C before TS /t/, in dilíG- *love*, neglíG- *neglect* and +ríG- *-rect*: dilés-se-, neglés-se-, +rés-se-; dilét-t-, neglét-t-, +rét-t-.

    C. In Non-Finite C before TS /t/ in díK- *say*: dét-t-.

    iv. /i/ > /a/:

    A. In Past C before TS /se/ and in Non-Finite C before TS /t/, in redíG- *edit*: redás-se-, redát-t-.

    B. In Non-Finite C before TS /t/, in esíG- *exact*: esát-t-.

    v. /a/ > /ɛ/ in Past C before TS /be/, in av- *have*: éb-be-.

    vi. /u/ > /o/ in Non-Finite C before TS /t/, in +duK- *-duct*, *-duce*: +dót-t-.

    d. ↓, in Past C before TS /e/, preceded by:

    i. No further change, in bév- *drink*, kád- *fall*, pióv- *rain*, vɔl- *wish*: bévv-e-, kádd-e-, pióvv-e, vóll-e-.

    ii. /om/ > /u/, in rómp- *break*: rúpp-e-.

    iii. /a/ > /e/, in sáp- *know*: sépp-e-.

    iv. /ɛ/ > /e/, in tɛn- *hold*, vɛn- *come*: ténn-e-, vénn-e-.

    e. Loss of final CC, preceded by /e/ > /i/, in Past C before TS /se/, in métt- *put*: mí-se-.

    3. In Non-Finite C:

    a. Arhyzotonic, before TV /u/:

    i. /v/ > /ss/ in vív- *live*: viss-ú-t-.

    ii. ↓ occurs in +vólv- *-volve*: +vɔl-ú-t-.

    b. TV /e/ > /i/, with:

    i. No change in stress, in +síst- *-sist*: +sist-í-t-.

    ii. Change in stress from arhyzotonic to rhyzotonic, in sɔl- *be wont*: sól-i-t-.

2.34. TENSE-SIGNS are:[17]

2.341. PRESENT:

1. /⊗á×/ in 1.-3.sg. and 3.pl. of:

a. Present A in verbs mentioned in §2.331.3.a: e.g. v-á-i *you go*; f-á× *he does*; s-án-no *they know*; án-no *they have*. With 1.sg. personal ending /a/ > /ɔ/ (§2.35.1): s-ɔ́× *I know*; ɔ́× *I have*; etc.

b. Present B of all verbs: e.g. kantɛr-á-i *you will sing*; kantɛr-á× *he will sing*; kantɛr-án-no *they will sing*; partir-á-i *you will depart*. With 1.sg. personal ending /a/ > /ɔ/: kantɛr-ɔ́× *I will sing*, etc.

2. TV > /iá/ in Present A 1.sg. of all verbs: e.g. kant-iá-mo *we sing*; part-iá-mo *we depart*; vɛnd-iá-mo *we sell*; abb-iá-mo *we have*; s-iá-mo *we are*.

3. 0 elsewhere: e.g., for Present A, kantá-te *you sing*; partí-te *you depart*; vɛndé-te *you sell*; dí-te *you say*. For Present B: kantɛré-te *you will sing*; partiré-te *you will depart*; vɛndɛré-te *you will sell*; diré-te *you will say*; kantɛré-mo *we will sing*; etc. With 1.sg. personal ending /⊗o/: kánt-o *I sing*; párt-o *I depart*; vénd-o *I sell*; etc. With 2.sg. personal ending /⊗i/: kánt-i *you sing*; párt-i *you depart*; vénd-i *you sell*; etc.

2.342. PAST.

1. In Past A:

a. In 1.-3.sg., 3.pl., 0 after éra- (:éss-) *be* (§2.331.5): éra *he used to be*; éra-no *they used to be*. With 1.sg. personal ending /⊗o/ and 2.sg. /⊗i/: éro *I used to be*; éri *you used to be*.

b. Elsewhere, /va/: e.g. kantá-va *he used to sing*; kanta-vá-mo *we used to sing*; kanta-vá-te *you used to sing*; kantá-va-no *they used to sing*; ɛra-vá mo *we used to be*; ɛra-vá-te *you used to be*; partí-va *he used to depart*; vɛndé-va *he used to sell*; etc. With 1.sg. personal ending /⊗o/: kantá-vo *I used to sing*; partí-vo *I used to depart*; vɛndé-vo *I used to sell*; etc. With 2.sg. personal ending /⊗i/: kantá-vi *you used to sing*; partí-vi *you used to depart*; vɛndé-vi *you used to sell*; etc.

2. In Past B:

a. In 1.-3.sg., 3.pl., /⊗é×/, followed by:

i. No further element in the tense-sign, in 1.sg.: e.g. kantɛr-é-i *I would sing*; partir-é-i *I would depart*; vɛndɛr-é-i *I would sell*; etc.

ii. /be/ in 3.sg. and 3.pl.: kantɛr-ébbe *he would sing*; kantɛr-ébbɛ-ro *they would sing*; partir-ébbe *he would depart*; partir-éb-bɛ-ro *they would depart*; etc.

3. In Past B and Past C:

a. In 1.pl., /×/. Thus, in Past B: kantɛré-m-mo *we would sing*; partiré-m-mo *we would depart*; vɛndɛré-m-mo *we would sell*; etc. In Past C: kantá-m-mo *we sang*; partí-m-mo *we departed*; vɛndé-m-mo *we sold*; fačé-m-mo *we did*; fú-m-mo *we were*; etc.

b. In 2.sg. and 2.pl., /st/. Thus, in Past B: kantɛré-st-i *you would sing* (sg.); kantɛré-st-e *you would sing* (pl.); partiré-st-i *you would depart* (sg.);

---

[17] In this section and §2.35, examples will be chosen for the clarity with which they exemplify the features under discussion, rather than for the sake of completeness.

partiré-s-te *you would depart* (pl.); vɛndɛré-st-i *you would sell* (sg.); vɛndɛré-s-te *you would sell* (pl.); etc.   In Past C: kantá-st-i *you sang* (sg.); kantá-s-te *you sang* (pl.); partí-st-i *you departed* (sg.); partí-s-te *you departed* (pl.); vɛndé-st-i *you departed* (sg.); vɛndé-st-e *you sold* (pl.); fačé-st-i *you did* (sg.); fó-s-te *you were* (pl.); etc.

    4. In Past C:

      a. In rhyzotonic forms (1.sg., 3.sg., 3.pl.) of strong verbs:

        i. 0, in fú- (:fó-:éss-) *be* (§2.333.1.b): fú-i *I was*, fú^x *he was*, fú-rɔno *they were*.

        ii. /e/, preceded by:

            A. 0, in the verbs listed in §2.333.2.a.i, ii: féč-e- *did*, víd-e- *saw*; and §2.333.2.d: bévv-e- *drank*, piɔ́vv-e- *rained*, vóll-e- *wished*, rúpp-e- *broke*, sépp-e- *knew*, ténn-e- *held*, vénn-e- *came*.

            B. /b/, in the verbs listed in §2.333.2.c.i.ᴅ: kɔnób-be- *knew*; kréb-be- *grew*; and §2.333.2.c.v: éb-be- *had*.

            c. /d/, in the verb dá- *give* (opt.; §2.333.2.a.iv): dié-de- *gave*.

            ᴅ. /s/, in the verbs mentioned with reference to Past C in §2.333.2, subsections a.v, viii; b; c.i.ᴀ-ᴄ, iii, iv;[18] and e.   Thus: espúl-se- *expelled*; apér-se- *opened*; kopér-se- *covered*; offér-se- *offered*; soffér-se- *suffered*; ár-se- *burned*, etc.; akkɔ́r-se- *noticed*, etc.; kié-se- *asked*, etc.; aččé-se- *lit*, etc.; fú-se- *melted*, etc.; kɔnčés-se- *conceded*, etc.; fís-se- *fixed*, etc.; dís-se- *said*; ⁺dús-se- *-duced*, *-ducted*; ⁺prés-se- *-pressed*; redás-se- *edited*; mí-se- *put*.   Also in the following verbs: dɔl- or dóLL- *hurt*, pár- *seem, appear* IIIax/Irr, ⁺par- *appear* II/ísK,[19] ⁺sum- *-sume* IIIb/Reg, trá^x *draw*, and val- *be worth*: dɔ́l-se-, pár-se-, ⁺sún-se-, trás-se-, vál-se-.

            ᴇ. /t/ in dé^x- (:dé-:dá-) *give*, sté- (:sté-:stá-) *stand* (§2.333.2.a.iii): dét-te-, stét-te-.

            ꜰ. /u/, in the verbs listed in §2.333.2.a.ix: ǧákk-ue- *lay*, nákk-ue- *came into being*, nɔ́kk-ue- *harmed*, piákk-ue- *pleased*, tákk-ue- *was silent*.

            ɢ. /v/, in par- *appear* IIIa/Irr (optional) and ⁺par- *appear* II/ísK:[20] par-ve-.

      b. In arhyzotonic forms:

        i. In 1., 3.sg. and 3.pl. of alternate forms of IIIb, /tte/: e.g. vɛndé-tte- *sold* (vɛndé-tt-i *I sold*; vɛndé-tte *he sold*; vɛndé-ttɛ-ro *they sold*).

        ii. In other forms, O: e.g. kantá-i *I sang*; kantá-rɔno *they sang*; partí-i *I departed*; partí-^{x} *he departed*; partí-rɔno *they departed*; vɛndé-i *I sold*: vɛndé^x *he sold*; vɛndé-rɔno *they sold*; with 3.sg. personal ending /a/ > /ɔ/ in conj. I, kantɔ́^{x} *he sang*.

---

  [18] Strong forms, with TS /se/, are found for métt- *put* optionally and rarely (més-se-); for fíGG- *fix*, they are found in the derivatives affíGG- *affix*, kročifíGG- *crucify*, infíGG- *infix*, prefíGG- *prefix*, suffíGG- *suffix*, and optionally in the simplex; for šínd- *split*, not in the derivative preššínd- *cut off, abstract*.

  [19] In the derivatives appar- *appear*, kɔmpar- *put in the appearance*, skɔmpar- *disappear*, traspar- *be transparent*.

  [20] In the derivatives listed in fn. 19 and in spar- *disappear*.

2.343. TIMELESS.

1. Timeless A:

a. In 1. and 2.pl., TV > /ia/: e.g. kant-iá-mo (*that*) *we sing*; part-iá-mo (*that*) *we depart*; vɛnd-iá-mo (*that*) *we sell*; s-iá-mo (*that*) *we be*; kant-iá-te (*that*) *you sing*; part-iá-te (*that*) *you depart*; vɛnd-iá-te (*that*) *you sell*; s-iá-te (*that*) *you be*; etc.

b. In 1.–3. sg. and 3.pl., TV >:

i. /i/ in Conj. I: e.g. kánt-i (*that*) *I, you, he sing*; kánt-i-no (*that*) *they sing*.

ii. /a/ in all other verbs: e.g. párt-a (*that*) *I, you, he depart*; párt-a-no (*that*) *they depart*; vénd-a (*that*) *I, you, he sell*; vénd-a-no (*that*) *they sell*; šélg-a (*that*) *I, you, he choose*; vád-a-no (*that*) *they go*; etc.

2. Timeless B:

a. In 1.pl., /si/: e.g. kantássimo (*that*) *we sang*; partíssimo (*that*) *we departed*; vɛndés-si-mo (*that*) *we sold*; fós-si-mo (*that*) *we were*.

b. In 2.pl., /s/: e.g. kantá-s-te (*that*) *you sang*; partí-s-te (*that*) *you departed*; vɛndé-s-te (*that*) *you sold*; fó-s-te (*that*) *you were*; etc.

c. In other persons, /se/: e.g. kantás-sc (*that*) *he sang*; kantás-sɛ-ro (*that*) *they sang*; partís-se (*that*) *he departed*; etc.

2.344. IMPERATIVE.

1. In 2.sg.:

a. /ˣ/ in da- *give*, sta- *stand*, di- (:díK-) *say*, fa- (:fáč-) *do* (§2.331.4) and va- (:vad-:and-) *go* (§2.331.8): dáˣ, díˣ, fáˣ, stáˣ, váˣ.

b. Zero in all other verbs: e.g. kanta *sing!*; párti *depart!*; véndi *sell!* (with 2.sg. personal ending /⊗i/; sí-i *be!*; abb-i *have!*.

2. In 1.pl., TV > /ia/ in all verbs: e.g. kant-iá-mo *let's sing!*; part-iá-mo *let's depart!*; vɛnd-iá-mo *let's sell!*; etc.

3. In 2.pl.:

a. TV > /a/ in si- (:éss-) *be* and abbi- (:av-) *have*: si-á-te *be!*; abbi-á-te *have!*.

b. 0 in all other verbs, e.g. kantá-te *sing!*; partí-te *depart!*; vɛndé-te *sell!*; dá-te *give!*; etc.

2.345. NON-FINITE.

1. On Stem A, with TV /i/ and /e/ > /ɛ/

a. Non-Finite[1] has /nd/; e.g. kantá-nd- *singing*; parté-nd- *departing*; vɛndé-nd- *selling*.

b. Non-Finite[2] has /nt/: e.g. kantá-nt- *singer*; assisté-nt- *assistant* (:assíst-assist IIIb/Reg/S[2]). TV /i/ and /e/ > /iɛ/ in a few archaic forms, now rare but occurring as bases for derivatives: e.g. udiént- *hearing*:ud- *hear* II/Irr/W, as in udiénţa *audience*.

2. On Stem B, 0: e.g. kantáre *to sing*; partíre *to depart*; kadére *to fall*; véndɛre *to sell*; pórre *to put*.

3. On Stem C, with TV > 0 in strong verbs (§2.321):

a. /s/ in the following verbs:

i. Those listed in the following subsections of §2.333:

A. 2.a.v: espúl-s- *expelled*.

B. 2.b.i.A, ii, iii: ár-s- *burned*, etc.; aččés-s- *lighted*, etc.; fú-s- *melted*, etc.

C. 2.c.i.A, iii.A: kɔnčés-s- *conceded*, etc.

ii. Also pár- *seem, appear* IIIax/Irr, ⁺pár- *appear* II, and vál- *be worth*: pár-s-, vál-s-.

b. /t/ in all other verbs, including all regular verbs, the strong verbs listed in §2.333 and not mentioned in subsection a above, and mɔr- *die*: e.g. kantá-t- *sung*; partí-t- *departed*; vɛndú-t- *sold*; mór-t- *dead*; etc. But in v Ɛn- *come*, TV /i/ > /u/: vɛn-ú-t- *come* (§2.322.III).

2.35. PERSONAL ENDINGS are:

1. In 1.sg.:

a. /a/ > /ɔ/ after TS /⊗áˣ/: e.g. s-ɔ̃ˣ *I know*; d-ɔ̃ˣ *I give*; st-ɔ̃ˣ *I stand*; v-ɔ̃ˣ *I go*; f-ɔ̃ˣ *I do*; kantɛr-ɔ̃ˣ *I shall sing*; partir-ɔ̃ˣ *I shall depart*; vɛndor-ɔ̃ˣ *I shall sell*; pɔrr-ɔ̃ˣ *I shall put*; etc.

b. /i/ in Past B and C and Timeless C (with loss of /e/ of a preceding TS): e.g. kantɛré-i *I would sing*; partiré-i *I would depart*; kantá-i *I sang*; partí-i *I departed*; vɛndé-i, vɛndétt-i *I sold*; fú-i *I was*; féč-i *I did*; diéd-i *I gave*; dís-si *I said*; nákku-i *I was born*; párv-i *I appeared*.

c. 0 in Timeless A:²¹ e.g. kánti *(that) I sing*; párta *(that) I depart*; vénda *(that) I sell*; sía *(that) I be*; váda *(that) I go*.

d. /⊗o/ elsewhere: e.g. kánt-o *I sing*; párt-o *I depart*; vénd-o *I sell*; són-o *I am*; kantáv-o *I used to sing*; partí-vo *I used to depart*; vɛndé-vo *I used to sell*; ér-o *I was*.

2. In 2.sg.:

a. 0 in:

i. Timeless A: e.g. kánti *(that) you sing*; párta *(that) you depart*; vénda *(that) you sell*; sía *(that) you be*.

ii. Imperative, in conj. I and after TS /ˣ/ (§2.344.1.a): e.g. kánta *sing!*; dáˣ *give!*; díˣ *say!*; fáˣ *do!*; stáˣ *stand!*; váˣ *go!*.

b. /⊗i/ elsewhere: e.g. kánt-i *you sing*; kantáv-i *you used to sing*; kantɛrá-i *you will sing*; kantɛrést-i *you would sing*; kantást-i *you sang*; kantáss-i *(that) you sang*; part-i *you depart*; partív-i *you used to depart*; vénd-i *you sell*; vɛndév-i *you used to sell*; sé-i *you are*; ér-i *you used to be*; etc.

3. In 3.sg.:

a. /a/ > /ɔ/ in Past C of verbs of conj. I: e.g. kantɔ̃ˣ *he sang*.

b. 0 (before which TV /i/ > /e/ in Pres. A of conj. II) elsewhere: e.g. kánta *he sings*; kantáva *he used to sing*; kánti *(that) he sing*; kantɛráˣ *he will sing*; kantɛrébbe *he would sing*; kantásse *(that) he sang*; párte *he departs*; partíva *he used to depart*; vénde *he sells*; vɛndéva *he used to sell*; Ɛ̃ˣ *he is*; éra *he used to be*; puɔ̃ˣ *he can*; fáˣ *he does*; etc.

4. In 1.pl., /mo/: e.g. kantiá-mo *we sing, (that) we sing, let's sing!*; kantavá-mo *we used to sing*; kantɛré- mo *we will sing*; kantɛrém-mo *we would sing*; kan-tám-mo *we sang*; kantássi-mo *(that) we sang*; partiá-mo *we depart, (that) we*

---

²¹ Use of ending 0 in Past A 1.sg. (e.g. kantáva *I used to sing*) is now archaic or sub-standard.

depart, let's depart; vɛndiá-mo *we sell, (that) we sell, let's sell!;* vɛndevá-mo *we used to sell;* siá-mo *we are, (that) we be, let's be!;* etc.

5. In 2.pl., /te/: e.g. kantáte *you sing, sing!;* kantavá-te *you used to sing;* kantiá-te *(that) you sing;* kantɛré-te *you will sing;* kantɛrés-te *you would sing;* kantás-te *you sang;* partí-te *you depart;* partivá-te *you used to depart;* vɛndé-te *you sell;* vɛndevá-te *you used to sell;* sié-te *you are;* etc.

6. In 3.pl.:

a. /ro/ in Past B, Past C and Timeless C: e.g. kantɛrébbɛ-ro *they would sing;* partirébbɛ-ro *they would depart;* vɛndɛrébbɛ-ro *they would sell;* vɛndétto-ro *they sold;* vólle-ro *they wished;* apérsɛ-ro *they opened;* ğákkuɛ-ro *they laid;* kantássɛ-ro *(that) they sang;* partíssɛ-ro *(that) they departed;* vɛndéssɛ-ro *(that)*

TABLE VII
MORPHOLOGICALLY DETERMINED PREPOSITIONAL ALTERNANTS

Before L- *the* (with loss of /i/ in il, m.sg.)	Elsewhere	Examples
dɛ*, *of*	d(i),	dɛllíbro *of the book;* dɛlluómo *of the man;* deilíbri *of the books;* dɛllakárta *of the paper;* but dilíbri *of books*
nɛ*, *in*	in,	nɛllíbro *in the book;* nɛlluómo *in the man;* neilíbri *in the books;* nɛllakárta *in the paper;* but inlíbri *in books*
kɔ*, *with*[22]	kɔn,	kɔllíbro *with the book;* kɔlluómo *with the man;* koilíbri *with the books;* kɔllakárta *with the paper;* but kɔnlíbri *with books*
pɛ*, *by, for*[22]	pɛr,	pɛllíbro *for the book;* pɛlluómo *for the man;* peilíbri *for the books;* pɛllakárta *for the paper;* but pɛrlíbri *for books*

they sold. But the use of /ro/ alone in Past C, after tense-signs other than those ending in /e/, is now archaic or non-standard, as in kantá-ro *they sang;* partí-ro *they departed;* fú-ro *they were.*

b. /no/ elsewhere:

i. Added to the 3.pl. personal ending /ro/ (forming a double ending -rono), in Past C after tense-signs other than those ending in /e/: e.g. kantá-rono *they sang;* partí-rono *they departed;* fú-rono *they were.*

ii. Alone, in other tenses (with preceding TV /e/ or /i/ > /ɔ/): e.g. kánta-no *they sing;* kantáva-no *they used to sing;* kánti-no *(that) they sing;* kantɛrán-no *they will sing;* pártɔ-no *they depart;* partíva-no *they used to depart;* párta-no *(that) they depart;* partirán-no *they will depart;* véndɔ-no *they sell;*

[22] Optional; at present, use of kɔ* instead of kɔn, before a definite article is somewhat archaic, and use of pɛ* instead of pɛr, is wholly archaic or sub-standard.

vɛndéva-no *they used to sell*; vénda-no (*that*) *they sell*; vɛnderán-no *they will sell*; só-no *they are*; éra-no *they used to be*; ván-no *they go*; etc.

2.4. INDECLINABLES.

2.41. PREPOSITIONS are of the following types:

1. Those in which the preposition has variants whose use is determined by phonological or morphological factors:

    a. Phonological factors determine the use of:

       i. a^x, *to* before a consonant ∼ ad, before a vowel: e.g. allúi *to him*, ammé^x *to me*, but adáltri *to others*.

       ii. di, *of* before a consonant (except before L- *the*, see Table VII) ∼ d, before a vowel: e.g. dimólti *of many*, but dalkúni *of some*.

    b. Morphological factors determine the use of the alternants shown in Table VII. The preposition kɔn, *with* has also the special alternant $^+$ko occurring in the compounds méko *with me*, téko *with thee* etc. (§3.225.2.b.i).

2. Those in which the preposition has only one form: e.g. da^x, *from*; fra^x, or tra^x, *among*; sénca *without*.

2.42. CONNECTIVES (usually termed 'coordinating conjunctions', and also including some forms traditionally termed 'adverbs') are likewise of two types:

1. Those having two phonologically determined alternants: ed, *and* (opt.) and od *or* (rare) before vowel ∼ e^x, and o^x, elsewhere: e.g. e(d)áltri *and others*, but ɛllúi *and him*, eččandó^x *and he went there*.

2. Those having only one alternant: e.g. nón, *not*; má^x, *but*.

2.43. ADVERBS, CONJUNCTIONS AND MINOR-CLAUSE Forms have only one alternant each: e.g. béne *well* adv.; mále *badly* adv.; ke^x∼ *that*; sí^x *yes*; nó^x *no*; ái *ow!*; pšt *psst, hey!*. The adverbs či, and vi, are phrasally bound, and are substitute ('pronominal') forms; they replace preposition-plus-object phrases (§4.21) introduced by a^x, *at, to*; in, *in*; kɔn, *with*; and su^x, *on*: e.g. nónrispósialle-súeparóle *I didn't answer* (lit. *to*) *his words* ∼ nónčirispósi or nónvirispósi *I didn't answer* (lit. *to*) *them*. But purists condemn the substitution of či, or vi,, instead of a bound personal indirect object pronoun, for a phrase containing a personal pronoun or noun referring to an animate object, as in buttáiunóssoalkáne *I threw a bone to the dog* ∼ čibuttáiunósso *I threw him a bone* (condemned by purists) instead of ʎibuttáiunósso. Similarly, the adverb ne, replaces phrases introduced by the prepositions di, *of* and da^x, *from* (including those referring to persons or animate objects, without objections from the purists): e.g. libɛriámočidalléi *let's get away* (lit. *free ourselves*) *from her* ∼ libɛriámočene *id*.

When cited in their root-forms, indeclinables will be classified according to their stem-vowels, with the same numbers as those assigned to the stem-vowels in §2.121: thus, bén- *well* adv/III; benín- *just right* adv/II; sénc- *without* prep/I; fuór- *outside* adv or prep/IV; pɛr, *for* prep/VI.

CHAPTER III. DERIVATION

Derivation of Italian inflected forms is accomplished by affixation and compounding. Each derived form belongs to one of the form-classes described in Chapter II, with the exception of certain bound prefixes and bases. An underlying form to which a suffix is added or which occurs as a constituent of a compound, is termed a BASE; a base not subdivisible into further elements is a PRIMARY base. In the discussion of derivatives, especially those formed by affixation, bases will be cited without inflectional endings wherever desirable for the sake of clarity, and with indication of the form-classes to which they belong.

3.0. ALTERNANT FORMS OF BASES occur in a number of derivatives, especially by affixation, and are listed here according to the alternations of phonemes which take place in them.

3.01. SPECIAL ALTERNANTS OF NON-FINITE C, based on certain verbs or verbal bases, and used only in derivation, show the following alternations of phonemes:

1. Before TS /s/:

   a. ↓ , in:

sɛnt- *feel* II/Reg/W	aččɛnd- *light*	
+ ɛr- *-here* ⎫	fɛnd- *split*	
plaud- *-plaud* ⎬ II/ísK/W	pɛnd- *hang*	
+ sɔrb- *(ab)sorb* ⎭	prɛnd- *take* ⎬ IIIb/Reg/S[1, 2]	
vid+: vɛd- *see* IIIa/Reg/S[1, 2]	+ spɔnd- *-spond*	
vɛrt- *turn* IIIb/Reg	šɛnd- *(de)scend*	
	tɔrK- *twist*	

Thus: sɛns+, +es+, plaus+, sɔrs+, vis+, vɛrs+, aččɛns+, fɛns+, pɛns+, prɛns+, spɔns+, šɛns+, tɔrs+.

   b. □, in +gred- *-gress, step* and pat- *suffer* II/ísK/W; sɛd- *sit* IIIa/Reg/W; and čɛd- *cede, -ceed, yield* IIIb/Reg/W: +grɛss+, pass+, sɛss+, čɛss+.

   c. /et/ > /is/ in mɛtt- *put, send* IIIb/Reg/S[1, 2]: miss+.

   d. /ɛ/ > /u/ in +vɛll- *strip, pull off* IIIb/Reg/S[1, 2]: +vuls+.

   e. /im/, /ik/ > /ɛs/ in +'plik- *-plicate* I/Reg/W and +prím- *-press* IIIb/ Reg/S[1] (:prém- *id.*): +plɛss+, +prɛss+.

   f. /o/ > /u/ in kórr- *run* IIIb/Reg/S[1, 2]: kurs+.

2. Before TS /t/:

   a. No change in root, in:

vɛn- *come* II/Irr/S[1, 2]	kól- *cultivate* IIIb	
+ ǧɛr- *-gest* ⎫	(b)uR+ *burn* ⎫	
kap- *take, grasp* ⎮	+ sul+ *-sult* ⎬ quasi-III	
+ loku- *speak* ⎬ II/ísK/W	tɔRR+ *burn* ⎭	
+ sɛr- *-sert* ⎮		
+ stitu- *stitute* ⎮		
+ tribu- *tribute* ⎭		

39

Thus: vɛnt⁺, ⁺ǧest⁺, kapt⁺, ⁺sɛrt⁺, ⁺stitut⁺, ⁺tribut⁺, kɔlt⁺, ⁺(b)ust⁺, ⁺lokut⁺, ⁺sult⁺, tɔst⁺.

b. ↓, in sanč- *sanction* II/ísK/W; mɔv- *move*, ténd- *stretch*, téss- *weave*, all of IIIb/Reg: ⁺sant⁺, mɔt⁺, tɛnt⁺, tɛst⁺.

c. □, in ⁺čep- -*ceive, cept* II/ísK/W; ⁺čév- -*ceive* IIIb/Reg/W; vív- *live* IIIb/Reg/S¹, ²; díK- *say* IV/Irr/S¹, ²; ⁺dúK- -*duct, -duce* IV/Reg/S¹, ²; and the verbal base spɛk⁺ *look, -spect*: čɛtt⁺, vitt⁺, ditt⁺, ⁺dutt⁺, spɛtt⁺.

d. /iɛ/ > /ues/ in kiéd- *ask* IIIb/Reg/S¹, ²: kuest⁺.

e. /g/ > /k/ in ségu- *follow* II/Reg/W: ⁺sekut⁺.

f. /nG/ and /nK/ > /t/ in fínG- *feign*, vínK- *conquer* IIIb/Reg/S¹, ²: fint⁺, vitt⁺.

g. /omp/ > /ut/ in rómp- *break* IIIb/Reg/S¹, ²: rutt⁺.

h. /ɔ/ > /u/ in kɔ́l- *cultivate* IIIb/Reg: kult⁺.

j. /s/ > /ns/ in tós- *shear* I/Reg/W: tons⁺.

k. /esK/ > /is/ in mésK- *mix* IIIb/Reg/W: mist⁺.

l. /v/ > /u/ in fav⁺ *favor*: faut⁺.

m. /t/ is added in ve⁺ *carry*: vett⁺.

3.02. OTHER BASES show:

1. Loss:

a. Vowels:

i. In derivation, two like vowels coalesce to form a single vowel, especially /i/ + /i/ > /i/ and /u/ + /u/ > /u/: e.g. prí⁺ *pri-(or)* + ⁺'im- numeral suffix adj/I–II > prímo *first* adj/I–II.

ii. An initial vowel is lost:

A. In ekui⁺ *equi-* > ⁺kui⁺ after s⁺ *dis-*, privative in skuilíbr- *unbalance* I/Reg/W:ekuilíbr- *equilibrate* I/Reg/W; ést- *this* (archaic) > st- in the compounds stamáne, and stamattína *this morning*, stanɔ́tte *tonight*, staséra *this evening*, stavɔ́lta *this time*.

B. Optionally, in a number of forms, most of which are archaic or sub-standard in contrast to the full forms, e.g.:

I. /i/: struménto *instrument* m/IIb: istruménto *id.*

II. /e ɛ/: pístɔla *epistle, letter* f/Ia: epístɔla *id.*; resía *heresy* f/Ia: ɛresía *id.*; státe *summer* f/IIIb: estáte id.; strémo *extreme* adj/I–II: estrémo *id.*

III. /a/: rabésko *arabesque* m/IIb: arabésko *id.*; strɔ́logo *astrologer*: astrɔ́logo *id.*

IV. /o/: spedále *hospital* m/IIIb: ospedále *id.*

iii. A medial vowel is lost (optionally, except as stated):

A. /i/, in spásim- *spasm* m/IIb ∼ spásm- *id.*; sálič- *willow* m/IIIb ∼ sálč- (optional in simplex and in saličéto salčéto *willow-grove* m/IIb; regular in salčáio *willow-hedge* m/IIb, salčíɲɲo *willowy* adj/I–II).

B. /ɛ/, in témpɛra *temper* f/Ia; véspɛro *evening, vesper(s)* m/IIb; spɛróne *spur* m/IIIb: témpra, véspro, spróne.

iv. A final vowel is lost:

A. /a/, in stá- *stand* IV/Irr/S¹, in a number of derivatives after prefixes, e.g. díst- *be distant*, kɔ́nst- *consist*, etc., all I/Reg/W.

B. /ɔ/, in benzɔ⁺ *benzo-* > bɛnʐ⁺, in bɛnʐína *benzine, gasoline* f/Ia.
b. Consonants:
  i. In final position:
    A. ↓ occurs in scattered derivatives of:

ídɔl- *idol*
líbr- *book*
mağístr- *master* ⎫ m/IIb
minístr- *minister*⎭
bóv- *ox* m/IIIb
minɔ́s *Minos* m/VId

kuadr⁺: kuáttr- *four* num/IId
tréˣ *three* num/VId
réGG- *rule, direct*⎫
tɔ́rK- *twist*   ⎬ IIIb/Reg/S¹, ²
vív- *live*   ⎭
pav⁺ *fear*

Derivatives showing the shortened bases: idɔ́latra *idolater* m/Ib; libéllo *little book, libel* m/IIb; mağistéro *mastery, mastership* m/IIb; ministéro *ministry* m/IIb; boário *boarian, for the sale of cattle* adj/I–II; boattiére *cattle-merchant, -herder* m/IIIb; minɔ́iK- *Minoan* adj/I–II; kuader⁺ (in kuadɛrlétto *square patch* m/IIb; kuadérno *note-book* m/IIb; kuadérna *series of four numbers* f/Ia); trédiči *thirteen* num/IVd; reğía *administration* (especially *tobacco monopoly*) f/Ia; tɔrménto *torment* m/IIb; víta *life* f/Ia; paúra *fear* f/Ia.
    B. /ngu/ is lost in saláss- *let blood* I/Reg/W = sa(ngu-) *blood* m/IIIb + láss- (archaic): lášš- *let* I/Reg/W.
    C. ↓↓ occurs in scattered derivatives of:

médi- *half* adj/I–II
kuinku⁺: čínku- *five* num/IIId
tréˣ *three* num/VId
ɔ́pɛr- *work* f/Ia
fɔ́sfɔr- *phosphorus* m/IIb
kuiét- *quiet* ⎫
palúd- *swamp* ⎬ f/IIIb
pólvɛr- *dust* ⎭

análiT- *analysis* f/IVd
naʐʐarét *Nazareth* m/VId
⁺táˣ -*ty* f/VId
činɛr⁺ *ashes*
bév- *drink* IIIb (x)/Reg/S¹

Examples of derivatives showing the shortened bases: metáˣ *half* f/VId; kuinário *quinary* adj/I–II; kuínto *fifth* adj/I–II; kuíndiči *fifteen* num/VId; tríno *trine* adj/I–II; opúskɔlo *opuscule*, fosfáto *phosphate*, fosfíto *phosphite*, fosfúro *phosphide*, all m/IIb; kuieššénte *quiescent* adj/IIIb; palústre *palustrine* adj/IIIb; pólve *dust* (archaic) f/IIIb; analísta *analyst* m/Ia; analíʐʐ- *analyze* I/Reg/W; naʐʐaréno *Nazarene* adj/I–II; all derivatives in ⁺os- -*ous*, -*ose* adj/I–II on nouns in ⁺táˣ -*ty*, e.g. kalamitóso *calamitous*:kalamitáˣ *calamity*; činíğa *hot ashes mixed with embers* f/Ia; béttɔla *drinkshop* f/Ia.
  ii. In medial position:
    A. /v/ > 0 in paóne *peacock* m/IIIb ~ pavóne *id.*
    B. /n/ > 0 in ⁺vik⁺:vínK-*overcome, conquer* IIIb/Reg/S¹, ²: pɛrvikáče *obstinate* adj/IIIb.
2. Replacement:
  a. Single Phonemes:
    i. Vowels:

A. /i/ >:

I. /e/ in ɔle⁺:óli- oil m/IIb and pedikɔl⁺: pidókki- *louse* m/IIb: e.g. ɔleáčeo *oleaceous*, ɔleaǧinóso *oleaginous*, ɔleário *of oil*, ɔléiK- *oleic*, ɔleóso *oil-bearing*, all adj/I–II, etc.; pedikɔláre *pedicular* adj/IIIb.

II. /ɛ/ in arɛng⁺: aríng- *harangue* f/Ia and ǧovɛn⁺:ǧóvin- *young* adj/IIIb, in arɛngário *speaker's stand*, *pulpit* m/IIb and ǧovɛntúˣ *youth* f/VId.

III. /ɔ/ (optionally) in martório *martyrdom* ∼ martírio *id.* m/IIb.

IV. /l/ in numerous but scattered derivatives of:

kiár- *clear* ⎫
pián- *level, plane* ⎬ adj/I–II
pién- *full* ⎭
giándɔl- *gland* ⎫ f/Ia
piánt- *sole (of foot)* ⎭

esémpi- *example* ⎫
giáčč- *ice* ⎬ m/IIb
kióstr- *cloister* ⎬
témpi- *temple* ⎭
fiór- *flower* m/IIIb
kiám- *call* I/Reg/W
kiúd- *close* IIIb/Reg/S[1, 2]

Examples of derivatives showing the alternants of these bases: prekláro *illustrious* adj/I–II; planimetría *planimetry* f/Ia; plɛnário *plenary* adj/I–II; glandɔláre *glandular* adj/IIIb; plantígrado *plantigrade* adj/I–II; esɛmpláre *exemplary* adj/IIIb; glačále *glacial* adj/IIIb; klaustrále *cloistral* adj/IIIb; tɛmpláre *Templar* m/IIIb; flɔrále *floral* adj/IIIb; klamóre *clamor* m/IIIb; ⁺klúd- *-clude*, as in okklúd- *occlude* IIIb/Reg/S[1, 2], etc.

V. /ɔl/ in maskɔl⁺:maski- *male* adj/I–II, in maskɔlíno *masculine* adj/I–II.

VI. /r/ in par⁺:pai- *pair* m/IIc, in paríʎʎa *couple* f/Ia.

B. /e/ >:

I. /i/ in a considerable number of bases, including:

déɲɲ- *worthy* adj/I–II
mén- *less* adj/IId
tre⁺: tréˣ *three* num/VId
ančéll- *handmaiden* ⎫
čétr- *cithara* ⎬ f/Ia
sélv- *forest* ⎭
péɲɲ- *pledge* ⎫
sén- *breast, curve* ⎬ m/IIb
séɲɲ- *signal* ⎬
vétr- *glass* ⎭

léɲɲ- *wood* m/IIc
čénɛr- *ashes* m/IIIb
féd- *faith* ⎫
péč- *pitch* ⎬ f/IIIb
sét- *thirst* ⎭
⁺čep- *-cept* II/ísK/W
tém- *fear* IIIa/Reg/W
véd- *see* IIIa/Reg/S[1]
prém- *press* IIIb/Reg/S[1]

Examples of derivatives based on the alternants: diɲɲitá⁺ *dignity* f/VId; minóre *lesser* adj/IIIb; tríade *triad* f/IIIb; ančilláre *ancillary* adj/IIIb; čitarédo *singer with the cithara* m/IIb; silváno *sylvan* adj/I–II; píɲɲɔr- *fake as pledge, foreclose* I/Reg/W; sinuóso *sinuous* adj/I–II; siɲɲífik- *signify* I/Reg/W; vítreo *vitreous* adj/I–II; líɲɲeo *ligneous* adj/I–II; činɛrário *cinerary* adj/I–II; fíd- *trust* I/Reg/W; píčeo *pitch-like* adj/I–II; sitibóndo *thirsty* adj/I–II; partéčip-

participate I/Reg/W; tímido *timid* adj/I–II; provvidénte *provident* adj/IIIb; opprím- *oppress* IIIb/Reg/S[1, 2].

II. /ɛ/ in mɛnt⁺:mént- *mind* f/IIIb, in dɛménte *demented* adj/IIIb.

III. /a/ (optionally) in salv⁺:sélv- *forest* f/Ia, in salvátiK- ~ sɛlvátiK- *wild, savage* adj/I–II.

IV. /u/ (optionally) in uguále ~ eguále *equal* adj/IIIb.

V. /ie/ in pariét⁺:parét- *wall* f/IIIb, in parietále *parietal* adj/IIIb and parietária *wall-plant* f/Ia.

VI. /ği/ in sağitt⁺:saétt- *arrow* f/Ia, in sağittále *sagittal* adj/IIIb and sağittário *bowman, Sagittarius* m/IIb.

VII. /ig/ in ⁺nigr⁺:nér- *black* adj/I–II, in denígr- *denigrate* I/Reg/W.

C. /ɛ/ or /Ɛ/:

I. /i/ in:

éku- *fair* adj/I–II	čél- *sky* ⎱ m/IIb
méʎʎ- *better* adj/IIIb	račém- *bunch of grapes* ⎰
mamméll- *breast* f/Ia	sƐd- *sit* IIIa/Reg/W
	tƐn- *hold* IIIa/Irr/S¹

Thus: iníku- *unfair* adj/I–II; miʎʎóre *better* adj/IIIb; mammilláre *mamillary* adj/IIIb; čiléstro *sky-blue* adj/I–II; račímɔlo *little bunch* m/IIb; presidénte *president* m/IIIb; pɛrtináče *pertinaceous* adj/IIIb, etc.

II. /a/ in:

ebré- *Hebrew* adj/I–II	moséˣ *Moses* m/VId
tɛnáʎʎ- *claw* f/Ia (opt.)	⁺iétt- *-ject* I/Reg/W
spɔndé- *spondee* ⎱ m/IIb	
troké- *trochee* ⎰	

Thus: ebráiK- *Hebraic* adj/I–II; tanáʎʎa *claw* (~ tɛnáʎʎa); spɔndáiK- *spondaic*, trokáiK- *trochaic* and mosáiK- *Mosaic* adjs/I–II; iattánca *boastfulness* f/Ia.

III. /ɔ/ in vɔlɔnt⁺:vɔlént- *willing* adj/IIIb, in vɔlɔntáˣ *will* f/VId and (optionally) vɔlɔntiéri ~ vɔlɛntiéri *willingly* adv/IV.

IV. /ie/ in alliév⁺:allév- *raise up* and liɛv⁺: lév- *raise*, both I/Reg/W, in alliévo *pupil* and liévito *leaven*, both m/IIb.

D. /a/ >:

I. /i/ in:

amíK- *friendly* ⎱ adj/I–II	ağ- *act* II/ísK/W
dát- *given* ⎰	sáp- *know* ⎱ IIIa/Irr/S¹
fáčil- *easy* ⎱ adj/IIIb	táč- *be silent* ⎰
ğóvan- *young* (opt.) ⎰	dá- *give* IV/Irr/S¹
	fáč- *do* IV/Irr/S[1, 2]

Thus: inimíK- *hostile* adj/I–II; édito *published*, dédito *given over*, both adjs/ I–II; diffíčile *difficult* adj/IIIb and diffikɔltáˣ *difficulty* f/VId; ğóvine (~ ğóvane) *young* adj/IIIb; redíğ- *edit, redact* IIIb/Reg/S[1, 2]; desipiénte *stupid* adj/IIIb;

retičénte *reticent* adj/IIIb; réddito *return* (*e.g. on capital*) m/IIb; effičénte *efficient* adj/IIIb; etc.

      ii. /ε/ in:

amíK- *friendly*}
fátt- *done* } adj/I–II
bárb- *beard* f/Ia

árm- *arm, weapon* f/Ib
ánn- *year* }
dánn- *harm* } m/IIb

Thus: nεmíK- *hostile, enemy* adj/I–II; pεrfétto *perfect* adj/I–II; imbérbe *beardless*, inérme *unarmed*, biénne *biennial*, indénne *unharmed*, all adj/IIIb.

      iii. /u/ in +suls+: sáls- *salty* adj/I–II and +sult+: sált- *jump* I/Reg/W, in insúlso *insulse* adj/I–II; insúlto *insult* and sussúlto *jerk*, both m/IIb.

      E. /ɔ/ >:
         i. /u/ in:

ísɔl- *island* }
nócc- (pl.) *wedding*} f/Ia
ɔrín- *urine* (opt.) }

lɔ́t- *mud* (opt.)}
ómεr- *shoulder*} m/IIb
érkɔl- *Hercules* m/IIIb

Thus: insuláre *insular* adj/IIIb; nuciále *nuptial* adj/IIIb; urína (~ ɔrína) *urine* f/Ia; lúto (~ lɔ́to) *mud* m/IIb; lúteo *yellowish* adj/I–II; lutulénto *muddy* adj/I–II; umεrále *humeral, of the shoulder* adj/IIIb; erkúleo *Herculean* adj/I–II.

      ii. /au/ in:

kód- *tail* f/Ia
kióstr- *cloister*}
lɔrét- *Loreto* } m/IIb

ór- *gold* (opt.)}
tór- *bull* (opt.)} m/IIb
lód- *praise* (opt.) I/Reg/W

Thus: kaudáto *caudate* adj/I–II; klaustrále *cloistral* adj/IIIb; lauretáno *of Loreto* adj/I–II; áuro (~ óro) *gold* m/IIb; áureo *golden* adj/I–II; táuro (~ tóro) *bull* m/IIb; láude (~ lóde) *praise* f/IIIb; etc.

      F. /o/ > /u/ in:

fósk- *dark* }
mólt- *many*} adj/I–II
sólk- *furrow* m/IIb

króč- *cross* }
pólv- *dust* } f/IIIb
pólvεr- *dust*}
kórr- *run* IIIb/Reg/S[1, 2]

Thus: offúsk- *obfuscate* I/Reg/W; múltiplo *multiple* adj/I–II; trisúlko *trisulcate* adj/I–II; kručále *crucial* adj/IIIb; pulvískɔlo *fine dust* m/IIb; pulvεrulénto *dusty* adj/I–II; kurríkɔlo *curriculum* m/IIb.

      G. /u/ >:
         i. /i/ in εsil+:ésul- *exile* (person) m/IIIb, in esílio *exile* (condition) m/IIb.

      ii. /o ɔ/ in lɔnG+:lunG+:lúng- *long* adj/I–II; do+:dú- *two* num/IIId; argɔ+:argu- *argue* II/ísK/W: e.g. lɔnǧitúdine *longitude* f/IIIb; dódiči *twelve* num/IVd; argɔménto *argument* m/IIb.

      iii. /au/ in aud+:ud- *hear* II/Irr/W and klaus+:kius- *closed* adj/I–II: e.g. auditívo *auditive* adj/I–II; klausúra *closure* f/Ia; etc.

ɪᴠ. /uv/ in diluv⁺:dilu- *add water* II/ísK/W, in dilúvio *deluge*
m/IIb.

ᴠ. /v/ (optionally) in nevr⁺:neur⁺ *nerve*: e.g. nevralǧía (∼ neu-
ralǧía) *neuralgia* f/Ia; etc.

  ii. Consonants change with respect to:
    ᴀ. Voice:
      ɪ. Voicing takes place in:
        α. /t/ > /d/ in mɛnd⁺:mént- *lie* II/ísK/W; líd- ∼ lít- *shore,
beach* m/IIb; podér-:potér- *to be able* m/IIIb (infin.): thus, mɛndáče *mendacious* adj/IIIb; lído *beach, Lido* m/IIb; podére *farm* m/IIIb, and with meaning
strength in podɛróso *powerful* adj/I–II, podestáˣ *mayor* m/IVd.
        β. /k/ > /g/ in egu⁺:éku- *fair* adj/I–II, in eguále *equal* adj/IIIb.
      ɪɪ. Unvoicing takes place in:
        α. /d/ > /t/ in patr⁺:pádr- *father* m/IIIb; matr⁺:mádr- *mother*
f/IIIb: e.g. pátria *fatherland* f/Ia; patriárka *patriarch* m/Ib; património *patri-
mony* m/IIb; matričída *matricide* m/Ib; matrípɲa *stepmother* f/Ia; etc.
        β. /g/ > /k/ in lak⁺:lág- *lake* m/IIb; lɔk⁺:lɔg- *place* m/IIb;
⁺seku⁺:ségu- *follow* II/Reg/W: e.g. lakústre *lacustrine* adj/IIIb; lokále *local*
adj/IIIb; lɔ́k- *locate* I/Reg/W; kɔnsekutívo *consecutive* adj/I–II; etc.
    ʙ. Manner of articulation: C > :
      ɪ. Plosive, in auspik⁺:áuspič- *auspex* m/IIIb; maid⁺:máis *maize*
m/VId; ⁺fik⁺:fáč- *do* IV/Irr/S¹˒²; od⁺:ɔl⁺ *smell*; thus, áuspik- *auspicate* I/Reg/
W; maídiK- *of corn* adj/I–II; ⁺′fik- *-fy* I/Reg/W, as in sipɲífik- *signify*, etc.;
maidísmo *pellagra* m/IIb; odóre *odor* m/IIIb.
      ɪɪ. Assibilate (before front vowel: /K G/, §1.621), in bases built
on:

lúng- *long*			čírk- *circus*	
mánk- *left*	} adj/I–II		múk- *mucus*	} m/IIb
ráuk- *raucous*			vísk- *bird-lime*	
vákk- *cow*	} f/Ia		róg- *draw up* I/Reg/W	
váng- *spade*				

Thus: lúnǧi *afar* adv/IV; mančíno *left* adj/I–II; raučédine *hoarseness* f/IIIb;
vaččíno *pertaining to cows* adj/I–II; vanǧíle *footpiece of spade* m/IIIb; čirčénse
of the circus, circensian adj/IIIb; múčido *foul-smelling, rancid* adj/I–II; viššido
viscid adj/I–II; róǧito *drawing up* m/IIb.
      ɪɪɪ. /r/, in prur⁺:prúd- *itch* IIIb/Reg; sal- kráut- (pl.) *sauerkraut*
m/IIb; pur⁺:pús *pus* m/VId; thus, prúrito *itching* m/IIb; pruríǧine *itching*
f/IIIb; salkráuti ∼ sarkráuti (pl.) *sauerkraut* m/IIb; purulénto *purulent*
adj/I–II.
      ɪᴠ. /s/, in kiɛs⁺:kiéd- *ask, seek* IIIb/Reg/S¹˒² and pos⁺:pón-
put IV/Irr/S¹˒², in kiésito *investigation, problem* m/IIb and ⁺pósit- *-posit* m/IIb
e.g. in depósito *deposit*).
    ᴄ. Position of articulation:
      ɪ. Labial or dental > palatal in pióǧǧ⁺:pióv- *rain* f/Ia; pipɲ⁺:pín-
pine m/IIb; kapɲ⁺:kán- *dog* m/IIIb; papɲ⁺:pán- *bread* m/IIIb; uguaʎʎ⁺:
uguál- *equal* adj/IIIb; viʎʎ⁺:víl- *vile* adj/IIIb; miʎʎ:míll- *1000* num/IIIc;

bariʎʎ+:baríl- *barrel* m/IIIb; širópp- ∼ sirópp- *syrup* m/IIb. Thus: pióǧǧa *rain* f/Ia; pínɲa *pine-tree* f/Ia; kápɲa *bitch* f/Ia; kaɲɲolíno *little dog* m/IIb; paɲɲótta *loaf of bread, livelihood* f/Ia; uguáʎʎ- *make equal* I/Reg/W; viʎʎákko *base* adj/I–II; bariʎʎóne *big barrel* m/IIIb; širóppo *syrup* m/IIb.

    ii. /G/ > /v/ in vólvolo *volvulus* m/IIb:vólG- *turn* IIIb/Reg/S[1, 2].

    D. Voice and manner of articulation:

    i. /p/ > /v/ in levr+:lépr- *hare* f/IIIb, in levriéro levriére *greyhound* m/IIb or m/IIIb.

    ii. /v/ > /p/ or /G/ in sap+ and saG+:sav+ *wise*: e.g. sap- *know* IIIa/Irr/S[1]; sagáče *sagacious* adj/IIIb; sáǧǧo *wise* adj/I–II.

    iii. /t/ > /ẓ/ in ẓooẓ+:ẓoot+ *zoot-* (*animal*), in epiẓoozía *epizootic* f/Ia.

    iv. /č/ > /g/ in peg+:péč- *pitch* f/IIIb, in pégola *pitch* f/Ia.

    E. Manner and position of articulation:

    i. /t/ > /č/ in +korč+:kórt- *short* adj/I–II, in (r)akkórč- skórč- *shorten*, both I/Reg/W or II/ísK/W.

    ii. /d/ > /GG/ in véGG- (archaic):véd- *see* IIIa/Reg/S[1, 2].

    iii. /kk/ > /cc/ in becc+:békk- *beak* m/IIb, in béccik- *peck at* I/Reg/W.

    iv. /g/ > /v/ in ruv+:rúg- *furrow, wrinkle*, in rúvido *wrinkled* adj/I–II.

    v. /K/ > /t/ in mest+:mésK- *mix* IIIb/Reg/W, in mést- *mix* I/Reg/W.

    F. Voice, manner, and position of articulation: /m/ > /t/ in salt+: sálm- *psalm* m/IIb, in saltér(i)o *psalter* m/IIb.

    G. Svarabhakti: /r/ > /Vr/, the V being:

    i. /a/ in čitar+:čétr- *cithara* f/Ia, e.g. in čitarísta *player on the cithara* m/Ib; čitaréǧǧ- *play the cithara* I/Reg/W; etc.

    ii. /ɛ/ in a number of derivatives based on:

sáKr- *sacred* adj/I–II	patr+:pádr- *father* m/IIIb
áKr- *bitter, sharp* ⎱ adj/IIIb	matr+:mádr- *mother* f/IIIb
čélebr- *well-known* ⎰	sóvr- *above, over* adv/I
ástr- *star* ⎱ m/IIb	
líbr- *book* ⎰	

Examples of derivatives: sačɛrdóte *priest* m/IIIb; ačérrimo *very sharp, very bitter* adj/I–II; čelebérrimo *very well known* adj/I–II; asterísko *asterisk* m/IIb; asteróide *asteroid* m/IIIb; libérkolo *little book* m/IIb; patérno *paternal* and matérno *maternal* adjs/IIIb; sovérkio *excessive* adj/I–II.

    iii. /ə/ in kuattɔr+:kuáttr- *four* num/IId, in kuattórdiči *fourteen* num/IVd.

    H. Vocalization: C > /u/ in: nau+:náv- *ship* f/IIIb; sɔlu+:sólv- *dissolve* IIIb/Reg/W; vɔlu+:vólG- *turn* IIIb/Reg/S[1, 2]: thus, naumakía (*mock*) *naval battle* f/Ia; náufrag- *shipwrecked person* m/IIb; sɔlúbile *soluble* and vɔlúbile *turning, voluble* adjs/IIIb.

J. C >:

I. /ˣ/ in fraˣ⁺:fraG⁺ *break*, in framménto *fragment* m/IIb.

II. CC in ⁺ammar⁺:amár- *bitter* adj/I–II; malatt⁺:malát- *sick* adj/I–II; réǧǧ⁺:réǧ- *kingly* adj/I–II; miššɛll⁺:miššél- *mixture* f/Ia; lučč⁺:lúč- *light* f/IIIb: thus, rammárik- *embitter* I/Reg/W; malattía *sickness* f/Ia; réǧǧa *palace* f/Ia; miššelláneo *miscellaneous* adj/I–II; lúččik- *shine* I/Reg/W.

III. Consonant cluster:

α. /t/ > /st/ in ɔnɔmast⁺:ɔnɔmat⁺ *name*, in ɔnɔmástiK- *onomastic, pertaining to names* adj/I–II.

β. /d/ > /sk/ in kask⁺:kád- *fall* IIIb/Reg/S¹, in kásk- *fall* I/Reg/W.

γ. /r/ > /šš/ in arbošš⁺:árbɔr- *tree* m/IIIb, in arboššéllo *shrub* m/IIb.

δ. /s/ > /ns/ in insul⁺:ísɔl- *island* f/Ia; spɔns⁺:spós- *spouse* m/IIb; mɛns⁺:més- *month* m/IIIb; mans⁺:⁺más- *remained* and tens⁺:tés- *stretched*, both Non-Finite C: thus, insuláre *insular* adj/IIIb; spɔnsále *marital* adj/IIIb; mɛnsíle and mɛnsuále *monthly* adjs/IIIb; mansióne *dwelling* (archaic), *function* and tɛnsióne *tension*, both f/IIIb.

IV. /č/ > /ku/ in kuinku⁺:čínku- *five* num/IIId:

α. Together with ↓↓, in kuíndiči *fifteen* num/IVd; kuinário *having five elements, quinary* adj/I–II.

β. Alone, e.g. in kuinkuénne *of five years' duration* adj/IIIb; kuinkuaǧ⁺ *fifty*, as in kuinkuaǧésimo *fiftieth* adj/I–II.

κ. /ˣ/ >:

I. /t/ in noɛt⁺:noɛˣ *Noah* m/VId, in noétiK- *of Noah* adj/I–II; and ⁺tat⁺:⁺táˣ -*ty* f/VId, in fakɔltatívo *facultative*, kualitatívo *qualitative* and kuantitatívo *quantitative* adjs/I–II and in karitatévɔle *charitable* adj/IIIb.

II. /d/ in čittad⁺:čittáˣ *city* f/VId, in čittadino *of a city, citizen* adj/I–II; čittadína *little city* f/Ia.

III. /G/ in reG⁺:réˣ *king, ruler* m/VId: e.g. réǧ- *kingly* adj/I–II; reǧína *queen* f/Ia; reǧíme *regime* m/IIIb; régɔla *rule* f/Ia.

IV. /GG/ in reGG⁺:réˣ *king, ruler* m/VId, in réGG- *rule, govern* IIIb/Reg/S¹, ².

b. Clusters of Phonemes:

i. Diphthongs:

A. /ié ɛ/ or /uó ɔ/ > /ɛ ɔ/ in a number of derivatives based on:

liét- *joyful, fertile* adj/I–II
liév- *light* adj/IIIb
diéč- *ten* num/IV
bandiér- *banner* ⎫
fiér- *wild beast* ⎬ f/Ia
piétr- *stone* ⎭
miél- *honey* ⎫
piéd- *foot* ⎬ m/IIb
sɛd- *sit* IIIa/Reg/W

nuóv- *new* ⎫
vuót- *empty* (opt.) ⎬ adj/I–II
ruót- *wheel* ⎫
skuól- *school* ⎬ f/Ia
fuók- *fire* ⎫
luóg- *place* ⎪
suón- *sound* ⎬ m/IIb
uóm- *man* ⎭

uóv- *egg* m/IIc   nɔK- *harm* IIIb/Irr/S[1]
kuór- *heart* m/IIIc   fuór- *outside* adv/IV

Examples of derivatives: letícia *joy* f/Ia; letáme *fertilizer* m/IIIb; allévi- *alleviate* I/Reg/W; dečína *about ten* f/Ia; bandɛruóla *streamer*; fɛróče *ferocious* adj/IIIb; petriéro *stone-throwing* adj/I–II; mɛláto *honeyed* adj/I–II; séd- *allay* I/Reg/W; innóv- *innovate* I/Reg/W; votáme *collection of empty things* m/IIIb; arrót- *sharpen* I/Reg/W; skɔláro *student* m/IIb; fokísta *fireman* m/Ib; allóg- *place, lodge* I/Reg/W; sɔnáta *sonata* f/Ia; ɔmáččo *nasty man* m/IIb; ovário *ovary* m/IIb; kɔráta *giblets* f/Ia; nočívo *harmful* adj/I–II; fɔrestiéro *stranger* m/IIb; etc.

     B. /ie/ ∼ /e/ in abéte ∼ abiéte *fir* m/IIIb.

     C. /iɛ/ > :

        I. /i/ in ⁺dič-:diéči *ten* num/IId: úndiči *eleven*, dódiči *twelve*, trédiči *thirteen*, kuattórdiči *fourteen*, kuíndiči *fifteen*, sédiči *sixteen*, all num/IVd; dičassétte *seventeen* num/IIId; dičótto *eighteen* num/IId; dičannóve *nineteen* num/IIId.

        II. /ɛl/ in mɛll⁺:miél- *honey* m/IIIb, in mɛllífɛro *honey-bearing* and mɛllífluo *mellifluous* adjs/I–II.

     ii. Double consonants > :

        A. Single consonants:

           I. /tt/ > /t/ before △ (but not in Roman pronunciation): e.g. adott- *adopt* I/Reg/W + ⁺△ión- *-ion* f/IIIb = adocióne *adoption* (Romanesco adoccióne), etc.

           II. In derivatives based on:

dúbbi- *doubtful* adj/I–II   fáčč- *face* f/Ia (opt.)
⁺énn- *of . . . years' duration* adj/IIIb   fetíčč- *fetish* m/IIb
kuáttr- *four* num/IId   léǧǧ- *law* f/IIIb

Examples of derivatives: dúbit- *doubt* I/Reg/W; čɛntɛnário *centenarian* adj/I–II; kuatriduáno *four days old* adj/I–II; fač(č)ále *facial* adj/IIIb; fetičísmo *fetichism* m/IIb; leǧíttimo *legitimate* adj/I–II; leǧísta *one skilled in law* m/Ib.

        B. C(C) > /ss/, in mass⁺:máǧǧ- *greater* and pɛss⁺:péǧǧ- *worse*, both adjs/IId, and pross⁺:prop⁺ *near*: mássimo *very large*, péssimo *very bad*, próssimo *nearest, next*, all adjs/I–II.

     iii. Individual combinations of phonemes (some of which include alternations already mentioned for single phonemes in §3.02.2.a):

        A. /ač/ > /ik/ in ⁺fik⁺:fáč- *do* IV/Irr/S[1, 2]: ⁺'fiK- *-ficent, -ficious* adj/I–II; ⁺'fik- *-fy* I/Reg/W.

        B. /bi/ > /ul/ in nebul⁺:nébbi- *cloud* f/Ia: nebulóso *nebulous* adj/I–II.

        C. /br/ > /i/ in labi⁺:lábbr- *lip* m/IIc: labiále *labial* adj/IIIb; làbiodɛntále *labio-dental* adj/IIIb.

        D. /dič/ > /ʑʑ/ in doʑʑ⁺:dódič- *twelve* num/IVd: doʑʑína *dozen* f/Ia.

E. /dr/ > /rr/ in parr⁺:pádr- *father* m/IIIb: parričída *parricide*
m/Ib.

F. /eg/ > /ik/ in frik⁺:frég- *rub* I/Reg/W: frikatívo *fricative* adj/
I–II.

G. /ekk/ > /iKK/ in siKK⁺:sékk- *dry* adj/I–II: siččitá⁺ *dryness*
f/VId; essíkk- *exsiccate, dry out* I/Reg/W.

H. /ekki/ > /iʎʎ/ in oriʎʎ⁺:orékki- *ear* m/IIb: oriʎʎére *pillow* m/IIIb.

J. /ell/ > /iʎʎ/ in kapiʎʎ⁺:kapéll- *hair* m/IIb: e.g. kapiʎʎatúra
mass of hair f/Ia; skapíʎʎ- *dishevel* I/Reg/W; etc.

K. /ent/ > /iğ/ in viğ⁺:vént- *twenty* num/VId: viğésimo *twentieth*
adj/I–II.

L. /et/ > /ed ad/ in red⁺ rad⁺:rét- *net* f/IIIb: redácca radácca *mop*
f/Ia.

M. /ett/ > /it/ in liter⁺:létter- *letter* f/Ia: oblíter- *obliterate* I/Reg/W.

N. /ev/ > /ib/ in bib⁺:bév- *drink* IIIb(x)/Reg/S¹: e.g. bíbulo *bibulous*
adj/I–II; bíbita *drink* f/Ia.

O. /ɛGG/ > /iG/ in korriG⁺:korréGG- *correct* IIIb/Reg/S¹, ²: korri-
ğéndo *reformatory inmate* m/IIb.

P. /ɛn/ > /eɲɲ/ in teɲɲ⁺:tɛn- *hold* IIIa/Irr/S¹: e.g. kontéɲɲo
mien, behavior m/IIb: ritéɲɲo *reserve* m/IIb; etc.

Q. /ɛni/ > /eɲɲ/ in ğeɲɲ:ğéni- *genius*: e.g. inğéɲɲo *ability* m/IIb;
konğéɲɲo *ensemble* m/IIb; etc.

R. /ğğ/ >:

I. /di/ in odi⁺:óğğ- *today* adv/IV: odiérno *of today* adj/I–II.

II. /g/ in greg'':gréğğ- *herd* f/IIIb; leg⁺:léğğ- *law* f/IIIb; e.g.
gregário *gregarious* adj/I–II; aggrég- *aggregate* I/Reg/W; legále *legal* adj/IIIb;
leguléio *shyster* m/IIb.

III. /i/ in mai⁺:mağğ- *greater* adj/IId: maiúskolo *majuscule, capital*
(*letter*) adj/I–II; maiorásko *share of the eldest* m/IIb.

S. /ieč/ > /ɛk/ in dɛk⁺:diéč- *ten* num/IVd: dékuplo *decuple* and
dekumáno *tenth* adjs/I–II; dekúria *decuria* f/Ia.

T. /in/ > /ut/ in mattut⁺:mattín- *morning* m/IIb: mattutíno *of
the morning* adj/I–II.

U. /io io/ > /lu/ in plumb⁺:piómb- *lead* m/IIb and pluv⁺:pióv- *rain*
f/Ia: plúmbeo *leaden* adj/I–II; plúvio *rainy* adj/I–II; pluviále *pluvial* adj/IIIb.

W. /iuˣ/ > /lur/ in plur⁺:piúˣ *more* adv/VI: e.g. plurále *plural* adj/
IIIb.

Y. /ka/ > /či/ in ⁺čipit⁺:kapit⁺:káp- *head* m/IIb: e.g. ančípite
doubtful, tričípite *three-headed* adjs/IIIb.

Z. /(k)ki/ >:

I. /kol/ in maskol⁺:máski- *male* adj/I–II and makol⁺:mákki- *spot*
f/Ia: maskolíno *masculine* adj/I–II; immakoláto *immaculate* adj/I–II.

II. /kul/ in makul⁺:mákki- *spot* f/Ia and okul⁺:ókki- *eye* m/IIb;
immakuláto *immaculate* adj/I–II; okuláto *cautious* adj/I–II; okuláre *ocular*
adj/IIIb; okulísta *oculist* m/Ib.

III. /ʎʎ/ in véʎʎo *old* (poet.) adj/I–II:vékkio *id.*

AA. /ieg/ > /lik/ in ⁺plik⁺:piég- *fold* I/Reg/W: e.g. kómplik- *complicate* I/Reg/W.

BB. /lm/ > /m/ in kom⁺:kólm- *summit* m/IIb:kəmíɲɲɔlo *gable* m/IIb.

CC. /ʎʎ/ > /li/, before a back vowel, in scattering forms based on:

bíʎʎ- *billiard* (opt.) ⎱ f/Ia   číʎʎ- *eyebrow* m/IIb, c
famíʎʎ- *family* (opt.) ⎰   spóʎʎ- *despoil, undress* I/Reg/W
fíʎʎ- *son* ⎱ m/IIb
míʎʎ- *millet* ⎰

Thus: biliárdo biʎʎárdo *billiard* m/IIb; familiáre famiʎʎáre *familiar* adj/IIIb; filiále fiʎʎále *filial* adj/IIIb; fíli- fíʎʎ- *filiate, give birth* I/Reg/W; affíli- *affiliate* I/Reg/W; miliáre *miliar (of fever)* adj/IIIb; čiliáre *ciliar* adj/IIIb; spəliacióne spəʎʎacióne *spoliation* f/IIIb.

DD. /m/ > /t/, e.g. in plast⁺:plásm- *plasm(a)* m/Ia and ɛntusiast⁺:ɛntusiásm- *enthusiasm* m/IIb: plástiK- *plastic* adj/I–II; ɛntusiástiK- *enthusiastic* adj/I–II.

EE. /ne ni/ > /ɲɲ/ in liɲɲ⁺:líne- *line* f/Ia and vɛɲɲént- ∼ vɛniént- *coming* adj/IIIb: liɲɲáǧǧ- *lineage* m/IIb; vɛɲɲénte *coming*.

FF. /nG/ > /ɲɲ/ in piáɲɲ- ∼ piánG- *weep* and spéɲɲ- ∼ spénG- *extinguish*, both IIIb/Reg/S¹, ².

GG. /nt/ > /mit/ in komit⁺:kónt- *count* m/IIIb: kəmitále *pertaining to a count* adj/IIIb; kəmitáto *county* m/IIb.

HH. /nt/ > /si/ in sɛmasi⁺:sɛmant⁺ *meaning*: sɛmasiɔloǧía *semasiology* f/Ia.

JJ. /ɲɲ/ > /n/ in kən⁺:kəɲɲ⁺ *know*; kənósK- *know* IIIb/Reg/S¹, ².

KK. /offi/ > /uffl/ in ⁺suffl⁺:sóffi- *blow* I/Reg/W: insúffl- *insufflate* I/Reg/W.

LL. /olč/ > /ulk/ in dulk⁺:dólč- *sweet* adj/IIIb: dúlko *sweet* adj/I–II.

MM. /oʎʎ/ > /uli/ in muli⁺:móʎʎ- *wife* f/IIIb: mulíebre muliébre *feminine* adj/IIIb.

NN. /ov/ > /eb/ in deb⁺:dov- *owe* IIIa/Irr/W: débito *due* adj/I–II.

OO. /ɔkki/ > /ikəl/ in pedikəl⁺:pidókki- *louse* m/IIb: pedikəláre *pedicular* adj/IIIb.

PP. /ɔr/ > /uǧ/ in ruǧ⁺:rɔr⁺ *dew*: ruǧáda *dew* f/Ia.

QQ. /ɔv/ > /aup/ in pauper⁺:póvɛr- *poor* adj/I–II: paupɛrísmo *pauperism* m/IIb.

RR. /Ɔv/ > /ɔb/ in mɔb⁺:mƆv- *move* IIIb/Reg/S¹, ²: móbile *mobile* adj/IIIb.

SS. /reˣ/ > /ɛr/ in tɛr⁺:tréˣ *three* num/VId: térco *third* adj/I–II.

TT. /šš/ > /ss/ in láss- (archaic) ∼ lášš- *leave* I/Reg/W.

UU. /sk/ > /sK/ in pasK⁺:pásk- *pasture* m/IIb: pásK- *graze* IIIb/Reg/W.

VV. /ttr/, in derivatives of kuáttr- *four* num/IId, >:

I. /t/ in kuat⁺:kuatérna *list of four* f/Ia.

II. /dr/ in kuadr⁺:e.g. kuádr- *square off* I/Reg/W; kuadraǧ⁺ *forty*, as in kuadraǧésimo *fortieth* adj/I–II.

III. /r/ in kuar⁺:kuárto *fourth* adj/I–II; kuaránta *forty* num/I.

WW. /cc/ > /ǧ/ in palážo *palace* m/IIb ∼ palácco *id.*

YY. /uɔi/ > /ɔr/ in kɔr⁺:kuɔi- *leather* m/IIb: kɔrácca *cuirass, armor* f/Ia; kɔráme *leather-work* m/IIIb.

ZZ. /uri/ > /ɔl/ in mɛrkɔl⁺:mɛrkúri- *Mercury* m/IIIb: mɛrkɔledí˟ *Wednesday* m/VId.

AAA. /ut/ > /o/ in tot⁺:tútt- *all* adj/I–II: totále *total* adj/IIIb.

3. Addition:

a. Vowels:

i. /a/ in ɔtta⁺:ótt- *eight* num/IId; prɔsa⁺:prós- *prose* f/Ia; ǧuda⁺:ǧúd- *Judah* m/Ib; teba⁺:téb- (pl.) *Thebes* f/Ia; ottaédro *octahedron,* ottágono *octagon,* both m/IIb; prosáiK- *prosaic* adj/I–II; prosaísta *prose-writer* m/Ib; ǧudáiK- *Judaic* adj/I–II; ǧudaísmo *Judaism* m/IIb; ǧudaíz̧z̧- *Judaize* I/Reg/W; tebáide *Thebaid* f/IIIb.

ii. /i/ in nídio *nest* m/IIb ∼ níd- *id.*

iii. /u/ to the following (of m/IIb except where otherwise indicated) before the suffixes:

A. ⁺ári- *ary* adj/I–II: sált- *jump* m/IIb; mórt- *death* f/IIIb.

B. ⁺ós- *-ous, -ose* adj/I–II:

anfrátt- *broken* (of terrain) fléss- *bent* } adj/I/II tórt- *twisted* únt- *smeared* afféтt- *feeling*	flát- *belch* flútt- *flood, wave* lútt- *mourning* móstr- *monster* frútt- *fruit* m/IIc mónt- *mountain* m/IIIb

C. ⁺ét- *having quality of being . . .* adj/I–II: máns- *docile* adj/I–II.

D. ⁺ál- *-al* adj/IIIb:

kás- *case*	séss- *sex*
kɔnčétt- *concept*	tést- *text*
lak⁺:lág- *lake*	vís- *vision, face*
pročéss- *process*	mán- *hand* f/IIb
púnt- *point*	mens⁺:més- *month* m/IIIb
séns- *sense*	

E. ⁺aǧ⁺ *-ty*: sétt- *seven* num/IIId.

F. ⁺ári- *-ary* m/IIb: prónt- *ready* adj/I–II; sánt- *holy* adj/I–II.

G. ⁺′0- *perform action involving . . .* I/Reg/W: ákk- *bow;* sít- *site;* eččétt- *except* prep/II.

H. ⁺0- *perform action involving . . .* II/ísK/W: min:mén- *less* adj/IId.

J. ⁺ári- *-ary* adj/I–II and ⁺ós- *-ous* adj/I–II: vɔlutt⁺:vɔluttá˟ *voluptuousness* f/VId.

K. ⁺ári- *-ary* adj/I–II and ⁺ál- *-al* adj/IIIb: ánn- *year;* ús- *use, custom.*

L. ⁺ál- *-al* adj/IIIb and ⁺′0- *perform action involving . . .* I/Reg/W: ábit- *habit;* aččént- *accent;* efféтt- *effect;* grád- *degree, grade.*

M. +ári- -ary adj/I–II, +ós- -ous adj/I–II and +ál- -al adj/IIIb: pórt- port.

N. +ári- -ary adj/I–II, +ós- -ous adj/I–II and +′0- perform action involving . . . I/Reg/W: tumúlt- tumult.

O. +ári- -ary adj/I–II, +ál- -al adj/IIIb and +′0- perform action involving . . . I/Reg/W: átt- act; čéns- census.

Examples of derivatives:

mɔrtuário mortuary
settuaǧenário septuagenarian
tɔrtuóso tortuous
vɔluttuóso voluptuous
tumultuóso tumultuous
mansuéto tame
} adj/I–II

kɔnčettuále conceptual
annuále annual
abituále habitual
attuále actual, present
} adj/IIIb

prɔntuário reference book m/IIb

sítu- situate
aččéntu- accentuate
tumúltu- be tumultuous
áttu- actuate
} I/Reg/W

diminu- diminish II/ísK/W

minuéndo minuend m/IIb:minu+ diminish

b. Consonants and combinations of phonemes (in reverse alphabetical order):

i. /d/, in kɔrd+:kɔr+:kuɔ́r- heart m/IIIb; a(b)- be(č)čed+:á(ˣ) + čé ABC: e.g. kɔrdiále cordial adj/IIIb; a(b)be(č)čedário primer m/IIb.

ii. /ad/, in spɔrad+:spɔ́r- spore f/Ia: spɔrádiK- sporadic adj/I–II.

iii. /ɔd/, in spasmɔd+:spásm- spasm m/IIb: spasmódiK- spasmodic adj/I–II.

iv. /il/, in skifil+:skíf- repugnant adj/I–II: skifiltáˣ excessive delicacy f/VId.

v. /ɔl/, in fokɔl+:fɔk:fuɔ́k- fire m/IIb: fokɔláio focus (e.g. of diffusion) m/IIb; fokɔláre hearth m/IIIb.

vi. /m/, in salm+:sál- salt m/IIIb: salmástro salty adj/I–II; salmístr- salt I/Reg/W.

vii. /ɛm/, in settɛm+:sétt- seven num/IIId: settémpliče sevenfold adj/IIIb.

viii. /n/, in sɛn+:sé- six num/IV: sɛnário of six elements adj/I–II.

ix. /an/, in messian+:messí- Messiah m/Ib: messiániK- messianic adj/I–II; messianísmo messianism m/IIb.

x. /in/, in bases built on the following, all of m/IIIb:

addóm- abdomen	nóm- name
ǧérm- germ	sángu- blood
lúm- light	sém- seed

Examples of derivatives: addɔminále *abdominal* adj/IIIb; ǧerminále *germinal* adj/IIIb; luminóso *luminous* adj/I–II; nɔminále *nominal* adj/IIIb; sanguinário *sanguinary* adj/I–II; seminário *seminary* m/IIb.

    xi. /ɛr/, in bases built on:

rap- *turnip*		lát- *side*		
páʎʎ- *straw*	f/Ia	pónd- *weight*	m/IIb	
		pép- *pepper*		

Examples of derivatives: raperóncɔlo *rampion* m/IIb; paʎʎeríno *straw-colored* adj/I-II; paʎʎeríččo *straw mattress* m/IIb; laterále *lateral* adj/IIIb; pɔnderóso *ponderous* adj/I–II; pónder- *ponder* I/Reg/W; peperíno *gray volcanic stone* m/IIb; peperóne *pepper* (vegetable) m/IIIb.

    xii. /ɛR/, in funɛR⁺:fun⁺ *disaster*: e.g. funerário *funerary*, funéreo *funereal*, funerále *funeral*, funésto *disastrous* adjs/I–II; mɔdɛR⁺:mód- *manner*: e.g. móder- *moderate* I/Reg/W, modést- *modest* adj/I–II.

    xiii. /ɔr/, in bases built on the following, all m/IIb:

ág- *needle*	nérb- *sinew*
káp- *head*	pétt- *chest*
kórp- *body*	sólf- *sulphur*
lít(t)- *shore, beach*	stérk- *excrement*
márm- *marble*	

Examples of derivatives: agɔráio *needle-box* m/IIb; kapɔrále *corporal* m/IIIb; kɔrpɔrále *corporal* adj/IIIb; lit(t)ɔrále *littoral* m/IIIb; marmóreo *marmoreal* adj/I–II; nerbɔrúto *sinewy* adj/I–II; sɔlfóriK- *sulphuric* adj/I–II; sterkɔrário *pertaining to, using excrement* adj/I–II.

    xiv. /s/ in sɛs⁺:sé- *six* num/IVd: sésto *sixth* adj/I–II.

    xv. /es/ in potes⁺:pɔt⁺ *powerful*, in potestá⁺ *power, authority* f/VId.

    xvi. /ss/ in sɛss⁺:sé- *six* num/IVd: sessánta *sixty* num/Id; sessaǧenário *of sixty years' duration* adj/I–II; sessénne *of six years' duration* adj/IIIb.

    xvii. /t/ in bases built on:

román- *Roman* adj/I–II		ego⁺ *ego*	
lín- *linen* m/IIb		es⁺ *ex-, out*	
frás- *phrase*		in⁺ *in-*	prefixes
pós- *gnosis*	f/IVd	pos⁺ *post-*	
kafféˣ *coffee* m/VId			

Examples of derivatives:rɔmántiK- *romantic* adj/I–II; línteo *of linen* adj/I–II; antifrástiK- *antiphrastic* adj/I–II; póstiK- *gnostic* adj/I–II; kaffettiéra *coffee-pot* f/Ia; egotísmo *egoism* m/IIb; est⁺ *outside*, int⁺ *inside*, post⁺ *post-*, as in esterióre *exterior*, interióre *interior*, posterióre *posterior* adjs/IIIb.

xviii. /at/ in a number of bases, such as those built on the following nouns or suffixes of types:

A. f/Ia: ákku- *water*
ále- *die*
ási- *Asia*
flémm- *phlegm*
káttedr- *cathedra*
línf- *lymph*
lún- *moon*

réum- *rheum*
síntɔm- *symptom*
spérm- *sperm*
stígm- stímm- *stigma*
šísm- *schism*
tém- *theme*
tráum- *trauma*

B. m/Ib: ásm- *asthma*
činɛm- *cinema*
diafrámm- *diaphragm*
dógm- dómm- *dogma*
+ém- -*eme*
ɛnígm- enímm- *enigma*
+grámm- -*gram*
klím- *climate*
krɔ́m- *chrome, color*
miásm- *miasma*
paradígm- *paradigm*
prísm- *prism*

ʒéugm- *zeugma*
ʒígɔm- ʒigɔ́m- *zygoma*

C. Nominal bases:
ɛm+ *blood*
fan+ *temple*
numism+ *coin, medal*
pneum+ *lung*
pragm+ pramm+ *fact*
sinallagm+ *obligation on both sides*
sɔm+ *body*
stɔm+ *mouth*

Examples of derivatives:

D. In +'iK- -*ic* adj/I–II: akkuátiK- *aquatic*; asiátiK- *Asiatic*; flɛmmátiK- *phlegmatic*; kattedrátiK- *of a cathedra* (*e.g. professorial*); linfátiK- *lymphatic*; lunátiK- *lunatic*; asmátiK- *asthmatic*; činɛmátiK- *cinematic*; diaframmátiK- *diaphragmatic*; dogmátiK- *dogmatic*; ʒeugmátiK- *zeugmatic*; etc. etc.

E. In +atóri- -*atory* adj/I–II: aleatório *aleatory*.

F. In +ísm- -*ism* m/IIb: dogmatísmo *dogmatism*; fanatísmo *fanaticism*; pragmatísmo *pragmatism*; reumatísmo *rheumatism*; etc.

G. In +íʒʒ- -*ize* I/Reg/W: dogmatíʒʒ- *uphold as a dogma*; fanatíʒʒ- *arouse fanaticism*.

xix. /et/ in luet+:lú- *lues* f/IIIb; prɔlet+:prɔ́l- *offspring* f/IIIb; činet+: čin+ *kin-, movement*; piret+:pir+ *pyr-, fire*; splɛnet+:splɛn+ *spleen*: luétiK- *luetic*, prɔletário *proletarian*, činétiK- *kinetic*, antipirétiK- *antipyretic, antifever*, splɛnétiK- *splenetic*, all adjs/I–II.

xx. /it/ in primit+:prím- *first* adj/I–II; kapit+:káp- *head* m/IIb; rak+ *spine*; posit+:pos+:pón- *put, place* IV/Irr/S[1, 2]: e.g. primitívo *primitive* adj/I–II; kapitále *capital* adj/IIIb; rakítiK- *rickety* adj/I–II; rakítide *rickets* f/IIIb; positívo *positive* adj/I–II; positióne *position* f/IIIb.

xxi. /ɔt/ in eskarɔt+:éskar- *scab, eschara* f/Ia; dɛmɔt:dém- *deme, people* m/IIb: eskarótiK- *escharotic*, dɛmótiK- *demotic* adjs/I–II.

xxii. /eT/ in mimeT+:mím- *mime* m/IIb; frɛnɛT+:frɛn+ *phren-, brain*: e.g. mimétiK- *mimetic* adj/I–II; mimési *mimesis* f/IVd; frɛnétiK- *frenetic* adj/I–II; frɛnesía *frenzy* f/Ia.

xxiii. /ot/ in ağğot⁺:ágğ- *agio* m/IIb: ağotágğo *agiotage* m/IIb.

xxiv. /aˣ/ (with concomitant shift of stress) in the free alternants lilláˣ ~ líll- *lilac* f/Ia; rağáˣ ~ ráğ- *rajah* m/Ib.

xxv. ẓ in kakk⁺:kák- *shit* I/Reg/W: kákk- *dung* f/Ia.

xxvi. △ in frɔnẓ⁺:frónd- *bough, leaf* f/Ia: frɔnẓúto *leafy* adj/I–II; frónẓɔlo *excessive ornament* m/IIb.

3.1. AFFIXATION. The structure of all forms derived by affixation is: ROOT = BASE (another root) + AFFIX. The form-class and stress of the root is determined by that of the final element: thus, kandɛlábro *candelabrum* m/IIb = kandél- *candle* f/Ia + ⁺ábr- *-abrum* m/IIb. The base may in its turn be another derived form: thus, in akkattɔnágğo *beggary* m/IIb (= akkattón- *beggar* m/IIIb + ⁺ágğ- *-age* m/IIb), the base akkatton- in its turn = akkátt- *beg* I/Reg/W + ⁺ón- *agent* m/IIIb. Often several prefixes or suffixes are added successively in this way: e.g. libɛrkɔluččáččo *worthless little book* = libɛr⁺ (alternant of líbr- *book* m/IIb, §3.02.2.a.ii.G.II) + ⁺'kɔl- dim. m/IIb + ⁺účč- contemptuous m/IIb + ⁺áčč- pejorative m/IIb.

A derivative by affixation has one primary stress. In derivatives by suffixation, if the stress is indicated on the suffix when the latter is cited separately, the stress is on the suffix in derivatives built therewith; cf. kandɛlábro *candelabrum*, akkattɔnágğo *beggary* and libɛrkɔluččáččo *worthless little book*, in the preceding paragraph. If the stress is indicated by /'/ written before the suffix, the stress is on the syllable immediately preceding, normally with automatic replacement of a close-mid by an open-mid vowel: thus, karbóniK- *carbonic* adj/I–II = karbón- *carbon* m/IIIb + 'iK- *-ic* adj/I–II. Otherwise, the stress remains on the base (except in arhyzotonic verb-forms).

3.11. SUFFIXATION involves the addition to a base of one of the following suffixes, which are here listed according to the form-classes to which they belong, and subdivided according to the form-classes of the bases to which they are added.

3.111. SUBSTANTIVES (i.e. both nouns and adjectives) are formed:

1. On substantives or adverbs and on verbs, with:

a. ⁺éčč- adj/I–II and f/Ia and m/IIb, with the meanings:

i. As adjective, *having the character of . . ., like . . .*, in pekɔréččo *sheep-like*:pékɔr- *sheep* f/Ia.

ii. As noun f/Ia, *place of or for . . .*, preceded by ⁺ar⁺, in pɔrkaréčča *hog farm*:pórK- *hog* m/IIb.

iii. As noun m/IIb, (*collective*) *action of . . .*, in pekɔréččo *trouble*:pékɔr- *sheep* f/Ia; ladrɔnéččo *thievery*:ladrón- *thief* m/IIIb; čikaléččo *chattering* (*of many people together*):čikál- *chatter* I/Reg/W.

iv. The suffix is preceded by ⁺ar⁺ in pɔrkaréčča *hog-farm* (cf. ii, above) and by ⁺ɛr⁺ in the following adjectives, derived from bases of:

A. f/Ia:festɛréččo *festive* (contemptuous):fést- *feast*; kostɛréččo *pertaining to the ribs*:kóst- *rib*; villɛréččo *rustic*:víll- *villa*.

B. m/IIb: boskɛréččo *forest* (adj.):bósk- *woods, forest*; kampɛréččo *rustic* (archaic):kámp- *field, country*; vɛrnɛréččo *of winter*:vérn- *winter*.

c. I/Reg/W: ǧovɛréččo *healthy*:ǧóv- *be well, be useful*; manǧeréččo *for eating, edible*:mánǧ- *eat*.

D. IIIa/Reg/W: godɛréččo *enjoying material things*:gód- *enjoy*.

E. IIIb/Reg/W: vɛndɛréččo *easily sold*:vénd- *sell*.

b. +íčč- adj/I–II and m/IIb, with the meanings:

i. As adjective, pejorative or diminutive: *lightly, easily, somewhat, poorly* . . ., especially on past participles, as in the following based on:

A. Adj/I–II: biankíččo *whitish*:biánk- *white*; biɔndíččo *blondish*:biónd- *blond*; kastaɲɲíččo *somewhat chestnut-colored*:kastáɲɲ- *chestnut-çolored*; pallidíččo *palish*:pállid- *pale*; etc.

B. Adj/I–II (past part.): abboccatíččo *badly sketched*:abboccát- *sketched*; abbrɔnzatíččo *slightly bronzed*:abbrɔnzát- *bronzed*; annakkuatíččo *diluted*:annakkuát- *watered*; kaskatíččo *frail*:kaskát- *fallen*; etc. etc.

c. f/Ia: massíččo *massive*:máss- *mass*.

ii. As noun, diminutive or *thing made of* . . ., in the following based on nouns of:

A. f/Ia: kanníččo *hurdle*:kánn- *cane*; gratíččo *wickerwork*:grát- *grating*; kiakkiɛríččo *gossip*:kiákkiɛr- *chatter*; paʎʎɛríččo *straw mattress*:paʎʎɛr+:páʎʎ- *straw*; pastíččo *pastry, mess*:pást- *paste*; tɛrríččo *topsoil*:tɛrr- *earth*.

B. m/IIb: ɔrlíččo *irregular rim, edge*:órl- *rim, edge*.

c. m/IIIb: sabbiɔníččo *sandy earth* (contemptuous):sabbión- *sandy earth*.

D. f/IIIb: karníččo *piece of meat left on skin of flayed animal*:kárn- *flesh, meat*; vitíččo *tendril*:vít- *vine*.

iii. The suffix is preceded by +it+ in rakkɔʎʎitíččo *gathered in haste*: rakkɔʎʎ- *gather* IIIb/Irr/S[1, 2].

c. +árd- -*ard, pertaining to* . . ., *of* . . . adj/I–II, f/Ia and m/IIb:

i. As adjective, based on:

A. Nouns, of types:

I. f/Ia in beffárdo *joking*:béff- *jest, joke*; buǧárdo *lying*:buǧí- *lie*; kodárdo *cowardly*:kód- *tail*; savoiárdo *Savoyard*:savói- *Savoy*; testárd- *hard-headed*: tést- *head*.

II. m/IIb in bastárdo *bastard*:bást- *pack-saddle*.

III. Nominal base in gaʎʎárdo *brave, sturdy*:gaʎʎ+ *bravery, strength*.

B. Verbs, in lekkárdo *greedy* (archaic):lékk- *lick* I/Reg/W; infingárdo *goldbricking, -er*:infínG- *pretend* IIIb/Reg/S[1, 2].

ii. As noun f/Ia, based on nouns of:

A. f/Ia, in bɔmbárda *mortar* (*type of gun*):bómb- *bomb*; kokkárda *cocarde*:kókk- *tip*; maliárda *witch*:malí- *magic*.

B. f/IIIb: kiavárda (*masonry*) *key*:kiáv- *key*.

iii. As noun m/IIb, based on:

A. Adj/I–II in vekkiárdo vɛʎʎárdo *old man*:vékki- véʎʎ- *old*.

B. Num/IIIc in miliárdo *milliard*:míl-:míll- *1000*.

c. Nouns of types:

I. f/Ia in biliárdo biʎʎárdo *billiard-table*:bíli- bíʎʎ- *billiard* (-*pocket*).

II. m/IIb in petárdo *petard*:pét- *fart*.

III. m/IIIb in kɔmunárdo *Communard* (*1871*):kɔmún- *Commune*.

d. ⁺ɛ- adj/I–II and, as noun, f/Ia and m/IIb, with meanings:

i. As adjective, -ean, -eic, -aic, pertaining to . . ., as in the following based on nouns of:

A. f/Ia: européo *European*:európ- *Europe*; pimpléo *Pymplean*: pímpl- *Pympla*.

B. m/I: ǧudéo *Jewish*:ǧud- *Judah*.

C. m/IIb: febéo *of Phoebus*:féb- *Phoebus*; mɛnippéo *Menippean*: mɛnípp- *Menippus*.

D. m/IIIb: ǧigantéo *gigantic*:ǧigánt- *giant*.

E. f/IIIb: plebéo *plebeian*:pléb- *plebs, common herd*.

F. Nominal bases: ebréo *Hebrew*:ebr⁺:ebra⁺ *Hebraic*; fariséo *Pharisaic*:faris⁺:farisa⁺ *Pharisa(ic)*.

ii. As noun f/Ia, -ea, -y, *thing pertaining to* . . ., as in the following based on:

A. Adj/IIIb: čikadéa *cicadea*:čikád- *cicada*.

B. f/Ia: ninféa *nymphaea*:nínf- *nymph*; skaléa (*monumental*) *flight of stairs*:skál- *stairs*; vallɔnéa *a kind of oak*:vallón- *Vallona*.

C. m/Ib: dukéa *duchy* (archaic):dúk- *duke*.

D. m/IIb: čɛntauréa *centaurea*:čɛntáur- *centaur*.

E. m/IIIb: kɔntéa *county, count's estate*:kónt- *count*; maréa *tide*:mársea; nɔméa *reputation*:nóm- *name*.

F. Nominal bases: livréa *livery*:livr⁺ *id*.; uréa *urea*:ur⁺ *ur(ine)*.

iii. As noun m/IIb, -(a)eus, -(a)eum, *person, place or thing pertaining to* . . ., as in the following based on:

A. f/Ia: muséo *museum*:mús- *muse*; ninféo *nymphaeum*:nínf- *nymph*; rɔméo *pilgrim* (archaic):róm- *Rome*.

B. m/I: mitréo *Mithraeum*:mítr- *Mithra*.

C. m/IIb: augustéo *Augusteum*:augúst- *Augustus*; babbéo *blockhead, fool*:bább- onomatopoetic, *daddy*; ǧubiléo *jubileum*:ǧúbil- *jubilation*; pritanéo *prytaneum*:pritán- *citizen lodged at public expense* (anc. Gk.).

D. f/IIIb: atɛnéo *Athenaeum, university*:atén- *Athene*; kɔrtéo *cortège*: kórt- *court* (reverence).

E. Nominal bases: ǧinečéo *gynaeceum*:ǧineK⁺ *woman*; mɔrféo *Morpheus*:mɔrf⁺ *sleep*; ɔrféo *Orpheus*:ɔrf⁺.

iv. The suffix is preceded by:

A. ⁺ik⁺ in manikéo *Manichaean* adj/I–II:mán- *Mani* m/IVd.

B. ⁺ist⁺ in piaɲɲistéo *long, objectionable weeping* m/IIb:piáɲɲ- *weep* IIIb/Irr/S¹, ².

e. ⁺áǧǧ- -age adj/I–II and m/IIb:

i. As adjective, in sɛlváǧǧo *wild, savage*:sélv- *forest*.

ii. As noun, based on:

A. adj/I–II: salvatáǧǧo *salvage*:salvát- *saved*.

B. f/Ia: ballottáǧǧo *second balloting*:ballótt- *ballot*; karɛnáǧǧo *careening*:karén- *hull*; piumáǧǧo *plumage*:piúm- *feather*; stalláǧǧo *stallage*:stáll- *stall*; tɛláǧǧo *quality of cloth*:tél- *cloth*; viáǧǧo *voyage, trip*:ví- *way*; villáǧǧo *village*:víll- *villa*.

C. m/Ib: ɛremitáǧǧo *hermitage*:ɛremít- *hermit*.

D. m/Id: vɔltáǧǧo *voltage*:vólt- *volt, Volta*.

E. m/IIb: aǧǧotáǧǧo *agiotage*:aǧǧot⁺:áǧǧ- *agio*; ǧardináǧǧo *gardening*:ǧardín- *garden*; messáǧǧo *message*:méss- *envoy*; ɔmáǧǧo *homage*:ɔm⁺:uómman; ɔrtáǧǧo *garden produce*:órt- *garden*; sɛrváǧǧo *servitude, slavery*:sérv-servant; stroccináǧǧo *usury*:stroccín- *usurer*; tiráǧǧo *draft*:tír- *act of drawing*; vassalláǧǧo *vassalage*:vassáll-*vassal*.

F. m/IIIb; akkattɔnáǧǧo *beggary*:akkattón- *beggar*; kɔráǧǧo *courage*:kɔr:kuór- *heart*; ostáǧǧo *hostage*:óst- *enemy*; paesáǧǧo *landscape*:paés- *country*; pedáǧǧo *toll*:pɛd:piéd- *foot*; spionáǧǧo *espionage*:spión- *spy*.

G. Nominal base: tatuáǧǧo *tattooing*:tatu⁺ *tattoo*.

H. I/Reg/W: abbɔrdáǧǧ- *boarding (attack)*:abbórd- *board*; ammaráǧǧo *'landing' on water*:ammár- *'land' on water*; fissáǧǧo *fixing* (photogr.):físs- *fix*; miráǧǧo *mirage*:mír- *look at*; mɔnetáǧǧo *(act, cost of) coining*:mɔnét- *coin*; mɔntáǧǧo *montage*:mónt- *mount*; passáǧǧo *passage*:páss- *pass*; pattináǧǧo *skating*:pattín- *skate*; viráǧǧo *turning, fixing* (photogr.):vír- *turn*.

J. Adv/III: ɔltráǧǧo *outrage*:óltr- *beyond*.

iii. The suffix is preceded by ⁺i⁺ in karriáǧǧo *cartage, carriage*:kárr-car(t) m/IIb.

f. ⁺′i- adj/I–II, f/Ia and m/IIb, normally preceded by △ after /Vt nt rt nk/, with the following meanings:

i. As adjectives, *-ic, -ian, of or pertaining . . .*, as in the following based on:

A. Adj/IIIb: vílio *cheap*:víl- *vile*.

B. f/Ia: plúvio *rainy*:pluv:pióv- *rain*.

C. m/IIb: arkilókio *Archilochian*:arkílok- *Archilochus*; číprio *Cyprian* (archaic):čípr- *Cyprus*; kɔríncio *Corinthian*:kɔrínt- *Corinth*; ikário *Icarian*:íkar-*Icarus*; nettúnio *Neptunian*:nettún- *Neptune*; ɔlímpio *Olympian*:ɔlímp- *Olympus*; pário *Parian*:pár- *Paros*; satúrnio *Saturnian*:satúrn- *Saturn*.

D. m/IIIb: adónio *Adonic* (verse):adón- *Adonis*; alkmánio *Alcmanic*:alkmán- *Alcman*; čensório *censorious, of a censor*; mártio *Martian*:márt- *Mars*; motório *pertaining to motion or motors*:motór- *motor*.

E. Substantival bases: sáǧǧo sávio *wise* (:saG⁺):sav⁺ *id.*; sácio *sated*: sat⁺ *enough*.

ii. As noun f/Ia, *-ia, -y, -ness, condition of . . .*, as in the following based on:

A. Adj/I–II: angústia *narrowness, anguish*:angúst- *narrow*; argúcia *keenness*:argút- *keen*; astúcia *astuteness*:astút- *astute*; barbária *barbarity*:bárbar-*barbarian*; grácia *grace, thanks*:grát- *pleasing, grateful*; laššívia *lascivity*:laššív-*lascivious*; pɛrícia *skill*:pɛríto *skilled*.

B. Adj/IIIb: audáča *boldness*:audáč- *bold*; indústria *industry*:indústr-*industrious*; inércia *inertia*:inért- *inert*; kɔnkórdia *concord*:kɔnkórd- *concordant*.

C. m/IIb: kɔlónia *colony*:kɔlón- *colonist*.

D. m/IIIb: kustódia *custody*:kustód- *custodian*; pátria *fatherland*: patr⁺:pádr- *father*.

E. Nominal base: órǧa *orgy*:ɔrG⁺ *org-, work*.

F. IIIa/Reg/W: sédia *seat, chair*:sɛd⁺:sƐd- *sit*.

G. Verbal base: fúria *fury*:fur[+] *rage*.

Also in a number of local or ethnic names, such as the following, based on:

H. Adj/I–II: fránča *France*:fránk- *Frank(ish)*; kalábria *Calabria*: kálabr- *Calabrian*; rússia *Russia*:rúss- *Russian*; skócia *Scotland*:skót- *Scottish*; túrkia *Turkey*:túrk- *Turkish*.

J. Adj/IIIb: arkádia *Arcadia*:árkad- *Arcadian*.

K. m/IIb: olímpia *Olympia*:olímp- *Olympus*.

iii. As noun m/IIb, *-ium, -ion, action of* . . ., as in the following based on:

A. Adj/I–II: eserčício *exercise*:esérčit- *exercised, conducted*.

B. Adj/IIIb: biénnio *biennium*:biénn- *triennial*; činkuanténnio *period of fifty years*:činkuanténn- *of fifty years' duration*; siléncio *silence*:silént- *silent*; etc.

C. f/Ia: potássio *potassium*:potáss- *potash*; puerpério *puerperium*: puérper- *woman in or after childbirth*.

D. m/Ib: [+]čídio *act of killing* . . .: [+]číd- *-cide, killer of* . . . .

E. m/IIb: vískio *bird-lime*:vísk- *id*.

F. m/IIIb: esílio *exile*:esil[+]:ésul- *exile* (person); karbónio *carbon*: karbón- *coal*; koniúǧo *conjugal state*:kóniuǧ- *spouse*; martírio *martyrdom*:mártir- *martyr*; ospício *hospice*:óspit- *guest*.

G. m/VId: nikélio *nickel*:níkel *id*.

H. Nominal bases: armónio *harmonium*:armon[+] *harmony*; bizáncio *Byzantium*:bizant[+] *id*.; komício *comitium*:komit[+] *companion*.

J. I/Reg/W: abomínio *abomination*:abómin- *abominate*; adultério *adultery*:adúlter- *adulterate*; augúrio *augury*:áugur- *augur*; desidério *desire*:desíder- *desire*; domínio *dominion*:dómin- *dominate*; prečipício *precipice*:prečípit- *precipitate*; vitupério *vituperation*:vitúper- *vituperate*.

K. IIIb/Reg/S[1, 2]: konvívio *convivium, banquet*:konvív- *live together*; vilipéndio *act of vilipending*:vilipénd- *vilipend*.

L. Verbal bases: [+]lókuio *-loquy*:loku[+] *speak*; stúdio *study*:stud[+] *study*.

iv. The suffix occurs with preceding /Vt/ or /nt/ unchanged in lítio *lithium* m/IIb:lit[+] *stone* and in koríntio *Corinthian* adj/I–II:korínt- *Corinth* m/IIb.

v. It occurs with preceding /k/ > /t/ in ǧudício *judgment* m/IIb:ǧúdik- *judge* I/Reg/W, and in [+]fício- *-fice* m/IIb:[+']fik- *-fy* I/Reg/W, e.g. edifício *edifice*:edífik- *build*.

vi. It occurs concomitantly with prefixation in provínča *province* f/Ia: vínK- *conquer* IIIb/Reg/S[1, 2], and in certain nouns of m/IIb, such as the following based on nouns of:

A. f/Ia: interkolúnnio *space between two columns*:kolunn[+]:kolónn- *column*; prošščénio *proscenium*:šén- *scene, stage*.

B. m/IIb: internódio *space between two knots*:nód- *knot*; provérbio *proverb*:vérb- *word, verb*.

C. f/IIIb: subúrbio *suburb*:úrb- *city*.

D. Nominal bases: interstítio *interstice*:stit[+] *stit-, standing*; epigástrio *epigastrium* and ipogástrio *hypogastrium*:gastr[+] *stomach*.

g. ⁺ái- adj/I–II, f/Ia and m/IIb, with the meanings:

i. As adjective -*like*, -*y*: pɔrráio *bulb-like* (of a type of onion):pórr- *wart*, *leek* m/IIb; pɔlvɛráio *dust-raising, dusty*:pólvɛr- *dust* f/IIIb.

ii. As noun f/Ia, indicating *place containing, for, planted with . . .; condition of being . . .; instrument for . . .*, as in the following based on:

A. Adj/I–II: kaldáia *boiler*:káld- *hot*; vekkiáia *old age*:vékki- *old*.

B. f/Ia: anguilláia *place full of snakes*:anguíll- *snake*; etc.

C. m/IIb: ačɛráia *maple-plantation*:áčɛr- *maple*; aʎʎáia *garlic-patch*: áʎʎ- *garlic*; burráia *buttery*:búrr- *butter*; kačáia *cheese-room*:káč- *cheese*; etc.

D. m/IIIb: bariláia *barrel-room*:baríl- *barrel*, etc.

E. I/Reg/W: alcáia *towrope*:álc- *raise*.

iv. As noun m/IIb, indicating *place of, for . . ., full of . . .*, as in the following based on:

A. Adj/I–II: viváio *vivarium, fish-bowl*:vív- *alive*.

B. f/Ia: akkuáio *sink*:ákku- *water*; kalčináio *limepit*:kalčín- *slaked lime*; mɛrdáio *shit-pile*:mérd- *shit*; troiáio *pig-pen*:trói- *sow*; vespáio *wasps' nest*:vésp- *wasp*; vipɛráio *snake-pit, -nest*:vípɛr- *viper*; etc.

C. m/IIb: agɔráio *needle-box*:agɔr⁺:ág- *needle*; baččelláio *beanfield*: baččéll- *bean*; bagaʎʎáio *baggage-truck*:bagáʎʎ- *baggage*; kavɔláio *cabbage-patch*: kávɔl- *cabbage*; pɔrkáio *filthy place*:pórK- *pig*; prunáio *plum grove*:prún- *plum tree*; etc.

D. m/IIIb: popɔnáio *melon-patch*:popón- *melon*; sɔláio *drying-room*: sól- *sun*; vɛrmáio *place teeming with worms*:vérm- *worm*.

E. f/IIIb: karnáio *charnel-house, slaughter*:kárn- *meat*; pulčáio *place full of fleas*:púlč- *flea*; sɛrpáio *place full of snakes*:sérp- *serpent, snake*.

v. The suffix is preceded by ⁺ɔl⁺ in certain derivatives, such as the following based on:

A. f/Ia: kalcɔláio *shoemaker*:kálc- *footgear*; kartɔláio *stationer*:kárt- *paper*.

B. m/IIb: arkɔláio *reel*:árk- *bow, arch*.

h. ⁺ki- adj/I–II and m/IIb, with meanings:

i. As adjective, *having quality of being . . .*, in sovérkio *excessive*:sover⁺: sóvr- *over* adv/I.

ii. As noun, -*cle*, diminutive, in karbónkio *carbuncle*:karbón- *coal, carbon* m/IIb; kopérkio *cover*:kɔpr- *cover* II/Reg/S[1, 2].

iii. The suffix is preceded by:

A. ⁺ák⁺ in pennákkio *cockade*:pénn- *feather* f/Ia; boccákkio *swollen, empty, worm-eaten plum*:bócc- *swelling, lump* m/IIb; spaurákkio *scarecrow*: spaúr- *frighten* I/Reg/W or II/ísK/W; mɔrdákkio *muzzle, gag*:mórd- *bite* IIIb/ Reg/S[1, 2].

B. ⁺ék⁺ in parékkio *some* adj/I–II:pár- *equal* adj/IVd; and in the nouns pennékkio *quantity of flax put on spinning-wheel*:pénn- *feather* f/Ia; sɔlékkio *sunshade (with hands)*:sól- *sun* m/IIIb.

C. ⁺ík⁺ in the nouns m/IIb mɔllíkkio *swampy stretch*:móll- *soft* adj/IIIb; kannɔlíkkio *kind of edible bivalve*:kánnɔl- *little cylinder, a kind of pastry* m/IIb; kročíkkio *crossroads*:króč- *cross* f/IIIb; kavíkkio *peg*:kav⁺ *pin*.

D. ⁺ók⁺ in santókkio *bigot*:sánt- *holy* adj/I–II; ranókkio *frog*:rán- *id.* f/Ia; batókkio *big stick, bell-clapper*:bat⁺ *stick, blow*; marmókkio *brat, kid*:marm⁺ *obnoxious person.*

E. ⁺ísk⁺ in nevískio *sleet*:név- *snow* f/IIIb.

j. ⁺ói- adj/I–II, f/Ia and m/IIb, with meanings:

i. As adjective, *-ory*, in skɔrsóio *slipping, slip* (*-knot*):Non-Finite C of skórr- *slip, run off* IIIb/Reg/S¹, ².

ii. As noun f/Ia, *place having* . . ., in tettóia *shelter, cave*:tétt- *roof* m/IIb; and strettóia *tight place*:Non-Finite C of strínG- *squeeze* IIIb/Reg/S¹, ².

iii. As noun m/IIb, *place or instrument of action*, in the following based on Non-Finite C of verbs of types:

A. II/Reg/S¹, ²: kopertóio *coarse blanket*:kɔpr- *cover.*

B. IIIb/Reg/S¹, ²: frantóio *olive-press*:fránG- *break*; rasóio *razor*:rád- *shave*; skrittóio *office, writing-room, desk*:skrív- *write.*

iv. The suffix is preceded by ⁺t⁺ in the following nouns based on Stem A of verbs (with TV /e/ > /i/):

A. Nouns of f/Ia (meaning *place or instrument of action*) on verbs of I/Reg/W: akkɔrčatóia, skɔrčatóia *short cut*:akkórč-, skórč- *shorten*; appianatóia *smoother, trowel*:appián- *smooth*; natatóia *fin*:nát- *swim*; paratóia *dam, cataract* :pár- *stop*; passatóia *runner* (*carpet*):páss- *pass.*

B. Many nouns of m/IIb, such as the following based on verbs of:

I. I/Reg/W: abbrevɛratóio *watering-trough*:abbévɛr- *water*; akkɔratóio *slaughtering-knife*:akkór- *strike to the heart*; affogatóio *smothering*(*ly hot*) *place*:affóg- *smother*; appianatóio, spianatóio *smoother, roller*:appián-, spián- *smoothe*; kakatóio *toilet*:kák- *shit*; kastratóio *gelding-knife*:kástr- *castrate*; nettatóio *cleaning-instrument*:nétt- *clean*; etc.

II. IIIb/Reg/W: aččenditóio *lamp-lighter*:aččénd- *light.*

v. It is preceded by ⁺at⁺ in matitatóio *pencil-holder*:matít- *pencil* f/Ia.

k. ⁺óri- adj/I–II, f/Ia and m/IIb, with meanings:

i. As adjective, *-orious*, in notório *notorious*:nót- *known* adj/I–II; mɛritório *meritorious*:mérit- *merit* m/IIb; and in a number of adjectives formed on Non-Finite C of verbs, e.g. of types:

A. I/Reg/W: akkusatório *accusatory*:akkús- *accuse*; čirkɔlatório *circulatory*:čírkɔl- *circulate*; kɔndannatório *condemnatory*:kɔndánn- *condemn*; etc.

B. II/ísK/W: ammɔnitório *admonitory*:ammɔn- *admonish.*

C. IIIb/Reg/S¹, ²: aččessório *accessory*:aččéd- *accede*; assɔlutório *absolutory*:assɔlút-:assólv- *absolve*; suččessório *successory*:suččéd- *succeed*; etc.

ii. As noun f/Ia, *action characteristic of* . . ., in baldória *feasting, revelry*: báld- *bold* adj/I–II; gallória *noisy merriment*:gáll- *rooster* m/IIb.

iii. As noun m/IIb, *-ory, -orium*, in forms based on:

A. Nouns: offɛrtório *offertory*:offért- *offer* f/Ia; čibório *ciborium*:číb- *food* m/IIb; rɔmitório *hermitage*:rɔmít- *hermit* m/IIb.

B. Verbs, on Non-Finite C: krɛmatório *crematory*:krém- *cremate* I/Reg/W; ɔratório *oratory*:ór- *pray* I/Reg/W; auditório *auditorium*:aud⁺:ud- *hear* II/Irr/W; mɔrtório *funeral*:mɔr- *die* II/Irr/W; aspɛrsório *aspersory*:

aspérG- *asperse* IIIb/Reg/S[1, 2]; rottório *obnoxious person*:rómp- *break* IIIb/Reg/S[1, 2]; traiettório *trajectory*:traiétt[+] *throw across.*

    iv. The suffix is preceded by:

      A. [+]at[+] in aleatório *aleatory* adj/I–II:ále- *die* f/Ia.

      B. [+]it[+] in tɛrritório *territory* m/IIb:tɛ́rr- *earth, land* f/Ia.

    l. [+]ásk- adj/I–II, f/Ia and m/IIb, with meanings:

      i. As adjective, *-asque, of* . . ., in forms based on geographical terms and place-names, such as riviɛrásko *coast-dwelling*:riviɛ́r- *coast* f/Ia; bɛrgamásko *Bergamasque*:bérgam- *Bergamo* f/II; komásko *Comasque*:kóm- *Como* f/II.

      ii. As noun f/Ia, *object tasting* . . ., in amaráska *maraschino*:amár- *bitter* adj/I–II.

      iii. As noun m/IIb, *share of* . . ., in maǧǧorásko *inheritance of the first-born*:maǧǧór- *greater, older* adj/IIIb; minorásko *inheritance of the younger brother*: minór- *lesser, younger* adj/IIIb; and *gust of* . . . in piovásko *gust of wind and rain*:pióv- *rain* f/Ia.

      iv. The suffix is preceded by [+]i[+] (absorbed in the preceding /GG/, §1.411.3) in fuǧǧásko *fugitive*:fúGG- *flee* II/Reg/W.

    m. [+]éll- adj/I–II, f/Ia and m/IIb, with meaning of a diminutive when formed on substantives, and of *instrument for* . . . when formed on verbs:

      i. As adjective, on adjectives, e.g. in morɛ́llo *blackish*:mór- *dark, Moorish* adj/I–II; pikkiatɛ́llo *pixilated, somewhat crazy*:pikkiát- *struck, crazy* adj/I–II (past part.); occasionally also on nouns, e.g. vɛrǧinɛ́llo *little virgin* (adj.):vérǧin- *virgin* f/IIIb.

      ii. As noun f/Ia:

      A. On verb, in tirɛ́lla *rein*:tír- *draw* I/Reg/W.

      B. On nouns: e.g. in ačetosɛ́lla *wild sorrel, wood-sorrel*:ačetós- *sorrel* f/Ia; kartɛ́lla *coupon, folder*:kárt- *paper* f/Ia; kasɛ́lla *pigeon-hole*:kás- *house* f/Ia; katinɛ́lla *basin, ewer*:katín- *bucket* m/IIb; abetɛ́lla *cut and lopped fir*:abét- *fir* m/IIIb; karbonɛ́lla *small coals*:karbón- *coal* m/IIIb; kancọnɛ́lla *jest*:kancón- *song, joke* f/IIIb; etc.

      iii. As noun m/IIb:

      A. On nouns, e.g. of types:

        i. f/Ia: kappéllo *hat*:kápp- *cape*; kartéllo *poster, sign*:kárt- *paper*; kaséllo (*railway lineman's*) *hut*:kás- *house*; favoléllo *fabliau*:fávol- *fable*; listéllo *listel*:líst- *strip, list*; ombréllo *umbrella*:ómbr- *shade*; etc.

        ii. m/IIb: čɛrkiéllo *little circle*:čérki- *circle*; karréllo *bogie, line-trolley*: kárr- *car*; libéllo *little book*:lib[+]:líbr- *book*; etc.

      B. On verbs of I/Reg/W in: pestéllo *pestle*:pést- *grind, powder*; kuadréllo *square*:kuádr- *square off.*

      iv. The suffix is preceded by:

      A. [+]č[+], with gender:

        i. f/Ia in vaššɛ́lla *vessel*:vás- *vase, container for liquids* m/IIb; parčɛ́lla *parcel, little part*:párt- *part* f/IIIb; and in a number of derivatives on bases in /n/ of f/IIIb: e.g. ambitiončɛ́lla *little ambition*:ambitión- *ambition*; amministraciončɛ́lla *little administration*:amministración- *administration*; aspiraciončɛ́lla *little aspiration*:aspiración- *aspiration*; etc.

II. m/IIb in arboššéllo *shrub*:arbos⁺:árbɔr- *tree* m/IIIb, and in a number of derivatives on bases in /n/ of m/IIIb: e.g. ladrɔnčéllo *little thief*: ladrón- *thief*, etc.

B. ⁺ič⁺ in a number of diminutives, after bases ending in /Ct Cd/, as in the following of types:

I. Adj/I–II: grandičéllo *biggish*:gránd- *big* adj/IIIb.

II. f/Ia: astičélla *little shaft*:ást- *shaft* f/Ia; kɔrdičélla *little cord*:kórd- *cord, rope* f/Ia; spɔrtičélla *little bag*:spórt- *shopping bag* f/Ia; artičélla *little art*: árt- *art* f/IIIb; fantičélla *little servant girl*:fánt- *servant girl* f/IIIb; partičélla *little part, particle*:párt- *part* f/IIIb; etc.

III. m/IIb: mɔntičéllo *little mountain*:mónt- *mountain* m/IIIb.

C. ⁺z⁺ in dɔnzélla *young lady* f/Ia, dɔnzéllo *young gentleman* m/IIb: dónn- *lady, gentleman* f/Ia or m/IIb.

D. ⁺iǧ⁺ in damiǧélla *young lady*:dám- *lady* f/Ia.

E. ⁺ik⁺ in ketikélla *quiet* (occurring only in the locution allaketikélla *on the quiet*):két- két- *quiet* adj/I–II.

F. ⁺ar⁺ in the following of f/Ia: dɔnnarélla *worthless woman*:dónn- *woman* f/Ia; saltarélla *country dance of Lazio*:sált- *jump* m/IIb; trɛmarélla *trembling*:tremár- *to tremble* m/IIIb (infin.)

G. ⁺ɛr⁺ in the following of:

I. f/Ia: akkuɛrélla *drizzle, light rain, aquarelle*:ákku- *water, rain* f/Ia; assɛrélla *little board*:áss- *board* f/IIIb; kakɛrélla *turd of dung*:kák- *shit* I/Reg/W; passɛrélla *(light) bridge*:páss- *pass* I/Reg/W.

II. m/IIb, on bases of m/IIb: bukɛréllo *little hole*:búk- *hole*; fat-tɛréllo *little fact*:fátt- *fact*; saltɛréllo *little jump*:sált- *jump*.

H. ⁺ist⁺ in kiavistéllo *bolt*:kiáv- *key* f/IIIb.

I. ⁺iv⁺ in pedivélla *pedal-bar*:ped⁺:piɛd- *foot* m/IIIb.

K. ⁺ov⁺ in manovélla *handle*:mán- *hand* f/IIb.

n. ⁺'ɔl- diminutive, adj/I–II, f/Ia and m/IIb, as in:

i. Adjectives, based on:

A. Substantives: trítɔlo *in tiny bits*:trít- *minced* adj/I–II; ǧúɲɲɔl- *pertaining to a kind of June pear*:ǧúɲɲ- *June* m/IIb; píkkɔl- *little*:piKK⁺ *small*.

B. Verbs: trémɔlo *tremulous*:trém- *tremble* I/Reg/W.

ii. As noun f/Ia, based on:

A. Nouns, of types:

I. f/Ia: ávɔla *grandmother*:áv- *id.*; ǧìravóltɔla *complete turn, spin*: ǧìravólt- *id.*; góččɔla *droplet*:góčč- *id.*; kákkɔla *drop of mucus or rheum*:kákk- *shit*; kôstɔla *rib*:kóst- *id.*; etc.

II. f/IIIb: pégɔla *pitch*:peg⁺:péč- *pitch*.

B. Verbs, in frégɔla *spawning* (with /é/ instead of /ɛ́/):frég- *rub* I/Reg/W; spáccɔla *brush*:spácc- *sweep* I/Reg/W; travéggɔle *'seeing things'* (pl.) (with /é/):travéGG-:travéd- *missee* IIIa/Reg/S[1]; régɔla *rule*:rɛG⁺:réGG- *rule* IIIb/Reg/S[1, 2].

iii. As noun m/IIb, based on:

A. Nouns of:

I. f/Ia: bíndɔlo *reel, water-wheel, meddler*:bínd- *reel, pulley*; číččɔlo *fleshy excrescence*:číčč- *meat* (childish term); kánnɔlo *kind of* (*cylindrical*) *pastry*: kánn- *cane, tube*; čímɔlo *tender part* (*esp. top*) *of edible plant*:čím- *top*; kódɔlo *handle* (with /ó/):kód- *tail*; etc.

   ii. m/IIb: ávɔlo *grandfather*:áv- *id.*; bámbɔlo *doll*:bámb- *ingenuous person, child*; bóccɔlo *cocoon*:bótt- *swelling, lump*; kapítɔlo *chapter*:kapit[+] káp- *head*; etc.

   B. Verbs of:

    i. I/Reg/W: skámpɔlo *scrap, remnant*:skámp- *escape, be left over*; túffɔlo *a kind of diving bird*:túff- *dive*.

    ii. IIIb/Reg/S[1, 2]: číngɔlo (*priest's*) *cord, girdle*:čínG- *gird*; péndɔlo *pendulum*:pénd- *hang*; púngɔlo *goad*:púnG- *prick*; vólgɔlo *package, roll*:vólG- *turn*; vólvɔlo *volvulus*:vɔlv[+]:vólG- *turn*.

   iv. The suffix is preceded by:

    A. [+]△[+], in minúccɔlo *minute piece* m/IIb:minút- *minute* adj/I–II; pénzɔlo *dangling*:pénd- *hang* IIIb/Reg/S[1, 2].

    B. [+]áčč[+], in kováččɔlo *nest* m/IIb:kóv- *brood* I/Reg/W.

    C. [+]ánd[+], in nidiándɔlo *nest-egg* m/IIb:nídi- *nest* m/IIb; ɔliándɔlo *oil-vendor* m/IIb:óli- *oil* m/IIb.

    D. [+]ɛ́[+], in auréɔla *aureole* f/Ia:áur- *gold* m/IIb.

    E. [+]úff[+], in batúffɔlo *package* m/IIb:bat[+] *stick, rod*.

    F. [+]ɛruǧ[+], in akkuɛrúǧɔla *drizzle, slight rain* f/Ia:ákku- *water* f/Ia.

    G. [+]k[+], in the following nouns m/IIb, based on:

     i. Nouns m/IIb: libérkɔlo *worthless little book*:lib[+]:líbr- *book*; tubérkɔlo *tubercle*:túber- *tuber*.

     ii. Verbs I/Reg/W: čɛnákɔlo *cenacle, Last Supper*:čén- *dine*; mirákɔlo *miracle*:mír- *wonder*; ostákɔlo *obstacle*:óst- *be in the way*; ɔrákɔlo *oracle*:ór- *pray*; propuɲɲákɔlo *defense*:propúɲɲ- *defend*; ričettákɔlo *receptacle*: ričétt- *receive*; seɲɲákɔlo *sign, symbol*:séɲɲ- *indicate*; spettákɔlo *spectacle*:spétt- *concern, (look)*; tɛntákɔlo *tentacle*:tént- *grasp*.

    H. [+]ák[+], in vɛrnákɔlo *vernacular* adj/I–II: vɛrn[+] *common*.

    J. [+]ék[+], in baẓẓékɔlo *bagatelle* f/Ia:báẓẓ- *id.* f/Ia; mɔlékɔla *molecule* f/Ia:mól- *mass* f/IIIb.

    K. [+]ík[+], in:

     i. The adjective ridíkɔlo *ridiculous*:ríd- *laugh* IIIb/Reg/S[1, 2].

     ii. The nouns f/Ia klavíkɔla *clavicle*:kláv- *club* f/Ia; partíkɔla *host* (in communion):párt- *part* f/IIIb; pɛllíkɔla *film*:péll- *skin* f/IIIb.

     iii. The nouns of m/IIb, based on:

      α. Nouns: gratíkɔlo *little grating*:grát- *grating* f/Ia; artíkɔlo *article*:árt- *joint* m/IIb; faššíkɔlo *fascicle*:fášš- *bundle* m/IIb; vɛntríkɔlo *ventricle, stomach*:véntr- *belly* m/IIIb; retíkɔlo *reticule*:rét- *net* f/IIIb; fɔllíkɔlo *follicle*: fɔll[+] *foll-*.

      β. Verbs: kurríkɔlo *curriculum* (*e.g. vitae*):kurr[+]:kórr- *run* IIIb/Reg/S[1, 2]; veíkɔlo *vehicle*:ve[+] *carry*.

    L. [+]ákk[+] in dɔnnákkɔla *worthless little woman* f/Ia and dɔnnákkɔlo *id.* m/IIb:dónn- *woman* f/Ia.

    M. [+]ókk[+] in bɛrnókkɔlo *bump, lump* m/IIb:bɛrn[+] *lump*.

n. ⁺únk⁺ in the nouns m/IIb: ranúnkɔlo *a kind of poisonous plant*:ránfrog f/Ia (through comparison with shape); fɔrúnkɔlo *foruncle, little abscess*: fór- *hole* m/IIb; pedúnkɔlo *peduncle, stem*:ped⁺:piéd- *foot* m/IIIb.

o. ⁺isk⁺ in pulvískɔlo pɔlvískɔlo *fine dust* m/IIb (:pulv⁺):pólv- *dust* (poet.) f/IIIb.

p. ⁺úsk⁺ in:

i. The adjectives, based on adjs/IId: maiúskɔlo *majuscule, capital*: mai⁺:mágğ- *greater*; minúskɔlo *minuscule*:min⁺mén- *less*.

ii. The nouns m/IIb: opúskɔlo *opuscule*:ɔp⁺:ópɛra *work* f/Ia; kɔrpúskɔlo *corpuscle*:kórp- *body* m/IIb; krepúskɔlo *crepuscule, twilight*:krép- *burst* I/Reg/W.

q. ⁺úk⁺, in the nouns:

i. f/Ia: dɔnnúkɔla *worthless little woman*:dónn- *woman* f/Ia; karrúkɔla *pulley*:kárr- *car* m/IIb.

ii. m/IIb: abatúkɔlo *worthless little priest*:abát- *priest* m/IIIb; ğɔrnalúkɔlo *worthless little newspaper*:ğɔrnál- *newspaper* m/IIIb.

r. ⁺iʎʎ⁺, in aččendíʎʎɔlo *tinder* m/IIb:aččénd- *light* IIIb/Reg/S[1, 2].

s. ⁺áɲɲ⁺, in appikkáɲɲɔlo attakkáɲɲɔlo *hanger, pretext* m/IIb: appíkk- attákk- *attach* I/Reg/W.

t. ⁺íɲɲ⁺, in the nouns m/IIb: kɔmíɲɲɔlo *gable*:kom⁺:kólm- *top, summit* m/IIb; nɔmíɲɲɔlo *nickname*:nóm- *name* m/IIIb; lučíɲɲɔlo *wick*:lúč- *light* f/IIIb.

u. ⁺óɲɲ⁺, in the following adjectives, based on:

i. Adjs/I–II: aẓẓurróɲɲɔlo *bluish*:aẓẓúrr- *blue*; ğallóɲɲɔlo *pale yellow*:ğáll- *yellow*; magróɲɲɔlo *thinnish*:mágr- *thin*.

ii. Adj/IIIb: verdóɲɲɔlo *greenish*:vérd- *green*.

iii. f/IIIb: čɛneróɲɲɔlo *ash-colored*:čénɛr- *ashes*.

w. ⁺íp⁺, in kasípɔla *hovel* ʃ/Ia:kás- *house* f/Ia; manípolo *handful* m/IIb:mán- *hand* f/IIb/.

x. ⁺óp⁺, in manópɔla *cuff* f/Ia:mán- *hand* f/IIb.

y. ⁺úp⁺, in kasúpɔla *hovel* f/Ia:kás- *house* f/Ia.

z. ⁺t⁺, in pústɔla *pustule* f/Ia:pús *pus* m/VId.

aa. ⁺ént⁺, in čɛneréntɔla *Cinderella* f/Ia:čénɛr- *ashes* f/IIIb.

bb. ⁺átt⁺, in linguáttɔla *a kind of flat fish* f/Ia:língu- *tongue* f/Ia; ğokáttɔlo *toy* m/IIb:ğók- *game, pastime* m/IIb.

cc. ⁺ičátt⁺, in the nouns m/IIb: kɔrpičáttɔlo *vile little body*:kórp- *body* m/IIb; vɛrmičáttɔlo *little worm*:vérm- *worm* m/IIIb.

dd. ⁺étt⁺, in béttɔla *wineshop*:b⁺:bév- *drink* IIIb(x)/Reg/S[1].

ee. ⁺ótt⁺, in the following nouns of:

i. f/Ia: pallóttɔla *ball, bullet*:páll- *ball* f/Ia; vióttɔla *by-way*:ví- *way, road* f/Ia; kɔllóttɔla *nape, back of the neck*:kóll- *neck* m/IIb.

ii. m/IIb: vióttɔlo *path*:ví- *way, road* f/Ia.

ff. ⁺ɛrótt⁺, in the nouns m/IIb: bambɛróttɔlo *(big) child*:bámb- *child, ingenuous person* m/IIb; pianɛróttɔlo *(staircase) landing*:pián- *floor, level place* m/IIb.

gg. ⁺ínc⁺, in kodíncɔlo *little tail*:kód- *tail* f/Ia.

HH. ⁺ónc⁺, in the nouns of m/IIb: raperóncɔlo rapóncɔlo *rampion* (:raper⁺):ráp- *turnip* f/Ia; medikóncɔlo *worthless doctor*:médiK- *doctor* m/IIb; abatóncɔlo *worthless priest*:abát- *priest* m/IIIb; pretóncɔlo *worthless priest*:prét- *priest* m/IIIb; lattóncɔlo *suckling animal*:látt- *suckle* I/Reg/W.

JJ. ⁺ácc⁺, in pretáccɔlo *worthless priest*:prét- *priest* m/IIIb.

o. ⁺(u)ól- adj/I–II, f/Ia and m/IIb, with the meanings:

i. As adjective, *pertaining to, like . . .*, in čilieg̓ólo *cherry (colored)*:čiliég̓- *cherry* f/Ia; kampaɲɲólo *rural, rustic*:kampáɲɲ- *country* f/Ia; spaɲɲuólo *Spanish*:spáɲɲ- *Spain* f/Ia; marcuólo *of March*:márc- *March* m/IIb.

ii. As noun f/Ia, diminutive, as in the following based on nouns f/Ia: ai(u)óla *ornamental flower-bed*:ái- *threshing-floor, open space*; antipatióla *little antipathy*:antipatí- *antipathy*; badióla *little abbey*:badí- *abbey*; fiʎʎ(u)óla *daughter*:fíʎʎ- *id.*; etc.

iii. As noun m/IIb:

A. *-ol*, e.g. in mɛntólo *menthol*:mént- *mint* f/Ia; naftólo *naphthol*:náft- *naphtha* f/Ia.

B. Diminutive, as in the following based on nouns m/IIb: armadiólo *little closet*:armádi- *closet*; fiʎʎ(u)ólo *son*:fíʎʎ- *id.*; laččólo *little snare, trap*:láčč- *snare, trap*; pog̓g̓ólo *terrace, balcony*:póg̓g̓- *hill*; etc.

iv. The suffix is preceded by:

A. ⁺ičč⁺ in astiččóla *little shaft, panhandle* f/Ia:ást- *shaft* f/Ia; donniččóla *(ignorant, gossipy) little woman* f/Ia:dónn- *woman* f/Ia; vɛrmiččólo *little worm* m/IIb:vérm- *worm* m/IIIb.

B. ⁺i⁺ in the following, of:

I. f/Ia: kaprióla *capriole, tumble*:kápr- *goat* f/Ia; karrióla *wheelbarrow*: kárr- *car(t)* m/IIb.

II. m/IIb: vaiólo *smallpox*:vái- *darkish* adj/I–II; kapriólo *roebuck*: kápr- *goat* f/Ia; vetriólo *vitriol*:vétr- *glass* m/IIb; beriólo *water-dish (in bird cage)*:bér- *to drink* m/IIIb (infin.).

C. ⁺ai⁺, forming a compound suffix ⁺aiól- adj/I–II *pertaining to . . .* or m/IIb indicating (usually) profession or activity, as in the following of:

I. Adj/I–II: akkuaiólo *aquarian*; as m/IIb, *water-vendor*:ákku- *water* f/Ia; rissaiólo *prone to fights*:ríss- *fight* f/Ia; lattaiólo *milk (of teeth)*:látt- *milk* m/IIIb.

II. f/Ia: kakaióla *diarrhea*:kák- *shit* I/Reg/W.

III. m/IIb: barkaiólo *boatman*:bárk- *boat* f/Ia; biskaiólo *frequenter of gambling joint*:bísk- *illegal gambling joint* f/Ia; bɔrsaiólo *highwayman*:bórs- *purse* f/Ia; armaiólo *seller, repairer, maker of arms*:árm- *arm, weapon* f/Ib; baɲɲaiólo *bath-keeper*:báɲɲ- *bath* m/IIb; etc.

D. ⁺ar⁺ in fumaróla *gaseous emanation* f/Ia:fúm- *smoke* m/IIb; barkarólo *boatman* m/IIb:bárk- *boat* f/Ia; dɛntaruólo *teething-ring*:dént- *tooth* m/IIIb.

E. ⁺ɛr⁺ in kassɛr(u)óla kaccɛr(u)óla *casserole*:kass⁺ kacc⁺ *kettle*; musɛruóla *muzzle*:mús- *snout, nose* m/IIb; puntɛruólo *awl*:púnt- *sewing* m/IIb.

F. ⁺anc⁺ in tristancuólo *sorry (poor, worthless)*:tríst- *bad* adj/I–II.

p. +′ul- -*ulous* adj/I–II, -*ula* f/Ia and -*ulus* m/IIb:

  i. As adjective, based on:

    A. Adj/I–II: ačídulo *acidulous*:áčid- *acid*.

    B. Verbs of types:

      I. I/Reg/W: trémulo *tremulous*:trém- *tremble*.

      II. II/ísK/W: gárrulo *garrulous*:garr- *chatter*.

      III. IIIb: bíbulo *bibulous*:bib+:bév- *drink*; krédulo *credulous*:kréd- *believe*; péndulo *pendulent*:pénd- *hang*; strídulo *stridulent*:stríd- *be strident*.

      IV. Verbal base: kuέrul- *querulous*:kuεr+ *complain*.

  ii. As noun f/Ia, based on nouns of f/Ia: čéllula *cellule*:čéll- *cell*; fórmula *formula*:fórm- *form*; kampánula *campanula, bell-flower*:kampán- *bell*; kánnula *enema-tube*:kánn- *tube*; lúnula *little moon*:lún- *moon*; spórtula *dole*:spórt- (*food-*)*bag*; stípula *stubble*:stíp- *fagot* (archaic).

  iii. As noun m/IIb, based on:

    A. Nouns m/IIb: glóbulo *globule*:glób- *globe*; lókulo *niche* (e.g. in catacombs):lók- *place*; módulo *module, blank*:mód- *manner*.

    B. Noun m/IIc: óvulo *ovule*:óv- *egg*.

    C. Verbal base: túmulo *tumulus, mound*:tum+ *swell up*.

q. +án- -*an, -anous, -ain* adj/I–II, f/Ia and m/IIb:

  i. As adjective, in the following based on:

    A. Adj/I–II: altáno *high*:ált- *id*.; kuartáno *quartain* (of fever):kuárt- *fourth*; medíano *median*:médi- *middle*; meẓẓáno *in the middle*:méẓẓ- *half*; nostráno *of ours*:nóstr- *our*; tεrcáno *tertain* (of fever):tέrc- *third*; toskáno *Tuscan*:tósk- *id*.

    B. Nouns, especially proper or geographical names, as in the following based on nouns of types:

      I. f/Ia: albáno *Alban*:álb- *Alba*; amεrikáno *American*:amérik- *America*; balcáno *whitefooted*:bálc- *whitefoot*; piováno *pertaining to rain*:pióv- *rain*; rɔmáno *Roman*:róm- *Rome*; etc.

      II. m/IIb: agostáno *of August*:agóst- *August*; balcáno *scatter-brained, bouncy*:bálc- *jolt, bounce*; kopεrnikáno *Copernican*:kopérnik- *Copernicus*; nestɔriáno *Nestorian*:nestóri- *Nestorius*; etc.

  ii. As noun f/Ia, based on:

    A. Adj/I–II: kaldána *midday heat, sudden flush of anger*:káld- *hot*.

    B. Nouns: kɔllána *necklace*:kóll- *neck* m/IIb; pedána *footstool*:ped+: piéd- *foot* m/IIIb; fɔntána *fountain*:fónt- *spring, fount(ain)* f/IIIb.

    C. Verb I/Irr/W: andána *path*:and- *go*.

  iii. As noun m/IIb, based on:

    A. Adj/I–II: kaldáno *brazier*:káld- *hot*.

    B. Nouns of types:

      I. f/Ia: kappεlláno *chaplain*:kappéll- *chapel*.

      II. m/IIb: bakkáno *uproar*:bákk- *Bacchus*; kapitáno *captain*:kapit+ :káp- *head*; kastεlláno *castellan*:kastéll- *castle*.

      C. Verbs in:

      I. Root: vɔláno *shuttlecock*:vól- *fly* I/Reg/W; skriváno *scribe, amanuensis*:skrív- *write* IIIb/Reg/S[1, 2].

ii. Non-Finite C: čarlatáno *charlatan*:čárl- *chat(ter)* I/Reg/W.

iv. The suffix is preceded by:

A. +anč+ in ridančáno *burlesque*:ríd- *laugh* IIIb/Reg/S[1, 2].

B. +iǧ+ in the following:

i. Adjectives, derived from nouns of types:

α. f/Ia: markiǧáno *of the Marche*:márk- (pl.) *the Marche*; parmiǧáno *Parmesan*:párm- *Parma*.

β. m/IIb: pianiǧáno *of the plain*:pián- *plain*.

γ. m/IIIb: kɔlliǧáno *of hills, hilldwelling*:kɔ́ll- *hill*.

δ. f/IIIb: alpiǧáno *Alpine (inhabitant)*, mountaineer:álp- *Alp*; kɔrtiǧáno *courtly*:kórt- *court*; partiǧáno *partisan*:párt- *party*; valliǧáno *of the valley*:váll- *valley*.

ε. m/IVd: lodiǧáno *of Lodi*:lɔ́d- *Lodi*.

ii. Nouns m/IIb: borgiǧáno *bourgeois, town-dweller*:bórg- *burgh* m/IIb; artiǧáno *artisan*:árt- *art, trade* f/IIIb.

c. +i+ (further preceded by △ after /k/, /Vt/), in:

i. Adjectives, such as the following based on nouns of types:

α. m/IIb: agostiniáno *Augustinian*:agostín- *Augustine*; ambrosiáno *Ambrosian*:ambros+:ambróǧ- *Ambrose*; erasmiáno *Erasmian*:erásm- *Erasmus*; ikariáno *Icarian*:íkar- *Icarus*; kristiáno *Christian*:kríst- *Christ*; marčáno *of St. Mark*:márk- *Mark*; etc.

β. m/IIIb: drakɔniáno *Draconian*:drakón- *Draco*; katɔnián- *Catonian*:katón- *Cato*; etc.

γ. m/IVd: bodɔniáno *Bodonian*:bodón- *Bodoni*; etc.

δ. Adv/IVd: anciáno *elder, ancient, senior*:ánc- *before*.

D. +l+ in tamburláno *clothes-dryer* m/IIb:tambúr- *drum* m/IIb.

E. +ɔl+ in grossɔláno *coarse, vulgar* adj/I–II:gróss- *big, large* adj/I–II; pɔrtɔláno *pilot's book, maps etc.* m/IIb:pórt- *port* m/IIb.

F. +iʎʎ+ in kasiʎʎáno *living in the same (apartment-) house as ...* adj/I–II:kás- *house* f/Ia.

G. +t+ (with loss of preceding C) in lɔntáno *distant* adj/I–II:lɔnG+: lúng- *long* adj/I–II.

H. +it+ in the adjectives puritáno *Puritan(ical)*:púr- *pure* adj/I–II; samaritáno *Samaritan*:samári- *Samaria* f/Ia.

J. +acc+ in terraccáno *inhabitant of a village* m/IIb:térr- *country, village* f/Ia.

r. +ín- adj/I–II, f/Ia and m/IIb, with the basic meaning of a diminutive, but with also other subordinate meanings.

i. As adjective, with the meanings:

A. Diminutive, e.g. in the following based on adjectives of types:

i. I–II: aẓẓurríno *light blue*:aẓẓúrr- *blue*; amikíno *little friend*: amik+:amíK- *friendly*; bɛllíno *little and pretty*:bɛ́ll- *beautiful*; buɔníno *good and little*:buón- *good*; etc.

ii. IIIb: grandíno *biggish*:gránd- *big*; verdíno *greenish, light green*: vérd- *green*; etc.

B. -ine, pertaining to . . ., as in the following based on:

    I. Adj/I–II: albíno *albino*:álb- *white* (poet.).

    II. Adj/IIIb: papalíno *papal*:papál- *id.*

    III. Nouns of types:

       α. f/Ia: akuilíno *aquiline*:ákuil- *eagle*; barbíno *strange, peculiar*: bárb- *beard*; etc.

       β. m/IIb: adultɛríno *adulterine*:adultéri- *adultery*; alabastríno *alabastrine*:alabástr- *alabaster*; arǧentíno *of silver*:arǧént- *silver*; baččɛllíno *of beans, bean-bearing*:baččéll- *bean*; brɔnʐíno *bronze-like*:brónʐ- *bronze*; kɔrvíno *corvine*:kórv- *crow*; etc.

       γ. m/IIIb: abietín- *abietine*:abiét- *fir.*

       δ. m/IVd: alkalíno *alkaline*:álkal- *alkali*; pariǧíno *Parisian*: paríǧ- *Paris.*

    IV. Verb, on Non-Finite B: kučiríno *for sewing*:kúč- *sew* II/Reg/W.
  ii. As noun f/Ia, with the meanings:

    A. Diminutive, as in the following based on nouns of:

    I. f/Ia: aččettína *little hatchet*:aččétt- *hatchet*; seǧǧolína *little chair*: séǧǧol- *chair*; tavɔlína *little table*:távɔl- *table*; travɛrsína *little bar*:travérs- *bar*; etc. etc.

    II. f/Ib: alína *little wing*:ál- *wing.*

    III. m/IIb: čedrína *a type of shrub*:čedr- *cedar*; kastɛllína *little heap*: kastéll- *castle.*

    IV. f/IIb: manína *little hand*:mán- *hand.*

    B. Feminine, as in ɛroína *heroine*:ɛró- *hero* m/IIIb; reǧína reína *queen* (:reG⁺):ré× *king* m/VId.

    C. -ine, substance having or causing quality of . . ., as in the following based on:

    I. Adj/IIIb: brillantína *brilliantine*:brillánt- *brilliant*; nasalína *an anti-cold preparation*:nasál- *nasal.*

    II. Nouns of types:

       α. f/Ia: fibrína *fibrine*:fíbr- *fiber.*

       β. m/IIb: ɔleína *olein*:ɔle⁺:óli- *oil.*

       γ. m/IIIb: kotɔnína *a kind of coarse cotton cloth*:kotón- *cotton.*

       δ. m/VId: kaffeína *caffein*:kaffé× *coffee.*

       ε. Substantival bases: kaseína *casein*:kase⁺ *cheese*; mɔrfína *morphine*:mɔrf⁺ *sleep*; narkotína *narcotine*:narkɔT⁺ *narcot-, narcosis*; neurína *neurine*:neur⁺ *neur-, nerve*; nikotína *nicotine*:nikot⁺ *Nicot*; pepsína *pepsin*:pepT⁺ *digestion*; sakkarína *saccharine*:sakkar⁺ *sugar*; stearína *stearine*:stear⁺ *stear-, fat, tallow.*

    D. Art of . . ., act of . . ., ensemble of . . ., in the following, based on:

    I. Adj/I–II: sɛlvaǧǧína *wild animals*:sɛlváǧǧ- *wild.*

    II. m/IIb: medičína *medicine*:médiK- *doctor.*

    III. m/IIIb: aruspičína *diviner's art*:arúspič- *haruspex*; karnefičína *execution, slaughter*:karnéfič- *executioner.*

    E. Group of (about) . . ., in nouns based on:

i. The adjs/I–II térc- *third* and sést- *sixth*: tɛrcína *terzina*, sestína *sestina*.

ii. Numerals above *four*: e.g. činkuína *group of five*:cínku- *five* num/IIId; diečína *about 10*:diéč- *ten* num/VId; doẓẓína *dozen*:doẓẓ⁺:dódič- *twelve* num/VId; činkuantína *about fifty*:činkuánt- *fifty* num/Id; etc.

F. Place, act of . . ., in guardína *guard-room*:guárd- *guard, keep* I/Reg/W; rapína *rapine*:rap- *rape* II/ísK/W.

iii. As noun m/IIb, with the meanings:

A. Diminutive, as in the following based on nouns of:

i. f/Ia: ačč́ettíno *little hatchet*:ačč́étt- *hatchet*; anatríno *duckling*: ánatr- *duck*; bokkíno *little mouth, cigarette-holder*:bókk- *mouth*; bottegíno *little shop, box-office*:bottég- *shop*; čɛríno *(wax) match*:čér- *wax*; figuríno *little figure, figurine*:figúr- *figure*; kasíno *little house, casino*:kás- *house*; etc.

ii. m/IIb: aɲɲɛllíno *lambkin*:aɲɲéll- *lamb*; invɔltíno *little package*: invólt- *package*; kappɛllíno *little hat*:kappéll- *hat*; kɔrníno *little horn*:kórn- *horn*; etc. etc.

iii. m/IIIb: abatíno *little priest*:abát- *priest*; fantíno *jockey*:fánt- *boy*; kavaliɛríno *little knight*:kavaliér- *knight*; paníno *roll*:pán- *bread*; etc.

B. *Grove of* . . ., in abietíno *fir-grove*:abiét- *fir* m/IIIb.

c. *Coin worth . . . monetary units, made of* . . ., in činkuantíno *50-centesimi coin*:činkuánt- *fifty* num/Id; činkuíno *5-centesimi coin*:čínku- *five* num/IIId; nikɛlíno *nickel coin*:nikél *nickel* m/VId or nikéli- *id.* m/IIb.

D. *Person acting in connection with* . . ., as in the following based on:

i. Nouns of:

α. f/Ia: čabattíno *shoe-repairer*:čabátt- *old shoe*; čɛrtosíno *Charterhouse monk*:čɛrtós- *Charterhouse*; kanapíno *hemp-comber*:kánap- *hemp*; pappíno *hospital orderly*:pápp- *pap, invalid food*.

β. m/IIb: baɲɲíno *bath-attendant*:báɲɲ- *bath*.

ii. Verbs of I/Reg/W: e.g. akkattíno *beggar*:akkátt- *beg*; appičč́ikíno *hail-fellow-well-met person*:appíčč́ik- *stick, catch poorly*; arrotíno *scissors-grinder*: arrót- *sharpen (on wheel)*; attakkíno *quarrelsome person*:attákk- *attack*; fikkíno *meddler*:fíkk- *stick, shove*; galoppíno *errand-boy*:galópp- *gallop*; lustríno *boot-black*:lústr- *shine (shoes)*; vageǧǧíno *courter, admirer*:vagéǧǧ- *court, admire*; etc.

iv. The suffix is preceded by:

A. ⁺ald⁺ in truffaldíno *cheater, swindler*:trúff- *cheat, swindle* I/Reg/W.

B. ⁺č⁺ in diminutives after bases ending in /n/: e.g. kɔrɔnčína *little crown*:kɔrón- *crown* f/Ia; bokkɔnčíno *little mouthful*:bokkón- *mouthful* m/IIIb; čičɛrɔnčíno *little cicerone*:čičɛrón- *cicerone* m/IIIb; ambiciɔnčína *little ambition*: ambición- *ambition* f/IIIb; kancɔnčína *little song*:kancón- *song* f/IIIb; etc.

c. ⁺ič⁺ in some diminutives, especially after bases ending in /rC/, such as the following based on:

i. Adj/I–II: mɔrtičíno *dead child*:mórt- *dead*.

ii. f/Ia: astičína *little shaft*:ást- *shaft*; kɔrdičína *little cord*:kórd- *cord*; spɔrtičína *little bag*:spórt- *bag*; vakkičína *little cow*:vákk- *cow*; etc.

iii. m/IIb: kɔrpičíno *little body*:kórp- *body*.

iv. m/IIIb: fiɔričíno *little flower*:fiór- *flower*; kuɔričíno *little heart*: kuɔ́r- *heart*; lumičíno *little light*:lúm- *light*.

v. f/IIIb: artičína *little art*:árt- *art*; assičína *little board*:áss- *board*.

D. ⁺nd⁺ in lavandíno *washbowl*:láv- *wash* I/Reg/W.

E. ⁺al⁺ in naftalína *naphthaline*:náft- *naphtha* f/Ia.

F. ⁺ɔl⁺ in certain diminutives: e.g. akkuɔlína *drizzle, slight rain* f/Ia: ákku- *water, rain* f/Ia; bestiɔlína *little beastie*:bésti- *beast* f/Ia; biettɔlína *little wedge* f/Ia:biétt- *wedge* f/Ia; krinɔlína *crinoline*:krín- *hair* m/IIb or m/IIIb; bakɔlíno *little (silk-) worm* m/IIb:bák- *(silk-) worm* m/IIb; fɛrrɔlíno *little iron* m/IIb:férr- *iron* m/IIb; etc.

G. ⁺ar⁺ in lɔngarína *long iron rod* f/Ia:lɔnG⁺:lúng- *long* adj/I–II; okarína *ocarina*:ók- *goose* f/Ia.

H. ⁺ɛr⁺ in mɔnkeríno *stump* m/IIb:mónk- *amputated* adj/I–II; damɛríno *dandy* m/IIb:dám- *lady* f/Ia; ballɛríno *dancer* m/IIb:báll- *dance* I/Reg/W.

J. ⁺itr⁺ in akkuitríno *surface penetration of water* m/IIb:ákku- *water* f/Ia.

K. ⁺astr⁺ in bekkastríno *long, narrow shoe* m/IIb:békk- *beak* m/IIb.

L. ⁺t⁺ in vespɛrtíno *of the evening* adj/I–II:vésp(ɛ)r- *evening, vesper(s)* m/IIb.

M. ⁺ant⁺ in parlantína *facility in speaking, gift of gab* f/Ia:párl- *speak* I/Reg/W.

N. ⁺st⁺ in pristíno *pristine* adj/I–II:pri⁺ *first*.

O. ⁺ast⁺ in mediastíno (also mediástino) *mediastine bone* m/IIb:médi- *in the middle* adj/I–II.

P. ⁺r⁺ in dottrína *doctrine, learning* f/Ia:dótt- *learned* adj/I–II.

Q. ⁺u⁺ in babbuíno *baboon, stupid fellow* m/IIb:bább- onomatopoetic m/IIb.

s. ⁺áɲɲ- *-ish, (thing) like . . ., means of . . .*, adj/I–II, f/Ia and m/IIb, in the following of types:

i. Adj/I–II: lungáɲɲ⁺ *longish* (in lungaɲɲáta *long-winded performance* f/Ia):lúng- *long* adj/I–II; tɛrráɲɲo *earthen* (rare or archaic):térr- *earth* f/Ia; grifáɲɲ- *raven-like, sharp*:gríf- *beak, snout* m/IIb.

ii. f/Ia: mɔntáɲɲa *mountain*:mónt- *mount(ain)* m/IIIb.

iii. m/IIb: viváɲɲo *edge of cloth*:vív- *alive* adj/I–II; kalkáɲɲo *heel*:kálk- *tread* I/Reg/W.

t. ⁺iér- adj/I–II, f/Ia, m/IIb and IIIb, with the following meanings:

i. As adj/I–II, *-y, -ish, for . . .*, in the following based on:

A. Adj/I–II: altiéro *haughty*:ált- *high*; primiéro *primary*:prím- *first*; straniéro *foreign*:strán- *strange*.

B. Nouns of types:

I. f/Ia: battaʎʎéro *pugnacious*:battáʎʎ- *battle*; karovaniéro *for caravans*:karován- *caravan*; mɛncɔɲɲéro *lying*:mɛncóɲɲ- *lie*; petriéro *stone-hurling* (of cannon etc.):pɛtr⁺:piétr- *stone*; poppiéro *of the stern, poop*:pópp- *poop, stern*; prodiéro *pertaining to the prow*:pród- *prow*; tɛrriéro *pertaining to land*:térr- *land, earth*; vєliéro *sailing*:vél- *sail*; (av)vєnturiéro *adventuresome*: (av)vєntúr- *adventure*.

    ii. m/IIIb: timɔniéro *pertaining to the rudder*:timón- *rudder*.

    iii. f/VId: vєritiéro *truthful*:vєrit+:vєritá[x] *truth*.

    c. Verbs I/Reg/W: čarliéro *talkative*:čárl- *chat(ter)*; passeǧǧéro *transitory, passenger*:passéǧǧ- *pass* (archaic), *walk*.

  ii. As noun f/Ia, *thing for . . ., container* based on:

    A. Nouns, such as the following of types:

      I. f/Ia: ampɔlliéra *jar-holder*:ampóll- *ampulla, wine-* or *oil-jar*; arančéra *place for orange plants during winter*:aránč- *orange*; balєniéra *whaling-vessel*:balén- *whale*; etc.

      II. m/IIb: bigattiéra *room for silk-worms*:bigátt- *silk-worm*; kaminiéra *fire-screen, wood-box, mantel-mirror*:kamín- *fireplace, chimney*; cukkєriéra *sugar-bowl*:cúkkєr- *sugar*; etc.

      III. m/IIIb: allumiéra *alum mine*:allúm- *alum*; saliéra *salt-cellar*: sál- *salt*; etc.

      IV. f/IIIb: frɔntiéra *frontier*:frónt- *front*.

      V. m/VId: bɔmbɔniéra *bonbonnière*:bɔmbón *bonbon*; kaffettiéra *coffee-pot*:kaffett+:kaffé[x] *coffee*; teiéra *tea-pot*:té[x] *tea*; etc.

    B. Verbs I/Reg/W, in pregiéra *prayer*:prég- *pray*; rasiéra *smoother*: rás- *smooth* (*top of grain barrel etc.*).

  iii. As noun m/IIb, indicating agent or result, based on verbs I/Reg/W: pєnsiéro *thought*:péns- *think*; troviéro *trouvère*:tróv- *find*.

  iv. As noun m/IIb or IIIb (of which one or the other is often archaic), indicating *person or thing connected with . . .*, in the following based on nouns of types:

    A. f/Ia: avvєnturiéro avvєnturiére *knight-errant*:avvєntúr- *adventure*; bankiéro (arch.) bankiére *banker*:bánk- *bank*; barbiéro (arch.) barbiére *barber*: bárb- *beard*; čimiéro čimiére *ornament on top of helmet*:čím- *top, summit*; levriéro levriére *greyhound*:levr+:lépr- *hare*; sɔmiéro *beast of burden*, sɔmiére *sounding board*:sóm- *burden*.

    B. Nominal base: sparviéro sparviére *sparrow-hawk, falcon*:sparv+ *sparrow*.

  v. As noun m/IIIb, indicating *person or thing connected with . . .* (especially by profession), as in the following based on:

    A. Adj/I–II: kuartiére *quarter*:kuárt- *fourth*; sestiére *region* (1/6 of town):sést- *sixth*.

    B. Nouns of types:

      I. f/Ia: alabardiére *hauberdier*:alabárd- *hauberd*; brakiére *truss* (*for hernia*):brák- *breeches*; etc.

      II. m/IIb: arčére *archer*:arK+:árk- *bow*; artifičére *soldier making inflammable materials*:artifíč- *artifice*; etc.

      III. m/IIIb: pɔntiére *soldier connected with bridge-making*:pónt- *bridge*.

      IV. f/IIIb: alpiére *Alpineer* (*soldier*):álp- *Alp*; bračére *brazier*:bráč- *embers, coals*; etc.

v. m/VId: kaffettiére *coffee-house keeper*:kaffɛtt⁺:kaffɛ́ˣ *coffee*.

VI. Nominal bases: artiʎʎére *artillery-man*:artiʎʎ⁺ *artillery*; aviére *soldier of the air forces*:av⁺ *bird, av(iation)*; baččelliére *bachelor (academic degree)*:baččell⁺ *bachel-*; etc.

c. Verb I/Reg/W, in kančelliére *chancellor*:kančéll- *cancel*.

vi. The suffix is preceded by:

A. ⁺ast⁺ ⁺est⁺ in fərastiéro fərestiéro *outsider, stranger, foreigner* m/IIb (or fərastiére fərestiére m/IIIb, archaic):fər:fuór- *outside* adv/IV.

B. ⁺att⁺ in: mulattiére *muleteer*:múl- *mule* m/IIb; boattiére *cowherder, -merchant*:bo:bóv- *ox* m/IIIb; kanattiére *dog-watcher, -tender*:kándog; panattiére *baker*:pán- *bread*.

u. ⁺ós- *-ose, -ous* adj/I–II and f/Ia:

i. As adjective, based on:

A. Adjectives: bɛllikóso *bellicose*:bélliK- *warlike* adj/I–II; gravóso *grievous*:gráv- *heavy* adj/IIIb.

B. Nouns, e.g. of types:

I. f/Ia: aččidióso *slothful*:aččídi- *sloth*; afóso *sultry*:áf- *sultriness*; albuminóso *albuminous*:albúmin- *albumen*; alteccóso *haughty*:altécc- *haughtiness*; angoššóso *anxious, in anguish*:angóšš- *anxiety, anguish*; etc.

II. m/IIb: ačetóso *vinegary*:ačét- *vinegar*; angolóso *angular*:ángol-*angle*; mərbóso *sickly*:mórb- *disease*; tedióso *tedious*:tédi- *tedium*; etc.

III. m/IIIb: adipóso *adipose*:ádip- *fat*; amoróso *amorous, loving*: amór- *love*; kaləróso *hot*:kalór- *heat*; məntuóso *mountainous*:montu⁺:mónt-*mountain*; etc.

IV. f/IIIb: pinguedinóso *fatty*:pinguédin- *fat*; putredinóso *corrupt*: putrédin- *corruption*.

v. f/VId: kalamitóso *calamitous*:kalamit⁺:kalamitáˣ *calamity*.

c. Verbs I/Reg/W: piangolóso *weeping*:piángol- *cry somewhat*; pikkóso *punctilious*:píkk- *pique (oneself on something)*; pioviǧǧinóso *rainyish*:piovíǧǧin-*rain a little*; sənnakkióso *sleepy*:sənnákki- *sleep a little, doze*; vitupɛróso *vituperative*:vitúper- *vituperate*.

D. Adv/II: ritróso *backwards, recalcitrant*:ritr⁺:rétr- *backward*.

ii. As noun, in čellulósa *cellulose*:čéllul- *cellule* f/Ia; ačetósa *sorrel*:ačét-*vinegar* m/IIb.

iii. The suffix is preceded in the following adjectives by:

A. ⁺i⁺ in pɛrfidióso *perfidious*:pérfid- *id.* adj/I–II; grandióso *grandiose*: gránd- *great* adj/IIIb; tɛndɛncióso *tendentious*:tɛndénc- *tendency* f/Ia; mistɛrióso *mysterious*:mistér- *mystery* m/IIb; bilióso *bilious*:bíl- *bile* f/IIIb.

B. ⁺△i⁺ in kapcióso *captious*:kapt⁺ *taken*:kap- *take, understand* II/ísK/W.

C. ⁺aǧin⁺ in əleaǧinóso *oleaginous*:əle⁺:óli- *oil* m/IIb.

D. ⁺iǧin⁺ in lattiǧinóso *like watery milk*:látt- *milk* m/IIb.

E. ⁺ɛr⁺ in nodɛróso *knotty*:nód- *knot* m/IIb; vələntɛróso *of good will*: vələnt⁺:vələntáˣ *will* f/VId.

w. ⁺ʹit- *-it, -ed, resultant from the action of . . .*, adj/I–II, f/Ia and m/IIb:

i. As adjective, based on verbs of types:

A. IIIa: débito *due*:deb⁺:dóv- *owe*; sólito *accustomed*:sƆl- *be accustomed*; táčito *tacit, silent*:táč- *be silent*.

B. IIIb: léčito líčito *licit*:léč- líč- *be allowed*.

ii. As noun f/Ia, based on:

A. Noun, in órbita *orbit*:órb- *orb, circle* f/IIIb.

B. Verbs of type IIIb/Reg/:

I. W, in čérnita *choice, selection*:čérn- *choose, select*; méššita *mixing (of liquors), bar* (with /é/):mésK- *mix*; rivéndita *resale*:rivénd- *resell*; véndita *sale*:vénd- *sell*.

II. S, in bíbita *drink*:bib⁺:bév- *drink*; kréššita *growth* (with /e/): krésK- *grow*; náššita *birth*:násK- *come into being*; pérdita *loss*:pérd- *lose*; réndita *income*:rénd- *give back, render*; spéndita *spending*:spénd- *spend*; vínčita *winning, victory*:vínK- *win*.

iii. As noun m/IIb, based on verbs of types:

A. I/Reg/W: anélito *panting, desire*:anél- *pant, desire*; ğéttito *casting*: gétt- *cast, throw*; lášito *legacy*:lášš- *leave*; liévito *leaven*:liév⁺:lév- *raise*; pálpito *palpitation*:pálp- *feel*; préstito *loan*:prést- *lend*; róğito *drawing up (of legal document)*:roğ⁺:róg- *draw up*; trémito *trembling move*.

B. I/Irr/W: ándito *corridor, hallway*:and- *go*.

C. II/ísK/W: ámbito *circle*:amb- *go around*; brámito *bellow*:brambellow; čirkúito *circuit*:čirku- *go around*; esérčito *army*:esɛrč- *exercise, conduct*.

D. IIIa: ábito *habit*:ab⁺:av- *have*.

E. IIIb: báttito *beating*:bátt- *beat;* frémito *shudder*:frém- *be agitated, shudder*; ğémito *groan, trickle*:ğém- *groan, trickle*; krédito *credit* (with /é/):kréd- *believe*; kuésito *problem, investigation*:kuɛs⁺:kiéd- *ask*; prémito *pressure (of intestines in evacuation)*:prém- *press*; prúrito *itching*:prur⁺:prúd- *itch*; strépito *uproar*:strép- *raise an uproar*.

F. Verbal bases: fómito *cause, source*:fom⁺ *foment*; mérito *merit*:mɛr⁺ *earn, deserve*; mónito *warning*:mon⁺ *warn*.

iv. The suffix is preceded by ⁺u⁺ in fortúito *fortuitous*:fort⁺ *chance*.

y. ⁺étt- diminutive, *-et*, adj/I–II, f/Ia and m/IIb:

i. As adjective, on adjectives, as in the following based on:

A. Adj/I–II: ačɛrbétto *bitterish*:ačérb- *bitter*; amarétto *bitterish*:amár- *bitter*; ambiciosétto *somewhat ambitious*:ambiciós- *ambitious*; asprétto *somewhat harsh*:áspr- *harsh*; ličɛnciosétto *a bit too free*:ličɛnciós- *over-free*; poverétto *poor little*:póvɛr- *poor*; etc.

B. Adj/IIIb: fačilétto (a) *little easy*:fáčil- *easy*; ğovanétto *young*: ğóvan- *young*; etc.

ii. As noun f/Ia, e.g. in the following based on:

A. Nouns of types:

I. f/Ia: akkuétta *slight rain*:ákku- *water, rain*; bollétta *little coupon, check, receipt*:bóll- *bull*; donzɛllétta *little damsel*:donzéll- *damsel*; etc.

II. f/Ib: alétta *little wing*:ál- *wing*.

III. m/IIb: karrétta *cart*:kárr- *car*; sigarétta *cigarette*:sígar- *cigar*.

IV. m/IIIb: marétta *slight sea*:már- *sea*.

B. Verbs: vedétta *vedette, lookout*:véd- *see* IIIa/Reg/S¹; vɛndétta *vendetta*:vɛnd⁺ *avenge*.

iii. As noun m/IIb, e.g. in the following based on:

A. Nouns of types:

I. f/Ia: piallétto *trowel*:piáll- *plane*.

II. m/IIb: aɲɲɛllétto *little lamb*:aɲɲéll- *lamb*; agétto *little needle, syringe or needle thereof*:ág- *needle*; karrétto *cart*:kárr- *car*; etc.

III. m/IIIb: animalétto *little animal*:animál- *animal*; kanalétto *little canal*:kanál- *canal*; etc.

b. Verb II/ísK/W, in sɔrbétto *sherbet*:sɔrb- *sip*.

iv. The suffix is preceded by ⁺ɛrl⁺ in kuadɛrlétto *square patch*:kuad⁺: kuadr⁺:kuáttr- *four* num/IId.

z. ácc- adj/I–II, f/Ia and m/IIb, with the meanings:

i. As adjective, color of . . ., in pa(v)ɔnácco *purple*:pa(v)ón- *peacock* m/IIIb.

ii. As noun f/Ia, pejorative or *thing connected with* . . ., in the following based on:

A. Nouns of type:

I. f/Ia: biskácca *illegal gambling joint*:bísk- *id.*; tɛrrácca *terrace*:térr- *earth*.

II. m/IIb: kɔrácca *cuirass, armor*:kɔr⁺:kuói- *leather*; ramácca *broom*: rám- *branch*.

III. f/IIIb: radácca redácca retácca *mop* (:rad⁺:red⁺):rét- *net*.

B. Verb I/Reg/W, in votácca *dipper*:v(u)ót- *empty*.

iii. As noun m/IIb, pejorative or *thing made of* . . ., in the following based on:

A. Nouns: kodácco *troop, train* (pej.):kód- *tail* f/Ia; amɔrácco *low love-affair*:amór- *love* m/IIIb.

B. Verb I/Irr/W, in andácco *way, behavior*:and- *go*.

aa. ⁺ív- *ive, -ed* adj/I–II; *group of* . . . f/Ia:

i. As adjective, based on:

A. Adj/I–II, in tardívo *tardy, belated*:tárd- *late*.

B. Nouns, of types:

I. f/Ia: festívo *festive*:fést- *feast*; stallívo *kept in a stall*:stáll- *stall*.

II. m/IIb: boskívo *wooded, pertaining to forests*:bósk- *woods, forest*; ɔrtívo *cultivated as a garden*:órt- *garden*; visívo *pertaining to sight*:vís- *sight, face*.

III. f/IIIb: vallívo *in a valley*:váll- *valley*.

c. Adv/IIb, in retrívo *backward, delayed*:rétr- *back*.

D. Verbs, on:

I. Root, in verbs of types:

α. I/Reg/W: adottívo *adoptive*:adótt- *adopt*; abusívo *abusive*:abús- *abuse*; affettívo *affective*:affétt- *affect*; kattívo *captive, bad*:kátt- *capture, get*; etc.

β. IIIb/Reg/S¹, ²: sɔrǧívo *pertaining to a spring*:sórG- *spring up*.

γ. IIIb/Irr/S¹: nočívo *harmful*:nɔč- *harm*.

ii. Non-Finite² A, in stantívo *stale*:stá- *stand* IV/Irr/S.¹

iii. Non-Finite C or alternant, in verbs of types:

α. II/ísK/W: attívo *active*:att⁺:aǧ- *act*; passívo *passive*:pass⁺: pat- *suffer*.

β. IIIb/Reg/S¹, ²: afflittívo *afflictive*:afflíGG- *afflict*; allusívo *allu-sive*:allúd- *allude*; kənǧuntívo *conjunctive*:kənǧúnG- *conjoin*; kərruttívo *corrup-tive*:kərrutt⁺:kərrómp- *corrupt*; kərsívo *cursive, italic*:kórr- *run*; soǧǧuntívo *subjunctive*:soǧǧúnG- *subjoin*.

ii. As noun, in kəmitíva *company*:kəmit⁺ *companion*.

iii. The suffix is preceded in:

A. Adjectives based on:

I. Nouns, by ⁺at⁺ in nərmatívo *normative*:nórm- *norm* f/Ia; səlatívo *with southern exposure*:sól- *sun* m/IIIb.

II. Verbs, in:

α. Stem A (with TV /e/ > /i/), by ⁺t⁺ in a number of adjectives, e.g.: abbreviatívo *abbreviative*:abbrévi- *abbreviate* I/Reg/W; kopiatívo *copying*: kópi- *copy* I/Reg/W; abəlitívo *abolitive*:abəl- *abolish* II/ísK/W; addəlčitívo *serving to sweeten*:addəlč- *sweeten* II/ísK/W; vəlitívo *volitive*:vɔl- *wish* IIIa/ Irr/S¹; akkreššitívo *augmentative*:akkrésK- *augment, increase* IIIb/Reg/S¹; etc. etc.

β. Non-Finite C or alternant, by ⁺it⁺ in fattitívo *factitive*:fáč-do IV/Irr/S¹,²; sensitívo *sensitive*:sens⁺:sént- *feel* II/Reg/W.

B. Nouns based on verbs (in Stem A), by ⁺t⁺ in aspettatíva *wait*:aspétt- *wait* I/Reg/W; attrattíva *attractiveness*:attráˣ- *attract* IV/Irr/S¹, ².

bb. ⁺áč- *-acious, -ax* adj/IIIb and m/IIIb:

i. As adjective, in the following based on:

A. Adj/I–II, in veráče *veracious*:vér- *true*.

B. Nouns: nid(i)áče *which has not yet left the nest*:níd(i)- *nest* m/IIb; saláče *salacious*:sál- *salt* m/IIIb.

c. Substantival base: sagáče *sagacious*:saG⁺ *wise*.

D. Verbs, such as the following of types:

I. I/Reg/W: falláče *fallacious*:fáll- *deceive*; puɲɲáče *pugnacious*: púɲɲ- *fight*; vəráče *voracious*:⁺vór- *devour*.

II. II/Reg/W: seguáče *follower*:ségu- *follow*.

III. II/ísK/W: mɛndáče *mendacious, lying*:mɛnd⁺:mɛnt- *lie*.

IV. IIIa/Irr/S¹: pertináče *pertinacious*:pertin⁺:tin⁺:tɛn- *hold*; tɛnáče *tenacious*:tɛn- *hold*.

V. IIIb/Reg/S¹, ²: mərdáče *mordacious*:mórd- *bite*; pervikáče *ob-stinate*:pervik⁺:vik⁺:vínK- *conquer*; viváče *vivacious*:vív- *live*.

VI. Verbal bases: audáče *audacious*:aud⁺ *dare*; edáče *eating, de-vouring*:ed⁺ *eat*; effikáče *efficacious*:effik⁺ *effect*; fɛráče *fertile*:fɛr⁺ *bear*; lokuáče *loquacious*:loku⁺ *speak*; perspikáče *perspicacious*:perspik⁺ *see clearly*.

ii. As noun, in bəráče *borax*:bór- *boron* m/IIb; fərnáče *furnace*:fórn- *oven* m/IIb.

cc. ′il- -*ile*, -*able*, -*ible* adj/IIIb and m/IIIb:

   i. As adjective, in the following based on verbs in:

   A. Root or alternant, in móbile *mobile*:mɔb:mɔv- *move* IIIb/Reg/S[1, 2]; téssile *textile*:téss- *weave* IIIb/Reg/W; víǧile *vigilant*:víG- *be in vigor* IIIb/Reg; fáčile *easy*:fáč- *do* IV/Irr/S[1, 2]; dóčile *docile*:dɔč[+] *teach, guide*; fráǧile *fragile*: fraG[+] *break*; núbile *marriageable*:nub[+] *marry*; stérile *sterile*:stɛr[+] *be sterile*; útile *useful*:ut[+] *use*.

   B. Non-Finite C or alternant, of the following verbs of types:

   I. I/Reg/W: pɔrtátile *portable*:pórt- *carry*; vɛrsátile *versatile*:vérs- *turn*; vibrátile *vibratory*:víbr- *vibrate*; vɔlátile *volatile*:vól- *fly*.

   II. IIIa: séssile *sessile*:sɛss[+]:sɛd- *sit*.

   III. IIIb: físsile *fissile, easily split*:fiss[+]:fénd- *split*; míssile *missile*: miss[+]:métt- *put (forth)*; pénsile *hanging*:pɛns[+]:pénd- *hang*; prénsile *prehensile*: prens[+]:prénd- *take*; táttile *tactile*:tatt[+]:tánG- *touch*; téstile *textile* (rare):test[+]: téss- *weave*; tórtile *twistable*:tórK- *twist*.

   IV. IV: dúttile *ductile*:dutt[+]:dúK- -*duce, -duct*; kɔntráttile *contractile, -able*:kɔntrá[x] *contract*; retráttile *retractile*:retratt[+] *drawn back*:trá[x] *draw*.

   V. Verbal base: fóssile *fossile*:fɔss[+] *dug out* (as n., *ditch*).

   ii. As noun, on a verb root in proiéttile *projectile*:proiétt- *hurl, project* I/Reg/W.

   iii. The suffix is preceded by:

   A. [+]b[+] in adjectives based on verbs in:

   I. Root or alternant in sɔlúbile *soluble*:sɔlu[+]:sólv- *dissolve* IIIb/ Reg/S[1]; vɔlúbile *turning, voluble*:vɔlu[+]:vólG- *turn* IIIb/Reg/S[1, 2]; stábile *stable*: stá- *stand* IV/Irr/S[1].

   II. Stem A (with TV /e/ > /i/) in many adjectives, such as the following based on verbs of type:

   α. I/Reg/W: abitábile *habitable*:ábit- *live*; abɔminábile *abomin-able*:abómin- *abominate*; ammirábile *admirable*:ammír- *admire*; etc.

   β. II/ísK/W: abɔlíbile *abolishable*:abɔl- *abolish*; etc.

   γ. IIIb: aččɛndíbile *ignitible*:aččénd- *light*; amovíbile *removable*: amov[+] *remove*:mɔv- *move*; etc.

   δ. IV: addučíbile *adducible*:addúK- *adduce*; appɔníbile *attachable*: appón- *attach*; etc.

   ε. Verbal bases: tɛrríbile *terrible*:tɛrr[+] *take fright, affright*; šíbile *knowable*:ši[+] *know*.

   B. [+]áb[+] in the following adjectives based on:

   I. Nouns: taskábile *pocket-size, pocketable*:tásk- *pocket* f/Ia; tea-trábile *performable, suitable for the theater*:teátr- *theater* m/IIb.

   II. Verb in Non-Finite C (alternant), in respɔnsábile *responsible*: respɔns[+]:rispónd- *respond* IIIb/Reg/S[1, 2].

   c. [+]íb[+] in the following adjectives based on verbs in:

   I. Stem A (alternant) in possíbile *possible*:póss-:pɔt- *be able* IIIa/ Irr/W.

ii. Non-Finite C or alternant, on verbs of types:

α. II/ísK/W, in passíbile *disposed to suffer, punishable*:pass⁺: pat- *suffer*; plausíbile *worthy of praise*:plaus⁺:plaud- *applaud*.

β. IIIb/Reg/S¹˒², in ammissíbile *admissible*:ammiss⁺:amméttˍ *admit*; kɔrruttíbile *corruptible*:kɔrrutt⁺:kɔrrómp- *corrupt*; preskrittíbile *prescribable*:preskrív- *prescribe*.

γ. IV/Irr/S¹˒², in putrefattíbile *putrefiable*:putrefáč- *putrefy*.

δ. Verbal base: kɔmbustíbile *combustible*:kɔmbúst- *burned*: kɔmbuR⁺ *burn*.

D. ⁺éns⁺ in the noun uténsile *utensil*:ut⁺ *use*.

E. ⁺t⁺ in the adjective fértile *fertile*:fɛr⁺ *bear*.

F. ⁺at⁺ in the adjectives umbrátile ɔmbrátile *in the shade, shaded* (:umbr⁺):ómbr- *shade* f/Ia; fluviátil- *of rivers*:fluvi⁺ *river*.

dd. ⁺ánt- adj/IIIb and m/IIIb, with the following meanings:

i. As adjective, *pro- . . ., partisan of . . .*, as in the following based on:

A. Adjectives of types:

i. I–II: austriakánte *pro-Austrian*:austríaK- *Austrian*; tedeskánte *pro-German*:tedésk- *German*.

ii. IIIb: belliǧeránte- *belligerent*:bɛllíǧer- *id*.

B. Nouns of types:

i. f/Ia: kruskánte *follower or member of the Crusca*:krúsk- *Accademia della Crusca*.

ii. m/IIb: bakkánte *Bacchante*:bákk- *Bacchus*; partitánte *follower of a party*:partít- *(political) party*.

ii. As noun, *one acting in connection with . . ., profiting by . . ., exercising the profession of . . .*, as in the following based on nouns of types:

A. f/Ia: bettɔlánte *innkeeper, wineshop keeper*:béttɔl- *wineshop*; birbánte *rascal, scoundrel*:bírb- *cheat*; bottegánte *shop-keeper*:bottég- *shop*; brigánte *brigand*:bríg- *trouble, quarrel*; pɔlitikánte *meddler in politics*:pɔlítik- *politics*; sɛratánte *beneficiary of a performance*:sɛrát- *evening*; traǧediánte *tragedian*: traǧédi- *tragedy*.

B. m/IIb: kasɛllánte *railway lineman*:kaséll- *railway lineman's hut*; ɔrekkiánte *one who plays by ear, dilettante*:ɔrékki- *ear*; teatránte *actor*:teátr- *theater*.

C. m/IIc: braččánte *day-laborer*:bráčč- *arm*.

D. m/IIIb: pedánte *pedant*:pɛd⁺:piéd- *foot*; podɛránte *farm-owner*: podér- *farm*.

E. f/IIIb: nottánte *night-nurse*:nótt- *night*.

iii. The suffix is preceded by ⁺bɔl⁺ in the adjective mirabɔlánte *astounding* (humorous):mír- *wonder* I/Reg/W.

2. On substantives or adverbs, with:

a. ⁺áčč- pejorative, adj/I–II, f/Ia and m/IIb:

i. As adjective, on adjectives, e.g. of types:

A. I–II: bɔnáččo *goodish*:bɔn⁺:buɔ́n- *good*; kattiváččo *nasty*:kattív- *bad*; pigračč0 *bad and lazy*:pígr- *lazy*; stupidáččo *nastily stupid*:stúpid- *stupid*; etc.

B. IIIb: insɔlɛntáč̣čo *nasty and insolent*:insɔlénte *insolent*; liberaláč̣čo *nasty liberal*:liberál- *liberal*; vɛrdáč̣čo *unpleasantly green*:vérd- *green*; etc.

ii. As noun f/Ia, on feminine nouns, e.g. of types:

A. Ia: annatáč̣ča *hell of a year*:annát- *year's activity*; arpiáč̣ča *vicious harpy*:arpí- *harpy*; tavɔláč̣ča *bad table*:távɔl- *table*; etc. etc.

B. IIb: manáč̣ča *bad hand*:mán- *hand*.

C. IIIb: aciɔnáč̣ča *evil action*:ación- *action*; kancɔnáč̣ča *nasty song*: kancón- *song*; partáč̣ča *bad part*:párt- *part*; etc.

iii. As noun m/IIb, on nouns of types:

A. f/Ia, in kampanáč̣čo *cow-bell*:kampán- *bell*; katɛnáč̣čo *bolt*:katén- *chain*.

B. m/IIb: libráč̣čo *nasty book*:líbr- *book*; medikáč̣čo *nasty doctor*:médiK- *doctor*; ɔrgɔʎʎáč̣čo *evil pride*:ɔrgóʎʎ- *pride*; etc. etc.

C. m/IIIb: abatáč̣čo *nasty priest*:abát- *priest*; amɔráč̣čo *evil love*:amór- *love*; studɛntáč̣čo *nasty student*:studént- *student*; etc.

b. óč̣č- augmentative adj/I–II, f/Ia and m/IIb:

i. As adjective, in bɛllóč̣čo *coarsely beautiful*:béll- *beautiful* adj/I–II.

ii. As noun f/Ia, in fiʎʎóč̣ča *god-daughter*:fíʎʎ- *daughter* f/Ia.

iii. As noun m/IIb, in kartóč̣čo *paper bag, paper cornel*:kárt- *paper* f/Ia; bambóč̣čo *chubby child, puppet*:bamb- *ingenuous person, child* m/IIb; karróč̣čo *carroccio*:kárr- *car(t)* m/IIb; fantóč̣čo *straw-man, puppet*:fánt- *child* m/IIb.

c. +úč̣č- disparaging or diminutive, adj/I–II, f/Ia or m/IIb:

i. As adjective, on adjectives, e.g. of types:

A. I–II: ambiciosúč̣čo *contemptibly ambitious*:ambiciós- *ambitious*; bɛllúč̣čo *pretty in a cheap way*:béll- *beautiful*; freskúč̣čo *disagreeably fresh*:frésk- *fresh*; etc.

B. IIIb: diffičilúč̣čo *somewhat unpleasantly difficult*:diffíčil- *difficult*; etc.

ii. As noun f/Ia: e.g. in animúč̣ča *poor little soul*:ánim- *soul* f/Ia; kannúč̣ča *thin, slender reed*:kánn- *reed* f/Ia; kartúč̣ča *worthless bit of paper, cartouche*: kárt- *paper* f/Ia; alúč̣ča *poor little wing*:ál- *wing* f/Ib; etc.

iii. As noun m/IIb, as in the following based on nouns of types:

A. f/Ia: kappúč̣čo *cowl*:kápp- *cape*.

B. m/IIb: avvokatúč̣čo *worthless little lawyer*: avvokát- *lawyer*; kantúč̣čo *dark, narrow corner*:kánt- *corner*; meʐʐúč̣čo *contemptible expedient*:méʐʐ- *means*; mostrúč̣čo *unpleasant little monster*:móstr- *monster*; etc.

C. m/IIIb: abatúč̣čo *contemptible little priest*:abát- *priest*; dottɔrúč̣čo *good-for-nothing little doctor*:dottór- *doctor*; studɛntúč̣čo *worthless little student*: studént- *student*; etc.

d. +íng- +éng- *pertaining to . . ., characteristic of . . .*, adj/I–II and m/IIb, in the following:

i. As adjective, based on:

A. Adj/I–II: sɔlíngo *solitary*:sól- *alone*.

B. f/Ia: guardíngo *cautious*:gúardi- *guard*; and, preceded by +al+, in kasalíngo *homely, home-made*:kás- *house*.

80 DESCRIPTIVE ITALIAN GRAMMAR

c. m/IIb: maǧǧéngo *of May* (referring to first cut of hay):máǧǧ-
May; ramíngo *jumping from branch to branch, wandering*:rám- *branch*.

ii. As noun, preceded by ⁺l⁺, in kamɛrlíngo kamɛrléngo *chamberlain*:
kámɛr- *chamber* f/Ia.

e. ⁺ári- *-ary, -arian, -al*, adj/I–II and m/IIb:

i. As adjective: e.g. in the following based on substantives and adverbs
of types:

A. Adj/I–II: abdikatário *abdicatory*:abdikát- *abdicated* (past part.);
avvɛrsário *adversary*:avvɛrs- *adverse*; bɔnário *affable*:bɔn⁺:buón- *good*; etc.

B. m/IIb: agrário *agrarian*:ágr- *field*; alimɛntário *alimentary*:alimɛ́nt-
food; ausiliário *auxiliary*:ausíli- *help;* etc.

C. m/IIIb: boário *boarian*:bo⁺:bóv- *ox*.

D. f/VId: autɔritário *authoritarian*:autɔrit⁺:autɔritá˟ *authority*; and
similarly unitário *unitary*:unitá˟ *unit(y)*; vɔlɔntário *voluntary*:vɔlɔntá˟ *will*; etc.

E. adv/I: kɔntrário *contrary*:kóntr- *against*.

ii. As noun; e.g. in the following based on nouns of type:

A. f/Ia: akkuário *aquarium*:ákku- *water*; antifɔnário *antiphonarium*:
antífɔn- *antiphon*; bɔllário *collection of (papal) bulls*:bóll- *(papal) bull*; čifrário
key to cipher:čífr- *cipher*; etc.

B. m/IIb: armamɛntário *collection of surgical instruments*:armamɛ́nt-
armament; etc.

C. Nominal base: abbečedário *primer*:abbeček⁺ *ABC*.

iii. The suffix is preceded by:

A. ⁺i⁺ in:

I. Adjectives: tɛrciário *tertiary*:tɛ́rc- *third* adj/I–II; atrabiliário
atrabilious:atrabíl- *black bile* f/IIIb; fɔndiário *pertaining to real estate*:fónd-
rural real estate m/IIb.

II. Nouns: breviário *breviary*:brév- *brief* m/IIIb; apiário *apiary*:áp-
bee f/IIIb; vestiário *wardrobe*:vést- *clothing* f/IIIb.

B. ⁺ɛn⁺ in mɛrčɛnário *mercenary* adj/I–II:mɛ́rč- *goods, reward* f/IIIb.

C. ⁺it⁺ in sɔlitário *solitary* adj/I–II:sól- *alone* adj/I–II.

f. ⁺íci- adj/I–II, f/Ia and m/IIb, with the meanings:

i. As adjective, *-itious, -ive, having the characteristics of . . ., pertaining to
. . .*, as in the following based on:

A. Adjectives of types:

I. I–II, in akkɔmodatício *accommodating*:akkɔmodát- *accommodated*
(past part.); aɲɲatício *characteristic of agnates*:aɲɲát- *agnate*; fattício *factitious*:
fátt- *done*.

II. IIIb, in natalício *pertaining to a birthday*:natál- *natal*; vitalício
for life:vitál- *pertaining to life*.

III. Adjectival bases, in fittício *fictitious*:fitt⁺ *pretended* (:fínG- *pretend* IIIb/Reg/S¹, ²); suppositício *supposititious*:suppɔsit⁺ *supposed* (:suppón-
suppose IV/Irr/S¹, ²).

B. Nouns of types:

I. m/IIb, in avvɛntício *adventitious*:avvɛ́nt- *advent, chance*; lega-
tício *of a legate*:legát- *legate*; tribunício *tribunician*:tribún- *tribune*.

ɪɪ. m/IIIb, in ğenɛralício *of a general* (*of an order*):ğenɛrál- *general*; kardinalício *of a cardinal*:kardinál- *cardinal*; maɲɲatício *of a magnate*:maɲɲát- *magnate*; pastorício *pertaining to shepherds*:pastór- *shepherd*; patrício *patrician*: patr⁺:pádr- *father*; torrɛntício *like, of a torrent*:torrént- *torrent*.

c. Adverbial base, in propício *propitious*:prop⁺ *near*.

ii. As noun f/Ia, *-ice, -ity, -ship, -ness*, as in the following based on:

A. Adjectives of types:

ɪ. I–II: amičícia *friendship*:amíK- *friend(ly)*; avarícia *avarice*:avár- *miserly*; blandície *caresses* (pl.):blánd- *soft, caressing*; furbícia *cunning*:fúrb- *sly, crafty*; ğustícia *justice*:ğúst- *just*; letícia *joy*:let⁺:liét- *joyful*; malícia *malice*:mál- *evil*; mestícia *sadness*:mést- *sad*; mondícia *cleanliness, neatness*:mónd- *clean*; pigrícia *laziness*:pígr- *lazy*; primícia *first fruit*:prím- *first*; pudičícia *modesty*: pudíK- *modest*; sevícia *cruelty*:sév- *savage*; stoltícia *stupidity*:stólt- *stupid*.

ɪɪ. IIIb: mollícia *softness*:móll- *soft*; tristícia *sadness*:tríst- *sad*.

B. Nouns of types:

ɪ. f/Ia: massɛrícia *furniture*:massɛrí- *running a household, farm*.

ɪɪ. Nominal base: puɛrícia *childhood*:puɛr⁺ *child*.

iii. As noun m/IIb, *-ice*, abstract, in novítio *novice*:nov⁺:nuóv- *new*; palmício *palm-tree, -decoration*:pálm- *palm* f/Ia; sodalício *company*:sodal⁺ *companion*.

iv. The suffix is preceded by:

A. ⁺il⁺ in fortilícia *little fortress*:fórt- *strong* adj/IIIb.

B. ⁺ir⁺ in likuirícia *licorice*:liku⁺ *liquid*.

g. ⁺'iK- *-ic* adj/I–II, f/Ia and m/IIb:

i. As adjective, as in the following based on:

A. Adj/I–II: arábiK- *Arabic*:árab- *Arab(ic)*; úniK- *only, unique*:ún- *one*.

B. Nouns of types:

ɪ. f/Ia: akkadémiK- *academic*:akkadémi- *academy*; ağográfiK- *hagiographic*:ağografí- *hagiography*; alğébriK- *algebraic*:álğebr- *algebra*; etc.

ɪɪ. m/Ib: akrobátiK- *acrobatic*:akróbat- *acrobat*; altruístiK- *altruistic*:altruíst- *altruist*; faššístiK- *fascistic*:faššíst- *Fascist*; kabalístiK- *cabalistic*:kabalíst- *cabalist*; kamítiK- *Hamitic*:kamít- *Hamite*; etc. etc., esp. on nouns in ⁺ist- *ist*.

ɪɪɪ. m/IIb: ačétiK- *acetic*:ačét- *vinegar*; aɛrostátiK- *aerostatic*: aɛróstat- *aerostat*; alfabétiK- *alphabetical*:alfabét- *alphabet*; bákkiK- *bacchic*: bákk- *Bacchus*; filíppiK- *Philippic*:filípp- *Philip*; etc.

ɪᴠ. m/IIIb: alkóliK- *alcoholic*:álkol- *alcohol*; babéliK- *Babelic*:babél- *Babel*; kadavériK- *cadaveric*:kadávɛr- *cadaver*; karbóniK- *carbonic*:karbón- *carbon, coal*; etc.

ᴠ. m/VId: alkoóliK- *alcoholic*:álkool *alcohol*.

ᴠɪ. Substantival bases: akústiK- *acoustic*:akust⁺ *hearing*; armóniK- *harmonic*:armon⁺ *harmon(y)*; etc.

ii. As noun f/Ia, diminutive or collective, in móllika *soft part of bread*: móll- *soft* adj/IIIb; lástrika *pavement*:lástr- *paving block* f/Ia; fábbrika *factory*: fábbr- *worker, smith* m/IIb; kántika *cantica*:kánt- *canto, song* m/IIb; ráffika *gust of wind*:ráffi- *hook* m/IIb; mánika *sleeve*:mán- *hand* f/IIb; briččika *trifle*: brič(č)⁺ *small bit.*

iii. As noun m/IIb, *-ico* or diminutive in pórtiK- *portico*:pórt- *door* f/Ia; kántiK- *song, canticle*:kánt- *song* m/IIb.

iv. The suffix is preceded by:

A. The SV of the base in vɔltáiK- *Voltaic* adj/I–II:vólta *Volta* m/Id; raméiK- *of copper or brass*:ráme *copper, brass* m/IIIb.

B. ⁺él⁺ in faméliK- *hungry*:fám- *hunger* f/IIIb.

C. ⁺íl⁺ in saličíliK- *salicylic* adj/I–II:sálič- *willow* f/IIIb.

D. ⁺án⁺ in grekániK- *Greek only by origin or imitation* adj/I–II:gréK- *Greek* adj/I–II.

E. ⁺ión⁺ in ɔlimpióniK- *Olympionic* adj/I–II:ɔlímp- *Olympus* m/IIb.

F. ⁺r⁺ in rúbrika *rubric* f/Ia:rub⁺ *red.*

G. ⁺t⁺ in rústiK- *rustic* adj/I–II:ruR⁺ *country.*

H. ⁺át⁺ in the following:

I. Adjectives, based on nouns of:

α. f/Ia: lunátiK- *lunatic*:lún- *moon*; sɛlvátiK- salvátiK- *wild, savage* (:salv⁺):sélv- *forest*; stallátiK- *pertaining to a stall*:stáll- *stall.*

β. m/IIb: luʎʎátiK- *maturing in July*:lúʎʎ- *July*; maǧǧátiK- *of May, fallow*:máǧǧ- *May.*

II. Noun f/Ia, meaning *provision of . . .*, in panátika *provision of food*:pán- *bread* m/IIIb.

III. Nouns m/IIb, meaning *money, fee, tax, rights for . . ., provision for . . .*, based on nouns of:

α. f/Ia: baliátiK- *wages for suckling*:báli- *wet-nurse*; makkiátiK- *wood-cutting rights or fee (for maquis)*:mákki- *maquis*; testátiK- *poll-tax*:tést- *head*; viátiK- *viaticum*:ví- *way, journey.*

β. m/IIb: fokátiK- *family tax, hearth tax*:fɔk⁺:fuók- *fire*; ǧogátiK- *wages for plowing*:ǧóg- *yoke*; spillátiK- *pin-money*:spíll- *pin.*

γ. m/IIIb: kɔmpanátiK- *things eaten with bread*:pán- *bread.*

J. ⁺ét⁺ in:

I. Adj/I–II: seɲɲalétiK- *pertaining to characteristics*:seɲɲál- *signal, characteristic* m/IIIb; paritéliK- *having equal representation*:parit⁺:paritáˣ *parity* f/VId; fɔnétiK- *phonetic*:fɔn⁺ *phone, sound.*

II. Noun f/Ia: pɛllétika *loose skin (on edible meat)*:péll- *skin* f/IIIb.

K. ⁺ást⁺ in a number of adjectives, especially those with parallel formations in ⁺ásmo *-asm* m/IIb (§3.114.6.000): e.g. ɔrǧástiK- *orgiastic*:órǧ- *orgy* f/Ia; prosástiK- *in prose*:prós- *prose* f/Ia; skɔlástiK- *scholastic*:skɔl⁺:skuól- *school* f/Ia; in such adjectives as ɛntusiástiK- *enthusiastic* ‖ ɛntusiásm- *enthusiasm*; sarkástiK- *sarcastic* ‖ sarkásm- *sarcasm*; and in fantástiK- *fantastic*:fantásm- *phantasm* m/Ib.

L. ⁺ést⁺ in dɔméstiK- *domestic* adj/I–II:dɔm⁺ *house.*

M. ⁺íst⁺ in:

I. Many adjectives, such as bɔrsístiK- *pertaining to the stock exchange*:bórs- *stock-exchange* f/Ia; fiɛrístiK- *pertaining to a fair*:fiér- *fair* f/Ia;

aɛroplanístiK- *aeroplanistic*:aɛroplán- *aeroplane* m/IIb; kalčístiK- *pertaining to soccer*:kálč- *soccer* m/IIb; etc.[1]

II. The noun patrístika *patristics, study of the Church Fathers* f/Ia: patr⁺:pádr- *father* m/IIIb.

N. ⁺ɔ́t⁺ in čɛrvɛllótiK- *bizarre, unreasonable* adj/I–II:čɛrvéll- *brain* m/IIb.

o. ⁺éut⁺ in farmačéutiK- *pharmaceutical* adj/I–II:fármaK- *pharmacist* m/IIb.

h. ⁺ákk- pejorative adj/I–II and f/Ia:

i. As adjective, in pɔlákko *Polish*:pɔl⁺ *Pol(and)*; viʎʎákko *base*:viʎʎ⁺:víl- *vile* adj/IIIb.

ii. As noun, in cambrákka *low chambermaid, whore*:cámbr- *room* (archaic) f/Ia; salákka *pilchard*:sál- *salt* m/IIIb.

j. ⁺ísk- -*isk*, -*iscine* adj/I–II and m/IIb:

i. As adjective, in prísko *priscine, of olden times*:pri⁺ *first, earlier*.

ii. As noun, in pietrísko *broken stones*:piétr- *stone* f/Ia; astɛrísko *asterisk*:astɛr⁺ *aster-*:ástr- *star* m/IIb.

k. ⁺én- -*ene* adj/I–II and f/Ia:

i. As adjective, formed on certain place names, as in damaššéno *damascene*:damásK- *Damascus* m/II; naẓẓaréno *Nazarene*:naẓẓar⁺:naẓẓarét *Nazareth* m/VI; saračéno *Saracen*:sarač⁺ *id*.

ii. As noun, in amaréna *amarena (a kind of cherry)*:amár- *bitter* adj/I–II.

l. ⁺érn- -*ernal*, -*ern*, -*erna* adj/I–II, f/Ia and m/IIb:

i. As adjective, in modérno *modern*:mód- *way, fashion* m/IIb; fratérno *fraternal*:frát- *brother* m/IIIb; etérn- *eternal*:et⁺:etáˣ *age* f/VId; odiérno *of today*:ɔdi⁺:ɔ́ǧǧ- *today* adv/IV.

ii. As noun f/Ia, in kavérna *cavern*:káv- *hollow* adj/I–II; kuadérna *series of four numbers*, kuatérna *list of four (people, etc.)* (:kuad⁺):kuat⁺:kuáttr- *four* num/IId; bastérna *a kind of wagon*:bást- *pack-saddle, load* m/IIb; lučérna *lamp*:lúč- *light* f/IIIb; ǧibérna *cartridge-case*:ǧib⁺ *game*; lačérna *Roman cloak*:lač⁺ *id*.; tavérna *tavern*:tav⁺ *house*.

iii. As noun m/IIb, in kuadérno *note-book (originally of four pages)*:kuad⁺:kuadr⁺:kuáttr- *four* num/IId; kuintérno *five-page note-book*:kuínt- *fifth* adj/I–II.

m. ⁺íɲɲ- -*ish*, -*ine*, *not wholly* . . . adj/I–II, f/Ia and m/IIb:

i. As adjective, e.g. in the following based on:

A. Adjectives of types:

I. I–II: aspríɲɲo *bitterish*:áspr- *bitter, harsh*; ǧallíɲɲo *yellowish*:ǧáll- *yellow*; malíɲɲo *malign*:mál- *evil*; rossíɲɲo *reddish*:róss- *red*.

II. IIIb: dolčíɲɲo *sweetish*:dólč- *sweet*; vɛrdíɲɲo *greenish*:vérd- *green*.

B. Nouns of types:

I. f/Ia: kapríɲɲo *goatlike, caprine*:kápr- *goat*; ɔlivíɲɲo *olive-ish*:ɔlív- *olive*; tɛrríɲɲo *earth-colored*:térr- *earth*.

[1] Cf. discussion and further examples in Migliorini, 'Il suffisso -*ístico*', Saggi sulla Lingua del Novecento² 90–133 (Firenze, 1942).

ɪɪ. m/IIb: fɛrrípɲo *iron-like*:férr- *iron*; lupíɲɲo *lupine, wolfish*:lúp-*wolf*; cɔlfíɲɲo *sulphur-colored*:cólf- *sulphur*; vetríɲɲo *vitrine, glassy*:vétr- *glass*.

ɪɪɪ. m/IIIb: salíɲɲo *saline*:sál- *salt*; sanguíɲɲo *bloody, sanguine*: sángu- *blood*.

ɪᴠ. f/IIIb: salčíɲɲo *willowy*:sálč- *willow*.

ii. As noun f/Ia, in stamíɲɲa *tamis*:stám- *stamen* m/IIIb; matríɲɲa madríɲɲa *step-mother* (:matr⁺):mádr- *mother* f/IIIb; vitíɲɲa *a type of vine*:vít-*vine* f/IIIb.

iii. As noun m/IIb, in patríɲɲo padríɲɲo *step-father* (:patr⁺):pádr-*father* m/IIIb.

n. ⁺ár- -*er*, -*eer*, adj/I–II, f/Ia and m/IIb:[2]

i. As adjective, in mɔntanáro *of the mountains, mountaineer*:mɔntán-*mountainous* adj/I–II.

ii. As noun f/Ia, *action, thing or place pertaining to* . . ., in kandelára *feast of the Purification*:kandél- *candle* f/Ia; sɔlfára *sulphur-wine*:sólf- *sulphur* m/IIb; tɔnnára *tuna-net*:tónn- *tuna-fish*; kaɲɲára *devilish uproar*:kaɲɲ⁺:kán-*dog* m/IIIb.

iii. As noun m/IIb, *one exercising profession or trade of* . . . e.g. in the following based on nouns of types:

ᴀ. f/Ia: čočáro *Ciociaro, person wearing coarse shoes* (*ciocie*):čóč- *coarse shoe*; kɔrsáro *corsair*:kórs- *trip, voyage*; marináro *mariner*:marín- *fleet*; skɔláro *scholar, student*:skɔl⁺:skuɔ́l- *school*; sɔmáro *donkey*:sóm- *burden*.

ᴮ. m/IIb: aʎʎáro *garlic-vendor*:áʎʎ- *garlic*; aɲɲɛlláro *lamb-butcher*: aɲɲéll- *lamb*; kalamáro *inkstand, inkfish*:kálam- *pen*; mačelláro *butcher*:mačéll-*abattoir, butcher's shop*; palɔmbáro *diver*:palómb- *a kind of fish*; piffɛráro *fifer*: píffɛr- *fife*.

ᴄ. m/IIIb: bováro *cowherd, oxherd*:bóv- *ox*; karbɔnáro *coal-vendor, Carbonaro*:karbón- *coal*.

iii. The suffix is preceded by:

ᴀ. ⁺ɔl⁺ in kartɔláro *stationer*:kárt- *paper* f/Ia.

ᴮ. ⁺at⁺ in sɔlfatára *sulphur-mine, solfatara*:sólf- *sulphur* m/IIb.

o. ⁺ástr- -*ish, incomplete(ly)* . . . adj/I–II, f/Ia and m/IIb:

i. As adjective, e.g. in the following based on:

ᴀ. Adjectives, of types:

ɪ. I–II: biankástro *whitish*:biánk- *white*; durástro *hardish*:dúr- *hard*; rossástro *reddish*:róss- *red*; etc.

ɪɪ. IIIb: dɔlčástro *sweetish*:dólč- *sweet*; vɛrdástro *greenish*:vɛ́rd-*green*.

ᴮ. Nouns, of types:

ɪ. f/Ia: ɔlivástro *olive-ish*:ɔlív- *olive*.

ɪɪ. m/IIIb: salmástro *salty*:salm⁺:sál- *salt*.

ii. As noun f/Ia, in the following based on nouns f/Ia: fiʎʎástra *step-daughter*:fíʎʎ- *daughter*; sɔrɛllástra *half-sister*:sɔréll- *sister*.

---

[2] Historically and geographically, this suffix is a non-Tuscan development of Latin -*ārius*, parallel to and in some words alternating with the Tuscan development ⁺ái- (§3.111.1.g).

iii. As noun m/IIb, in the following based on nouns of types:

A. f/Ia: mɛntástro *wild mint*:mént- *mint*; pilástro *pilaster*:píl- *column*.

B. m/Ib: poetástro *poetaster*:poét- *poet*.

C. m/IIb: filosofástro *incompetent philosopher*:filósof- *philosopher*; fratɛllástro *half-brother*:fratéll- *brother*; grammatikástro *ignorant, pedantic grammarian*:grammátiK- *grammarian*; etc.

D. m/IIIb: ǧovinástro *badly brought up young man*:ǧóvin- *young man*; salikástro *wild willow*:salik⁺:sálič- *willow*.

p. át- adj/I–II, f/Ia and m/IIb, with the meanings:

i. As adjective, *-ate, provided with . . .*, as in the following based on nouns of types:

A. f/Ia: astáto *armed with a lance*:ást- *lance, shaft*; kanfɔráto *camphorated*:kánfɔr- *camphor*; togáto *wearing a toga*:tóg- *toga*; unguláto *ungulate*, ungiáto *having (finger-, toe-) nails* (:ungul⁺):úngi- *(finger-, toe-) nail*; vɛrtebráto *vertebrate*:vértebr- *vertebra*.

B. f/Ib: aláto *alate, winged*:ál- *wing*.

C. m/IIb: azotáto *containing nitrogen*:azót- *azote, nitrogen*; akuleáto *aculeate*:akúle- *sting*; kapitáto *capitate*:kapit⁺:káp- *head*; ɔleáto ɔliáto *oiled, dressed with oil* (:ɔle⁺):óli- *oil*.

D. f/IIIb: tigráto *with a striped skin*:tígr- *tiger*.

This suffix also occurs in a number of parasynthetic adjectives formed with the prefix s⁺ privative (§3.132.5.g), e.g. in sgraciáto *graceless, unadorned*:grácigrace f/Ia; skreancáto *ill-bred*:kreánc- *good breeding* f/Ia; sgarbáto *ill-mannered, discourteous*:gárb- *good manners, courtesy* m/IIb; skostumáto *ill-mannered*: kostúm- *(good) manners* m/IIIb; sfrɔntáto *shameless*:frónt- *forehead* f/IIIb; spassiɔnáto *dispassionate*:passión- *passion* f/IIIb; spietáto *pitiless*:piet⁺:pietáˣ *pity* f/VId; etc.

ii. As noun f/Ia:

A. *Duration of . . .*, in nouns based on nouns referring to periods of time: sɛráta *(whole) evening*:sér- *evening* f/Ia; annáta *year's activity, income*:ánn-*year* m/IIb; ǧɔrnáta *(whole) day*:ǧórn- *day* m/IIb; nottáta *night*:nótt- *id.* f/IIIb.

B. *Action (often sudden or unpleasant), thing(s) connected with, made of or characteristic of . . ., -ade*, as in the following based on:

I. Adj/I–II: amerikanáta *mad prank, typically American behavior*: amerikán- *American*; italianáta *typically Italian behavior*:italián- *Italian*; etc.

II. Nouns of types:

α. f/Ia: aččugáta *anchovy sauce*:aččúg- *anchovy;* akkuáta *sudden shower*:ákku- *water, rain;* arančáta *orangeade*:aránč- *orange*.

β. m/IIb: agáta *needleful*:ág- *needle*; aʎʎáta *garlic sauce*:áʎʎ-*garlic*; albɛráta *tree-lined road*:álbɛr- *tree*; asináta *trip on a donkey, asinine act*: ásin- *donkey*; bɔrgáta *collection of houses*:bórg- *burgh*; etc.

γ. m/IIIb: balkɔnáta *balconade, railed balcony*:balkón- *balcony*; kantɔnáta *street-corner*:kantón- *corner*; kɔráta *vital organs*:kɔr⁺:kuór- *heart*; etc.

iii. As noun m/IIb, *-ate, condition or rank or ensemble of . . .*, as in the following based on:

A. Adjectives of types:

   I. I–II: anɔnimáto *anonymity*:anɔnim- *anonymous*.

   II. IIIb: čelibáto *celibacy*:čélib- *celibate*; potɛntáto *potentate*:potént- *potent, powerful*.

B. Nouns of types:

   I. f/Ia: kɔlɔnnáto *colonnade*:kɔlónn- *column*.

   II. m/IIb: akkɔlitáto *order of acolytes*:akkólit- *acolyte*; alunnáto *student body*:alúnn- *student*; ammiraʎʎáto *rank of admiral, admiralty*:ammiráʎʎ- *admiral*; kalifáto *caliphate*:kalíf- *caliph*; klɔráto *chlorate*:klór- *chlorine*; etc.

   III. m/IIIb: braččantáto *day-laborers (as a group)*:braččánt- *day-laborer*; kančɛlleráto *chancellorate*:kančɛllɛr+:kančɛlliér- *chancellor*; markesáto *marquisate*:markés- *marquis*; etc.

   IV. f/IIIb: mɛrkáto *market*:mɛrk+:mérč- *goods, wares*.

   V. Nominal bases: e.g. in čitráto *citrate*:čitr+ *citr(on)*; etc.

  iv. The suffix is preceded by:

   a. +izz+ in palizzáta *palisade* f/Ia:pál- *stake* m/IIb.

   B. +eg+ in variegáto *variegated* adj/I–II:vári- *various* adj/I–II.

   c. + eǧǧ+ in kaseǧǧáto *built-up area, building* m/IIb:kás- *house* f/Ia.

   D. +i+ in uniáto *Uniat*:ún- *one* adj/I–II; notariáto *rank, position of notary*:notár- *notary* m/IIb.

 q. ótt- *quite . . ., small and sturdy . . .* adj/I–II, f/Ia and m/IIb:

  i. As adjective, e.g. the following based on adjectives of types:

   A. I–II: durótto *quite hard*:dúr- *hard*; grassótto *short and fat*:gráss- *fat*; vekkiótto *sturdy and old*:vékki- *old*; etc.

   B. IIIb: sɛmpličótto *rather stupid*:sémplič- *simple, stupid*.

  ii. As noun f/Ia, e.g. in the following based on nouns of:

   A. f/Ia: sɛrvótta *husky servant girl*:sérv- *servant girl*; etc.

   B. m/IIIb: paɲɲótta *loaf of bread, livelihood*:paɲɲ+:pán- *bread*.

  iii. As noun m/IIb, also meaning *worker in . . .* e.g. in the following based on nouns of:

   A. f/Ia: akuilótto *eaglet*:ákuil- *eagle*; galeótto *galley-slave*:galé- *galley*; kasótto *cabin*:kás- *house*; pančótto *double-breasted vest*:pánč- *belly*; pɔliciótto *policeman*:pɔlicí- *police*; cukkótto *skull-cap*:cúkk- *gourd, head*.

   B. m/IIb: asinótto *big ass*:ásin- *ass*; kaccótto *punch, thump*:kácc- *penis*; passɛrótto *young sparrow*:pásser- *sparrow*; etc.

   c. m/IIc: braččótto *round, fat arm*:bráčč- *arm*.

   D. m/IIIb: arsenalótto *arsenal worker*:arsɛnál- *arsenal*; bikkiɛrótto *biggish glass*:bikkiér- *glass, tumbler*; ǧovanótto *sturdy young man*:ǧóvan- *young man*; siɲɲɔrótto *petty tyrant*:siɲɲór- *lord*; etc.

   E. f/IIIb: leprótto *young rabbit*:lépr- *hare*.

  iv. The suffix is preceded by +ɛr+ in kalcɛrótto *sock* m/IIb:kálc- *stocking* f/Ia.

 r. ócc- *augmentative (implying coarseness)* adj/I–II, f/Ia and m/IIb:

  i. As adjective: grandócco *great big* (Rom.):gránd- *big*.

  ii. As noun f/Ia, based on nouns of types:

A. f/Ia: barbócca *chinband* (*of helmet*), *lower lip* (*of horse*):bárb- *beard*; gallócca *bubble*:gáll- *id.*; pikkócca *alpenstock*:píkk- *pike*; tavɔlótt- *palette*:távɔl- *table*.

B. m/IIb: karrócca *carriage*:kárr- *car*(*t*); tinócca *little barrel*:tín- *barrel*.

iii. As noun m/IIb, based on nouns of types:

A. m/IIb: maritócco *a kind of cake*:marít- *husband*.

B. m/IIIb: barilócco *keg*:baríl- *barrel*.

C. Nominal bases: bɛrlingócco *a kind of pastry*:bɛrling+ *gluttony*; gargarócco *throat*:gargar+ *id.*

s. úcc- adj/I–II, f/Ia and m/IIb, with the following meanings:

i. As adjective, -*ute*, in agúcco *acute*:ág- *needle* m/IIb.

ii. As noun f/Ia, diminutive and pejorative: e.g. in paniúcca *limed stick*: páni- *bird-lime* f/Ia; vɔʎʎúcca *contemptible desire*:vɔʎʎ- *desire* f/Ia.

iii. As noun m/IIb, diminutive and pejorative: e.g. avvokatúcco *worthless little lawyer*:avvokát- *lawyer* m/IIb; animalúcco *worthless little animal*:animál- *animal* m/IIIb; etc.

iv. The suffix is preceded by +estr+ in kalčestrúcco *concrete*:kálč- *lime* f/IIIb.

t. +'id- -*id* adj/IIIb, f/IIIb and m/IIIb:

i. As adjective, in the following based on nouns of:

A. m/IIb: anéllide *ring-like and segmented* (*of a kind of worm*):anéll- *ring*.

B. m/IIIb: napɔleónide *of the family of Napoleon*:napɔleón- *Napoleon*.

C. Nominal bases: aráknide *arachnid*:arakn+ *spider*; parótide *parotid*: parɔt+ *parot-*.

ii. As noun m/IIIb, in bólide *meteor*:bɔl+ *id.*

iii. As noun f/IIIb, in the following based on nouns of:

A. f/Ia: kariátide *Caryatid*:kariat+:kári- *Caria*; tebáide *Thebaid*: teba+:téb- *Thebes* (pl.).

B. m/Ib: ɛnéide *Aeneid*:ɛné- *Aeneas*.

C. m/IIb: sílfide *sylph* (f.):sílf- *sylph* (m.); tiránnide *tyranny*:tiránn- *tyrant*.

D. Nominal bases: glóttide *glottis*:glɔtt+ *glott-*; karótide *carotid* (*artery*):karɔt+ *carot-*; rákid- *spinal column*:rak+ *spine*.

u. +óid- -*oid* adj/IIIb, m/IIIb and f/IIIb:

i. As adjective, e.g. in the following based on:

A. Adj/I–II: mattóide *somewhat crazy*:mátt- *crazy*.

B. Nouns of types:

i. f/Ia: albuminóide *albuminoid*:albúmin- *albumen*; čellulóide *celluloid*:čéllul- *cellule*; kɔllóide *colloid*:kóll- *glue*; kɔnkóide *conchoid*:kónk- *conch-shell*; etc.

ii. m/Ib: dɛltóide *deltoid*:délt- *delta*.

iii. m/IIb: čilindróide *cylindroid*:čilíndr- *cylinder*.

iv. m/IIc: ovóide *ovoid*:óv- uóv- *egg*.

v. Nominal bases: adɛnóide *adenoid*:adɛn+ *tonsil*; sfɛnóide *sphenoid* :sfɛn+ *wedge*.

ii. As noun m/IIIb, in sfɛróide *spheroid*:sfér- *sphere* f/Ia; astɛróide *asteroid*:astɛr+ *aster-*:ástr- *star* m/IIb; alkalóide *alkaloid*:álkal- *alkali* m/IVd; ǧeóide *geoid*:ǧe+ *earth*.

iii. As noun f/IIIb, in čiklóide *cycloid*:číkl- *cycle, circle* m/IIb; vaiolóide *chicken-pox*:vaiól- *smallpox* m/IIb; araknóide *arachnoid (membrane)*:arakn+ *spider (web)*; koróide *choroid (membrane of eye)*:kor+ *chor-*; mastóide *mastoid*: mast+ *breast*.

w. +ál- adj/IIIb and m/IIIb, with the following meanings:

i. As adjective, *-al, of or pertaining to* . . ., as in the following based on:

A. Adjectives of types:

I. I–II: nostrále *of our own*:nóstr- *our*; totále *total*:tot+:tútt- *all*; solidále *in agreement*:sólid- *full, firm*; vičinále *of the region, of the neighborhood*: vičín- *neighboring*.

II. IIIb: komunále *communal*:komún- *common*.

B. Nouns of types:

I. f/Ia: abbaciále *abbatial*:abbací- *abbey*; animále *spiritual*:ánim- *soul*; aciɛndále *of the business*:aciénd- *business, concern*; etc. etc.

II. m/IIb: abissále *abyssal, abysmal*:abíss- *abyss*; abituále *habitual*: abitu+:ábit- *habit*; anále *anal*:án- *anus*; arsɛnikále *arsenical*:arséniK- *arsenic*; etc. etc.

III. m/IIIb: orizzontále *horizontal*:orizzónt- *horizon*; pedále *pedal*: pɛd+:piéd- *foot*; etc.

IV. f/IIIb: addicionále *additional*:addición- *addition*; mortále *mortal*: mórt- *death*; passionále *pertaining to or caused by passion*:passión- *passion*; etc.

V. m/VId: regále reále *royal* (:reg+):réˣ *king*.

VI. Nominal bases: pineále *pineal*:pine+ *pineum*; reále *real*:re+ *thing*; etc.

ii. As noun, *-al; thing pertaining to, having, like or for* . . ., *big* . . ., as in the following based on:

A. Adj/I–II: kuartále (*actors'*) *pay*:kuárt- *fourth*; strakkále *breechband, brace*:strákk- *worn out*.

B. Nouns of types:

I. f/Ia: animále *animal*:ánim- *soul*; antifonále *antiphonal*:antífon- *antiphon*; guančále *pillow*:guánč- *cheek*; kasále *hamlet*:kás- *house*; piaccále (*large*) *square, plaza*:piátt- *public square*; portále *portal*:pórt- *door*; tɛndále *big tent*:ténd- *tent*; viále *avenue*:ví- *way, street*.

II. m/IIb: annále *annal*:ánn- *year*; kambiále *bill of exchange*:kámbi- *exchange*; pianále *plain-like area*:pián- *plain*; puɲɲále *dagger*:púɲɲ- *fist*; puntále *point, tip*:púnt- *point* sɛɲɲále *signal*:séɲɲ- *sign*.

III. m/IIc: braččále *bracelet*:bráčč- *arm*; ditále *thimble*:dít- *finger*.

IV. Nominal base: skaffále (*book*) *shelf*:skaff+ *id*.

iii. The suffix is preceded by:

A. +e+ in the adjectives rateále *by installments*:rát- *installment* f/Ia; floreále *floral*:flor+:fiór- *flower* m/IIIb.

B. +i+ (further preceded by △ after /t/, except after /st/) in a number of adjectives, such as the following based on:

I. Adj/IIIb: čelestiále *celestial* (*in mystic, religious meaning*):čelést-*celestial*; potenciále *potential*:potént- *potent*.

II. Nouns of types:

α. f/Ia: differenciále *differential*:differénc- *difference*; kredenciále *credential*:kredénc- *credence*; nuciále *nuptial*:nucc⁺:nócc- *wedding* (pl.)

β. m/IIb: bronkiále *bronchial*:brónk- *bronchial tube*; mondiále *of the world*:mónd- *world*.

γ. m/IIIb: governatorále *gubernatorial*:governatór- *governor*; ǧoviále *jovial*:ǧóv- *Jove*; kordiále *cordial*:kord:kuór- *heart*; torrenciále *torrential*:torrénte *torrent*.

δ. f/IIIb: partiále *partial*:párt- *part*.

ε. Nominal base: badiále *abbatial*:bad⁺ *abbot*.

C. ⁺or⁺ in kaporále *corporal* m/IIIb:káp- *head* m/IIb.

D. ⁺ev⁺ ⁺ašš⁺ ⁺ešš⁺ in karnevále karnaššále karneššále *carnival*:kárn-*meat* f/IIIb.

y. ⁺íl- adj/IIIb and m/IIIb, with the following meanings:

i. As adjective, *-ile, pertaining to . . .*, as in the following based on:

A. Adjectives of types:

I. I–II: maskíle *masculine*:máski- *male*.

II. IIIb: ǧovaníle *youthful*:ǧóvan- *young*.

B. Nouns of types:

I. f/Ia: femminíle *feminine*:fémmin- *woman, female*; vedovíle *of a widow*:védov- *widow*.

II. m/IIb: arčiveskovíle *of an archbishop*:arčivéskov- *archbishop*; bisestíl- *bisextile*:bisést- *bisextile day*; fabbríle *pertaining to a worker*:fábbr-*worker, smith*; notaríle *of or pertaining to a notary*:notár- *notary*; servíle *servile*:sérv- *servant, slave*; veskovíle *episcopal*:véskov- *bishop*; viríle *virile*:vir- *man*.

III. m/IIIb: mensíle *monthly*:mens⁺:més- *month*; merkantíle *mercantile*:merkánt- *merchant*; ostíle *hostile*:óst- *enemy*; sinノoríle *upper-class, of a gentleman or lord*:sinノór- *gentleman, lord*; tenoríle *of or pertaining to a tenor*: tenór- *tenor*.

IV. f/IIIb: febbríle *febrile*:fébbr- *fever*; ǧentíle *noble, gentle, kind*: gént- *people, race*.

V. Nominal bases: čivíle *civil*:civ⁺ *citizen*; pueríle *puerile*:puer⁺ *child*; seníle *senile*:sen⁺ *old man*.

C. Adv/II, in sottíle *subtle*:sótt- *under*.

ii. As noun, *place for or characterized by . . .*, as in the following based on nouns of types:

A. f/Ia: areníle *beach*:arén- *sand*; fontaníle *place having a spring or fountain*:fontán- *fountain*; kampaníle *bell-tower*:kampán- *bell*; kapríle *goat-fold*:kápr- *goat*; sedíle *seat*:sédi- *chair*; staffíle *stirrup-strap*:stáff- *stirrup*; vanǧíle *footpiece of mattock*:vanǧ⁺:váng- *mattock*.

B. m/IIb: fieníle *hayloft*:fién- *hay*; porčíle *pig-sty*:pórK- *hog*.

C. m/IIIb: kaníle *kennel*:kán- *dog*; pontíle (*boat-*) *landing*:pónt-*bridge*.

D. f/IIIb: kortíle *courtyard*:kórt- *court*.

E. Nominal bases: bačíle *basin*:bač⁺ *id.*; ovíle *sheep-fold*:ov⁺ *sheep*.

iii. The prefix is preceded by ⁺ar⁺ in podestaríle *of a podestà* adj/IIIb: podest⁺:podestáˣ *podestà, mayor* m/VId.

z. ⁺ár- *-ar, -ary* adj/IIIb and m/IIIb:

i. As adjective, in many formations, such as the following based on nouns of:

A. f/Ia: ančilláre *ancillary*:ančill:ančéll- *maid*; aššelláre *axillar*:aššéll- *axilla, armpit*; čelluláre *cellular*:čéllul- *cellule;* etc.

B. m/IIb: alimɛntáre *alimentary*:alimént- *nourishment*; angoláre *angular*:ángol- *angle*; artikoláre *articular*:artíkol- *article, joint*; titoláre *titular*:títol- *title*; etc. etc.

C. Nominal bases: anuláre *annular*:anul⁺ *ring*; balneáre *balnear*:balne⁺ *bath*; etc.

ii. As noun m/IIIb, preceded by ⁺ol⁺, in kasoláre *poor, mean country house*:kás- *house* f/Ia; and by ⁺an⁺, in lupanáre *lupanar, brothel*:lúp- *she-wolf, (whore)* f/Ia.

iii. The suffix is also preceded by the following elements in adjectives:

A. ⁺i⁺ in atrabiliáre *atrabiliar*:atrabíl- *black bile* f/IIIb; miliáre *mile-*:míl-:míll- *1000* num/IIIc.

B. ⁺il⁺ in basiláre *basilar*:bás- *base* f/IIIb.

C. ⁺ikol⁺ in vɛrmikoláre *vermiform*:vérm- *worm* m/IIIb; lɛntikoláre *lens-shaped, -like*:lént- *lens* f/IIIb.

aa. ⁺és- *-ese, -ish, having or characterized by* . . ., adj/IIIb and m/IIIb:

i. As adjective, e.g. in the following based on:

A. Adj/I–II: kalabrése *Calabrese*:kálabr- *Calabrian*; etc.

B. Nouns of types:

I. f/Ia: bandɛrése *having own troops*:bandɛr⁺:bandiér- *banner*; frančése *French*:fránč- *France*; maltése *Maltese*:mált- *Malta*; modɛnése *Modena*:módɛn- *Modena*; etc.

II. m/IIb: borgése *bourgeois*:bórg- *burgh*; maǧǧése *of May, fallow*:máǧǧ- *May*; etc.

III. m/IIIb: ǧapponése *Japanese*:ǧappón- *Japan*; etc.

IV. m/IVd: kamaldolése *of Camaldoli*:kamáldol- *Camaldoli*.

V. m/VId: siamése *Siamese*:siám *Siam*; etc.

VI. Nominal bases: bavarése *Bavarian*:bavar⁺ *Bavar(ia)*; portogése *Portuguese*:portog⁺ *Portug(al)*; svedése *Swedish*:sved⁺ *Swed(en)*; etc.

ii. As noun, in turkése *turquoise*:túrk- *Turkish* adj/I–II; laudése *writer of laude*:láud- *lauda* f/Ia; markése *marquis*:márk- *borderland* f/Ia.

3. On verbs, with:

a. ⁺′nd- *to be* . . . adj/I–II, f/Ia and m/IIb, based on Stem A of verbs (with TV /i/ > /ɛ/):

i. As adjective, e.g. in the following based on verbs of:

A. I/Reg/W: abominándo *abominable*:abómin- *abominate*; ammirándo *admirable*:ammír- *admire*; (e)vitándo *to be avoided*:(e)vít- *avoid*; onorándo *venerable*:onór- *honor*; ordinándo *to be ordained*:órdin- *ordain*; vɛnɛrándo *venerable*:vénɛr- *venerate*.

B. II/ísK/W: revɛréndo *reverend*:revɛr⁺:rivɛr- *revere*; stupéndo *stupendous*:stup- *be amazed*.

C. IIIb/Reg/S¹, ²: dekɔrréndo *to begin* (*starting from a given date*): dekórr- *pass*.

D. Verbal bases (quasi-III): kɔléndo *honorable*:kɔl⁺ *cultivate*; ɔrréndo *frightful, horrendous*:ɔrr⁺ *be affrighted*; pudéndo *private, to be kept hidden*:pud⁺ *be ashamed*.

ii. As noun f/Ia, in the following based on verbs of:

A. I/Reg/W: edukánda *pupil in convent school*:éduk- *educate*; filánda *spinning-wheel*:fíl- *spin*; lavánda *washing*:láv- *wash*; lokánda *inn*:lók- *lodge, locate*; mɔnakánda *candidate for nunhood*:mónak- *make into a nun*; mutánde (pl.) *underwear*:mút- *change*; vɔlánda *dust* (*of wheat in winnowing*):vól- *fly*.

B. II/ísK/W: áǧénda *agenda*:aǧ- *act*.

C. IIIb/Reg/S¹, ²: kiudénda *enclosure*:kiúd- *close*; leǧǧénda *legend*: léGG- *read*; repriménda *reprimand*:reprím- *repress*.

D. IV/Irr/S¹, ²: faččénda *thing to be done, affair*:fáčč-:fáč- *do*.

E. Verbal base (quasi-III): mɔlénda *quantity of grain to be milled*:mɔl⁺ *mill, grind*.

iii. As noun m/IIb, in laureándo *candidate for doctorate*:láure- *confer doctorate on* ... I/Reg/W; minuéndo *minuend*:⁺minu- *diminish* II/ísK/W; dividéndo *dividend*:divíd- *divide* IIIb/Reg/S¹, ²; kɔrriǧéndo *inmate* (*of reformatory*):kɔrriG⁺:kɔrréGG- *correct* IIIb/Reg/S¹, ²; addéndo *addendum*:add⁺ *add* quasi-III.

iv. Replacement of TV occurs:

A. With /a/ > /ɛ/, in trɛméndo *tremendous* adj/I–II:trém- *tremble* I/Reg/W.

B. With /e/ > /a/, in bevánda *drink* f/Ia:bév- *drink* IIIb(x)/Reg/S¹; vivánda *food*:vív- *live* IIIb/Reg/S¹, ².

b. ⁺'t- (with loss of preceding /č K v/) *-ed, having undergone or resulting from action of* ... adj/I–II, f/Ia, m/IIb:

i. As adjective, in modésto *modest*:modɛR- *moderate* I/Reg/W; minúto *minute*:⁺minu- *diminish* II/ísK/W.

ii. As noun f/Ia, in prostitúta *prostitute*:prostitu- *prostitute* II/ísK/W; trasférta *transfer*:trasfɛr- *transfer* II/ísK/W; vít- *life*:vív- *live* IIIb/Reg/S¹, ².

iii. As noun m/IIb, in libérto *freedman*:líber- *free* I/Reg/W; sálto *jump*: sál- *go up* II/Irr/W; sostitúto *substitute*:sostitu- *substitute* II/ísK/W; statúto *statute*:statu- *establish* II/ísK/W; pásto *meal*:pásK- *graze, feed* IIIb/Reg/W; and with the meaning of *person engaged in* ..., in sárto *tailor*:sarč- *patch, put in shape* II/ísK/W.

3.112. ADJECTIVES are formed:

1. On substantives and verbs, with:

a. ⁺'id- *-id, having the characteristics of* ... I–II:

i. On the following substantives:

A. Adjectives, of types:

I. I–II: márčido *rotten*:márč- *decayed*; tórbido *turbid*:tórb- *disturbed, muddied*.

        ii. IIIb: grávida (f.) *pregnant*:gráv- *heavy*.

     B. Nouns, of types:

        i. f/Ia: rípido *steep*:ríp- *bank*; rúvido *wrinkled*:ruv[+]:rúg- *wrinkle, crease*.

        ii. m/IIb: fúmido *smoky*:fúm- *smoke*; ğélido *gelid*:ğél- *icy cold*; mórbido *soft*:mórb- *disease*; múčido *evil-smelling*, *rancid*:muč[+]:múk- *mucus*; víššido *viscid*:visK[+]:vísk- *bird-lime*.

        iii. m/IIIb: flórido *flowering, flourishing*:flor[+]:fiór- *flower*.

        iv. Substantival bases: lívido *livid*:liv[+] *lividness*; límpido *limpid*: limp[+] *pure*; líkuido *liquid*:liku[+] *fluid*; pútrido *putrid*:putr[+] *rotten*; ríğido *rigid*: riG[+] *stiff*; úmido *humid*:um[+] *damp*.

     ii. On the following verbs and verbal bases:

A. langu- *languish* ⎫
   stup- *be amazed, dull*⎰ II/ísK/W
   tép- t Ɛp- *be tepid* IIIa
   tim[+]:tém- *fear* IIIa/Reg/W
   sap- *taste, know* IIIa/Irr/S[1]
   vál- *be strong* IIIa/Irr/S[1,2]
   férv- *be fervent* ⎫
   fúlG- *shine* ⎬ IIIb/Reg
   splénd- *resplend*⎰
   alG[+] *be cold* ⎫
   fet[+] *stink*
   nit[+] *shine*
   ɔrr[+] *be affrighted*
   pall[+] *be pale*
   ranK[+] *be rancid* ⎬ quasi-III
   skuall[+] *be squalid*
   tɔrp[+] *be dull*
   tum[+] *swell up*
   turG[+] *be turgid* ⎰

B. rap- *snatch, steal* ⎫
   vinč- *bend* ⎰ II/ísK/W
   lúč- *shine* IIIb/Reg/S[1]
   vív- *live* IIIb/Reg/S[1,2]
   pav[+] *be afraid*
   put[+] *stink* ⎫
   tɔrr[+] *be hot, rush* ⎬ quasi-III
   trɛp[+] *tremble* ⎰

Thus: lánguido *languid*; stúpido *stupid*; tépido tiépido *tepid*; tímido *timid*; sápido *tasty*; válido *valid*; férvido *fervid*; fúlğido *refulgent*; spléndido *splendid*; álğido *freezing cold*; fétido *fetid*; mádido *dripping wet*; nítido *shining*; órrido *horrid*; pállido *pallid, pale*; ránčido *rancid*; skuállido *squalid*; tórpido *torpid*; túmido *tumid*; túrğido *turgid*; rápido *rapid*; vínčido *soft, flexible*; lúčido *lucid*; vívido *vivid*; pávido *afraid*; pútido *stinking*; tórrido *torrid*; trépido *trembling, afraid*.

     b. [+]ónd- -*und, having* . . . I–II:

        i. Alone, in ğókóndo *jocund*:ğók- *pleasure, game* m/IIb.

        ii. Preceded by:

           A. [+]ak[+] in irakóndo *iracund, bad-tempered*:ír- *wrath* f/Ia.

           B. [+]ek[+] in vɛrekóndo *modest, chaste*:vɛr[+] *fear*.

           C. [+]ik[+] in rubikóndo *rubicund*:rub[+] *red*.

c. ⁺áne- -aneous I–II, as in the following, based:

   i. Without concomitant prefixation, on nouns of type:

     A. m/IIb: kɔntɛmpɔráneo *contemporaneous*:kɔntɛmpɔr⁺:kɔntémp- *same time*; tɛmpɔráneo *temporary*:tɛmpɔr⁺:témp- *time*.

     B. m/IIIb: istantáneo *instantaneous*:istánt- *instant*.

     C. f/IIIb: kutáneo *cutaneous*:kút- *cutis*.

     D. Nominal base: spɔntáneo *spontaneous*:spɔnt⁺ *volition*.

   ii. With concomitant prefixation or composition, on nouns of type:

     A. f/Ia: mediterráneo *Mediterranean*:mediterr⁺ = médi- *middle* adj/I–II + térr- *land* f/Ia; sotterráneo *subterranean*:sotterr⁺ = soˣ *under* + térr- *earth, land* f/Ia.

     B. f/VId: koetáneo *coetaneous*:koeta⁺ = ko⁺ *co-* + et⁺:etáˣ *age*.

   iii. On verbs: frustráneo *useless, in vain*:frústr- *frustrate* I/Reg/W; kɔnsentáneo *suitable, fitting*:kɔnsént- *fit, consent* II/Reg/W; suččedáneo *substitutable*: suččéd- *succeed, replace* IIIb/Reg/W.

d. ⁺′ič- IIIb, with meanings:

   i. On adjectival base -*fold*: sémpliče *simple*:sémpl⁺ *id*.

   ii. On verb IIIb/Reg/S¹, ², -*able*:prémiče *easily breakable by pressing*: prém- *press*.

e. ⁺évɔl- IIIb, with the meanings:

   i. On substantives, -*ly*, -*like*, -*able*, as in the following based on:

     A. Adj/I–II: amikévɔle *friendly*:amíK- *friend(ly)*.

     B. Nouns of types:

       I. f/Ia: festévɔle *festive, cheerful*:fést- *feast, festival*; kɔlpévɔle *guilty*: kólp- *guilt, sin*; kruskévɔle *of or following the Crusca Academy*:krúsk- *Crusca*; sorellévɔle *sisterly*:sɔréll- *sister*.

       II. m/IIb: fratellévɔle *brotherly*:fratéll- *brother*; sɛrviciévɔle *willing to perform services*:sɛrvíci- *service*.

       III. f/VId: karitatévɔle *charitable*:karitat⁺:karitáˣ *charity*.

   ii. On verbs, -*ible*, -*able*, -*ant*, -*ent*, -*y*, as in the following formed on verbs of:

     A. I/Reg/W: abbɔndévɔle *abundant*:abbónd- *abound*; adattévɔle *adaptable*:adátt- *adapt*; kɔndannévɔle *condemnable*:kɔndánn- *condemn*; etc.

     B. II/Reg/W: fuġġévɔle *fleeting*:fúGG- *flee*; partévɔle *divisible*:párt- *divide*.

     C. II/ísK/W: aġévɔle *easy*:aġ- *act*; kapévɔle *capable*:kap- *grasp, understand*; etc.

     D. IIIb/Reg/W: čedévɔle *yielding*:čéd- *yield*; risplɛndévɔle *resplendent*:risplénd- *be resplendent*.

     E. IIIb/Reg/S¹, ²: rispɔndévɔle *answerable*:rispónd- *answer*; rɔmpévɔle *easily breakable, brittle*:rómp- *break*; skɔrrévɔle *flowing*:skórr- *flow*; etc.

f. ⁺ént- -*ent*, *characterized by* . . . IIIb, based on:

   i. Noun, in peccénte *ragged*:pécc- *rag* f/Ia; sɛrpénte *serpent*:sérp- *snake* f or m/IIIb.

   ii. Verbs, on:

     A. Root, in the following based on verbs of I/Reg/W: bručénte *burn-*

ing:brúč- *burn*; diffidénte *diffident*:diffíd- *distrust*; fidénte *trusting*:fíd- *trust*; konfidénte *confident*:konfíd- *confide*; lustrénte *shining*:lústr- *shine*; violénte *violent* (also violénto I–II):víol- *violate*.

B. Root + ⁺ísK⁺, in appariššénte *handsome*:appar- *appear* II/ísK/W.

iii. The suffix is preceded by:

A. ⁺i⁺ in the following, based on verbs of:

I. II/Reg/W: dormiénte *sleeping*:dórm- *sleep*.

II. II/Irr/W: saliénte *salient*:sál- *go up;* udiénte *hearing*:ud- *hear*.

III. II/Irr/S¹, ²: veniénte *coming*:vɛn- *come*.

IV. II/ísK/W: perčipiénte *percipient*:perčip⁺:perčep- *perceive*.

V. IIIa/Irr/S¹: sapiénte *wise*:sap- *know*.

B. ⁺△i⁺ in senciénte *sentient*:sént- *feel* II/Reg/W; paciénte *patient*:pat- *suffer* II/ísK/W.

C. ⁺il⁺ in pestilénte *pestilent*:pést- *pestilence* f/IIIb.

D. ⁺ešš⁺ in the following based on:

I. Adj/I–II: kuieššénte *quiescent*:kui⁺:kuiét- *quiet*; marčeššénte *rotting*:márč- *decayed*.

II. Nouns of types:

a. m/IIb: fluoreššénte *fluorescent*:fluór- *fluor*; fosforeššénte *phosphorescent*:fósfor- *phosphorus*; opaleššénte *opalescent*:opál- *opal*.

β. m/IIIb: arboreššénte *arborescent, with spreading branches*:árbor- *tree*.

III. Substantival base: putreššénte *putrescent*:putr⁺ *rotten*.

IV. Verbal base: eskandeššénte *irascible, suddenly irate*:eskand⁺ *heat up suddenly*.

2. On substantives, with:

a. ⁺′e- *-eous, -ean, -eal, of* . . . I–II, as in the following based on:

i. Adj/I–II: čerúleo *cerulean*:čérul- *id.*

ii. Nouns of types:

A. f/Ia: ákkueo *aqueous*: ákku- *water*; čéreo:čér- *wax*; etc.

B. m/IIb: arğénteo *of silver*:arğént- *silver*; áureo *golden*:áur- *gold*; brónzeo *of bronze*:brónz- *bronze*; korpóreo *corporeal*:korpor:kórp- *body*; etc.

C. m/IIIb: arbóreo *arboreous*:árbor- *tree*; česáreo *Caesarian*:čésar- *Caesar*; kalkáreo *calcareous, of limestone*:kalkár- *limestone*; etc.

D. f/IIIb: činéreo *ashen (in color)*:činɛr⁺:čénɛr- *ashes*; etc.

b. ⁺ésk- *-esque, -ish*, mostly pejorative (except on place-names or in time-references) I–II, as in the following based on:

i. Adjectives, of types:

A. I–II: (a)rabésko *Arabesque*:árab- *Arabian*; romanésko *(modern) Roman*:román- *Roman*.

B. IIIb: popolarésko *plebeian*:popolár- *popular*.

ii. Nouns, of types:

A. m/IIb: asinésko *asinine*:ásin- *ass*; avvokatésko *pettifogging*: avvokát- *lawyer*; bambinésko *childish*:bambín- *child*; barbarésko *barbaric*: bárbar- *barbarian*; činkuečɛntésko *of the Cinquecento*:činkuečént- *Cinquecento, 16th century*; etc.

B. m/IIIb: animalésko *animal-like*:animál- *animal*; (dən)kiššottésko *Quixotic*:(dən)kiššótt- (*Don*) *Quixote*; kaɲɲésko *dog-like*:kaɲɲ⁺:kán- *dog*.

c. ⁺ʼn- *nal* I–II, in estérno *external*:éstɛr- *outside* adj/I–II; patérno *paternal*: patɛr⁺:patr⁺:pádr- *father* m/IIIb; matérno *maternal*:matɛr⁺:matr⁺:mádr- *mother* f/IIIb; intérno *internal*:intɛr⁺ *inside*.

d. ⁺úrn- *-urnal* I–II, in tačitúrno *taciturn*:tačit- *tacit* adj/I–II; nottúrno *nocturnal*:nótt- *night* f/IIIb; diúrno *diurnal*:díˣ *day* m/VId.

e. ⁺ént- *-ent, characterized by* . . . I–II:
  i. Alone, in kruénto *bloody*:kru⁺ *blood*.
  ii. Preceded by:
    A. ⁺il⁺ in mačilénto *emaciated*:máč- *emaciation* f/IIId.
    B. ⁺əl⁺ in the following, based on nouns of types:
      I. m/IIb: puccəlénto *stinking*:púcc- *stench*; sənnəlénto *somnolent* (also sənnəlénte IIIb):sónn- sónn- *sleep*; turbəlénto *turbulent*:túrb- *whirlwind*; vinəlénto *having drunk too much wine*:vín- *wine*.
      II. m/IIIb: sanguinəlénto *bloody* (also sanguinəlénte IIIb):sanguin⁺: sángu- *blood*.
      III. f/IIIb: fraudəlénto frodəlénto *fraudulent*:fráud- fród- *fraud*.
    c. ⁺ul⁺ in the following, based on:
      I. Adj/I–II: amarulénto *bitterish* (rare):amár- *bitter*.
      II. Nouns of types:
        a. m/IIb: flatulénto *flatulent*:flát- *burp*; lutulénto *muddy*:lút- *mud*.
        β. f/IIIb: pulvɛrulénto pəlvɛrulénto *dusty* (:pulvɛr⁺):pólvɛr- *dust*.
        γ. m/VId: purulénto *purulent*:pur⁺:pús *pus*.
        δ. Nominal base: eskulénto *esculent, tasty*:esk⁺ *food*.

f. ⁺úst- *having quality of* . . . I–II, in vetústo *old*:vɛt- *old* (*-fashioned*) adj/I–II; vɛnústo *beautiful*:vɛn⁺ *beauty*.

g. ⁺él- *having quality of* . . . IIIb, in krudéle *cruel*:krúd- *crude* adj/I–II; fedéle *faithful*:féd- *faith* f/IIIb.

3. On adjectives and adverbs, with ⁺ést- *having character of* . . . I–II, in agrésto *sour*:ágr- *bitter* adj/I–II; fərésto *remote, wild*:fɔr⁺:fuór- *outside* adv/IV.

4. On adjectives, with:

a. ⁺ʼ0- *id.* I–II, with change in root: dúlk- *sweet* (Tusc.):dólč- *id.* IIIb.

b. ⁺ʼΔ- *-ce, derived from* . . . I–II, together with voicing of resultant assibilate, in rəmánzo *Romance*:rəmant⁺ *romant*(*ic*).

c. ⁺ʼb- *behaving, acting like* . . . I–II, in supérbo *haughty, proud*:súper- *above* I–II.

d. ⁺vắǧ- *having quality of* . . . I–II, in malváǧo *wicked*:mál- *bad* I–II.

e. ⁺ési- *-ish* I–II, in vanésio *conceited, foppish*:ván- *vain* I–II.

f. ⁺ík- *-ik* III, in bəlševíko *bolshevik*:bəlšev⁺ *more*; mɛnševíko *menshevik*: mɛnšev⁺ *less*.

g. ⁺ʼiK- *-ex* IIIb, on adjectives referring to number of times: e.g. čɛntúpliče *centuplex*:čéntupl- *centuple, hundred-fold*; dúpliče *duplex, double*:dúpl- *double*;

kuadrúpliče *quadruplex*:kuádrupl- *quadruple*; moltépliče *multiple(x)*:moltepl⁺: múltipl- *multiple*; etc.

 h. ⁺óll- diminutive I–II, in satóllo *full* (*of food*):sat⁺ *enough*.

 j. ⁺'im- *at the extreme of . . ., very . . .* I–II:

  i. Alone, based on:

   A. Adj/IId: mínimo *minimum, very small*:min⁺:mén- *less*.

   B. Adj/IIIb: ačérrimo *very bitter, sharp*:ačɛrr⁺:aKr- *bitter*; čelebérrimo *very well-known*:čelebɛrr:čélebr- *well-known*.

   c. Adjectival bases: íntimo *innermost, intimate*:int⁺ *inside*; óttimo *very good, excellent*:ott⁺ *opt-, best*; prímo *first*:pri⁺ *prior, beforehand*; último *last*:ult⁺ *far*.

  ii. Preceded by ⁺ss⁺, in mássimo *very great*:ma⁺:mážǧ- *greater* adj/IId; péssimo *very bad*:pɛ⁺:péǧǧ- *worse* adj/IId; próssimo *nearest, next*:pro⁺:prop⁺ *near*.

  iii. Preceded by ⁺íss⁺, in a great number of adjectives, formed on any common adjective, as in the following based on adjectives of types:

   A. I–II: ačɛrbíssimo *very bitter*:ačérb- *bitter*; buoníssimo *very good*: buón- *good*; kattivíssimo *very bad*:kattív- *bad*; primíssimo *very first*:prím- *first*; stupidíssimo *very stupid*:stúpid- *stupid*; etc. etc. etc.

   B. IIIb: fačilíssimo *very easy*:fáčil- *easy*; fortíssimo *very strong*:fórt- *strong*; ǧentilíssimo *very kind*:ǧentíl- *kind*; vɛrdíssimo *very green*:vérd- *green*; etc. etc.

 k. ⁺'om- superlative I–II, in ménomo (also ménomo) *least*:mén- *less* adj/ IId.

 l. ⁺áčin- *tending to be . . .* I–II, in duráčino *cling* (*of peaches, etc.*):dúr- *hard* I–II.

 m. ⁺órs- *going towards the . . . side* I–II, in destrórso *going to the right*:déstr- *right-hand* I–II; sinistrórso *going to the left*:sinístr- *left-hand* I–II.

 n. ⁺éšš- -*ish* I–II, in maléššo *sickish, inedible* (*a kind of nut*):mál- *bad* I–II.

 o. ⁺uét- *rendered . . .* I–II, in mansuéto *docile*:máns- *tame* I–II.

 p. ⁺ínku- *in the vicinity of . . .* I–II, in lonǧínkuo *distant, far away*:lonG⁺: lúng- *long* I–II; propínkuo *near*:prop⁺ *nearby*.

 q. ⁺v- *in the condition of being . . .* I–II, in sálvo *safe*:sal⁺ *safe, healthy*.

 r. ⁺0- *in the condition of being . . .* IIIb, in esénte *exempt*:esɛnt⁺ *exempted*.

 s. ⁺úbr- -*ubrious* IIIb, in salúbre *salubrious*:sal⁺ *safe, healthy*.

 t. ⁺ókr- -*ocre* IIIb, in mediókre *mediocre*:médi- *medium, middle* I–II.

 u. ⁺ór- -*er*, comparative IIIb:

  i. Alone, in minóre *lesser*:min⁺:mén- *less* IId.

  ii. Preceded by ⁺△i⁺, in the following based on adjectives of types:

   A. I–II: čɛrciór⁺ *more certain* (in čɛrciór- *inform* I/Reg/W):čért- *certain*; estɛrióre *exterior*:éstér- *outside, foreign*; postɛrióre *posterior*:póstɛr- *later, a member of posterity*; supɛrióre *superior*:súpɛr- *above*; vičinióre *nearer*:vičín- *nearby*.

   B. IId: maǧǧóre *greater*:máǧǧ- *id.*; miλλóre *better*:miλλ⁺:méλλ- *id.*; peǧǧóre *worse*:péǧǧ- *id.*

c. Adjectival bases: antɛrióre *anterior*:anter⁺ *before, previous*; čitɛrióre *citerior, hither*:čitɛr⁺ *on this side*; intɛrióre *interior*:inter⁺ *inside*; pocióre *more important, taking precedence*:pɔt⁺ *powerful, important*; prióre *prior*:pri⁺ *beforehand*; sɛnióre *older, senior*:sɛn⁺ *old (man)*; tucjór⁺ *safer* (in tucjɔrísmo *tutiorism* m/IIb):tut⁺ *safe*; ulterióre *ulterior*:ultɛr⁺ *farther*:ult⁺ *far*.

w. únku- -*ever* (indefinite) IIId, in kuantúnkue *however much*:kuánt- *how much* I–II; kualúnkue *what(so)ever*:kuál- *which, what* IIIb.

5. On numerals, adjectives based thereon, or adjectives or nouns referring to quantity, with:

a. ⁺ağ⁺ -*ty*, in the following based on:

i. Adj/I–II: nɔnağ⁺ *ninety* (in nɔnağɛnário *nonagenarian* and nɔnağésimo *ninetieth* adjs/I–II):nón- *ninth*; ottuağ⁺ *eighty* (in ottuağɛnário *octuagenarian* adj/I–II):ottu⁺:ottáv- *eighth*.

ii. Numerals, of types:

A. IId, in kuadrağ⁺ *forty* (in kuadrağésimo *fortieth* adj/I–II):kuadr⁺: kuáttr- *four*.

B. IIId, in settuağ⁺ *seventy* (in settuağɛnário *septuagenarian*, settuağésimo *seventieth* adjs/I–II):settu⁺:sétt- *seven*.

c. IVd, in sessağ⁺ *sixty* (in sessağɛnário *sexagenarian*, sessağésimo *sixtieth* adjs/I–II):sɛss⁺:sé- *six*.

b. ⁺'pl- -*ple, -fold* I–II:

i. Alone, in dúplo *double*:dú- *two* num/IIId; tríplo *triple*:tri⁺:tréˣ *three* num/VId.

ii. Preceded by ⁺i⁺, in múltiplo *multiple*:mult⁺:mólt- *many*.

iii. Preceded by ⁺u⁺, in the following based on:

A. Adj/I–II: kuíntuplo *quintuple*:kuínt- *fifth*; nónuplo *nonuple*:nón- *ninth*; séstuplo *sextuple*:sést- *sixth*.

B. Numerals, of types:

I. IId: čéntuplo *centuple*:čént- *100*; kuádruplo *quadruple*:kuadr⁺: kuáttr- *four*; ɔ́ttuplo *octuple*:ɔ́tt- *eight*.

II. IIId: séttuplo *septuple*:sétt- *seven*.

III. IVd: dékuplo *decuple*:dɛk⁺:diéč- *ten*.

c. ⁺'im- -*th* I–II:

i. Alone, in séttimo *seventh*:sétt- *seven* num/IIId; déčimo *tenth*:dɛč⁺: diéč- *ten* num/IVd.

ii. Preceded by ⁺és⁺, on the following bases:

A. All numerals above *ten*: e.g. undičésimo *eleventh*:úndič- *eleven* num/IVd; dodičésimo *twelfth*:dódič- *twelve* num/IVd; vɛntésimo *twentieth*:vént- *twenty* num/IVd; vɛntottésimo *twenty-eighth*:vɛntótto *twenty-eight* num/IId; čentésimo *100th*:čént- *100* num/IId; millésimo *1000th*:míll- *1000* num/IIIc; etc. etc.

B. On nouns, in ɛnnésimo *nth*:ɛ́nn- *n* m/IIIb; miljɔnésimo *millionth*: miljón- *million* m/IIIb.

d. ⁺–↓n- -*th* I–II, in nóno *ninth*:nóv- *nine* num/IIId.

e. ⁺t- -*th* I–II, in kuárto *fourth*:kuar⁺:kuáttr- *four* num/IId; kuínt- *fifth*: kuin⁺:kuinku⁺:čínku- *five* num/IIId; sést- *sixth*:sɛss⁺:sé- *six* num/IVd.

f. +c- -th I–II (with preceding /re^x/ > /ɛr/) in térco *third*:tré^x *three* num/ VId.

g. +áv- +u+ -th I–II, in ottáv- *eighth* (ottu+ in ottuaǧenário *octuagenarian* adj/I–II):ótt- *eight* num/IId.

6. On nouns, with:

a. +0- *of . . ., like . . ., having . . .* I–II:

    i. Alone, in the following based on nouns of:

    A. f/Ia: ambrósio *of ambrosia*:ambrósi- *ambrosia*; kastáɲɲ- *chestnut-colored*:kastáɲɲ- *chestnut*.

    B. f/IIIb: fído *faithful*:fid+:féd- *faith*; kuiéto *quiet* (adj.):kuiét- *quiet* (n.); mɛretríčo *of a whore, meretricious*:mɛretríč- *whore*.

    ii. In the following parasynthetic compounds:

    A. Stressed on the base, with the prefixes:

      i. an+ privative, in anónimo *anonymous*:ɔnim+ *name*.

      ii. in+ negative: insapóro *tasteless*:sapór- *taste* m/IIIb.

      iii. s+ provative, in skárno *very thin, (almost) fleshless*:kárn- *flesh, meat* f/IIIb.

      iv. sin+ *syn-*, in sinónimo *synonymous*:ónim+ *name*.

    B. Stressed on the prefix (i.e. having '), with the prefixes:

      i. ɔ^x+ *ob-*, in óvvio *obvious*:ví- *way* f/Ia.

      ii. pɛr+ *through*, in pérvio *pervious, passable*:ví- *way* f/Ia.

      iii. pre+ *pre-*, in prévio *previous*:ví- *way* f/Ia.

      iv. sin+ *syn-*, in sínkrɔno *synchronous*:krɔn+ *time*.

b. +áče- *-aceous* I–II:

    i. Alone, as in the following based on nouns of types:

    A. f/Ia: arǧilláčeo *argillaceous*:arǧíll- *clay*; ɛrbáčeo *herbaceous*:érb- *grass, herb*; farináčeo *farinaceous*:farín- *flour*; kartáčeo *of paper*:kárt- *paper*; mɛmbranáčeo *membranaceous*:mɛmbrán- *membrane*; etc.

    B. m/IIb: aʎʎáčeo *alliaceous, garlic-like*:áʎʎ- *garlic*; frumɛntáčeo *frumentaceous*:frumént- *grain*; ǧiʎʎáčeo *liliaceous*:ǧíʎʎ- *lily*.

    ii. Preceded by +i+, in kɔriáčeo *of leather, coriaceous*:kɔr+:kuói- *leather* m/IIb.

c. +íče- *similar to . . .* I–II, in sɛríčeo *silk-like*:sɛr+ *silk*.

d. +'af- *making, pertaining to the making of . . .* I–II, in órafo *goldsmith, pertaining to the making of gold*:ór- *gold* m/IIb.

e. +óǧ- pejorative I–II, in barbóǧo *doting, dotard*:bárb- *beard* f/Ia.

f. +árbi- pejorative I–II, in kapárbio *stubborn*:káp- *head* m/IIb.

g. +'aK- *-ac, -ian* I–II:

    i. Alone, as in the following based on nouns of:

    A. f/Ia: austríaK- *Austrian*:áustri- *Austria*; maníaK- *maniac(al)*:maní- *mania*; ɔlimpíak- *Olympiac*:ɔlímpi- *Olympia*.

    B. m/Ib: fidíaK- *of, worthy of Phidias*:fídi- *Phidias*.

    C. m/IIb: dɛmɔníaK- *demoniac(al)*:dɛmóni- *demon*; diɔnisíaK- *Dionysiac*:diɔnísi- *Dionysius*; idillíaK- *idyllic*:idílli- *idyll*; ilíaK- *iliac*:íli- *loin*; simposíaK- *of a symposium*:simpósi- *symposium*.

D. Nominal bases: ammɔníaK- *ammoniac(al)*:ammɔni⁺ *Ammon*; kardíaK- *cardiac*:kardi⁺ *heart*.

ii. Preceded by:

A. ⁺í⁺ in paradisíaK- *paradisiac*:paradís- *paradise* m/IIb.

B. ⁺lí⁺ in ǧenetlíaK- *pertaining to birth*:ǧeneT⁺ *genet-, origin, birth*.

h. ⁺étim- *-ly* I–II, in diétimo *daily*:díˣ *day* m/VId.

j. ⁺ítim- *having . . .* I–II, in finítimo *neighboring, having a common boundary*:fín- *boundary* m/IIIb.

k. ⁺íttim- *-itime, -itimate* I–II, in maríttimo *maritime*:már- sea m/IIIb; leǧíttimo *legitimate*:leG⁺:léǧǧ- *law* f/IIIb.

l. ⁺ɔ́tin- *characterized by . . .* I–II, in serótino *late*:sér- *evening, (lateness)* f/Ia.

m. ⁺órn- *tending towards . . .* I–II, in piovórno *rainy*:piɔv- *rain* f/Ia; musórno *stupid*:mús- *snout, mouth* m/IIb.

n. ⁺árr- *characterized by . . .* I–II, in biẓẓárro *bizarre*:bíẓẓ- *sudden short fit of anger* f/Ia.

o. ⁺s- *-y* I–II, in sálso *salty*:sál- *salt* m/IIIb.

p. ⁺t- *having quality of . . .* I–II, in funést- *baleful, dire*:funɛR⁺ *disaster*.

q. ⁺ést- *-estic* I–II, in mɔlésto *disagreeable*:mól- *weight* f/IIIb.

r. ⁺út- *-ute, having . . ., provided with . . .* I–II:

i. Alone, as in the following based on nouns of:

A. f/Ia: barbúto *bearded*:bárb- *beard*; fɔrcúto *strong*:fórc- *strength*; lanúto *woolly*:lán- *wool*; linguaččúto *sharp-tempered*:linguáčč- *nasty tongue*; etc.

B. m/IIb: bekkúto *beaked*:békk- *beak*; bɛrnokkɔlúto *having bumps*: bɛrnókkɔl- *bump, lump*; kappellúto *crested*:kappéll- *hat, crest*; čɛrvellúto *brainy*: čɛrvéll- *brain*; nasúto *having a big nose*:nás- *nose*; etc.

C. m/IIc: kɔrnúto *horned*:kórn- *horn*; mɛmbrúto *strong-limbed*:mémbr- *limb, member*; ossúto *big-boned*:ɔ́ss- *bone*; etc.

D. m/IIIb: pepúto *peppery*:pép- *pepper*.

ii. Preceded by:

A. ⁺△⁺, in frɔnzúto *having boughs*:frónd- *bough* f/Ia.

B. ⁺ɛr⁺, in nokkiɛrúto *knotty*:nókki- *knot (in wood)* m/IIb.

s. ⁺'u- *-ual* I–II, in ánnu- *annual*:ánn- *year* m/IIb.

t. ⁺0- *-(i)al, having . . .* IIIb, in parasynthetic compounds based on adjectives, nouns, substantival bases, prepositions or prefixes, as in the following in which the first element of the base is:

i. An adjective or adjectival base, as in lɔngánime *patient, persevering*: lɔnG⁺ (:lúng- *long* adj/I–II) + ánim- *spirit, courage* m/IIb; maǧǧɔrénne *of age*:maǧǧór- *greater* adj/IIIb + énn⁺ (:ánn- *year* m/IIb); minɔrénne *under age*:minór- *lesser* adj/IIIb + énn⁺ (:ánn- *year* m/IIb); pusillánime *pusillanimous*:pusill *cowardly* + ánim- *spirit, courage* m/IIb; kuadrilíngue *quadrilingual*: kuadr⁺ (:kuáttr- *four* num/IId) + /i/ + língu- *tongue* f/Ia; kuadrúpede *quadruped*:kuadr⁺ (:kuáttr- *four* num/IId) + /u/ + ped⁺ (:piéd- *foot* m/IIIb); etc.

ii. A preposition, as in akklíve *steep*:aˣ, *to* + klív- *ascent* m/IIb; kɔnfórme *conforming*:kɔn, *with* + fórm- *form* f/Ia; pɛrénne *perennial*:pɛr, *through* + énn⁺ (:ánn- *year* m/IIb); etc.

iii. A prefix, as in abnórme *abnormal*:ab⁺ *ab-* + nórm- *norm* f/Ia; bikórne *two-horned*:bi⁺ *bi-* + kórn- *horn* m/IIc; deménte *demented*:de⁺ *de-* + mént⁺ (:mént- *mind* f/IIIb); diskórde *discordant*:dis⁺ *dis-* + kórd⁺ (:kɔr⁺:kuór- *heart* m/IIIb); implúme *featherless*:im⁺ *not* + plúm- *feather* f/Ia; ribélle *rebel*: ri⁺ *re-, again* + béll⁺ *war*; etc.

u. ⁺óč- *-ocious, like or having* ... IIIb, in fɛróče *ferocious*:fɛr⁺:fiér- *wild beast* f/Ia; vɛlóče *rapid*:vɛl⁺ *speed*.

w. ⁺'ebr- ⁺ébr- *-ebral, -ereal* IIIb, in fúnebr- funébr- *funereal*:fun⁺ *funeral*; mulíebre muliébre *feminine*:muli⁺:móʎʎ- *wife* f/IIIb.

y. ⁺'ɛr- *developing with respect to* ... IIIb, in púbere *adolescent*:púb- *pubes* m/IIIb.

z. ⁺éstr- *-estrian, -ine, -ian* IIIb (in some adjectives, also I–II), in the following based on nouns of types:

i. f/Ia: silvéstre *sylvan*:silv⁺:sélv- *forest*; tɛrréstre *terrestrial*:térr- *earth*.

ii. m/IIb: čiléstro *sky-blue*:čil⁺:čél- *sky*; kampéstre *rustic*:kámp- *field, country*.

iii. m/IIIb: pedéstre *pedestrian*:ped⁺:piéd- *foot*.

iv. f/IIIb: alpéstre alpéstro *Alpine*:álp- *Alp*; rupéstre *of or on a rock*: rúp- *rock*.

v. Nominal base: ekuéstre *equestrian*:eku⁺ *horse*.

aa. ⁺ústr- *-ustrine* IIIb: lakústre *lacustrine*:lak⁺:lág- *lake* m/IIb; palústre *palustrine, pertaining to swamps*:pal⁺:palúd- *swamp* m/IIIb.

bb. ⁺éns- *-ensic, -ese, of* ... IIIb, in the following based on nouns of type IIb: čirčénse *pertaining to a circus (ancient)*:čirč⁺:čírk- *circus*; čistɛrčénse *Cistercian*:čistérč- *Cîteaux*; fɔrénse *forensic*:fór- *forum*; kastrénse *military*:kástr- *(ancient) camp*; ɔrténse *of, pertaining to gardens*:órt- *garden*; praténs- *of, pertaining to fields*:prát- *field*.

cc. ⁺ést- *pertaining to* ... IIIb, in agréste *rustic*:ágr- *field, countryside* m/IIb.

7. On pronominal bases (§2.21), with the following suffixes of type I–II, meaning *of, belonging to* ...:

a. ⁺í- in mío *my, mine*:m⁺ *me*.

b. ⁺'str- in nóstro *our(s)*:nó- *we, us*; vóstro *your(s)*:vó- *you*.

c. ⁺ú- in súo *his, her(s), its*:s⁺ *him(self), her(self), it(self)*; túo *thy, thine*:t⁺ *thee, thou*.

8. On indeclinables or corresponding bases, with:

a. ⁺ínseK- *-insic* I–II, in estrínseK- *extrinsic*:éstr- *extra* adv/I; intrínseK- *intrinsic*:intr⁺ *intra*.

b. ⁺rém- *-reme* I–II, in estrémo *extreme*:éstr- *extra, outside* adv/I; postrémo *last*:post⁺ *after, behind*; suprémo *supreme*:sup⁺ *over*:súˣ *up, over* adv/VI.

c. ⁺'um- *-humous* I–II, in póstumo *posthumous*:post⁺ *after*.

d. ⁺'ɛr- *comparative* I–II, in éstero *outside, foreign*:ɛst⁺ *out*:es⁺ *ex-*;

súpɛro *upper, above*:sup⁺ *over*:súˣ *up, over* adv/VI; intɛr⁺ *inter-*:int⁺ *inside*:in¹ *in* prep/VId; póstɛro *later, member of posterity*:post⁺ *post-, after*.

9. On verbs, on the following root- or stem-forms:

    a. On root or verbal base, with:

        i. ⁺0- -*ed* I–II, on verbs of I/Reg/W (so-called 'shortened past participles', with slightly more generic meaning and indicating less specific action than the past participle), as in ăččɛ́tto *accepted, acceptable*:ăččɛ́tt- *accept*; akkónčo *fit, proper*:akkónč- *put in order*; adúltɛro *adulterous*:adúltɛr- *adulterate*; dimɛ́ntiko *forgetful*:dimɛ́ntik- *forget*; káriko *loaded*:kárik- *load*; kólmo *full*:kólm- *heap up, fill*; etc.

        ii. ⁺únd- -*ing* I–II, in ɔriúndo *arising, originating*:ori⁺ *arise*.

        iii. ⁺óne- -*oneous* I–II, in ɛrróneo *erroneous*:ɛ́rr- *err* I/Reg/W.

        iv. ⁺úk- -*ucous* I–II, in kadúko *caducous, dilapidated*:kád- *fall* IIIa/Reg/S¹.

        v. ⁺íK- agent I–II, in amíK- *friendly*:ám- *be friendly, love* I/Reg/W; pudíK- *modest*:pud⁺ *be modest*.

        vi. ⁺ór- -*orous* I–II, in sɔnóro *sonorous*:sɔn- *sound* I/Reg/W; kanóro *canorous, melodious*:kan⁺ *sing*.

        vii. ⁺'u- -*uous* I–II, in resíduo *residual*:resid⁺:sɛd- *sit* IIIa/Reg or Irr/W; nókuo *harmful*:nɔk⁺:nɔ̌č- *harm* IIIb/Irr/S¹; prɔmískuo *promiscuous*:pro⁺ *pro-* + misk⁺:mésK- *mix* IIIb/Irr/W; dečíduo *deciduous*:dečid⁺ *fall down*; oččíduo *western, setting (of sun)*:oččid⁺ *set, go down*; pɛrspíkuo *perspicuous, clear*:pɛr⁺ *through* + spik⁺ *see*.

        viii. ⁺0- -*ate, -ating, -ous* IIIb, on verbs of I/Reg/W in değénɛre *degenerate(d)*:değénɛr- *degenerate*; partéčipe *participating*:partéčip- *participate*; prečípite *precipitous, precipitate*:prečípit- *precipitate*.

        ix. ⁺'ubr- -*ubrious* IIIb, in lúgubre *lugubrious*:lug⁺ *weep*.

    b. On root, Stem A and Stem C, with ⁺túr- *about to . . .* I–II, with the following distribution:

        i. On root, in vɛntúro *coming, to come*:vɛn- *come* II/Reg/S¹.

        ii. On Stem A (with TV /e/ > /i/), in mɔritúro *about to die*:mɔr- *die* II/Irr/S²; naššitúro *about to be born*:násK- *come into being* IIIb/Reg/S¹, ².

        iii. On Stem C, alternate, in futúro *future*:fú-:fó-:ɛ́ss- *be* IIIb/Irr/S¹.

    c. On Stem A, with ⁺bónd- -*bund, engaged in . . . -ing* I–II, in the following based on verbs of types:

        i. I/Reg/W: ɛrrabóndo *wandering*:ɛ́rr- *wander*; koğitabóndo *cogitative*:kóğit- *cogitate*; meditabóndo *meditating*:médit- *meditate*; nauseabóndo *nauseating*:náuse- *nauseate*; vagabóndo *vagabond*:vág- *wander*. TV /a/ > /e/ in trɛmebóndo *trembling*:trém- *tremble*.

        ii. II/Irr/S²: mɔribóndo *moribund*:mɔr-*die*.

        iii. IIIb/Reg/W: frɛmebóndo *agitated*:frém- *be agitated*; ğemebóndo *groaning*:ğém- *groan*.

        iv. Verbal bases, with TV /i/, in furibóndo *furibund, raging*:fur⁺ *rage*; pudibóndo *modest*:pud⁺ *be ashamed*; sitibóndo *thirsting*:sit⁺ *thirst* (:sét- *thirst* f/IIIb).

d. On Non-Finite[2] A, +0- *performing the action of . . . -ing, -er* IIIb ('present participle'), as in the following based on verbs of conjugations:

i. I: abitánte *inhabiting, inhabitant*:ábit- *inhabit*; abbondánte *abundant*: abbónd- *abound*; andánte *going, moving along*:and- *go*; kantánte *singing, singer*: kánt -*sing*; parlánte *talking*:párl- *talk*; etc.

ii. II: dorménte *sleeping*:dórm- *sleep*; servénte *serving*:sérv- *serve*.

iii. IIIa: avénte *having*:av- *have*; kadénte *falling*:kád- *fall*; tenénte *holding*:tɛn- *hold*; etc.

iv. IIIb: eččedénte *exceeding*:eččéd- *exceed*; končernénte *concerning*: končérn- *concern*; naššénte *nascent*:násK- *come into existence*; etc.

v. IV: dičénte *saying*:díK- *say*; fačénte *making*:fáč- *do*; ponénte *setting (of sun), east*:pón- *put, set*; etc.

e. On Non-Finite C, +0- -*ed* (indicating condition gotten into as a result of the action) I–II ('past participle'), on almost every verb of the language, as in the following based on verbs of conjugations:

i. I: abitáto *inhabited*:ábit- *inhabit*; abbondáto *abounded*:abbónd-*abound*; andáto *gone*:and- *go*; kantáto *sung*:kánt- *sing*; parláto *talked*:párl- *talk*; etc. etc. etc.

ii. II: dormíto *slept*:dórm- *sleep*; partíto *departed*:párt- *depart*; servíto *served*:sérv- *serve*; etc.

iii. IIIa: avúto *had*:av- *have*; kadúto *fallen*:kad- *fall*; tenúto *held*:tɛn-*hold*, etc.

iv. IIIb: fínto *pretended*:fínG- *pretend*; náto *born*:násK- *come into existence*; rétto *ruled*:réGG- *rule*; etc.

v. IV: détto *said*:díK- *say*; fátto *done*:fáč- *do;* trátto *drawn*:trá[x] *draw;* etc.

3.113. NUMERALS are formed on numerals with the suffix +nt- -*ty* Id:

1. Alone, in trénta *thirty*:tré[x] *three* num/VId.

2. Preceded by +á+, in the following based on numerals of types:

a. IId: kuaránta *forty*:kuar+:kuáttr- *four*; ottánta *eighty*:ótt- *eight*.

b. IIIc: millánta *1000, any large number*:míll- *1000*.

c. IIId: činkuánta *fifty*:čínku- *five*; settánta *seventy*:sétt- *seven*; novánta *ninety*:nóv- *nine*.

d. IVd: sessánta *sixty*:sɛss:sé- *six*.

3.114. NOUNS are formed on:

1. Other form-classes, with the suffix +0- m/VId, as in pagerɔ́[x] *note*, IOU = pagɛrɔ́[x] *I will pay* (:pág- *pay* I/Reg/W); váλλa *money-order* = váλλa *let it be worth* (:vál- *be worth* IIIa/Irr/S[1, 2]).

2. Substantives, verbs and adverbs with:

a. +íǧ- -*ness, quality of . . .* (pejorative) f/Ia, in the following based on:

i. Adjectives, of types:

A. I–II: altɛríǧa *haughtiness*:alt(i)ér- *haughty*; frankíǧa *frankness*: fránk- *frank*; kupidíǧa *cupidity*:kúpid- *greedy*; and in a parasynthetic compound with the preposition in₁ *in*, in ingordíǧa *voracity, greediness*:górd- *greedy*.

B. IIIb: grandíǧa *pride*:gránd- *big, great*.

ii. Noun f/IIIb, in činíǧa *hot ashes mixed with embers*:čin+:činɛr+:čéner-*ashes*.

iii. Verb II/ísK/W, in guarɛntíǧa *guaranty*:guarɛnt- *guarantee*.

b. ⁺í- *-y, -ness*, quality, place of action f/Ia, as in the following based on:

i. Adj/I–II: afɔnía *aphony*:áfɔn- *aphonic*; allegría *cheerfulness*:allégr- allégr- *cheerful*; anɔmalía *anomaly*:anɔmal- *anomalous*; bigamía *bigamy*:bígam- *bigamous*; malía *magic*:mál- *bad*; mattía *madness*:mátt- *mad*; etc. etc.

ii. Nouns, as in the following based on nouns of types;

A. m/IIb: aǧografía *hagiography*:aǧógraf- *hagiographer*, and similarly with all nouns ending in ⁺grafía *-graphy*; agrɔnɔmía *agronomy*:agrónɔm- *agronomer*; astrɔloǧía *astrology*:astróloG- *astrologer*, and similarly with all nouns ending in ⁺loǧía *-logy*; kɔrsía *passage*:kórs- *course*; etc.

B. m/IIIb: agɔnía *agony*:agón- *struggle*; barɔnía *barony*:barón- *baron*; kalɔría *calory*:kalór- *heat*; etc.

C. Nominal bases: armɔnía *harmony*:armɔn⁺ *harmon-*; badía *abbey*: bad⁺ *abbot*; etc.

iii. Verb or verbal base, in anfanía *crazy idea or doings*:anfán- *be busy* I/Reg/W; mɔría *pestilence and mass death*:mɔr- *die* II/Irr/S²; ǧɛnía (*low*) *breed, race*:ǧɛn⁺ *beget*.

iv. The suffix is preceded by:

A. ⁺△⁺ in many nouns, as the following based on:

I. Adjectives: analoǧía *analogy*:análog- *analogous* I–II; idiocía *idiocy*:idiót- *idiot* Ib; etc.

II. Nouns: akrobacía *acrobatics*:akróbat- *acrobat* m/Ib; mɛrkancía *merchandise*:mɛrkánt- *merchant* m/IIIb; aristokracía *aristocracy*:aristokrat⁺ *aristocrat*, and similarly with all other nouns in ⁺kracía *-cracy*; etc.

B. ⁺ɔrn⁺ in lekkɔrnía (also lekkórnia) *gluttony, dainty bit*:lékk- *lick* I/Reg/W.

C. ⁺ɛr⁺ in a great many nouns, especially those in ⁺ɛría *-ery, ensemble of . . ., action characteristic of . . ., place of . . .*,[3] as in the following based on:

I. Adjectives: fessɛría *stupidity*:féss- *stupid* I–II; giottɔnɛría *gluttony*:giottón- *glutton* IIIb; etc.

II. Nouns, of types:

a. f/Ia: birrɛría *beer-joint*:bírr- *beer*; krɛmɛría *cream-shop*:krém- *cream*; piccɛría *pizzeria*:pícc- *pizza*; etc.

β. m/Ib: kopistɛría *copying-room*:kopíst- *copyist*; modistɛría *modiste's shop*:modíst- *modiste*; etc.

γ. f/Ib: armɛría *armory, collection of weapons*:árm- *arm, weapon*.

δ. m/IIb: allokkɛría *stupidity, owlishness*:allókk- *owl*; araccɛría *place, ensemble of tapestries*:arácc- *tapestry*; avvokatɛría *pettifoggery*:avvokát- *lawyer*; pollɛría *poultry-market*:póll- *chicken*; etc.

ε. m/IIIb: akkattɔnɛría *beggary*:akkattón- *beggar*; bakkettɔnɛría *bigotry*:bakkettón- *bigot*; lattɛría *milk-shop*:látt- *milk*; ɔrefičɛría *goldsmith's shop*:ɔréfič- *goldsmith*; etc.

ζ. f/IIIb: mɛrčɛría *mercer's shop*:mérč- *goods*; vɛrničɛría *varnish-store*:vɛrníč- *varnish*.

---

[3] For a full listing of nouns indicating place of trade, etc., in *-ia -ería*, cf. K. McKenzie, 'Divertimento Filologico', Italica 17.42–48 (1940).

η. Nominal bases: biǧottɛría *jeweler's shop*:biǧott⁺ *jewel*; kinkaʎʎ-ɛría *five-and-ten store*:kinkaʎʎ⁺ *thing of small value*; linǧería *laundry*:linǧ⁺ *linen*.

III. Verbs of types:

α. I/Reg/W, in lavɛría *washing-place (for metals in mines)*:láv- *wash*; manǧería *graft*:máng- *eat*; raffinɛría *refinery*:raffín- *refine*; rubería *robbery*:rúb- *rob*.

β. IIIb: battería *battery*:bátt- *beat*; (s)kɔrrɛría *incursion*:(s)kórr- *run, dash about*.

D. ⁺ndɛr⁺ in lavandɛría *laundry*:láv- *wash* I/Reg/W.

E. ⁺agɔr⁺ in fantasmagɔría *phantasmagoria*:fantásm- *phantasm* m/Ib.

F. ⁺as⁺ in fantasía *fantasy, fancy, imagination*:fant⁺ *fancy*.

G. ⁺is⁺ in idropisía *dropsy*:ídrop- *id.* m/IIIb.

H. ⁺at⁺ in supremacía *supremacy*:suprém- *supreme* adj/I–II.

J. ⁺est⁺ in karestía *famine*:kár- *dear* adj/I–II; sagrestía sakrestía *sacristy* (:sagr⁺):sáKr- *sacred* adj/I–II.

c. él- abstract or collective f/Ia:

i. On adjectival bases, in tutéla *guardianship*:tut⁺ *safe*.

ii. On nouns, in tɔrdéla *a kind of turtle-dove*:tórd- *turtle-dove* m/IIb; klientéla *clientèle*:kliént- *client* m/IIIb; parɛntéla *relationship*:parént- *relative* m/IIIb.

iii. On verbs, based on:

A. Root, in sekuéla *sequence*:seku⁺:ségu- *follow* II/Reg/W; miššéla *mixture*:misK⁺:mésK- *mix* IIIb/Reg/W; kuɛréla *complaint*:kuɛr⁺ *complain*; lokuéla *speech*:loku⁺ *speak*.

B. Non-Finite C or alternant, in kuratéla *guardianship*:kúr- *care for* I/Reg/W; kɔrruttéla *corruption*:kɔrrutt⁺:kɔrrómp- *corrupt* IIIb/Reg/W.

d. ⁺áʎʎ- collective and pejorative f/Ia:

i. On adjectives, as in antikáʎʎa *old junk*:antík- *old, antique* I–II; minutáʎʎa- *collection of worthless things or people*:minút- *minute, unimportant* I–II; sodáʎʎa *unplowed land*:sód- *solid, firm* I–II; etc.

ii. On nouns, e.g. of types:

A. f/Ia: baváʎʎa *gag*:báv- *drool*; čurmáʎʎa *motley crew*:čúrm- *crew*; etc.

B. m/IIb: boskáʎʎa *thick woods with undergrowth*:bósk- *forest*; fɛrráʎʎa *scrap-iron*:fɛrr- *iron*; (s)birráʎʎa *gendarmerie*:(s)bírr- *gendarme*; etc.

C. m/IIIb: čaltrɔnáʎʎa *collection of evil-tongued persons*:čaltrón- *evil-tongued person*; kanáʎʎa *canaille, rabble*:kán- *dog*; etc.

D. Nominal base: marmáʎʎa *rabble*:marm⁺ *obnoxious person*.

iii. On verbs, indicating means or result of action: akkoccáʎʎa *heap, crowd*:akkócc- *heap together* I/Reg/W; avvisáʎʎa *hostile encounter*:avvís- *meet (of enemies)* I/Reg/W; tɛnáʎʎa *claw, hook*:tɛn- *hold* IIIa/Irr/S¹; battáʎʎa *battle*:bátt- *beat* IIIb/Reg/W.

e. ⁺íʎʎ- f/Ia, with the following meanings:

i. On nouns, diminutive, as in the following based on nouns of types:

A. f/Ia: flottíʎʎa *flotilla*:flótt- *fleet*; guɛrríʎʎa *guerrilla*:guérr- *war*;

kartíʎʎa *low card* (*in game*): kárt- *card, paper*; kɔnkíʎʎa *conch-shell*:kónk- *basin, jar*.

    B. m/IIb: brodíʎʎa *dish-water*:bród- *broth*; fangíʎʎa *oozy mud*:fáng- *mud*; ǧunkíʎʎa *jonquil*:ǧúnk- *reed*; mantíʎʎa *mantle*:mánt- *cloak*; kuadríʎʎa *quadrille*:kuádr- *square*.

    C. f/IIb: maníʎʎa *handle*:mán- *hand*.

    D. m/IIc: paríʎʎa *pair, couple*:par⁺:pái- *pair*.

    E. f/IIIb: bottíʎʎa *bottle*:bótt- *cask*.

    F. Nominal base: kavíʎʎa *ankle-bone*:kav⁺ *pin*.

    ii. On verbs, indicating result of action, with diminutive force, in mɔndíʎʎa *sweepings*:mónd- *clean* I/Reg/W; stampíʎʎa *printed form*, etc.:stámp- *print* I/Reg/W.

    iii. The suffix is preceded by:

    A. ⁺ott⁺ in pakkottíʎʎa *junk, quantity of worthless stuff*:pákk- *package* m/IIb.

    B. ⁺ov⁺ in goccovíʎʎa *binge*:gócc- *throat, stomach* m/IIb.

  f. ⁺'im- f/Ia, with the following meanings:

    i. On noun, diminutive, in bóẓẓima *chicken-feed mash, pasty mess*:bóẓẓ- *puddle* m/IIb.

    ii. On verb (Non-Finite C, alternant), object of action, in víttima *victim*: vitt⁺:vín*K*- *conquer* IIIb/Reg/S¹, ².

  g. ⁺úr- *-ure*, abstract f/Ia, as in the following based on:

    i. Substantives:

    A. Adjectives, of types:

      I. I–II: altúra *height*:ált- *high*; bassúra *lowness*:báss- *low*; bravúra *bravery*:bráv- *brave*; freskúra *coolish air*:frésk- *cool*; kaldúra *summer heat*:káld- *hot*; largúra *space*:lárg- *broad, wide*; pianúra *plain*:pián- *flat*; soẓẓúra *filth*:sóẓẓ- *filthy*.

      II. IIIb, in vɛrdúra *verdure, green vegetables*:vérd- *green*.

    B. Nouns m/IIb: avvokatúra *lawyer's profession*:avvokát- *lawyer*; čɛnsúra *censorship, censure*:čéns- *census*.

    ii. Verbs, in:

    A. Root: mɔntúra *uniform* (*military*):mónt- *mount* I/Reg/W¹; prɛmúra *solicitude*:prém- *press* IIIb/Reg/W; pročedura *procedure*:pročéd- *proceed* IIIb/Reg/W; paúr- *fear*:pa⁺:pav⁺ *fear*.

    B. Non-Finite C or alternant, in many nouns, such as the following based on verbs of types:

      I. I/Reg/W: abbaiatúra *barking*:abbái- *bark*; abbottɔnatúra *buttoning*:abbottón- *button*; akkoppiatúra *coupling*:akkóppi- *couple*; alcatúra *raising*:álc- *raise*; aratúra *plowing*:ár- *plow*; etc. etc.

      II. II/Reg/W: partitúra *partition,* (*musical*) *score*:párt- *divide*.

      III. II/Irr/S¹; avvɛntúra *adventure*:avvɛn- *happen*; vɛntúra *fortune*:vɛn- *come*.

      IV. IIIb/Reg/S¹, ²: kottúra *cooking*:kɔč- *cook*; mɔrsúra *eating* (*of acid*):mórd- *bite*; pittúra *painting*:pín*G*- *paint*; etc.

      V. IV/Irr/S¹, ²: fattúra *making, bill*:fáč- *do, make*.

iii. The suffix is preceded by:

A. ⁺t⁺, in nouns formed on Stem A of certain verbs (with TV > /i/), in fenditúra *act of splitting*:fénd- *split* IIIb/Reg/S¹, ²; dičitúra *words (of dis-* *course)*:díK- *say* IV/Irr/S¹, ²; fačitúra *work, doing*:fáč- *do* IV/Irr/S¹, ²; molitúra *milling*:mol *mill, grind.*

B. ⁺at⁺ in certain nouns based on nouns of types:

I. f/Ia: kostatúra *rib-structure*:kóst- *rib*; sabbiatúra *sand covering*: sábbi- *sand*; venatúra *veining (in marble etc.)*:vén- *vein*.

II. m/IIb: nervatúra *nerve-structure*:nérv- *nerve*.

III. m/IIc: ossatúra *bony structure*:óss- *bone*.

h. ⁺énc- *-ence* f/Ia:

i. On adj/I–II, in onorifičénca *honorification*:onorífiK- *honorific*; šeménca *stupid act*:šém- *stupid, imbecile*.

ii. On verbs, in kointeressénca⋅ *co-interest* (n.):kointeréss- *co-interest* (vb.) I/Reg/W; sekuénca seguénca *sequence, hymn* (:seku⁺):ségu- *follow* II/ Reg/W.

j. ⁺icc- *action of . . ., thing characterized by . . .* f/Ia:

i. On noun m/IIIb, in kanícca *baying of hounds*:kán- *dog*.

ii. On verb II/Reg/W, in putícca *natural emanation of sulphuric acid*:pút- *stink*.

k. íst- *-ist* m/Ib:

i. On adjectives, as in the following based on adjectives of types:

A. I–II: belličísta *war-monger*:bélliK- *warlike*; bizantinísta *Byzantin-ist*:bizantín- *Byzantine*; latinísta *Latinist*:latín- *Latin*; positivísta *positivist*: positív- *positive*; purísta *purist*:púr- *pure*; etc. etc.

B. IIIb: komunísta *communist*:komún- *common*; materialísta *material-ist*:materiál- *material*; racionalísta *rationalist*:racionál- *rational*; sočalísta *social-ist*:sočál- *social*; etc.

ii. On nouns, as in the following based on nouns of types:

A. f/Ia: akkademísta *academist*:akkadémi- *academy*; àkkuaplanísta *aquaplanist*:àkkuaplán- *aquaplane*; alkimísta *alchemist*:alkími- *alchemy*; al-ǧebrísta *algebrist*:alǧébr- *algebra*; etc.

B. m/IIb: abbakísta *arithmetician*:ábbak- *abacus*; čìnkuečentísta *per-son of the sixteenth century*:čìnkuečént- *sixteenth century*; ebanísta *worker in fine woods*:éban- *ebony*; faššísta *fascist*:fášš- *bundle, fascio*; flautísta *flautist*:flaút-*flute*; kalvinísta *Calvinist*:kalvín- *Calvin*; organísta *organist*:órgan- *organ*; etc.

C. f/IId: autísta *chauffeur*:áut- *auto*.

D. m/IIIb: affarísta *affairiste*:affár- *affair, business*; agonísta *com-batant*:agón- *struggle*; dantísta *Dantist*:dánt- *Dante*; etc.

E. f/IIIb: appendičísta *appendix-, serial-writer*:appendíč- *appendix*; artísta *artist*:árt- *art*; professionísta *professional person*:professión- *profession*; etc.

F. m/VId: barísta *bar-tender*:bár *bar*; kaffeísta *coffee-fiend*:kafféˣ *coffee*.

G. Nominal bases: analísta *analyst*:anal⁺ *anal(ysis)*; teísta *theist*:te⁺ *the-, god*.

ii. On verbs or verbal bases in arrivísta *arriviste*:arrív- *arrive* I/Reg/W; apprendísta *apprentice*:apprénd- *learn* IIIb/Reg/S[1, 2]; battísta *baptist*:batt[+] bapt(*ize*).

1. [+]í- *lively, hasty or continual activity in connection with* . . . m/IIb:

   i. On nouns, as in the following based on nouns of types:

     A. f/Ia: čanía *gossip*:čán- *vulgar low-class woman*.

     B. m/IIb: brividío *continual shivering*:brívid- *shudder*; ǧɛmitío *continual trickling*:ǧémit- *trickle*; tremitío *continual trembling*:trémit- *trembling movement*.

     C. m/IIIb: affarío *to-do*:affár- *affair*.

     D. f/IIIb: pɔlverío *dust-cloud*:pólvɛr- *dust*.

   ii. On verbs, in many nouns, such as the following based on verbs of types:

     A. I/Reg/W: abbaruffío *lively rumpus*:abbarúff- *raise a rumpus*; abbɔrraččío *hasty bungling*:abbɔrráčč- *bungle*; armeǧǧío *continual striving*:arméǧǧ- *struggle, strive*; balɛnío *continual lightning*:balén- *lighten*; martɛllío *continual hammering*:martéll- *hammer*; etc. etc.

     B. IIIb/Reg/S[1, 2]: leǧǧío *lectern, reading-desk*:léGG- *read*.

m. [+]óni- abstract m/IIb:

   i. Alone, only in kɔmprɛndónio *understanding* (*humorous*):kɔmpréndunderstand IIIb/Reg/S[1, 2].

   ii. Preceded by [+]im[+], in the following based on:

     A. Substantives:

       I. Adjectives: kastimónio *chastity*:kást- *chaste* I–II; akrimónio *acrimony*:áKr- *bitter, sharp* IIIb.

       II. Nouns: património *patrimony*:patr[+]:pádr- *father* m/IIIb; testimónio *testimony*:tést- *witness* m/IIIb; matrimónio *matrimony*:matr[+]:mádr- *mother* f/IIIb; merčimónio *illicit traffic*:mérč- *goods* f/IIIb.

       III. Substantival bases: čɛrimónio *cerimony*:čɛr[+] *id.*; parsimónio *parsimony*:pars[+] *stingy*.

     B. Verbal base, in kuɛrimónio *loud complaint*:kuɛr[+] *complain*.

n. [+']bɔl- -*ble* m/IIb:

   i. Alone, on Stem A of verb or verbal base, in patíbɔlo *scaffold*:patsuffer II/ísK/W; vokábɔlo *vocable, word*:vok[+] *call*.

   ii. Preceded by [+]í[+] in turíbɔlo *censer*:tur[+] *incense*.

o. [+]íʎʎ- m/IIb, with the following meanings:

   i. On nouns, diminutive, in kartíʎʎo *scroll-shaped ornament*:kárt- *paper* f/Ia; motíʎʎo *a little mud*:mót- *mud* f/Ia; fondíʎʎo *lees*:fónd- *bottom* m/IIb; vɛntríʎʎo *muscular part of birds' stomach, gizzard*:véntr- *belly* m/IIIb; navíʎʎo *ship, fleet, navigable canal*:náv- *ship* f/IIIb.

   ii. On verbs, instrument, place or result of action, in the following formed on:

     A. Root, in skandíʎʎo *measure of broken rock*:skánd- *measure* II/ísK/W; ǧačíʎʎo *pallet*:ǧáč- *lie* IIIa/Irr/S[1]; naskɔndíʎʎo *hiding-place*:naskóndhide IIIb/Reg/S[1, 2]; vinčíʎʎo *withe*:vinč[+] *bind*.

B. Non-Finite C, in ripostíʎʎo *hiding-place*:ripón- *put away* IV/Irr /S[1, 2].

p. ⁺úʎʎ- m/IIb, with the following meanings:

    i. On nouns, diminutive or contemptuous, in avancúʎʎo *little remainder*: avánc- *remainder* m/IIb; čespúʎʎo *clump of bushes*:čésp- *bush* m/IIb.

    ii. On verbs, result of action (contemptuous), based on:

        A. Root, in miskúʎʎo meskúʎʎo *mixture* (:mis$K$⁺):mésK- *mix* IIIb/ Reg/W.

        B. Non-Finite C (Alternant), in rimasúʎʎo *left-overs*:rimás-:rimán- *remain* IIIa/Irr/S[1, 2].

q. ⁺ísm- *-ism* m/IIb:

    i. On substantives, in many nouns, such as the following based on:

        A. Adjectives, of types:

           I. I–II: aɲɲostičísmo *agnosticism*:aɲɲóstiK- *agnostic*; albinísmo *albinism*:albín- *albino*; plebeísmo *plebeian act, speech*:plebé- *plebeian*; etc.

           II. IIIb: dualísmo *dualism*:dúal- *dual*; kɔmunísmo *communism*: kɔmún- *common*; racionalísmo *rationalism*:racionál- *rational*; etc.

        B. Nouns, as in the following based on nouns of types:

           I. f/Ia: animísmo *animism*:ánim- *soul*; eufɛmísmo *euphemism*: eufɛmí- *euphemy*; etc.

           II. m/Ib: akrobatísmo *acrobaticism*:akróbat- *acrobat*; dogmatísmo *dogmatism*:dogmat:dógm- *dogma*; etc.

           III. m/IIb: dialettísmo *dialectalism*:dialétt- *dialect*, evɛmɛrísmo *Euhemerism*:evémɛr- *Euhemerus*; feti(č)čísmo *fetishism*:fetíčč- *fetish*; etc.

           IV. m/IIIb: affarísmo *affairism*:affár- *affair*; alkɔlísmo *alcoholism*: álkɔl- *alcohol*; platɔnísmo *Platonism*:platón- *Plato*; etc.

           V. f/IIIb: abɔlicɔnísmo *abolitionism*:abɔlición- *abolition*; esibicɔnísmo *exhibitionism*:esibitión- *exhibition*; espansɔnísmo *expansionism*:espansión- *expansion*; etc.

           VI. m/IVd: makiavɛllísmo *Machiavellism*:makiavéll- *Machiavelli*.

        C. Substantival bases: egoísmo *egotism*:ego⁺ *ego*; fanatísmo *fanaticism*: fanat⁺:fan⁺ *temple*.

    ii. On pronouns, in altruísmo *altruism*:altrúi *someone else*.

    iii. On adverbs, as in apriorísmo *apriorism*:apriór- *a priori* adv/IV.

    iv. On verbs I/Reg/W, in illuminísmo *enlightenment* (18*th* c.):illúmin- *illuminate*; trasformísmo *transformism* (*Italian politics*):trasfórm- *transform*.

    v. The suffix is preceded by:

        A. ⁺e⁺ in assɛnteísmo *absenteeism*:assént- *absent* adj/IIIb.

        B. ⁺ač⁺ in iotačísmo *iotacism*:iót- *iota* m/Id; etačísmo *etacism*:éteta m/Id; itačísmo *itacism*:ít- *ita* m/Id.

        C. ⁺tač⁺ in rotačismo *rhotacism*:ró⁽ˣ⁾ *rho* m/VId.

        D. ⁺t⁺ in egotísmo *egoism*:ego⁺ *ego*.

r. ⁺ábr- *-abrum*, in kandɛlábro *candelabrum*:kandél- *candle* f/Ia; vɛntilábro *ventilator*:véntil- *ventilate* I/Reg/W.

s. ⁺úr- m/IIb, with the following meanings:

i. On nouns, *-ide*, as in the following based on nouns of:

A. m/IIb: brɔmúro *bromide*:brɔ́m- *brome*; klɔrúro *chloride*:klɔ́r- *chlor-(ine)*; fluɔrúro *fluoride*:fluɔ́r- *fluor*; fosfúro *phosphide*:fɔsf⁺:fɔ́sfɔr- *phosphor*; sɔlfúro *sulphide*:sólf- *sulphur*; etc.

B. Nominal bases: čanúro *cyanide*:čan⁺ *cyan-*; karbúro *carbide*:karb⁺ *carb-*; etc.

ii. On verbs I/Reg/W, *place for* . . ., in abitúro *cottage, miserable lodging*: ábit- *live, dwell*; trattúro *pasture land*:trátt- *treat*.

t. ⁺mént- *-ment, action or effect of* . . . m/IIb:

i. Alone, only on verbs:

A. On root or verbal base, in segménto *segment*:ség- *saw, cut* I/Reg/W; fragménto frammén to⁴ *fragment*:frag⁺ *break*; and with /u/ > /ɔ/, in argɔménto *argument*:argu- *argue* II/ísK/W.

B. On Stem A (with TV /e/ > /i/), in many derivatives, such as the following based on verbs of conjugations:

I. I: abbakiaménto *beating down*:abbáki- *beat down*; abbaiaménto *barking*:abbái- *bark*; abbɔnaménto *subscription*:abbɔ́n- *subscribe* (refl.); andaménto *gait*:and- *go*; etc.

II. II/Reg: kɔmpartiménto *compartment*:kɔmpárt- *divide*; sentiménto *feeling*:sént- *feel*; etc.

III. II/ísK: abbɛlliménto *embellishment*:abbɛll- *embellish*; finiménto *finishing*:fin- *finish*; smarriménto *daze*:smarr- *daze*; etc.

IV. IIIa: ǧačiménto *deposit* (*e.g. of minerals*):ǧáč- *lie*; sediménto *sediment*:sɛd- *sit*; tɛniménto *possession*:tɛn- *hold*.

V. IIIb: abbattiménto *felling, dejection*:abbátt- *deject*; akkɔʎʎiménto *reception*:akkóʎʎ- *receive*; kɔnoššiménto *knowledge*:kɔnósK- *know*; moviménto *movement*:mɔʋ- *move*; etc.

ii. Preceded by:

A. ↓ (of final C or /sK/), on root or verbal base in dekreménto *decrement, decrease*:dekrésK- *decrease* IIIb/Reg/S¹; inkreménto *increment, increase*: inkrésK- *cause regret* (*increase*) IIIb/Reg/S¹; tɔrménto *torment*:tɔ́rK- *twist* IIIb/Reg/S¹, ²; fɔménto *fomentation*:fɔm⁺ *foment*.

B. ⁺a⁺ in kasaménto *large (apartment) house*:ḳás- *house* f/Ia.

C. ⁺u⁺ in nokuménto *harm*:nɔč- *harm* IIIb/Irr/S¹; dokuménto *document*:dɔK⁺ *teach* quasi-III.

u. ⁺ʹiK- *-yx, -ice, -ex* m/IIIb:

i. On nouns or nominal bases, in láttiče *milk-like juice*:látt- *milk* m/IIIb; mátriK- *matrix*:matr⁺:mádr- *mother* f/IIIb; bómbiče *bombyx*:bomb⁺ *bumbling noise*.

ii. On verb IIIb/Reg, in vértiče *vertex, summit*:vért- *turn*.

w. ⁺ám- collective (often pejorative), *-amen* m/IIIb:

i. On nouns, as in the following based on nouns of type:

A. f/Ia: bestiáme *animals*:bésti- *animal*; čarpáme *collection of old junk*:čárp- *junk*; pietráme *collection of stones*:piétr- *stone*; etc.

⁴ Cf. §1.222.2.k, and fn. 7 to Chapter 1.

B. m/IIb: kapɛlláme *coloring or quality of hair*:kapέll- *hair*; kiodáme *collection of nails*:kiód- *nail*; kɔntadináme *rabble of peasants*:kɔntadín- *peasant*; etc.

C. m/IIc: ossáme *heap of bones*:óss- *bone*.

D. f/IIIb: bottáme *cooperage, collection of barrels*:bótt- *barrel, cask*; karnáme *mass of putrefied flesh*:kárn- *meat, flesh*; etc.

E. Nominal base: karkáme *carcass*:kark⁺ *dead flesh*.

ii. On adj/I–II: letáme *fertilizer*:lɛt⁺:liét- *joyous, (fertile)*.

iii. On verbs I/Reg/W: brulikáme *swarming, crawling mass or crowd*: brúlik- *swarm, crawl*; dettáme *dictamen, dictate*:détt- *dictate*; kaskáme *refuse, cuttings*:kásk- *fall*; legáme *bond*:lég- *bind*; etc.

y. ⁺úm- *-umen, collection of . . ., matter having characteristics or taste of . . .* (pej.) m/IIb:

i. On substantives, as in the following based on:

A. Adjectives, of types:

I. I–II: ačidúme *acid matter, acid taste*:áčid- *acid*; agrúme *bitter taste or thing, citrus fruit*:ágr- *bitter*; bastardúme *collection of bastards, bastard things*:bastárd- *bastard*; vekkiúme *old junk*:vékki- *old*; etc.

II. IIIb: vɛrdúme *green parts of plants, excessive green*:vérd- *green*.

B. Nouns, of types:

I. f/Ia: čɛrúme *cerumen, ear-wax*:čér- *wax*; pastúme *chicken-feed*: pást- *paste*; etc.

II. m/IIb: ačetúme *vinegary matter*:ačét- *vinegar*; bagaʎʎúme *heap of baggage*:bagáʎʎ- *baggage*; bečɛrúme *bunch of oafs*:béčɛr- *oaf*; etc.

III. m/IIIb: salúme *salt foods*:sál- *salt*; etc.

ii. On verb IIIb/Reg/S¹, ², in vɔlúme *volume*:vɔlu⁺:vólG- *turn*.

z. ⁺'in- abstract m/IIIb:

i. On nouns, in túrbine *whirlwind*:túrb- *id.* m/IIb; vérmine *worm* (archaic or substandard):vérm- *worm* m/IIIb.

ii. On verbs, in órdine *order*:ɔrd- *put in order, arrange* II/ísK/W; téndine *tendon*:ténd- *stretch* IIIb/Reg/S¹, ².

iii. The suffix is preceded by:

A. ⁺éd⁺ in the following based on:

I. Adjectives or adjectival bases of types:

α. I–II: raučédine *hoarseness*:rauč⁺:ráuk- *hoarse*; salsédine *saltiness*:sáls- *salty*; makrédine *thinness*:mákr- *thin*.

β. IIIb: akrédine *acridity, sharpness*:áKr- *sharp, bitter*; pinguédine *fatness*:píngu- *fat*.

γ. Bases: putrédine *rottenness*:putr⁺ *rotten*; tɔrpédine *torpedo*: tɔrp⁺ *id.*

II. Verbal base, in urédine *(plant) rust*:ur⁺ *burn*.

B. ⁺id⁺ in libídine *libido, unbridled desire*:lib⁺ *desire*.

C. ⁺ud⁺ in the following based on Adjs/I–II: desuetúdine *desuetude*:desuét- *unaccustomed*; kɔnsuetúdine *habit, custom*:kɔnsuét- *accustomed*; inkuietúdine *inquietude*:inkuiét- *restless*.

D. ⁺etúd⁺ in mansuetúdine *docility*:mansu⁺:máns- *docile*; valetúdine *health*:vál- *be in health* IIIa/Irr/S¹, ².

E. ⁺itúd⁺ in the following nouns based on:

I. Adjectives, of types:

a. I–II: altitúdine *altitude*:ált- *high*; amplitúdine *amplitude*:ámpl- *ample*; attitúdine *aptitude*:átt- *apt*; čɛrtitúdine *certitude*:čɛ́rt- *certain*; gratitúdine *gratitude*:grát- *grateful*; latitúdine *latitude*:lát- *broad*; lɔnǧitúdine *longitude*:lɔnG:lúng- *long*; mɔltitúdine *multitude*:mólt- *many*; sɔlitúdine *solitude*:sól- *alone*.

β. IIIb: fɔrtitúdine *fortitude*:fórt- *strong*; similitúdine *similitude*:símil- *similar*; turpitúdine *turpitude*:túrp- *shameful*.

II. Adverbial base, in vičissitúdine *vicissitude*:vičiss⁺ *vicissim*.

III. Verb, on Non-Finite C (alternant), in attitúdine *attitude*:att⁺: aǧ- *act* II/ísK/W.

F. ⁺ǧ⁺ in vɔráǧine *abyss*:⁺vór- *devour* I/Reg/W.

G. ⁺áǧǧ⁺ (in general, with pejorative connotation), in nouns based on:

I. Adjectives, of types:

a. I–II: ačči diosáǧǧine *slothfulness*:aččidióso *slothful*; astrusáǧǧine *abstruse discourse*:astrús- *abstruse*; lɛntáǧǧine *slowness*:lɛ́nt- *slow*; ridikɔláǧǧine *ridiculous behavior*:ridíkɔl- *ridiculous*; sfaččatáǧǧine *shamelessness*:sfaččát- *shameless*; stupidáǧǧine *stupidity*:stúpid- *stupid*; etc.

β. IId: dappokáǧǧine *worthlessness*:dappók- *worthless*.

γ. IIId: dabbɛnáǧǧinc *stupidity*:dabbén- *stupid, kindly, well-intentioned*.

II. Nouns, as in asináǧǧine *asinity*:ásin- *ass* m/IIb; fančulláǧǧine *childishness*:fančull- *child* m/IIb; lɔmbáǧǧine *lumbago*:lómb- *loin* m/IIb; etc.

III. Verbs I/Reg/W in kaskáǧǧine *drowsiness, weariness*:kásk- *fall*; traskuráǧǧine *neglect*:traskúr- *neglect*.

H. ⁺assáǧǧ⁺ in buassáǧǧine *doltishness, awkwardness*:bú- *ox* m/IIIb.

J. ⁺íǧǧ⁺ in lɛntíǧǧine *lentigo, freckle*:lént- *lens, lentil* f/IIIb.

K. ⁺úǧǧ⁺ in salsúǧǧine *saltiness*:sáls- *salty* adj/I–II; testúǧǧine *tortoise*:tést- *(shell), head* f/Ia.

L. ⁺íǧ⁺ in the following, based on:

I. Nouns, in impetíǧine *impetigo*:ímpet- *impetus* m/IIb; sɛrpíǧine *serpigo*:sérp- *snake* f or m/IIIb.

II. Verbs, in skaturíǧine *spring*:skatur- *burst forth (of water)* II/ísK/W; kalíǧine *dense steam, cloud*:kál- *be hot* (archaic) IIIa/Reg; pruríǧine *itching*:prur⁺:prúd- *itch* IIIb/Reg; vɛrtíǧine *vertigo, dizziness*:vért- *turn*; ɔríǧine *origin*:ɔri⁺ *arise*; ulíǧine *dampness*:ul⁺ *be damp*.

M. ⁺úǧ⁺ in albúǧine *albugo, whitish spot on cornea*:álb- *white* adj/I–II; lanúǧine *lanugo, down*:lán- *wool* f/Ia; fɛrrúǧine *iron-salt, rust*:férr- *iron* m/IIb; kalúǧǧine *down*:kal⁺ *id*.

aa. ⁺ón- m/IIIb, with the following meanings:

i. On substantives, normally augmentative, as in the following based on:

A. Adjectives: allegróne *continually cheerful person*:allégr- *cheerful*

I–II; biəndóne *big blond person*:biónd- *blond* I–II; vɛrdóne *heavy green (color)*: vérd- *green* IIIb.

B. Nouns, e.g. of the following types:

i. f/Ia: akuilóne *big eagle, kite, strong cross-mountain wind*:ákuil- *eagle*; arančóne *orange color*:aránč- *orange*; barbóne *big beard*:bárb- *beard*; bɛrtuččóne *big ape*:bɛrtúčč- *ape*; dənnóne *big woman*:dónn- *woman*; kartóne *carton, heavy paper*:kárt- *paper*; pilóne *pilaster, column*:píl- *pillar*; etc. etc.

ii. m/IIb: artikəlóne *big article*:artíkəl- *article*; goččəlóne *big drop*: góččəl- *drop*; libróne *big book*:líbr- *book*; etc.

iii. m/IIIb: animalóne *big animal*:animál- *animal*; padróne *boss, master*:pádr- *father*; pəntóne *pontoon*:pónt- *bridge*; etc.

iv. f/IIIb: assóne *big board*:áss- *board*; vəlpóne *crafty old fox*:vólp- *fox*; etc.

But in a few post-substantival derivatives, the meaning of this suffix is *one acting in connection with . . .*, as in baióne *jester*:bái- *jest* f/Ia; bagaʎʎóne *soldier or slave in charge of baggage*:bagáʎʎ- *baggage* m/IIb; pedóne *footsoldier, pedestrian*:ped⁺:piéd- *foot* m/IIIb.

ii. On verbs, agent (often pejorative), almost exclusively on verbs of I/Reg/W, as in abbərdóne *brazen-faced person*:abbórd- *approach*; abbərraččóne *bungler*:abbərračč- *bungle*; aǧǧeǧǧóne *muddler*:aǧǧéǧǧ- *muddle*; armeǧǧóne *Macher*:arméǧǧ- *bustle*; bestɛmmióne *continual swearer*:bestémmi- *blaspheme*; etc. etc.   Result of action is indicated in a few of these derivatives, as in barbikóne *main root*:bárbik- *take root*; kastróne *eunuch, gelding*:kástr- *castrate*. The base is of a type other than I/Reg/W in kiedóne *continual asker*:kiéd- *ask* IIIb/Reg/S[1, 2].

iii. On verbal phrase, in fànnullóne *good-for-nothing*:fánnúlla *does nothing*.

iv. The suffix is preceded by:

A. ⁺č⁺ in kərənčóna *big crown*:kərənčón⁺ *id.*:kərón- *crown* f/Ia.

B. ⁺i⁺ in the following, based on:

i. Nouns, of types:

α. f/Ia: kodióne *coccyx of bird*:kód- *tail*; lampióne *street-lamp, headlight*:lámp- *lamp* (archaic).

β. m/IIb: babbióne *big blockhead*:bább- onomatopoetic; kampióne *champion*:kámp- *field (of battle)*.

ii. Num/IIIc, in mi(l)lióne *million* (:mil⁺):míll- *1000*.

iii. Verbs, in vibrióne *vibrio, a kind of bacterium*:víbr- *vibrate* I/Reg/W; paššóne *abundance of food*:pásK- *feed, graze* IIIb/Reg/W.

C. ⁺okk⁺ in pačokkóne *fat, peaceful person*:páč- *peace* f/IIIb.

D. ⁺al⁺ in brakalóne *man whose pants are always falling down*:brák- *breeches* f/Ia.

E. ⁺iɲɲ⁺ in pediɲɲóne *chilblain on feet*:ped⁺:piéd- *foot*.

F. ⁺ar⁺ in ləngaróne *longitudinal beam*:lənG⁺:lúng- *long* adj/I–II.

G. ⁺ɛr⁺ ⁺ett⁺ in alɛróne alettóne *aileron*:ál- *wing* f/Ib.

H. ⁺c⁺ in villancóne *big boor*:villán- *boorish* adj/I–II.

J. ⁺acc⁺ in akkuaccóne *short, hard rain*:ákku- *water, rain* f/Ia.

bb. ⁺ór- *quality of* . . . m/IIIb, in the following based on:

    i. Substantives:

        A. Adjectives, of types:

            I. I–II: albóre *whiteness, dawn*:álb- *white*; alidóre *dryness, aridity*: álid- *arid*; amaróre *bitterness (of slightly turned wine)*:amár- *bitter*; aššuttóre *dryness*:aššútt- *dry*; ǧallóre *yellowness*:ǧáll- *yellow*; kiaróre *brightness*:kiár- *clear, bright*; malóre *sickness, ill*:mál- *bad*; rossóre *redness*:róss- *red*; sekkóre *dryness*:sékk- *dry*; spessóre *thickness*:spéss- *thick*; umidóre *dampness, humidity*: úmid- *humid*.

           II. IIIb: dɔlčóre *sweetness*:dólč- *sweet*.

        B. Noun f/Ia, in kremóre *cream of tartar*:krém- *cream*.

        C. Substantival bases, in kruóre *flowing blood*:kru⁺ *blood*; likuóre *liquor*:liku⁺ *fluid*; livóre *lividness*:liv⁺ *livid*; rigóre *rigor*:riG⁺ *stiff*; umóre *humor, wetness*:um⁺ *damp*.

    ii. Verbs:

        A. Those listed in §3.112.1.a.ii.A.

        B. Also the following:

ám- *love*		dɔl- *hurt*	
⁺báʎʎ- *dazzle*		tɛn- *hold*	IIIa/Irr/S¹
brúč- *burn*	I/Reg/W	stríd- *be strident* IIIb/Reg	
frízʒ- *smart*		prúd- *itch*	IIIb/Reg/W
kiám- *call*		víG- *be in strength*	
súd- *sweat*		árd- *burn* IIIb/Reg/S¹, ²	
bóll- *boil*	II/Reg/W	fraG⁺ *break, clatter*	
sént- *smell*		od⁺ (: ɔl⁺) *smell*	quasi-III
sop- *put to sleep* II/ísK/W		pud⁺ *be ashamed*	
kál- *be hot* IIIa/Reg/S¹		tɛrr⁺ *frighten*	

Thus, for the verbs listed in §3.112.1.a.ii.A: languóre *languor*; stupóre *stupor*; tepóre *tepor*; timóre *fear*; sapóre *flavor*; valóre *strength, worth*; fɛrvóre *fervor*; fulgóre *splendor*; algóre *extreme cold*; fetóre *stench*; madóre *wetness*; nitóre *brightness*; ɔrróre *horror*; pallóre *pallor*; rankóre *rancor*; skuallóre *squalor*; tɔrpóre *dullness, torpor*; tumóre *tumor*; turgóre *turgidity*. For those given in the immediately preceding list: amóre *love*; baʎʎóre *dazzling light*; bručóre *smarting, itching*; frizʒóre *pricking, smarting*; kiamóre *clamor*; sudóre *sweat*; bɔllóre *boiling*; sɛntóre *stench*; sopóre *sleep*; kalóre *heat*; dɔlóre *pain*; tɛnóre *tenor*; stridóre *strident noise*; prudóre *itching*; vigóre *vigor*; ardóre *ardor*; fragóre *clatter, uproar*; odóre *odor*; pudóre *modesty*; tɛrróre *terror*.

    cc. ⁺ór- -*or*, agent m/IIIb.[5]

    i. Alone, only on verbs:

        A. On root, in the following formed on verbs of types:

            I. I/Reg/W: kantóre *singer*:kánt- *sing*; kɔnfessóre *confessor*:kɔnféss- *confess*; professóre *professor*:proféss- *profess*.

---

[5] Differentiated formally from the ⁺ór- abstract m/IIIb discussed in the preceding subsection (bb), in that most nouns formed with ⁺ór- suffix of agent can form a feminine in either ⁺íče, ⁺éssa or ⁺a, whereas those with the ⁺ór- of sec. bb never do.

  ii. II/ísK/W: čɛnsóre *censor*:čɛns- *take a census*.

  iii. IIIb/Reg/S[1, 2]: riflettóre *reflector*:riflétt- *reflect*.

  B. On Non-Finite C or alternant, in a great many derivatives, such as the following formed on verbs of types:

   i. I/Reg/W: abbaiatóre *slanderer*:abbái- *bark, slander*; abbɔrraččatóre bungler:abbɔrračč- *bungle*; abbreviatóre *abbreviator*:abbrévi- *abbreviate*; abusatóre *abuser*:abús- *abuse*; amatóre *lover, amateur*:ám- *love*; etc. etc. etc.

   ii. II/Reg/W: dɔrmitóre *sleeper*:dórm- *sleep*; kopritóre *slater, tiler, thatcher*:kɔpr- kópr- *cover*; mɛntitóre *liar*:mént- *lie*; etc.

   iii. II/ísK/W: abɔlitóre *abolisher*:abɔl- *abolish*; kostruttóre *constructor*:kostrutt[+]:kostru- *construct*; nutritóre *nourisher*:nutr- *nourish*; traditóre *traitor*:trad- *betray*; etc. etc.

   iv. IIIb: adduttóre *adductor* (muscle):addutt[+]:addúK- *adduce*; antečessóre *predecessor*:antečɛss[+]:antečéd- *precede*; aššensóre *elevator*:aššens[+]:aššénd- *ascend*; kultóre *cultivator*:kult[+]:kól- *cultivate*; motóre *motor*:mɔt[+]:mɔv- *move*; rettóre *rector*:réGG- *direct*; etc.

   v. IV: datóre *giver*:dá- *give*; fattóre *maker*:fáč- *make*; impostóre *impostor*:impón- *impose*; etc.

  ii. Preceded by:

   A. [+]d[+] (with TV /e/ > /i/) in čurmadóre *charlatan*, (archaic) *magician*:čúrm- *enchant* I/Reg/W; trovadóre *troubadour* (archaic):tróv- *find, create poetry* I/Reg/W; kɔrridóre *racer*:kórr- *run* IIIb/Reg/S[1, 2]; skɔrridóre *runner*:skórr- *run* IIIb/Reg/S[1, 2].

   B. [+]t[+] in the following, based on:

    i. Root, in sostitutóre *substituter*:sostitu- *substitute* II/ísK/W.

    ii. Stem A (with TV /e/ > /i/), as in the following based on verbs of:

     α. II/Reg/S[1, 2]: apritóre *opener*:ápr- *open*.

     β. IIIa: riveditóre *reviewer, corrector*:rivéd- *review*; sostɛnitóre *sustainer*:sostɛn- *sustain*.

     γ. IIIb: fɔnditóre *melter, fuser*:fónd- *melt, fuse*; mɔrditóre *biter*:mórd- *bite*; pɛrditóre *loser*:pérd- *lose*; pɔrǧitóre *offerer*:pórG- *offer*; prɛnditóre *taker*:prénd- *take*; prɔmovitóre *promoter*:promɔv- *promote*; rakkɔʎʎitóre *collector*:rakkóʎʎ- *collect*; etc. etc.

     δ. IV: dičitóre *speaker, orator*:díK- *say*; fačitóre *maker*:fáč- *make*; rifačitóre *remaker, redoer*:rifáč- *remake, redo*.

     ε. Verbal bases (quasi-III): ǧɛnitóre *parent*:ǧɛn[+] *beget*; mɔlitóre *miller*:mɔl[+] *mill, grind*; mɔnitóre *monitor*:mɔn[+] *warn*; etc.

   c. [+]at[+], in settatóre *sectarian*:sétt- *sect* f/Ia.

  dd. [+]íč- *ix*, feminine agent f/IIIb:

   i. On nouns:

   A. On a great many nouns formed with the suffix ór- -*or*, agent m/IIIb (discussed in the preceding section, §3.114.2.cc), with /or/ > /r/:e.g. abbaiatríče *slanderer* (f.):abbaiatór- *id.* (m.); abbɔrraččatríče *bungler* (f.):abbɔrraččatór- *id.* (m.); abbreviatríče *abbreviator* (f.):abbreviatór- *id.* (m.); traditríče *traitress*:traditór- *traiter*; lettríče *feminine reader*:lettór- *reader*; etc. etc.

B. On nouns f/IIIb: matríče *matrix*:matr⁺:mádr- *mother*; naríče *nostril*:nár- *id*.

ii. On verb: nutríče *nurse*:nutr- *nourish* II/Reg or ísK/W.

ee. ⁺△ón- *-ion, action of* . . . f/IIIb:

i. Alone, in kancóne *song*:kánt- *sing* I/Reg/W.

ii. The last two phonemes of the suffix are preceded by ⁺i⁺, in the following based on:

A. Substantives: kaucióne *caution (bail, security)*:káut- *cautious* adj/ I–II; kɔmunióne *communion*:kɔmún- *common* adj/IIIb; mɛncióne *mention*: mént- *mind* f/IIIb.

ii. Verbs, on:

α. Root, in adocióne *adoption*:adótt- *adopt* I/Reg/W; opinióne *opinion*:opín- *opine* I/Reg/W; reğóne *region*:reG⁺:réGG- *rule* IIIb/Reg/S¹, ²; alluvióne *alluvion*:alluv⁺ *flood*.

β. Non-Finite C or alternant, in a great many derivatives: e.g. abbreviacióne *abbreviation*:abbrévi- *abbreviate* I/Reg/W; abdikacióne *abdication*:ábdik- *abdicate* I/Reg/W; abɛrracióne *aberration*:abérr- *be aberrant* I/ Reg/W; particióne *partition*:párt- *divide* II/Reg/W; abɔlicióne *abolition*:abɔl- *abolish* II/ísK/W; kɔnčecióne *conception*:kɔnčett⁺:kɔnčep- *conceive* II/ísK/W; čessióne *cession*:čɛss⁺:čéd- *cede* IIIb/Reg/W; abrasióne *abrasion*:abrád- *abrade* IIIb/Reg/S¹, ²; affissióne *affixation*:affíGG- *affix* IIIb/Reg/S¹, ²; dicióne *diction*:ditt⁺:díK- *say* IV/Irr/S¹, ²; facióne *faction*:fáč- *make, do* IV/Irr/S¹, ²; etc. etc.

ii. The extended suffix thus formed, ⁺△ión-, is further preceded by:

A. ⁺ğ⁺, in nouns based on Stem A of the following verbs:

fát- *enchant*		piánt- *plant*	
frég- *rub*		pót- *prune*	
gónfi- *inflate*		sémin- *sow*	I/Reg/W
impíkk- *hang (execute)*		uččéll- *hunt birds*	
inkánt- *enchant*	I/Reg/W	guarn- *furnish*	
káčč- *hunt*		imband- *prepare (food)*	II/ísK/W
líb- *pour*		stá- *stand* IV/Irr/S¹	
pésk- *fish*			

Thus: fatağóne *enchantment*; fregağóne *(medicinal) rubbing*; gɔnfiağóne *inflation*; impikkağóne *hanging*; inkantağóne *enchantment*; kaččağóne *venison*; libağóne *libation*; peskağóne *catch of fish*; potağóne *pruning*; sɛminağóne *sowing*; uččéll-ağóne *bird-hunting*; guarniğóne *garrison*; imbandiğóne *preparation of food, prepared food*; stağóne *season*.

B. ⁺ağ⁺ in the following based on nouns: fiɛnağóne *haying*:fién- *hay* m/IIb; karnağóne *complexion*:kárn- *flesh* f/IIIb.

C. ⁺it⁺ in dɛnticióne *dentition*:dént- *tooth* m/IIIb.

ff. '△i- *-ity, quality of* . . . f/IIId:

i. On adj/I–II: barbárie *barbarity*:bárbar- *barbarian*.

ii. On verbal base: kɔnğérie *congeries*:kɔngɛr⁺ *congest*; proğénie *progeny*: prɔğɛn⁺ *procreate*; spéče *species*:spɛk⁺ *look*.

iii. The suffix is preceded by $^+$ɛr$^+$ in tɛmpérie (*clear*) *state of the weather*: témp- *weather* m/IIb.

   gg. $^+$á^x *-ty, quality of* . . . f/VId:

     Alone, in vɛnustá^x *beauty*:vɛnúst- *beautiful* adj/I–II; etá^x *age*:et$^+$ *id.*

    ii. Preceded by:

       A. $^+$t$^+$, in the following based on adjectives of types:

            I. I–II, in bɛltá^x *beauty* (somewhat archaic):béll- *beautiful;* libɛrtá^x *liberty*:líbɛr- *free*; metá^x *half*:me$^+$:médi- *half, medium*; povɛrtá^x *poverty*:póvɛr- *poor*; pubɛrtá^x *puberty*:púbɛr- *adolescent*; sikurtá^x *security*:sikúr- *secure.*

           II. IIIb, in čiviltá^x *civilization*:čivil- *civil(ized)*; fedɛltá^x *faithfulness*: fedél- *faithful*; krudɛltá^x *cruelty*:krudél- *cruel*; realtá^x *reality*:reál- *real*; umiltá^x *humility*:úmil- *humble*; vɔlɔntá^x *will*:vɔlɔnt:vɔlént- *willing.*

       B. $^+$et$^+$, after adjectives of I–II ending in /i/ and also after sɔč- *associated* adj/I–II: ansietá^x *anxiety*:ánsi- *anxious*; bɔnarietá^x *affability*:bɔnári- *affable*; kapárbietá^x *stubbornness*:kapárbi-*stubborn*; notɔrietá^x *notoriety*:notóri- *notorious*; obbligatɔrietá^x *obligation* (legal term):obbligatóri- *obligatory*; pietá^x *piety*:pí- *pious*; proprietá^x *propriety, property*:própri- *own*; sacietá^x *satiety*:sáci- *satisfied, sated*; sɛrietá^x *seriousness*:séri- *serious*; sobrietá^x *sobriety*:sóbri- *sober*; sɔčetá^x *society*:sɔč- *associated*; sɔlidarietá^x *solidarity*:sɔlidári- *upholding a common cause*; šɛmpietá^x *stupidity*:šémpi- *stupid, simple*; tɛmerarietá^x *temerity*:tɛmɛrári- *overbold*; varietá^x *variety*:vári- *various.*

       C. $^+$iet$^+$, in e(b)brietá^x *ebriety, drunkenness*:έ(b)br- *drunken.*

       D. $^+$it$^+$, in many nouns based on:

           I. Adjectives, of types:

             α. I–II: ačɛrbitá^x *acerbity*:ačérb- *bitter, unripe*; ačiditá^x *acidity*: áčid- *acid*; amɛnitá^x *amenity*:amén- *pleasant*; assiduitá^x *assiduity*:assídu- *assiduous*; etc. etc.

             β. IIIb: abilitá^x *ability, skill*:ábil- *skillful*; abitabilitá^x *habitability*:abitábil- *habitable*; alakritá^x *alacrity*:álakr- alákr- *alacritous*; etc. etc.

             γ. IVd: paritá^x *parity*:pár- *equal.*

           II. Nouns, in asininitá^x *asininity*:ásin- *ass* m/IIb; autɔritá^x *authority*: autór- *author* m/IIIb.

       E. $^+$△it$^+$, after /k/, in čečitá^x *blindness*:čék- *blind* adj/I–II; kadučitá^x *caducity*:kadúk- *transient, caducous* adj/I–II.

       F. $^+$il$^+$, in skifiltá^x *persnicketiness*:skíf- *repugnant* adj/I–II.

       G. $^+$ɔl$^+$, in fakɔltá^x *faculty*:fak$^+$:fáč- *do, make* IV/Irr/S[1,2].

   3. Substantives or numerals, with:

    a. $^+$íg- *thing having characteristics of* . . . f/Ia, in lettíga *sedan-chair, stretcher* :létt- *bed* m/IIb; kuadríga *quadriga, chariot*:kuadr$^+$:kuáttr- *four* num/IId.

    b. $^+$úri- *abstract* f/Ia, in the following based on:

       i. Adj/I–II, in bɛllúria *apparent beauty*:béll- *beautiful*; bruttúria *ugly, dirty thing*:brútt- *ugly, unpleasant.*

       ii. Nouns, in lussúria *carnal desire*:lúss- *luxury* m/IIb; pɛllúria *down*: péll- *skin* f/IIIb.

       iii. Numerals, in čɛntúria *century* (*group of* 100):čént- *100* num/IId; dekúria *decuria* (*group of* 10):dɛk$^+$:diéč- *ten* num/IVd.

4. Substantives or adverbs, with:

a. ⁺ánc- -*ance, quality of being* ... f/Ia, in the following based on:

   i. Adjectives, of types:

     A. I–II, in baldánca *boldness*:báld- *bold*.

     B. IIIb, in kəmunánca *community, possession in common*:kəmún- *common*; maǧǧoránca *majority*:maǧǧór- *greater*; miʎʎoránca *betterness*:miʎʎór- *better*; minoránca *minority*:minór- *lesser*.

   ii. Nouns, of types:

     A. f/Ia, in vedovánca *widowhood*:védov- *widow*.

     B. m/IIb, in fratɛllánca *brotherhood*:fratéll- *brother*; maestránca *ensemble of master-workers*:maéstr- *master*.

     C. m/IIIb, in kostumánca *custom*:kostúm- *habit*.

   iii. Adv/III, in oltránca *outrage, excess*:óltr- *beyond*.

b. ⁺éri- -*ery* m/IIb:

   i. Alone, in the following based on nouns: battistério *baptistery*:battíst- *baptist* m/Ib; saltério *psalter*:salt⁺:sálm- *psalm* m/IIb; battério baktério *bacterium*:batt⁺ bakt⁺ *rod*; filattério *phylactery*:filatt⁺ *guard, protection*; falanstério *phalansterium*:falanst⁺ *id*.

   ii. Preceded by ⁺ič⁺, in primičério *leader (in religious brotherhood)*:prím- *first* adj/I–II.

c. ⁺ósi- -*ose* m/IIb:

   i. Alone, in destrósio *dextrose*:déstr- *right hand* adj/I–II; maltósio *maltose*:mált- *malt* m/IIb; sakkarósio *saccharose*:sakkar⁺ *sugar*; etc.

   ii. Preceded by ⁺ul⁺ in levulósio *levulose*:lev⁺ *left-hand*.

d. ⁺átt- diminutive m/IIb:

   i. Alone, in čɛrbiátto *young fawn*:čɛrbi- *stag* (archaic) m/IIb; mulátto *mulatto*:múl- *mule* m/IIb.

   ii. Preceded by ⁺iǧ⁺ in buǧigátto *dark little room*:búǧ- *empty* (archaic) adj/I–II.

e. ⁺úl- -*ule*, diminutive m/IIIb:

   i. Alone, in meẓẓúle *middle-piece (of bottom of cask)*:méẓẓ- *middle, half* adj/I–II; kanapúle *hemp-stalk*: kánap- *hemp* m/IIb; pedúle *part of sock covering foot*:pɛd⁺:piéd- *foot* m/IIIb.

   ii. Preceded by:

     A. ⁺i⁺, in grembiúle *apron*:grémb- *lap* m/IIb.

     B. ⁺occ⁺, in gorgoccúle *upper part of throat* (vulg.):górg- *throat* (archaic) f/Ia.

f. ⁺íci- -*ity, -ness* f/IIId, in kalvície *baldness*:kálv- *bald* adj/I–II; məllície *softness*:móll- *soft* adj/IIIb; kanície *hoariness, old age*:kan⁺ *white hair*.

g. ⁺0- abstract f/IVd, on nominal bases in /T⁺/, e.g. análisi *analysis*: análiT⁺ *analyt-*; diurési *diuresis*:diuréT⁺ *diuret-*; sépsi *sepsis*:sépT⁺ *sept-, poison*.

h. ⁺túˣ -*tue, -ness, quality of being* ... f/VId:

   i. Alone, in ǧovɛntúˣ *youth*:ǧovɛn⁺:ǧóvin- *young* adj/IIIb; virtúˣ *virtue, ability*:⁺vír- *man* m/IIb.

ii. Preceded by ⁺i⁺, in servitúˣ *servitude*:sérv- *servant, slave* m/IIb; skiavitúˣ *slavery*:skiáv- *slave* m/IIIb.

5. Adjectives or adverbs, with:

a. ⁺0- *science of* . . ., *thing derived from or characteristic of* . . ., *quality of being* . . . f (whether I < I–II or IIIb < IIIb), as in the following based on adjectives of types:

i. I–II: akústika *acoustics*:akústiK- *acoustic*; arǧentína *silver powder*: arǧentín- *of silver*; barkaróla *barcarolle*:barkaról- *boating, boatman*; bovína *bovine excrement*:bovín- *bovine*; fiákka *weakness*:fiákk- *weak*; kiérika *tonsure*: kiériK- *cleric(al)*; etc. etc.

ii. IIIb: autɔmóbile *auto(mobile)*:autɔmóbil- *automobile*; čeléste *celesta (musical instrument)*:čelést- *heavenly*.

iii. The suffix is preceded by ǯ in réǧǧa *palace*:réǧ- *royal* adj/I–II.

b. ⁺écc- *-ness, quality of being* . . . f/Ia, as in a(b)biettécca *abjectness*: a(b)biétt- *abject* adj/I–II; akutécca *acuteness*:akút- *acute* adj/I–II; allegrécca *joy*:allégr- *allégr- joyful* adj/I–II; ǧustécca *justness, exactness*:ǧúst- *just, exact* adj/I–II; šokkécca *foolishness*:šókk- *foolish* adj/I–II; aǧevɔlécca *ease*:aǧévɔl- *easy* adj/IIIb; etc. etc.

c. ⁺0- *abstract* m/Id, in núlla *nothing*:núll- *null* adj/I–II.

d. ⁺0- *thing having quality of* . . . m (whether II < I–II, or IIIb < IIIb), e.g. in aǧǧettívo *adjective*:aǧǧettív- *adjective* adj/I–II; assúnto *subject-matter, task*:assúnt- *assumed* adj/I–II; animále *animal*:animál- *spiritual, animal* adj/ IIIb; ballábile *piece of dance music*:ballábil- *danceable to* adj/IIIb; átto *act*:att⁺ *acted* (:aǧ- *act* II/ísK/W); etc. etc.

e. ⁺íd- *-ide* m/IIb, as in óssido *oxide*:ɔssi⁺ *oxy-, sharp*; etc.

f. ⁺órdi- *-ordium* m/IIb, in primórdio *beginning*:prím- *first* adj/I–II; esórdio *exordium*:es⁺ *ex-*.

g. ⁺ésim- *-ism* m/IIb, in the following based on:

i. Adj/I–II: kattɔličésimo *Catholicism*:kattɔlič⁺:kattóliK- *Catholic*; kristianésimo *Christianity*:kristián- *Christian*; toskanésimo *Tuscanism*:toskán- *Tuscan*; umanésimo *humanism*:umán- *human*.

ii. Adj/IIIb: protestantésimo *Protestantism*:protestánt- *Protestant*.

iii. Adjectival base: battésimo *baptism*:batt⁺ *bapt-*.

h. ⁺ádr- *one who takes* . . . m/IIb, in meʒʒádro *share-cropper*: méʒʒ- *half* adj/I–II.

j. ⁺čip- *-ceps, -ce* m/IIIb, in prínčipe *prince*:prím- *first* adj/I–II.

k. ⁺át- *-ate* m/IIIb, oṅ adj/I–II in maɲɲáte *magnate*:máɲɲ- *great*; ottimáte *optimate*:óttim- *best*; primáte *primate*:prím- *first*.

l. ⁺dót- *guardian, administrator of what is* . . . m/IIIb, in sačerdóte *priest*: sačɛr⁺:sáKr- *sacred* adj/I–II.

m. ⁺íd- *-ide* f/IIIb, as in anidríde *anhydride*:ánidr- *anhydrous* adj/I–II.

n. ⁺út- *-th, -ness* f/IIIb, in salúte *health*:sal⁺ *safe, healthy*.

o. ⁺um *-um* m/VIe, in álbum *album*:álb- *white* adj/I–II; médium (*spiritualistic*) *medium*:médi- *in the middle* adj/I–II.

6. Nouns or adverbs, with:

a. ⁺0- *feminine* f/Ia, on masculines of IIb or IIIb, as in allókka *female owl*:allókk- *owl* m/IIb; alliéva *female pupil*:alliév- *pupil* m/IIb; abbaiatóra *slanderous woman*:abbaiatór- *slanderer* m/IIIb; allegróna *continually cheerful woman*:allegrón- *continually cheerful man* m/IIIb; čičeróna *female cicerone*: čičerón- *cicerone* m/IIIb; etc. etc. Also in nouns used in exocentric phrases introduced by alla, *in the manner of* . . .: e.g. allaraffaélla *in Raphaelesque style*: raffaéll- *Raphael* m/IIb; allakaččatóra *hunter style*:kaččatór- *hunter* m/IIIb. In a few words, this ending has no specifically feminine meaning: albúmina *albumen*:albumin⁺:albúm- *white matter* m/IIIb (:álb- *white* adj/I–II); píɲɲa *pine-tree*:piɲɲ⁺:pín- *pine* m/IIb.

b. ⁺úč- abstract f/Ia, in fidúča *trust*:fid⁺:féd- *faith* f/IIIb.

c. ⁺ád- collective f/Ia, in ruǧáda *dew*:ruǧ⁺:rɔr⁺ *dew*; kɔntráda *long street*; *ward (of town, esp. Siena)*:kóntr- *opposite, against* adv/II.

d. ⁺'ad- f/Ia, in lámpad- *lamp*:lámp- *id.* (archaic) f/Ia.

e. ⁺'id- abstract f/Ia, in sóččida *share-grazing*:sóčč- *share-grazer* m/IIb.

f. ⁺úg- *-uce* f/Ia, in lattúga *lettuce*:látt- *milk* m/IIIb.

g. ⁺édi- *-edy* f/Ia, in traǧédia *tragedy*:traǧ⁺ *trag-*.

h. ⁺óffi- pejorative f/Ia (together with prefix s⁺ contemptuous), in skartóffia *(poor) paper*:kárt- *paper* f/Ia.

j. ⁺íni- *-inia* f/Ia, in lačínia *lacinia, hem of toga*:lač⁺ *cloak, coat*.

k. ⁺ékk- *place for* . . . f/Ia, in ǧudékka *ghetto, Jewish quarter*:ǧudé- *Jew* m/IIb.

l. ⁺íkk- diminutive f/Ia, in pastíkka *pastille, lozenge*:pást- *dough* f/Ia; martiníkka *hand-brake*:martín- *Martin* m/IIb.

m. ⁺astrókk- augmentative and pejorative f/Ia, in filastrókka *long, annoying series*:fíl- *row, series* f/Ia.

n. ⁺úk- diminutive f/Ia, in paʎʎúka *little bit of straw*:páʎʎ- *straw* f/Ia.

o. ⁺íll- diminutive f/Ia, in fibrílla *very thin fiber*:fíbr- *fiber* f/Ia.

p. ⁺érl- diminutive f/Ia, in postérla *postern-gate*:post⁺ *behind*.

q. ⁺émm- *land near* . . . f/Ia, in marémma *maremma, low-lying land near sea*:már- *sea* m/IIIb.

r. ⁺érm- *-erne* (augm.) f/Ia, in kasérma *barracks, caserne*:kás- *house* f/Ia.

s. ⁺ilén- *-ilena, long* . . . f/Ia, in kantiléna *long song, discourse*:kánt- *song* m/IIb.

t. ⁺'in- diminutive f/Ia, in lámina *thin metal strip*:lám- *blade* f/Ia.

u. ⁺ún- *-une, -una* f/Ia, in lagúna *lagoon*:lág- *lake* m/IIb; lakúna *lacuna*: lak⁺:lág- *lake* m/IIb; fɔrtúna *fortune*:fɔrt⁺ *chance*.

w. ⁺ángɛr- pejorative f/Ia, in poccángɛra *mud-puddle*:pócc- *puddle* f/Ia.

y. ⁺'pɛr- *-bearing* f/Ia, in puérpɛra *woman in or after childbirth*:puɛr⁺ *child*.

z. ⁺ágr- *-agra, disease connected with* . . . f/Ia, in pɛllágra *pellagra*:péll- *skin* f/IIIb; podágra *podagra*:pod⁺ *foot*.

aa. ⁺ór- *feast marked by* . . . f/Ia, in kandɛlóra *feast of Purification of Virgin* :kandél- *candle* f/Ia.

bb. ⁺étr- ⁺'etr- *-ethra* f/Ia, in urétra *uretra urethra*:ur⁺ *ur(ine)*.

cc. ⁺ás- *thing marking* . . . f/Ia, in čimása *finial, top ornament* (archit.): čím- *top, summit* f/Ia.

dd. ⁺áss- -ass(es) f/Ia, in mɛlássa molasses:mɛl⁺:miél- honey m/IIIb; karkássa carcass (esp. of thorax):kark⁺ dead flesh.

ee. ⁺éss- -ess, female . . ., wife of . . . f/Ia, on the following:

atlét- *athlete*		brigánt- *brigand*	
dúk- *duke*		dottór- *doctor*	
páp- *pope*	m/Ib	ɛlefánt- *elephant*	
poét- *poet*		ǧenɛrál- *general*	
bói- *executioner* m/Id		kónt- *count*	
avvokát- *lawyer*		mɛrkánt- *merchant*	m/IIIb
filósof- *philosopher*		óst- *host, innkeeper*	
gámbɛr- *crab*	m/IIb	pitón- *Python*	
médiK- *doctor*		prínčip- *prince*	
órk- órk- *giant*		professór- *professor*	
sɔnétt- *sonnet*		sačɛrdót- *priest*	

podest⁺:podestá⁺ *mayor* m/VId
(ab)bad⁺ *abbot*

Thus: atletéssa *female athlete*; dukéssa *duchess*; papéssa *she-pope*; poetéssa *poetess*; boiéssa *cruel woman*; avvokatéssa *female lawyer*; filosoféssa *woman philosopher* (ironical); medikéssa *woman doctor*; ɔrkéssa *giantess*; sɔnettéssa *caudate sonnet*; brigantéssa *brigand's wife, moll*; dottɔréssa *blue-stocking*; ɛlefantéssa *she-elephant*; ǧenɛraléssa *woman general, general's wife*; kɔntéssa *countess*; mɛrkantéssa *woman merchant*; ostéssa *innkeeper's wife*; pitɔnéssa *oracle, witch*; prinčipéssa *princess*; professɔréssa *woman professor, blue-stocking*; sačɛrdotéssa *priestess*; podestéssa *mayor's wife*; (ab)badéssa *abbess*.

ff. ⁺ét- *grove of . . ., land planted with . . .* f/Ia, in the following based on nouns m/IIb: ačɛréta *maple-plantation*:áčɛr- *maple*; albɛréta *land planted with trees*:álbɛr- *tree*; čɛrréta *oak-grove*:čérr- *a kind of oak*; kuɛrčéta *oak-grove*:kuérč- *oak-tree*; ɔlivéta *olive-grove* (rare):ɔlív- *olive-tree*; pinéta *pine-grove*:pín- *pine-tree*.

gg. ⁺ést- *(bad) state of . . .* f/Ia, in tɛmpésta *tempest*:témp- *weather* m/IIb.

hh. ⁺átt- *diminutive* f/Ia, in kulátta *breech (of gun), seat (of pants)*:kúl- *arse* m/IIb.

ii. ⁺óst- *abstract* f/Ia, in batósta *blow*:bat⁺ *stick, blow*.

jj. ⁺árk- -arch m/Ib:

i. Alone, e.g. in mɔnárka *monarch*:mɔn⁺ *one, mon-*.

ii. Preceded by ⁺i⁺, in ɛresiárka *heresiarch*:ɛresí- *heresy* f/Ia; patriárka *patriarch*:patr⁺:pádr- *father* m/IIIb.

kk. ⁺óm- -oma m/Ib: e.g. fibróma *fibroma*:fíbr- *fiber* f/Ia; aróma *aroma*:ar⁺ *odor*; karčinóma *carcinoma*:karčin⁺ *carcin-*; leukóma *leukoma*:leuK⁺ *white*; sarkóma *sarcoma*:sark⁺ *flesh*; trakóma *trachoma*: trak⁺ *trach-*; etc.

ll. ⁺ém- -eme m/IIb: e.g. glosséma *glosseme*:glóss- *gloss* f/Ia; filoséma *philosophical formula*:filósof- *philosopher* m/IIb; ɛritéma *freckle*:ɛrit⁺ *red, eryth-*; fɔnéma *phoneme*:fɔn⁺ *sound*; mɔrféma *morpheme*:mɔrf⁺ *morph-, form*; patéma *(inner) suffering*:pat⁺ *suffering*; postéma *accumulation of pus*:post⁺ *pus*; teɔréma *theorem*:teɔr⁺ *theor(y)*; etc.

mm. ⁺ásm- -asm(a), in fantásma phantasm:fant⁺ fancy; miásma miasma: mi⁺ mi-.

nn. ⁺ísm- -ism m/Ib, in aneurísma aneurism:aneur⁺ aneur-; prísma prism: pri⁺ prime.

oo. ⁺t- agent m/Ib, in náuta sailor:nau⁺:náv- ship f/IIIb.

pp. ⁺át- -ade m/Ib, in kamɛráta comrade:kámɛr- room f/Ia.

qq. ⁺ít- -ite m/Ib, as in the following based on nouns of type:

i. m/Ib: barnabíta Barnabite:bárnab- Barnaby; etc.

ii. m/IIb: čɛnobíta cenobite:čɛnóbi- monastery; ɛrɛmíta hermit:ɛrɛm- hermitage, solitary place; sɛrvíta Servite:sérv- servant; etc.

iii. m/IIIb: minɔríta Minorite:minór- lesser person.

iv. f/IIIb: sɛlɛníta inhabitant of the moon:sɛlén- Selene, moon.

v. m/IVd: levíta Levite:lév- Levi.

vi. f/IVd: sibaríta Sybarite:síbar- Sybaris.

vii. m/VId: ǧesuíta Jesuit:ǧesúˣ Jesus; kamíta Hamite:kám Ham; sɛmíta Semite:sém Shem; etc.

rr. ást- -ast m/Ib: e.g. pɛltásta peltast:pélt- light shield f/Ia; čineásta one interested in movies:číne movies m/IIId; ɛntusiásta enthusiast:ɛntusi⁺ enthusi- (asm); ǧinnásta gymnast:ǧinn⁺ gymn-; pedɛrásta pederast:pedɛr⁺:ped⁺ child.

ss. ⁺ó(t)t- lover of . . . m/Ib, in patrió(t)ta patriot:pátri- fatherland f/Ia.

tt. ⁺0- tree bearing . . . m (IIb < Ia or IIb, IIIb < IIIb), on fruit-names (of f/Ia, m/IIb or m/IIIb), as in the following tree-names of:

i. m/IIb, based on fruit-names of:

A. f/Ia: albáno Alban grape-vine:albán- Alban grape; albikókko apricot-tree:albikókk- apricot; aránčo orange tree:aránč- orange; banáno banana-tree: banán- banana; kastáɲɲo chestnut-tree:kastáɲɲ- chestnut; etc. etc.

B. m/IIb: fíko fig-tree:fík- fig.

ii. m/IIIb: nóče walnut-tree:nóč- walnut f/IIIb.

uu. ⁺0- m/IIb, on nouns of f/Ia, with the meanings:

i. Masculine, in dámo fiancé, lover:dám- lady; pékɔro ram:pékɔr- sheep.

ii. Augmentative, as in bakkétto big rod:bakkétt- rod, stick; bigónčo big wooden bowl:bigónč- wooden bowl; čéro big wax candle:čér- wax (candle); figúro objectionable person:figúr- figure; kanéstro big basket:kanéstr- basket; lámpo flash of lightning:lámp- lamp (archaic); etc. etc.

iii. Diminutive, as in bárko little boat:bárk- boat; bávero coat-collar: bávɛr- cape; kaldáio little kettle:kaldái- big kettle; kóso thingummy, whatsis, doohickey:kós- thing; etc.

vv. ⁺efíč- ⁺efíci- -efice m/IIb, in bɛnefíčo bɛnefício benefice:bén- good m/IIb.

ww. ⁺ifíč- ⁺ifíci- -ifice, -factory m/IIb, as in pastifíčo pastry-shop:pást- dough, pastry f/Ia; kotɔnifíčo cotton factory:kotón- cotton m/IIIb; panifíčo bakery:pán- bread m/IIIb; artifíčo artifício artifice:árt- art f/IIIb; pɔlvɛrifíčo (gun-) powder-factory:pólvɛr- powder f/IIIb; edifíčo edifício edifice:ed⁺ building.

yy. ⁺ád- ensemble, residence, territory of . . . m/IIb, in arčiveskovádo archbishop's palace:arčivéskov- archbishop m/IIb; kɔntádo territory around a town, *county*:kónt- *count* m/IIIb; parɛntádo *relatives* (collective):parént- *relative* m/IIIb.

zz. ⁺éd- *singer with* . . . m/IIb, in čitarédo *cithara singer*:čitar⁺:čétr- *cithara* f/Ia.

aaa. ⁺éẓẓ- diminutive m/IIb, in maréẓẓo *wavy strip of color*:már- *sea* m/IIIb; lakkéẓẓo *delicacy, flattery*:lakk⁺ *id.*

bbb. ⁺arg- *-argy* m/IIb, in letárgo *lethargy*:lét- *Lethe, sleep* f/IIIb.

ccc. ⁺íǧ- diminutive m/IIb, in barbíǧi (pl.) *little mustache*:bárb- *beard* f/Ia.

ddd. ⁺uléi- pejorative m/IIb, in leguléio *shyster*:leG⁺:léǧǧ- *law* f/IIIb.

eee. ⁺áli- *-al* m/IIb: e.g. klɔrálio *chloral*:klór- *chlorine* m/IIb.

fff. ⁺ičíli- *-icile* m/IIb, in dɔmičílio *domicile*:dɔm⁺ *house.*

ggg. ⁺ičíni- *thing made of* . . . m/IIb, in lattičínio *milk- or dairy-product*: látt- *milk* m/IIIb.

hhh. ⁺íbri- *subject for* . . . m/IIb, in ludíbrio *mockery*:lúd- *sport* m/IIb.

jjj. ⁺úbri- *tool to be grasped by* . . . m/IIb, in manúbrio *handle, handle-bar*: mán- *hand* f/IIb.

kkk. ⁺ási- *-asium* m/IIb, in ǧinnásio *gymnasium*:ǧinn⁺ *gymn-.*

lll. ⁺'il- *-ilus* m/IIb, in náutilo *nautilus*:náut- *sailor* m/Ib.

mm. ⁺íll- diminutive m/IIb, in spiríllo *a kind of spiral microorganism*:spír- *spiral* f/Ia; mirtíllo *myrtillum*:mírt- *myrtle* m/IIb; kodičíllo *codicil*:kódič- *code* m/IIIb; biríllo *bottle (in pool game)*:biri⁺ *gyration.*

nnn. ⁺čúll- diminutive m/IIb, in fančúllo *boy*:fánt- *child* m/IIIb.

ooo. ⁺ásm- *-asm* m/IIb, in kiásmo *chiasmus*:kíˣ *chi* (Greek letter name) m/VId; ɛntusiásmo *enthusiasm*:ɛntusi⁺ *enthusi-*; ɔrgásmo *orgasm, excitement*: ɔrg⁺ *work*; sarkásmo *sarcasm*:sark⁺ *sarc-, sneer.*

ppp. ⁺'an- *-ule, -an* m/IIb, in módano *module*:mód- *manner* m/IIb; órgano *organ*:ɔrg⁺ *work.*

qqq. ⁺úmɛn- *-umen* m/IIb, in ɛnergúmɛno *energumen, fanatic*:ɛnɛrG⁺ *energ(y)*; katekúmɛno *catechumen*:katek⁺ *catech(ism).*

rrr. ⁺'in- *-inum* m/IIb, in plátin- *platinum*:plat⁺ *silver.*

sss. ⁺ón- *-on* m/IIb, in patróno *patron*:patr⁺:pádr- *father* m/IIIb.

ttt. ⁺ɲ- *possession, action of* . . . m/IIb, in réɲɲo *kingdom, reign*:réˣ *king* m/VId.

uuu. ⁺ándr- *-ander*, in ɔleándro *oleander*:ɔle⁺:óli- *oil* m/IIb.

vvv. ⁺ɛr- *-(e)ry, place for* . . ., *rank of* . . . m/IIb, in the following based on nouns of types:

    i. m/Ib: battistéro *baptistery*:battíst- *baptist.*

    ii. m/IIb: maǧistéro *rank, position of master*:maǧist⁺:maǧístr- *master*; ministéro *ministry*:minist⁺:minístr- *minister*; saltéro *psalter*:salt⁺:sálm- *psalm.*

    iii. Nominal bases: čimitéro *cemetery*:čimit⁺ *cemet-*; mistéro *mystery*: mist⁺ *myst-*; mɔnastéro:mɔnast⁺ *monk.*

www. ⁺éstr- ⁺éstr- *action, thing connected with* . . . m/IIb, in kapéstro kapéstro *capistrum, halter*:káp- *head* m/IIb; maléstro *harm, damage*:mál- *evil* m/IIIb.

yyy. ⁺áss- pejorative m/IIb, in papásso *Greek orthodox* priest:páp- *priest, pope* m/Ib.

zzz. ⁺ét- *collection of* . . ., *grove of* . . . m/IIb, in many derivatives, such as the following based on nouns of types:

i. f/Ia: kannéto *cane-field*:kánn- *cane*; mačɛréto *pile of stones*:mačér- *stone(s)* (archaic).

ii. m/IIb: ačɛréto *maple-plantation*:áčɛr- *maple*; albɛréto *land planted with trees*:álbɛr- *tree*; arančéto *orange grove*:aránč- *orange-tree*; kastaɲɲéto *chestnut-grove*:kastáɲɲ- *chestnut-tree*; čɛrréto *oak-grove*:čérr- *a kind of oak*; etc. etc.

iii. m/IIIb: agruméto *citrus grove*:agrúm- *citrus fruit*; nočéto *walnut grove*:nóč- *walnut tree*.

aaaa. ⁺ít- *-ite, result of action done with* . . . m/IIb, in fosfíto *phosphite*: fɔsf⁺:fósfɔr- *phosphorus* m/IIb; assíto *repair or division made with boards*:áss- *board* f/IIIb.

bbbb. ⁺arícc- *way to* . . . m/IIb, in barkarícco *gangway, entrance port*:bárk- *boat* f/Ia.

cccc. ⁺ɛrícc- *one who deals with* . . . m/IIb, in kavallerícc- *horseman, riding-master*:kaváll- *horse* m/IIb.

dddd. ⁺'tru- *truum* m/IIb, in méstruo *menstrual flow*:més- *month* m/IIIb.

eeee. ⁺éfič- *-ificer, -ifex* m/IIIb, in ɔréfiče *goldsmith*:ór- *gold* m/IIb; pɔntéfiče *pontifex*:pónt- *bridge* m/IIIb; artéfiče *artificer*:árt- *art* f/IIIb; karnéfiče *executioner*:kárn- *meat, flesh* f/IIIb.

ffff. ⁺ilén- *-ylene* m/IIIb, in ačetiléne *acetylene*:ačét- *vinegar* m/IIb.

gggg. ⁺ón- *-one* m/IIIb, as in ačetóne *acetone*:ačét- *vinegar* m/IIb; elettróne *electron*:ɛléttr- *amber, electr-* m/IIb; peptóne *peptone*:pɛpT⁺ *digestion*.

hhhh. ⁺imón- *one who acts as* . . . m/IIIb, in testimóne *witness (public)*: tést- *witness* m/IIIb.

iiii. ⁺etér- *-eter* m/IIIb, in katetére *catheter*:kat⁺ *cath-*; uretére *ureter*:ur⁺ *ur(ine)*.

jjjj. ⁺sétt- abstract m/IIIb, in bausétte *barking, bow-wowwing*:báu *bow-wow* mcl or m/Vd.

kkkk. ⁺'ad- *-ad* f/IIIb, as in ɔlimpíade *Olympiad*:ɔlímpi- *Olympia* f/Ia; ğɛrɛmíade *Jeremiad*:ğɛrɛmí- *Jeremiah* m/Ib; ilíade *Iliad*:íli- *Ilium* m/IIb; tríade *triad*:tri⁺:tré*ˣ three* num/VI; dríade *dryad*:dri⁺ *tree*; mónade *monad*: mɔn⁺ *mon-, one*.

llll. ⁺'ɛr- *quality of* . . ., *goddess of* . . . f/IIIb, in vénɛre *beauty, Venus*:vɛn⁺ *beauty*.

mmmm. ⁺át- *season of* . . . f/IIIb, in estáte *summer*:est⁺ *id.*

nnnn. ⁺ít- f/IIIb, with the meanings:

i. *-ite*, in derivatives based on chemical, botanical, zoological terms: e.g. balistíte *balistite*:balíst- *balista* f/Ia; kalčíte *calcite*:kálč- *calcium* m/IIb; allumíte *alumite*:allúm- *alum* m/IIIb; ammoníte *ammonite*:ammón- *Ammon* m/IIIb; antračíte *anthracite*:antráč- *anthrax* m/IIIb; dinamíte *dynamite*:dinam⁺ *force*; dɔlomíte *dolomite*:dɔlɔm⁺ *Dolom(ieu)*; ɛmatíte *hematite*:ɛmat⁺:ɛm⁺ *blood*; epsɔmíte *epsom salts*:epsɔm⁺ *Epsom*; etc.

ii. *-itis*, in derivatives based on names of body parts: e.g. kɔnǧuntivíte *conjunctivitis*:kɔnǧuntív- *conjunctiva* f/Ia; brɔnkíte *bronchitis*:brónk- *bronchial tube* m/IIb; appɛndičíte *appendicitis*:appɛndíč- *appendix* f/IIIb; čistíte *cystitis*: číst- *bladder* f/IIIb or IVd; adɛníte *tonsilitis*:adɛn⁺ *tonsil*; artríte *arthritis*:artr⁺ *joint*; ɛntɛríte *enteritis*:ɛntɛr⁺ *intestines*; kɔlíte *colitis*:kɔl⁺ *colon*; etc.

oooo. ⁺ɔ́T- *-osis* f/IVd: e.g. klɔrósi *chlorosis*:klɔr- *chlorine* m/IIb; amaurósi *amaurosis*:amaur⁺ *amaur-*; čanósi *cyanosis*:čan⁺ *cyan-, blue*; mikósi *mycosis*: mik⁺ *myc-*; etc.

pppp. ⁺0- abstract m/IVd, in mestiéri *need*:mestiér- *trade, profession* m/IIIb.

qqqq. ⁺ías- *-iasis* f/IVd: e.g. ɛlmintíasi *helminthiasis*:ɛlmínt- *helminth* m/IIb; ɛlefantíasi *elephantiasis*:ɛlefánt- *elephant* m/IIIb; litíasi *lithiasis*:lit⁺ *stone*; psɔríasi *psoriasis*:psɔr⁺ *scale*.

rrrr. ⁺′im- *-im* m/VId, in íntɛrim *interim, meantime*:intɛr⁺ *between*.

ssss. ⁺ɔn *-on* m/VId, in kólɔn *colon (intestine)*:kɔl⁺ *colon*; míkrɔn *micron (millionth part of meter)*:mikr⁺ *small, micr(o)-*; néɔn *neon*:ne⁺ *new*.

tttt. ⁺íˣ m or f/VId, forming names of letters, added to the phoneme which the letter represents, in bíˣ *B*; číˣ *C*; díˣ *D*; ǧíˣ *G*; píˣ *P*; tíˣ *T*; víˣ *V* (modern).

uuuu. ⁺úˣ m or f/VId, forming a letter name on the phoneme /v/, in vúˣ *V*.

vvvv. ⁺ɛt⁺ and (before ⁺í- *-y* f/Ia) ⁺ɛss⁺, together with a⁺ privative, in apirétiK- *apyrectic (lacking fever)* and apiressía *apyrexia (absence of fever)*:pir⁺ *fever, fire*.

7. Numerals, with:

a. ⁺én- *period of . . . days* f/Ia, in kuaranténa *period of forty days, quarantine*:kuaránt- *forty* num/Id; novéna *novena*:nóv- *nine* num/IIId.

b. ⁺0- *distance of . . . (steps)* m/IIc, in míʎʎo *mile*:miʎʎ⁺:míll- *1000* num/IIIc.

c. ⁺ái- *group of . . ., approximately . . .* m/IIc:

   i. Alone, in miʎʎáio *about 1000*:miʎʎ⁺:míll- *1000* num/IIIc.

   ii. Preceded by ⁺in⁺, in other derivatives: e.g. čentináio *about 100*:čént- *100* num/IId.

d. ⁺émbr- *-ember* (in month names) m/IIIb, in novémbre *November*:nóv- *nine* num/IIId; settémbre *September*:sétt- *seven* num/IIId; dičémbre *December*:dič⁺:diéč- *ten* num/IVd.

e. ⁺óbr- *-ober* m/IIIb, in ottóbre *October*:ótt- *eight* num/IId.

8. Adverbs, with ⁺0- abstract m/IIIb, in béne *good*:bén- *well* adv/III; mále *evil*:mál- *badly* adv/III.

9. Prefixes, with ⁺′d- *-(a)d* f/IIIb, in miríade *myriad*:miria⁺ *10,000*.

10. Verbs:

a. On root or root alternant (rhyzotonic unless otherwise indicated):

   i. ⁺0- *action of . . ., instrument for . . .* f/Ia, as in the following based on verbs of types:

   A. I/Reg/W: abiúra *abjuration*:abiúr- *abjure*; amménda *amends*: amménd- *amended*; bɔnífika *reclamation (of land)*: bɔnífik- *reclaim*; kiáma *(roll) call*:kiám- *call*; kɔnǧúra *conspiracy*:kɔnǧúr- *conspire*; etc. etc.

B. IIIa/Irr/S¹: dóʎʎa *pain, sorrow*:dóʎʎ-:dɔl- *be in pain, hurt*; vóʎʎa *wish, desire*:vóʎʎ-:vɔl- *wish*.

C. IIIb(x)/Reg/S¹: béva *drink*:bév- *drink*.

ii. ⁺úǧ- *instrument for* . . . f/Ia, in grattúǧa *grater*:grátt- *grate* I/Reg/W.

iii. ⁺éli- *-ely* f/Ia, in kɔntumélia *contumely*:kɔntum⁺ *be haughty*:tum⁺ *swell up*.

iv. ⁺oɲɲ- *action of* . . . f/Ia, in mɛncóɲɲa *lie*:mént- *lie* II/Reg or ísK/W.

v. ⁺ámin- *result of* . . . f/Ia, in sudámina *heat rash*:súd- *sweat* I/Reg/W.

vi. ⁺ébr- *thing which* . . . f/Ia, in pálpebra *eyelid*:pálp- *feel*, (*palpitate*) I/Reg/W; vértebr- *vertebra*:vért- *turn* IIIb/Reg.

vii. ⁺'tu- *-tue* f/Ia, in státua *statue*:stá- *stand* IV/Irr/S¹.

viii. ⁺0- *agent* m/Ib, in compounds formed in ⁺čída *-cide* (:⁺číd- *kill*): e.g. insettičída *insecticide*; fratričída *fratricide*; matričída *matricide*; ɔmičída *homicide*; etc.

ix. ⁺ét- *-et* m/Ib, in poéta *poet*:po⁺ *make poetry*.

x. ⁺0- *action of* . . ., *result of* . . . m/IIb:

A. With no change in the root, in many derivatives, such as the following based on verbs of types:

I. I/Reg/W: abbáʎʎo *bedazzlement, mistake*:abbáʎʎ- *dazzle*; abbáio *barking*:abbái- *bark*; abbandóno *abandon*(*ment*):abbandón- *abandon*; akkátto *begging*:akkátt- *beg*; akkuísto *acquisition*:akkuíst- *acquire*; etc. etc.

II. II/Reg/W: abórto *abortion*:abort- *abort*.

B. With change in the root:

I. Diphthongization, in roots of I/Reg/W, in alliévo *pupil*:allév- *raise*; sɔlliévo *relief*:sɔllév- *raise, relieve*; niégo *refusal*:nég- *deny, refuse*; diniégo *denial*:dinég- *deny*.

II. /ɛn/ > /éɲɲ/, in kɔntéɲɲo *mien, behavior*:kɔntɛn- *contain, behave* (refl.) IIIa/Irr/S¹.

xi. ⁺△- *action of* . . . m/IIb, in púcco *stench*:pút- *stink* II/Reg/W.

xii. ⁺éǧǧ- *act of* . . . m/IIb, as in parkéǧǧo *parking*:párk- *park* I/Reg/W; postéǧǧo *establishment of posts*:póst- *post* I/Reg/W.

xiii. ⁺íǧ- *-ice, act of* . . . m/IIb, in sɛrvíǧo *service*:sérv- *serve* II/Reg/W; suffumíǧo *fumigation*:suffum⁺ *fumigate*.

xiv. ⁺ídi- *-ation* m/IIb, in falčídio *defalcation*:fálk- *cut* (*orig. with a scythe*) I/Reg/W.

xv. ⁺áʎʎ- *instrument for* . . . m/IIb, in the following derivatives of verbs of types:

A. I/Reg/W: sɛrráʎʎo *collection of animals*; *lock* (archaic):sérr- *lock up*; sɔnáʎʎo (*little*) *bell*:sɔn- *sound*; spiráʎʎo *air-vent*:spír- *blow, breathe*; vɛntáʎʎo *fan*:vɛnt- *blow, cause wind* (archaic).

B. II/ísK/W: skandáʎʎo *plumb-line* (*for sounding water*):skand- *measure*.

C. IIIb/Reg/W: battáʎʎo *bell-clapper*:bátt- *beat*.

D. IIIb/Reg/S¹, ²: pɛndáʎʎo *pendant*:pénd- *hang*.

xvi. ⁺ɔrígm- *action of* . . . m/IIb, in bɔrbɔrígmo *intestinal rumblings*: bɔrb⁺ *rumble*.

xvii. +ákr- *acrum* m/IIb, on verbs of I/Reg/W, in ambulákro *ambula-crum*:ámbul- *ambulate*; lavákro *lavacrum*:láv- *wash*; simulákro *simulacrum*: símul- *simulate*.

xviii. +'etr- *implement for* . . . m/IIb, in féretro *bier*:fɛr- *bear*.

xix. +últ- -*ult* m/IIb, in tumúlto *tumult*:tum+ *swell up*.

xx. +uént- -*uent, means of* m/IIb, in unguénto *unguent*:únG- *smear, anoint* IIIb/Reg/S[1, 2].

xxi. +△- *object of action* m or f/IIIb, in kóniuǧe *spouse*:kóniug- *conjugate, join* I/Reg/W.

xxii. +0- *actor, action of* . . . m/IIIb:

A. With /'/ and /ɛ/ > /i/, in préside *president*:presɛd- *preside* IIIa/Reg/W.

B. With prefix intɛr+ *inter-*, in interésse *interest*:éss- *be* IIIb/Reg/S[1].

xxiii. +ím- *object, means, effect of action, -ime(n)* m/IIIb, in the following based on verbs of types:

A. I/Reg/W: akkɔnčíme *repair, restoration*:akkɔ́nč- *put in order*; bekkíme *chicken-feed*:békk- *peck*; governíme *feed, fodder*:govérn- *care for*; kɔnčíme *fertilizer*:kɔ́nč- *put in order*; lattíme *eczematous malady*:látt- *suckle*; manǧíme *fodder*:mánǧ- *eat*.

B. II/ísK/W: marčíme *straw-and-dung compost*:marč- *rot*.

C. IIIb/Reg/[1, 2]: reǧíme *regime*:reG+:réGG- *rule*.

xxiv. +ón- *action of* . . . m/IIIb, in barkɔllóne *reeling, tottering*:barkɔ́ll- *reel* I/Reg/W.

xxv. +'ɛr- -*us* m/IIIb, in ǧénɛre *genus, kind*:ǧɛn+ *beget*.

xxvi. +íK- -*ix* f/IIIb, in appendíče *appendix*:appénd- *append* IIIb/Reg/S[1, 2].

xxvii. +ɛT- -*esis* f/IVd:

A. With stress on preceding syllable, in aféresi *apheresis*:fɛr+ *carry, bear*; ǧénesi *genesis*:ǧɛn+ *beget*; paréntesi *parenthesis*:parɛnt+ *put within*; parénesi *exhortation*:parɛn+ *exhort*.

B. With stress on suffix, in kosmési *cosmesis*:kosm+ *beautify*; poési *poesy*:po+ *make poetry*.

C. With indeterminate stress, in patɛT+ (in derivative patétiK- *pathetic* adj/I–II): pat- *suffer* II/ísK/W.

xxviii. +í[x] -*y* m/VId, in ǧurí[x] *jury*:ǧúr- *swear* I/Reg/W.

b. On Stem A, with:

i. +dér- *place of* . . . m/IIb, in imbarkadéro *landing-place*:imbárk- *embark* I/Reg/W.

ii. +'tr- *implement for* . . . m/IIb, in arátro *plow*:ár- *plow* I/Reg/W.

c. On Imperative, with +0- *performer of action* m/Id, in akkómoda *accomodating person*:akkómoda *accomodate!*; tɛnténna *hesitating person*:tɛnténna *hesitate!*.

d. On Non-Finite[2] A, with +△- -*ce, -cy* f/Ia, in very many derivatives, such as abbɔndánca *abundance*:abbónd- *abound* I/Reg/W; arrogánca *arrogance*: arróg- *arrogate* I/Reg/W; sɛnténca *opinion, sentence*:sént- *feel* II/Reg/W;

kadénca *cadence*:kád- *fall* IIIa/Reg/S¹; akkɔʎʎénca *reception*:akkóʎʎ- *receive* IIIb/Irr/S¹, ²; etc. etc.

e. On Stem B, with ⁺0- *action of . . ., to . . .* m/IIIb (the 'infinitive'), on almost all verb roots, such as the following of types:

i. I/Reg/W: kantáre *to sing*:kánt- *sing*; mangǎ́re *to eat*:mángǎ- *eat*; parláre *to speak, dialect*:párl- *speak*; etc. etc. etc.

ii. I/Irr/W: andáre *to go, gait*:and- *go*.

iii. II/Reg/W: dɔrmíre *to sleep*:dɔ́rm- *sleep*; partíre *to depart*:párt- *depart*; sentíre *to feel*:sént- *feel*; etc.

iv. II/ísK/W: arrikkíre *to enrich*:arríkk- *enrich*; finíre *to finish*:fin- *finish*; patíre *to suffer*:pat- *suffer*; etc.

v. IIIa: dɔlére *to suffer*:dɔ́l- *suffer*; kadére *to fall*:kád- *fall*; tɛnére *to hold*:tɛn- *hold*; etc.

vi. IIIb: báttere *to beat*:bátt- *beat*; éssere *to be, being*:éss- *be*; régǧere *to rule*:réGG- *rule*; etc.

vii. IV: dáre *to give*:dá- *give*; pórre *to put*:pón- *put*; stáre *to stand*:stá- *stand*; trárre *to draw*:trá^x *draw*; etc.

The defective verb ékko *here is, there is* (Imperative, non-contrastive as to person and number) has no infinitive formation, nor do a few roots and all verbal bases.

f. On Non-Finite C, with:

i. ⁺0- *action of . . ., result of . . .* f/Ia, in very many derivatives, such as the following based on verbs of types:

A. I/Reg/W: abbaiáta *barking, slander*:abbái- *bark, slander*; abboccáta *quick sketch*:abbócc- *sketch*; adunáta *gathering*:adún- *gather*; armáta *armada, army*:árm- *arm*; bakkettáta *beating*:bakkétt- *beat (with rod)*; etc. etc.

B. II/Irr/S¹: vɛnúta *coming*:vɛn- *come*; etc.

C. II/ísK/W: fɛríta *wound*:fɛr- *strike*; etc.

D. IIIa: kadúta *fall*:kád- *fall;* valúta *(foreign) currency*:vál- *be worth*; etc.

E. IIIb: agǧúnta *addition*:agǧúnG- *add*; akkólta *gathering*:akkóʎʎ- *receive*; attésa *wait*:atténd- *wait, attend*; kiúsa *enclosure*:kiúd- *close;* etc.

F. IV: dáta *date*:dá- *give*; pósta *mail*:pón- *put*.

ii. ⁺0- *result of action* m/IIb, on verbs of I/Reg/W, in aggregáto *aggregate*:aggrég- *aggregate*; alcáto *elevation (of building)*:álc- *raise*.

iii. ⁺ént- *abstract* m/IIIb, in valsénte *worth, value*:vál- *be worth* IIIa Irr/S¹, ².

3.115. PRONOUNS are formed with the elements enumerated in §2.2, and also with ⁺únku- *-ever* III (no pl.) in kiúnkue *whoever*:kí^x *who, he who* . . . .

3.116. VERBS are formed on:

1. Substantives and Verbs, with:

a. ⁺égǧ- *-ize, act like or in connection with . . ., be like . . ., make like . . .* I/Reg/W, as in the following verbs based on:

i. Adjectives, of types:

A. I–II: amarégǧ- *embitter*:amár- *bitter*; antikégǧ- *act old-fashioned*:

antík- *old, antique*; aʒʒurréǧǧ- *make, be bluish*:aʒʒúrr- *blue*; biɔndéǧǧ- *be, become blond(e)*:biónd- *blond(e)*; kaldéǧǧ- *favor warmly*:káld- *hot*; etc. etc.

   B. IIIb: grandéǧǧ- *be outstanding*:gránd- *big, great*; vɛrdéǧǧ- *become green*:vérd- *green*; etc.

   C. IVd: paréǧǧ- *make alike, equalize*:pár- *equal*.

  ii. Nouns, of types:

   A. f/Ia: albéǧǧ- *begin to dawn*:álb- *dawn*; ariéǧǧ- *aerate, have the air of . . ., seem like . . .*:ári- *air*; befféǧǧ- *mock*:béff- *joke, jest*; bɔrséǧǧ- *rob*:bórs- *purse*; etc. etc.

   B. f/Ib: aléǧǧ- *flutter, fly lightly*:ál- *wing*; arméǧǧ- *joust, bustle, dither*: árm- *arm, weapon*.

   C. m/IIb: bekkéǧǧ- *pitch (of boat)*:békk- *beak*; lampéǧǧ- *lighten*:lámp- *flash of lightning*; etc.

   D. f/IIb: manéǧǧ- *handle, manage*:mán- *hand*.

   E. m/IIIb: amɔréǧǧ- *make love* (often pej.):amór- *love*; favɔréǧǧ- *favor*: favór- *favor*; siɲɲɔréǧǧ- *rule over*:siɲɲór- *lord*; etc.

   F. f/IIIb: frɔntéǧǧ- *be opposite*:frónt- *front, forehead*; partéǧǧ- *side with*:párt- *party*; etc.

   G. Proper names: e.g. petrarkéǧǧ- *Petrarchize*:petrárk- *Petrarch* m/Id; bɛmbéǧǧ- *imitate Bembo*:bémb- *Bembo* m/IId; bɛrnéǧǧ- *write in Bernesque manner*:bérn- *Berni* m/IVd; etc.

  iii. Verb I/Reg/W, in mɔrmɔréǧǧ- *murmur gently*:mórmɔr- *murmur*.

 b. ⁺ik- causative, diminutive, *act with or by means of . . .* I/Reg/W, as in the following based on:

  i. Adjectives of types:

   A. I–II: mórsik- *bite, nibble*:mórs- *bitten*; etc.

   B. IIIb: kɔmúnik- *communicate*:kɔmún- *common*.

  ii. Nouns of types:

   A. f/Ia: bárbik- *take root*:bárb- *root, beard*; bárrik- *barricade*:bárr- bar; čámpik- *walk slowly and draggingly*:čámp- *paw*; rámpik- *climb up*:rámp- *paw*; etc.

   B. m/IIb: fúmik- *smoke* (tr.):fúm- *smoke*; beccik- *peck*:becc⁺:békk- *beak*; etc.

   C. f/IIIb: lúččik- *shine*:lučč⁺:lúč- *light*; névik- *snow*:név- *snow*; etc. With prefix di⁺ and /é/ > /ɛ́/:diméntik- *forget*:mént- *mind*.

  iii. Verbs of types:

   A. I/Reg/W: appíččik- *attach (insecurely)*:appíčč- *attach*; biáššik- *chew with excess of saliva*:biášš- *id.*; čánčik- *talk, chew with difficulty*:čánč- *talk idly*; méstik- *mix (colors)*:mést- *mix*; spíččik- *unstick*:spíčč- *empty*.

   B. IIIb/Reg/W: ǧémik- *trickle lightly*:ǧém- *trickle*.

   C. IIIb/Reg/S¹, ²: mórdik- *bite*:mórd- *bite*.

   D. Verbal bases: véndik- *avenge*:vɛnd⁺ *id.* With prefix s⁺, stráššik- *drag along*:trašš⁺ *drag*.

  iv. The suffix is preceded by ⁺ičč⁺, in dɔlíččik- *hurt a little*:dɔl- *hurt* IIIb/Irr/S¹.

  v. It is preceded by ⁺△⁺ in vérʒik- *turn green*:vérd- *green* adj/IIIb.

c. ⁺'ɔl- I/Reg/W, with the meanings:

i. On nouns, *do like . . ., act in the manner of or in connection with . . ., give . . .*, in the following based on nouns of type:

A. f/Ia: fɔrmíkɔl- *swarm*:fɔrmík- *ant*; nínnɔl- *play*:nínn- *sleep, lullaby*; rótɔl- *roll*:rɔt⁺:ruót- *wheel*.

B. m/IIb: guáiɔl- *yelp*:guái- *lament* (archaic), *trouble*; préccɔl- *price*: précc- *price*; véntɔl- *ventilate*:vént- *wind*.

ii. On verbs, diminutive, augmentative or repetitive, in the following based on verbs of:

A. I/Reg/W: frúgɔl- *rummage around*:frúg- *search*; ǧókɔl- *juggle*:ǧók- *play*; svágɔl- *amuse a little, with trifles*:svág- *amuse*; trémɔl- *tremble lightly*:trém- *tremble*; vágɔl- *wander around*:vág- *wander*; vóltɔl- *keep turning*:vólt- *turn*.

B. IIIb: báttɔl- *chatter loudly*:bátt- *beat, strike*; méskɔl- (also méskɔl-) *mix*:mésK- *mix*; piángɔl- *cry a little*:piánG- *weep*.

iii. The suffix is preceded by:

A. ⁺and⁺ ⁺ɔnd⁺ in ǧirándɔl- ǧiróndɔl- *go around here and there*:ǧír- *turn* I/Reg/W.

B. ⁺g⁺ in pígɔl- *cheep*:pí- *chirp* I/Reg/W.

C. ⁺k⁺ (with loss of preceding /d/) in pénkɔl- *waver*:pénd- *hang* IIIb/ Reg/S¹, ².

D. ⁺úk⁺ in piaɲɲúkɔl- *snivel*:piáɲɲ- *weep* IIIb/Irr/S¹, ².

E. ⁺ínc⁺, together with prefix s⁺ intensive, in skodíncɔl- *wag the tail*: kód- *tail* f/Ia.

F. ⁺ícc⁺ in skavíccɔl- *dig out carefully*:skáv- *excavate* I/Reg/W.

G. ⁺ónc⁺ in ballóncɔl- *dance poorly*:báll- *dance* I/Reg/W.

d. ⁺'ul- *-ulate* I/Reg/W, in óndul- *undulate*:ónd- *wave* f/Ia; spékul- *speculate*:spɛk⁺ *look*, spec-.

e. ⁺íʎʎ- *act like . . ., make . . .* I/Reg/W, in the following based on:

i. Noun m/IIb: gattíʎʎ- *quarrel*:gátt- *cat*.

ii. Verb, in:

A. Root: attɔrčíʎʎ- *twist up*:attórK- *twist* IIIb/Reg/S¹, ².

B. Non-Finite C: attɔrtíʎʎ- *twist up*:attórK- *twist* IIIb/Reg/S¹, ².

f. ⁺óʎʎ- diminutive I/Reg/W, in ǧermóʎʎ- *bud, sprout*:ǧérm- *germ* m/IIIb; bɔrbóʎʎ- *mutter, burble, rumble*:bɔrb⁺ *rumble*.

g. ⁺'in- diminutive I/Reg/W:

i. Alone, in tráššin- *drag along*:trašš⁺ *drag*.

ii. Preceded by:

A. ⁺íǧǧ⁺, in piovíǧǧin- *drizzle*:pióv- *rain* IIIb/Reg/S¹.

B. ⁺úm⁺, in fɛrrúmin- *weld*:férr- *iron* m/IIb.

h. ⁺'it- *-itate*, in the following based on:

i. Adjectives, of types:

A. I–II: dúbit- *doubt*:dúbi- dúbbi- *doubtful*; úsit⁺ (in inusitáto *unaccustomed* past part.):ús- *used, accustomed*.

B. IIIb: abílit- *habilitate, qualify*:ábil- *qualified, able*; aǧílit- *render agile*:áǧil- *agile*; debílit- *debilitate*:débil- *weak*; fačílit- *facilitate*:fáčil- *easy*; kapáčit- *capacitate*:kapáč- *capable*; lévit- *levitate*:lév- liév- *light*.

ii. Verbs, of types:

A. I/Reg/W: krépit- *crepitate, crackle*:krép- *burst*; vólit- *flit*:vól- *fly*.

B. II/ísK/W: áǧit- *agitate*:aǧ- *act*; esérčit- *exercise*:esɛrč- *exercise, conduct*.

C. II/ísK/W or IIIb/Reg: vómit- *vomit*:vɔm- *id*.

D. Verbal base: skálpit- *pound hoofs (of horses)*:skalp⁺:kalp⁺ *id*.

iii. The suffix is preceded by ⁺íč⁺ in febbríčit- *have a fever*:fébbr- *fever* f/IIIb.

j. ⁺étt- diminutive or causative, in the following based on:

i. Nouns: skulétt- *walk wiggling the buttocks*:kúl- *arse* m/IIb; uméttdampen:um⁺ *damp(ness)*.

ii. Verbs I/Reg/W: ballétt- *dance poorly*:báll- *dance*; fiskiétt- *whistle in snatches*:físki- *whistle*; piegétt- *plait, crease*:piég- *fold*; seǧett- *cut to a saw-like edge*:ség- *saw*; sgambétt- *cut capers*:sgámb- *caper*; campétt- *prance*:cámp- *stamp*; cappétt- *hoe lightly*:cápp- *hoe*.

2. Substantives and adverbs, with:

a. ⁺0- *perform action of . . ., connected with . . ., make . . .* I/Reg/W, in many verbs, such as the following based on:

i. Adj/I–II: báss- *lower*:báss- *low*; férm- *stop*:férm- *firm*; kiár- *make clear, explain*:kiár- *clear*; etc.

ii. Nouns of types:

A. f/Ia: ánim- *animate*:ánim- *spirit*; bóll- *stamp, seal*:bóll- *seal*; kɔrón- *crown*:kɔrón- *crown*; etc. etc.

B. f/Ib: árm- *arm*:árm- *arm, weapon*.

C. m/IIb: ábbak- *reckon, fantasticate*:ábbak- *abacus*; aččái- *steel*:aččái- *steel*; blókk- *block*:blókk- *block*; etc.

D. m/IIIb: órdin- *order*:órdin- *order*; ɔnór- *honor*:ɔnór- *honor*; sánguin- *bleed*:sanguin⁺:sángu- *blood*.

E. f/IIIb: kiáv- *nail; have sexual intercourse with . . .*:kiáv- *key*; rádik- *root*:rádiK- *root*; etc.

iii. Adverbs: éntr- *enter*:éntr- *within* adv/II; addéntr- *penetrate*:addéntr- *far in* adv/II; súpɛr- *overcome*:supɛr⁺ *super-, over-*.

This suffix occurs also in the majority of parasynthetic compounds consisting of prefix or preposition (§3.2) + substantive + verbal suffix: e.g. kɔmmíser- *commiserate*:mísɛr- *miserable* adj/I–II; esílar- *exhilarate*:ílar- *hilarious* adj/ IIIb; kɔnfigúr- *configurate*:figúr- *figure* f/Ia; kɔnčéntr- *concentrate*:čéntr- *center* m/IIb; ɛlímin- *eliminate*:limin⁺ *threshold*; pɛrnótt- *pass the night*:nótt- *night* f/IIIb.

b. ⁺△- causative I/Reg/W, in álc- *raise*:ált- *high* adj/I–II; d(i)rícc- *straighten*:d(i)rítt- *straight* adj/I–II; minúcc- *cut, break into little pieces*:minút- *minute* adj/I–II; rícc- *raise*:rítt- *upright* adj/I–II; bálc- *bound*:bált- *jolt, upset* f/Ia; tappécc- *carpet*:tappét- *carpet* m/IIb; avánc- *be left over, remain, advance*: avánt- *before* adv/IV.

c. ⁺ácc̆- pejorative causative I/Reg/W:

i. Alone, in spɔrkácc̆- *mess up, make filthy*:spórk- *dirty* adj/I–II; spadácc̆- *strike with the sword* (archaic):spád- *sword* f/Ia.

ii. Together with s⁺ intensive, in skuláčč- *pinch the arse of* . . . :kúl-*arse* m/IIb; smanáčč- *make exaggerated gestures*:mán- *hand* f/IIb.

d. ⁺ízẓ- *-ize* I/Reg/W, as in the following based on:

i. Adj/I–II: akutízẓ- *make acute*:akút- *acute;* etc.

ii. Nouns of types:

A. f/Ia: alkimízẓ- *practice alchemy on* . . . :alkími- *alchemy*; anatɔmízẓ-*anatomize*:anatɔmí- *anatomy*; etc.

B. m/Ib: anatɛmízẓ- *anathematize*:anátɛm- *anathema*; arɔmatízẓ-*aromatize*:arɔmat⁺:aróm- *aroma*; etc.

C. m/IIIb: agɔnízẓ- *agonize*:agón- *struggle*; autɔrícc- *authorize*:autór-*author*; kanɔnízẓ- *canonize*:kánɔn- *canon*; karattɛrízẓ- *characterize*:karáttɛr-*character*; patrízẓ- *take after one's father*:patr⁺:pádr- *father*; etc.

D. m/IIIb or VId: alk(o)ɔlízẓ- *alcoholize*:álkɔl- (IIIb) álkoɔl (VId) *alcohol*.

E. Nominal base: pɔlɛmízẓ- *polemicize*:pɔlɛm⁺ *war*.

This suffix occurs also in parasynthetic compounds: e.g. derattízẓ- *rid of rats*:rátt- *rat* m/IIb; detrɔnízẓ- *dethrone*:trón- *throne* m/IIIb.

e. ⁺′ig- *-igate* I/Reg/W, in the following based on:

i. Adj/IIIb: lévig- *levigate, smooth*:lév- liév- *light*; mítig- *mitigate*:mít-*mild*.

ii. Nouns of:

A. m/IIb: fúmig- *fumigate*:fúm- *smoke*; rémig- *row* (with /é/):rém-*oar*.

B. f/IIIb: lítig- *quarrel, litigate*:lít- *quarrel, fight*; návig- *navigate*:náv-*ship*.

f. ⁺′i- causative, *act in connection with* . . . I/Reg/W, in the following based on:

i. Adj/IIIb: umíli- *humiliate*:úmil- *humble*.

ii. Nouns f/Ia: čirkostánci- *narrate in detail*:čirkostánc- *circumstance*; píkki- *strike, hit*:píkk- *staff*; poténci- *make strong*:poténc- *potency*; sɛnténci-*judge, opine*:sɛnténc- *sentence, opinion*; stánci- *stabilize, put in order*:stánc-*standing place*.

g. ⁺′ɔr- causative; *take, gather* I/Reg/W:

i. Alone, in érbɔr- *gather herbs or grasses*:érb- *herb, grass* f/Ia; píɲɲɔr-*take as security, foreclose*:piɲɲ⁺:péɲɲ- *pledge* m/IIb.

ii. Together with the prefix e⁺ intensive, in edúlkɔr- *sweeten*:dúlk- *sweet* adj/I–II.

h. ⁺0- *perform action of* . . . , *connected with* . . . , *make* . . . , *-ish* II/ísK/W, in many derivatives, such as the following based on:

i. Adj/I–II: biank- *whiten*:biánk- *white*; bland- *soften, blandish*:blánd-*soft*; brun- *polish, brighten*:brún- *brown* (earlier *bright*); etc. etc.

ii. Nouns of types:

A. m/IIb: band- *proclaim, banish*:bánd- *ban*; bɔmb- *resound*:bómb-*resonance*; etc.

B. m/IIIb: favɔr- *favor*:favór- *favor*; kɔlɔr- *color*:kɔlór- *color*; etc.

c. f/IIIb: fin- *finish*:fín- *end*; etc.

d. m/IVd: kand- *candy*:kánd- *candied fruit*.

This suffix also occurs in many parasynthetic compounds, such as imbiənd- *make blond(e)*:biónd- *blond(e)* adj/I–II; diminu- *diminish*:minu+:mén- *less(er)* adj/IId; inčivil- *civilize*:čivíl- *civil(ized)* adj/IIIb; defin- *define*:fín- *end* f/IIIb; etc. etc.

j. +0- *perform action as . . ., involving . . .* II/Reg/W, in sérv- *serve*:sérv- *servant* m/IIb; vést- *clothe*:vést- *dress* f/IIIb.

k. +0- *perform action involving . . ., be* IIIb/Reg/S, in vív- *live*:vív- *alive* adj/I–II; pasK- *graze*:pasK+:pásk- *pasture* m/IIb; lúč- *shine*:lúč- *light* f/IIIb; réGG- *rule, govern*:reGG+:réˣ *king* m/VId.

3. Adjectives, with:

a. +'id- *-idate* I/Reg/W, in trúčid- *murder*:trúč- *cruel, pitiless* adj/IIIb.

b. +'an- *causative* I/Reg/W, together with s+ *privative* in skalmán- *over-excite*:kálm- *calm* f/Ia.

c. +'ur- *causative, -urate* I/Reg/W in sátur- *saturate*:sat+ *enough*.

d. +0- *be . . .* IIIa/Irr, in pɔt- *be able, can* (W):pɔt+ *able, powerful*; sap- *be wise, know* (S[1]):sap+:sav+ *wise*.

e. +ešš+ *-esce* quasi-III, only in certain present participles: e.g. marčeššénte *decaying*:marčešš+:márč- *decayed* adj/I–II; putreššénte *putrescent*:putrešš+:putr+ *rotten*; etc.

4. Nouns, with:

a. +'e- *act like . . ., make into . . .* I/Reg/W, in ráte- *divide into installments*:rát- *installment* f/Ia; róte- *revolve, rotate*:rɔt+:ruɔ́t- *wheel* f/Ia.

b. +é- *make . . ., frequent . . .* I/Reg/W, in dɔnné- *flirt*:dɔ́nn- *lady, woman* f/Ia; tɔrné- *tourney, joust*:tɔrn+:túrn- *turn* m/IIb.

c. +ékki- *diminutive* I/Reg/W, in sɔnnékki- *doze*:sɔ́nn- sɔ́nn- *sleep* m/IIb.

d. +'il- *-ilate* I/Reg/W, in véntil- *ventilate*:vént- *wind* m/IIb.

e. +óll- +úll- *act like . . .* I/Reg/W, in barkóll- barkúll- *reel*:bárk- *boat* f/Ia.

f. +očín- *act as . . .* I/Reg/W, in patročín- *protect, sponsor*:patr+:pádr- *father* m/IIIb.

g. +'ɛR- *-erate* I/Reg/W, in módɛR- *moderate*:mód- *way, manner* m/IIb.

h. +ístr- *prepare with . . .* I/Reg/W, in salmístr- *salt*:salm+:sál- *salt* m/IIIb.

j. +'u- *-uate* I/Reg/W, in abítu- *habituate*:ábit- *habit* m/IIb.

k. +'ov- *bring to . . .* I/Reg/W, in méntov- *mention*:mént- *mind* f/IIIb.

l. +ɔr- *perform the act of . . .* II/ísK/W, in partɔr- *give birth to . . .*:párt- *birth* m/IIb.

m. +△- *do the work of . . .* IIIb/Reg/S[1, 2], in kuɔ́č- *cook*:kuɔ́k- *cook* m/IIb.

5. Verbs:

a. On root, with:

i. +0- *causative* I/Reg/W:

A. With no change in root, in stríng- *make concise, tight*:strínG- *squeeze* IIIb/Reg/S[1, 2].

B. With change in the root:

I. /ɛ/ > /ɛ/, in séd- *calm, allay*:sɛd- *sit* IIIa/Reg/W.

ii. /d/ > /sk/, in kásk- *fall*:kád- *fall* IIIa/Reg/S.[1]

iii. /K/ > /t/, in mést- *mix*:mésK- *mix* IIIb/Reg/W.

c. With concomitant prefixation in parasynthetic compounds:

i. With no change in the root, in ossérv- *observe*:sérv- *serve* II/Reg/W; prédik- *preach*:díK- *say* IV/Irr/S[1, 2]; éduk- *educate*:⁺dúK- *-duce, -duct* IV/Reg/S[1, 2].

ii. With loss of final V and shift of stress to preceding syllable (but without lowering of mid-vowels), in derivatives of stá- *stand* IV/Irr/S[1]:díst- *be distant*; kɔntrást- *contrast, oppose, stand against*; óst- *be in the way*; rést- *remain*; sóst- *stand still*.

ii. ⁺íčč- repetitive I/Reg/W, in skalpíčč- *stamp repeatedly, shuffle*:skalp⁺: kalp⁺ *stamp*; stropíčč- *rub*:strop⁺ *rub*.

iii. ⁺ézʐ- *-ize* I/Reg/W:

A. Alone, in battézʐ- *baptize*:batt⁺ *bapt-*; ɔlézʐ- *be sweet-smelling*:ɔl⁺ *smell*.

B. With concomitant prefixation, in spetézʐ- *fart*:pét- *id.* I/Reg/W.

iv. ⁺ákki- pejorative, diminutive, as in the following based on verbs of I/Reg/W: abboccákki- *make rough sketches*:abbócc- *sketch*; bručákki- *scorch*: brúč- *burn*; fɔrákki- *make a lot of little holes*:fór- *hole*; gridákki- *gripe, beef*:gríd- *yell*; kampákki- *eke out a living*:kámp- *live (poorly)*; lavɔrákki- *work a little*:lavór- *work*; etc.

v. ⁺úkki- pejorative, diminutive, as in the following based on verbs of:

A. I/Reg/W: ǧokúkki- *play a little*:ǧók- *play*; imparúkki- *learn a little*:impár- *learn*; kampúkki- *eke out a living*:kámp- *live (poorly)*; lavɔrúkki- *work a little*:lavór- *work*; manǧúkki- *eat slowly, nibble*:mánǧ- *eat*; etc.

B. IIIb/Reg/S (with final /G/ or /GG/ > /ǧ/), in bevúkki- *drink a little too much*:bév- *drink*; leǧǧúkki- *read a little*:léGG- *read*; pianǧúkki- *weep a little*:piánG- *weep*; skrivúkki- *write a little*:skrív- *write*.

vi. ⁺úkk- diminutive I/Reg/W, in pilúkk- *pluck, pull off*:pil⁺:pél- *pluck (hair)* I/Reg/W.

vii. ⁺éll- diminutive I/Reg/W, on verbs I/Reg/W:

A. Alone, in ǧiréll- *wander around*:ǧír- *turn*; saltéll- *go by little jumps*: sált- *jump*.

B. Preceded by ⁺ɛr⁺, in fiskiɛréll- *whistle sotto voce*:físki- *whistle*; ǧokɛréll- *play distractedly*:ǧók- *play*; kantɛréll- *hum, sing sotto voce*:kánt- *sing*; trottɛréll- *trot along*:trótt- *trot*.

viii. ⁺úʎʎ- diminutive, pejorative I/Reg/W, in čančúʎʎ- *stammer*:čánč- *talk idly, with difficulty* I/Reg/W.

ix. ⁺'ɛr- causative I/Reg/W, in búkɛr- . . . *make a hole in* . . .:búk- *make a hole* I/Reg/W.

x. ⁺ént- intensive I/Reg/W, in pavént- *be frightened, take fright*:pav⁺ *fear*.

xi. ⁺ést- intensive I/Reg/W, in kalpést- *tread on, crush by treading*:kalp⁺ *stamp*.

xii. ⁺ótt- diminutive I/Reg/W, in bɔrbótt- *mutter, burble, rumble*:bɔrb⁺ *rumble*.

xiii. +ácc- pejorative I/Reg/W, on verbs of I/Reg/W in the parasynthetic compounds skakácc- *void excrement in several installments*:kák- *shit*; skiamácc-raise a *ruction*:kiám- *call*; svɔlácc- *fly around*:vól- *fly*.

xiv. +úcc- diminutive I/Reg/W, in taʎʎúcc- *cut to pieces*:táʎʎ- *cut* I/Reg/W.

xv. +0- causative II/ísK/W, together with the prefix in *in-*, in indɔl-*cause slow, continual pain*:dɔl- *hurt* IIIa/Reg/S[1].

xvi. +tu- causative II/ísK/W, in statu- *establish*:stá- *stand* IV/Irr/S[1].

xvii. +0- IIIb/Reg/W, in presiéd- *preside*:presɛd- *id.* IIIa/Reg/W.

xviii. +ósK- IIIb/Reg/S[1, 2], in kɔnósK- kɔɲɲósK- (archaic) *know* (:kɔn+):kɔɲɲ+ *id.*

b. On root and Non-Finite C, with +íkki- diminutive and pejorative I/Reg/W:

i. On Non-Finite C, in mɔrsíkki- *nibble*:mórd- *bite* IIIb/Reg/S[1, 2].

ii. On root, in other derivatives, such as the following based on verbs of:

A. I/Reg/W: abboccíkki- *make rough sketches*:abbócc- *sketch*; ammɔn-tíkki- *heap up, accumulate*:ammónt- *heap up, amount*; kampíkki- *eke out a living*:kámp- *live (poorly)*; dɛntíkki- *nibble*:dént- *bite*; lavɔríkki- *work a little*:lavór- *work*; puccíkki- *stink a little*:púcc- *stink*; saltíkki- *jump a little*:sált- *jump*; etc.

B. II/Reg/W: kučíkki- *sew poorly*:kúč- *sew*; dɔrmíkki- *snoozle*:dɔrm-*sleep*.

c. IIIa/Irr/S[1]: dɔlíkki- *hurt a little*:dɔl- *hurt*.

D. IIIb: bevíkki- *drink rather too much*:bév- *drink*; leǧǧíkki- *read a little*:léGG- *read*; skrivíkki- *write a little, with difficulty*:skrív- *write*.

c. On Non-Finite C or alternant, with the following suffixes of intensive meaning, all of type I/Reg/W:

i. +0-, in sált- *jump*:sál- *go up* II/Irr/W; divént- *become*:divɛn- *id.* II/Irr/S[1]; kapt- *capture, take*:kap- *grasp, understand* II/ísK/W sostént- *sustain*:sostɛn- *id.* IIIa/Irr/S[1]; céss- *stop*:céd- *yield* IIIb/Reg/W; vérs- *pour, turn*:vért- *turn* IIIb/Reg; vólt- *turn*:vólG- *turn* IIIb/Reg/S[1, 2]; kánt- *sing*:kan+ *id.*

ii. +ki-, in ráski- *scrape*:rád- *shave* IIIb/Reg/S[1, 2].

iii. +u-, in kuéstu- *beg*:kuɛst+:kiéd- *ask, seek* IIIb/Reg/S[1, 2].

iv. +'iv- -*ivate*, in kóltiv- *cultivate*:kól- *id.* IIIb/Reg/S[1, 2].

3.117. ADVERBS are formed on:

1. Adverbs or adverbial bases, with:

a. +'0- I (with preceding /s/ > /šš/), in póšša *afterwards*:pos+ *post-, after*.

b. +ín- diminutive, *just* ... II, in appuntíno *just right*:appúnt- *exactly* adv/II; bɛníno *nicely*:bén- *well* adv/III.

c. +ón- augmentative III, in bɛnóne *very well indeed*:bén- *well* adv/III.

d. +únku- indefinite, -*ever* III, in dovúnkue *wherever*:dóv- *where* adv/III; kɔmúnkue *however*:kóm- *how* adv/III.

2. Demonstrative bases, with +áˣ *location (farther away from person spoken to)* and +íˣ *location (nearer person spoken to)*, both adv/VI, in the forms shown in Table VIII.

3. Adjectives, with:

a. ⁺0- -*ly* I, in príma *first, before*:prím- *first* adj/I–II.

b. ⁺0- -*ly* III, in mássime *very greatly, especially*:mássim- *great* adj/I–II; bélle *handsomely, completely*:béll- *handsome, fine* adj/I–II.

c. ⁺0- -*ly* IV, on adj/I–II, in lúngi *afar*:lun$G$⁺:lúng- *long*; tárdi *late*:tárd- *late*.

d. ⁺imént- -*ly* IV in altriménti *otherwise*:áltr- *other* adj/I–II; pariménti *equally*:pár- *equal* adj/IVd.

4. Nouns and verbs, with ⁺ón- *like* . . ., -*ingly* IV (also III in those based on nouns), as in the following based on:

a. Nouns, in katɛllóne katɛllóni *stealthily*:katéll- *kitten* m/IIb; ğinokkióne ğinokkióni *kneeling*:ğinókki- *knee* m/IIc.

b. Verbs I/Reg/W, in brankɔlóni *gropingly*:bránkɔl- *grope*; dɔndɔlóni *rockingly, idlingly*:dóndɔl- *rock, idle*; ğirandɔlóni *wandering around*:ğirándɔl- *wander around*; kapitɔmbɔlóni *head over heels*:kapitómbɔl- *fall head over heels*; pɛnzɔlóni *danglingly*:pénzɔl- *dangle*; saltɛllóni *jumpingly*:saltéll- *go with little jumps*; strofinóni *rubbingly*:strófin- *rub*; tɛntɛnnóni *gropingly*:tɛnténn- *grope*; tɛntóni *feeling one's way*:tént- *feel*; vɔltɔlóni *turning*:vólt- *turn*.

TABLE VIII: DEMONSTRATIVE ADVERBS

	kost⁺ *that (iste)*	l⁺ *that (ille)*	ku⁺ *this (hic)*
With ending { +áˣ	koştáˣ *over there*	láˣ *there*	kuáˣ *here*
{ +íˣ	kostíˣ *over there*	líˣ *there*	kuíˣ *here*

5. Nouns IIIb, with ⁺0- -*ly* IV, in barkɔllóni *reelingly, staggeringly*:barkɔllón- *staggering, reeling*; bokkóni *face downwards*:bokkón- *big mouth*.

6. Verbs:

a. In Non-Finite[1] A, with ⁺iér- -*ingly* IV, in vɔlɛntiéri *willingly, gladly*: vɔl- *wish, will* IIIa/Irr/S[1].

b. In Non-Finite[2] A, with ⁺0- -*ing* II, the 'gerund':e.g. kantándo (*by*) *singing*; vɔléndo (*by*) *wishing*; etc.

3.118. PREPOSITIONS. The only preposition-forming suffix is ⁺0- III, on a present participle (§3.112.9.d) in duránte *during*:duránt- *lasting* (:dúr- *last* I/Reg/W); mediánte *by means of*:médi⁺ *mediate* (:médi- *middle* adj/I–II).

3.12. ABBREVIATION is the derivation of a form by the loss of one or more phonemic elements of the base, and is of the following types:

1. Loss of all but the first two syllables; the resulting form is masculine (if based on an adjective) or of the same gender as the base (if based on a noun), and has suffix ⁺′0- d (i.e. is invariable), as in the following based on:

a. Adj/I–II: zóo *zoo* m/IId:zoolóğiK- *zoological* (sc. ğardíno *garden* m/IIb).

b. Nouns of:

i. f/Ia: fóto *photo* f/IId:fòtografí- *photograph*; móto *motorcycle*:moto-čiklétt- *id*.

ii. m/Ib: náci *Nazi* m/IVd: nacionàlsočalíst- *National Socialist*.

2. Loss of all phonemes between the initial consonant or consonant-cluster and the vowel of the stressed syllable, with no change in gender or stem-vowel. This type of abbreviation occurs only in mónna *Monna* (archaic title for ladies): madónna *my lady* f/Ia, and in personal names: e.g. bráččo *Braccio*:brunáččo *nasty Bruno* m/IIb; dánte *Dante*:duránte *Durante* m/IIIb; bíče *Bice*:beatríče *Beatrice* f/IIIb; ǧánni *Gianni, Johnny*:ǧovánni *Giovanni, John* m/IVd; etc.

3. Loss of all syllables preceding the stressed syllable, without change of gender or stem-vowel. This type of abbreviation occurs only in personal names: e.g. vánna *Vanna*:ǧovánna *Giovanna, Johanna* f/Ia; bérto *Bert*:albérto *Albert*, robérto *Robert*, both m/IIb; néllo *Nello*:ǧovannéllo *little John* m/IIb; viéri *Vieri*:oliviéri *Oliver* m/IVd; etc.

3.13. PREFIXATION is accomplished with the following elements,[6] here sub-divided according to the types of derivatives in which they occur: endocentric alone (§3.131), exocentric alone (§3.132), and both endocentric and exocentric (§3.133).

3.131. ENDOCENTRIC derivation is accomplished for:

1. Both substantives and verbs, with:

a. ant[+] anti[+] *anti-, against, un-*; *ante-, before* . . ., in the following distribution: ant[+] only before the adjectives I–II ártiK- *Arctic*, ɛlmíntiK- *helminthic*, ɛmétiK- *emetic*, iǧéniK- *hygienic*, istériK- *hysteric(al)*; the noun f/Ia [+]onomasí- *onomasia*; and the noun m/Ib [+]agoníst- *-agonist*; and anti[+] elsewhere; occurring in:

i. Adjectives of types:

A. I–II: those listed in the first paragraph of this section and many others; e.g. antiaéreo *anti-aircraft*:aére- *aerial*; antiestétiK- *unaesthetic*:estétiK- *aesthetic*; antikattóliK- *anti-Catholic*:kattóliK- *Catholic*; antireliǧóso *anti-religious*:reliǧóso *religious*; etc.

B. IIIb: antikostitucionále *unconstitutional*:kostitucionále *constitutional*; antinacionále *anti-national*:nacionále *national*; etc.

ii. Nouns, e.g. of types:

A. f/Ia: antikámɛra *antechamber*:kámɛr- *room, chamber*; antipórta *outer door, vestibule*:pórt- *door*; antonomasía *antonomasia*:[+]onomasí- *-onomasia*; etc.

B. m/Ib: antipápa *anti-pope*:páp- *pope*; antagonísta *antagonist*:agoníst- *-agonist*.

C. m/IIb: antikórpo *anti-body*:kórp- *body*; antikrísto *anti-Christ*:krísto *Christ*; antipásto *antipasto*:pást- *repast, meal*; etc.

D. m/IIc: antibráččo *forearm* (obs.):bráčč- *arm*.

E. m/IIIb: antičiklóne *anticyclone*:čiklón- *cyclone*.

F. f/IIIb: antístrof- *antistrophe*:[+]'strof-:stróf- *strophe*.

G. f/IVd: antisépsi *antisepsis*:sépT- *sepsis*; antítesi *antithesis*:[+]'tɛs-:téT- *thesis*.

iii. Verbs: antíčip- *anticipate*:[+]'čip- *-cipate* I/Reg/W; antivɛn- *provide for, against*:vɛn- *come* II/Irr/S[1]; antivéd- *foresee*:véd- *see* IIIa/Reg/S[1, 2].

---

[6] These elements qualify as prefixes, as distinguished from initial elements of compounds (§3.2), in that they are always derivationally bound and occur only in this position.

b. ante⁺ *ante-, before,* in:

i. Adi/I–II: antɛnáto *born previously, ancestor*:nát- *born*; antepɛnúltimo *antepenultimate*:pɛnúltim- *penultimate*; anteskrítto *previously written, abovementioned*:skrítt- *written.*

ii. Nouns of types:

A. f/Ia: antefíssa *antefix*:físs- *-fix.*

B. m/IIb: antefátto *previous occurrence*:fátt- *fact, deed*; antesiɲɲáno *advance standard-bearer*:siɲɲán- *standard-bearer.*

C. m/IIIb: antɛmurále *outside wall*:murál- *wall.*

iii. Verbs: antečéd- *antecede*:čéd- *cede* IIIb/Reg/W; antepón- *put before, prepone*:pón- *put* IV/Irr/S¹· ².

c. bi⁺ *bi-, two-, double-,* as in:

i. Adjectives, of types:

A. I–II: bikɔrnúto *two-horned*:kɔrnút- *horned*; bisdrúččɔlo *having accent on fourth from last syllable*:sdrúččɔl- *having accent on third from last syllable.*

B. IIIb: bilabiále *bilabial*:labiál- *labial*; bimɛnsíle *bimonthly*:mɛnsíl- *monthly.*

ii. Nouns m/IIb: bikarbɔnáto *bicarbonate*:karbɔnát- *carbonate*; bióssido *bioxide*:óssid- *oxide.*

iii. Verb: bipárt- *divide in two*:párt- *divide* II/ísK/W.

d. bis⁺ *bis-, twice, double, imperfectly . . ., badly . . .,* as in:

i. Adj/I–II: biskótto *twice cooked, biscuit*:kótt- *cooked*; bislúngo *longer than wide* (often *irregular*):lúng- *long*; bistórto *distorted*:tórt- *twisted*; bisúnto *very greasy and dirty*:únt- *smeared*; bistóndo *not absolutely round*:tónd- *round.*

ii. Nouns m/IIb: bisávɔlo *great-great-grandfather*:ávɔl- *great-grandfather*; biskánto *jog, double angle*:kánt- *angle*; biskuǧíno *second cousin*:kuǧín- *cousin.*

iii. Verbs I/Reg/W: bisbíʎʎ- *whisper*:⁺bíʎʎ- *id.*; bistrátt- *maltreat*:trátt- *treat.*

e. čirko⁺ (before /sC/), elsewhere čirkɔn⁺ *circum-,* as in:

i. Adjectives, of types:

A. I–II: čirkɔnvičíno *surrounding*:vičín- *nearby*; čirkospétto *circumspect*:⁺spétt- *-spect.*

B. IIIb: čirkostánt- *surrounding*:stánt- *standing.*

ii. Nouns f/IIIb: čirkɔnlokucióne *circumlocution*:lokución- *locution*; čirkɔnvallacióne *circumvallation*:⁺vallación- *-vallation*; čirkɔnvɔlucióne *circumvolution*:⁺vɔlución- *volution.*

iii. Verbs of types:

A. II/Irr/S¹: čirkɔnvɛn- *circumvent*:vɛn- *come.*

B. IIIb/Reg/S¹· ²: čirkɔnčíd- *circumcise*:⁺číd- *-cise, cut*; čirkɔnfónd- *circumfuse*:fónd- *fuse*; čirkoskrív- *circumscribe*:skrív- *write, -scribe.*

C. IV/Irr/S: čirkónd- *surround*:dá- *give*; čirkɔndúK- *lead around*:⁺dúK- *lead.*

f. dɔ⁺ *de-, tomorrow,* in dɔmattína *tomorrow morning*:mattín- *morning* f/Ia; dɔmáni *tomorrow*:⁺mán- *morrow* m/IVd; dɔmánd- *demand, ask*:mánd- *command* I/Reg/W.

g. én+ *in-* (negative, intensive), in émpio *impious*:pí- *pious* adj/I–II; énfi- *inflate*:+fi- *-flate* I/Reg/W.

h. es+ *ex-*, as in:

i. Substantives: esátt- *exact*:átt- *act(ed)* adj/I–II; esantéma *exanthema*: antém- *-anthema* m/Ib; ésodo *exodus*:'od- *-odus, road* m/IIb.

ii. Verbs of types:

A. I/Reg/W: esáǧit- *agitate violently*:áǧit- *agitate*; eskóǧit- *excogitate*: kóǧit- *cogitate*; esklám- *exclaim*:+klám-:kiám- *call*; espórt- *export*:pórt- *carry*; espúrg- *expurgate*:púrg- *purge*.

B. IIIb/Reg/W or S: esíǧ- *demand*:+íǧ- *-act*; esklúd- *exclude*:+klúd- *-clude*:kiúd- *close*; eskút- *cite* (legal term):+kút- *-cute, shake*; espánd- *expand*: +pánd- *stretch*; espéll- *expel*:+péll- *drive*; esprím- *express*:+prím-:prém- *press*; espúnG- *expunge*:púnG- *prick*; esténd- *extend*:ténd- *stretch*; estíngu- *extinguish*: +tíngu- *id*.

C. IV/Irr/S: espón- *expose, expound*:pón- *put, place*; estráˣ- *extract*: tráˣ- *draw*.

j. infra+ *infra-*, as in:

i. Adj/I–II: infrarósso *infra-red*:róss- *red*; infraskrítto *written below*: skrítt- *written*.

ii. Verbs:

A. Alone, in inframétt- *interfere*:métt- *put* IIIb/Reg/S[1, 2].

B. Followed by /ˣ/, in infrappón- *put in between*:pón- *place, put* IV/ Irr/S[1, 2].

k. intra+ *intra-*, as in:

i. Substantives: intrauteríno *intrauterine*:uterín- *uterine* adj/I–II; intradósso *inside of vault arch*:dóss- *back* m/IIb.

ii. Verbs:

A. Alone, IIIb/Reg/S[1, 2]: intramétt- *put in*:métt- *put*; intraprénd- *undertake*:prénd- *take*.

B. Followed by /ˣ/, in intrattɛn- *entertain*:tɛn- *hold* IIIa/Irr/S[1]; intravvéd- *see dimly*:véd- *see* IIIb/Reg/S[1, 2].

l. ko+ *co-, com-, con-, with . . ., together with . . ., of the same . . .*, followed by:1) /ˣ/ before /l r/; 2) /m/ before labial consonants, except in kɔmánd- *command* I/Reg/W; 3) /n/ before /sC/ only in kónst- *consist, be evident* I/Reg/W, and before other non-labial consonants and consonant clusters; 4) zero elsewhere; as in:

i. Adjectives of types:

A. I–II: kɔrréo *guilty at the same time, co-defendant*:ré- *guilty*; kɔrrelatívo *correlative*:rɛlatív- *relative*; kɔrrespettívo *(co)respective*:respettív- *respective*; kɔmmísto *mixed together*:míst- *mixed*; kɔmpaesáno *of the same town or region*: paesán- *of a town or region*; kɔmplésso *complex*:+pléss- *-plex(ed)*; kɔndéɲɲo *suitable*:déɲɲ- *worthy*; kɔnkávo *concave*:káv- *hollow*; kɔnnáto *connate*:nát- *born*; koakkusáto *co-accused*:akkusát- *accused*; koátto *restricted*:+átt- *act(ed)*, *driven*; koɛlétto *elected together*:ɛlétt- *elected*; koetáneo *coetaneous*:+etáne- *of an age*.

B. IIIb: kɔllatɛrále *collateral*:latɛrál- *lateral*; kɔmprovinčále *of the same province*:provinčál- *provincial*; kɔnnaturále *having the same nature*:naturál- *natural*; kɔnnacɔnále *of the same nationality*:nacɔnal- *national*; kɔnsímile (*a*)*like*: símil- *similar*; kɔntitɔláre *co-titular*:titɔlár- *titular*.

ii. Nouns of types:

A. f/Ia: kɔnkáusa *co-cause*:káus- *cause*.

B. m/Ib: kɔmpatrióta *compatriot*:patriót- *patriot*.

C. m/IIb: kɔmpatróno *co-patron*:patrón- *patron*; kɔmpossésso *co-possession*:posséss- *possession*; kɔnčittadíno *co-*, *fellow-citizen*:čittadín- *citizen*; kɔndɔmínio *condominium*:dɔmíni- *dominion*; kɔnkámbio *exchange*:kámbi- (*ex*)-*change*; kɔntémpo *same time*:témp- *time*; etc.

D. m/IIIb: kɔllokutóre *collocutor*:lokutór- *speaker*; kɔmprotettóre *co-protector*:protettór- *protector*; kɔndirettóre *co-director*:direttór- *director*; koautóre *co-author*:autór- *author*; etc.

E. f/IIIb: kɔrrelacióne *correlation*:relación- *relation*; kɔmpassióne *com-passion*:passión- *passion, suffering*; koacióne *violence*:ación- *action*; etc.

F. f/VId: kɔmproprietá^x *joint property*:proprietá^x *property*; kɔnservitú^x *co-slavery*:sɛrvitú^x *slavery*; etc.

iii. Verbs:

A. With /'/, in the following of I/Reg/W: kóllok- *collocate*:lók- *locate*; kómput- *compute*:$^+$pút- -*pute*; kónst- *consist*:$^{+'}$st- (:stá- *stand* IV/Irr/S[1]).

B. With no shift in stress, e.g. in the following of types:

I. I/Reg/W: kɔllútt- *struggle together*:lútt- *struggle*; kɔmbáč- *fit together*:báč- *kiss*; kɔndánn- *condemn*:dánn- *damn*; koábit- *cohabit*:ábit- *live, inhabit*; etc. etc.

II. II/Reg or Irr: kɔmpárt- *share*:párt- *divide*; kɔnségu- *be conse-quent, obtain*:ségu- *follow*; kɔnsént- *consent*:sént- *feel*; kɔnvɛn- *agree, convene, be fitting*:vɛn- *come*; kɔnvért- *convert*:$^+$vért- -*vert*.

III. II/ísK/W: kɔmpar- *appear*:$^+$par- *appear*; kɔmpat- *feel com-passion for* ...:pat- *suffer*; kɔnčep- *conceive*:$^+$čep- -*ceive*; kɔnfɛr- *confer*:$^+$fɛr- -*fer*; kostitu- *constitute*:$^+$stitu- -*stitute*; kostru- *construct*:$^+$stru- -*struct*.

IV. IIIa: kɔndɔl- *condole*:dɔl- *hurt*; kɔntɛn- *contain*:tɛn- *hold*.

V. IIIb: kɔrréGG- *correct*:réGG- *rule, guide*; kɔmbátt- *combat*:bátt- *beat*; kɔnkórr- *concur, compete, run together*:kórr- *run*; koinčíd- *coincide*:inčíd- *incise, -incide*; etc.

VI. IV: kɔndúK- *conduce, conduct*:$^+$dúK- -*duce, -duct*; kɔnfáč- *be suitable*:fáč- *do*; kɔntrá^x- *contract*:trá^x- *draw*.

m. kɔntra^{x+} (before consonant), kɔntr$^+$ (before vowel) *contra-, counter-, anti-, against* ..., as in:

i. Adj/I–II: kɔntraére- *anti-aircraft*:aére- *aerial*.

ii. Nouns of types:

A. f/Ia: kɔntraddánca *counter-dance*:dánc- *dance*; kɔntrakkúsa *counter-accusation*:akkús- *accusation*; etc.

B. m/IIb: kɔntrabbásso *counter-bass, double bass*:báss- *bass*; kɔntrağ-ğénio *aversion*:ğéni- *genius, spirit*; kɔntrattémpo *contretemps*:témp- *time*; kɔntrammiráʎʎ- *rear-admiral*:ammiráʎʎ- *admiral*; kɔntrappéllo *second appeal*: appéll- *appeal*; kɔntrattákko *counter-attack*:attákk- *attack*; etc.

iii. Verbs of types:

A. I/Reg/W: kɔntrakkámbi- *exchange*:kámbi- *change*; kɔntríndik- *counter-indicate*:índik- *indicate*.

B. II/Irr/S¹, ²: kɔntravvɛn- *countervene*:vɛn- *come*.

C. IIIb/Reg/S¹, ²: kɔntraddistíngu- *recognize (by countersign)*:distíngu- *distinguish*.

D. IV/Irr/S¹, ²: kɔntraddíK- *contradict*:díK- *say*; kɔntraffáč- *counterfeit, imitate*:fáč- *do, make*; kɔntrappón- *set against*:pón- *put, place*.

n. mis⁺ *mis-, dis-, fail to* . . ., as in:

i. Substantives: misleále *disloyal* (archaic):leál- *loyal* adj/IIIb; misfátto *misdeed*:fátt- *deed* m/IIb.

ii. Verbs IIIb/Reg/S¹: miskɔnósK- *fail to recognize*:kɔnósK- *recognize, know*; miskréd- *disbelieve*:kréd- *believe*.

o. pretɛr⁺ *praeter-, beyond* . . ., as in:

i. Substantives IIIb:

A. Adjectives: preterintenciɔnále *unintentional*:intɛnciɔnál- *intentional*; preternaturále *preternatural*:naturál- *natural*.

B. Noun: pretɛrmissióne *omission*:missión- *mission* f.

ii. Verb: pretɛrmétt- *omit*:métt- *put* IIIb/Reg/S¹, ².

p. re⁺ *re-, again, back, away*, as in:

i. Noun: rékuie *rest, requiem*:⁺'kui- *quiet* f/IIId.

ii. Verbs:

A. Followed by /d/, in redíntegr- *reintegrate*:íntegr- *integrate* I/Reg/W; redargu- *reprove*:argu- *argue* II/ísK/W; redim- *crown*:⁺im- *id.* II/ísK/W; redíG- *edit, redact*:⁺íG- *-act* IIIb/Reg/¹, ²; redím- *redeem, bring back*:⁺ím- *buy* IIIb/Reg/S¹, ².

B. Alone, as in the following of types:

I. I/Reg/W: rekálčitr- *be recalcitrant*:⁺kálčitr- *kick*; reklám- *reclaim*:⁺klám-:kiám- *call*; reklín- *recline*:⁺klín- *-cline, lean*; etc.

II. II/ísK/W; reaǧ- *react*:aǧ- *act*; etc.

III. IIIb: rečéd- *recede*:čéd- *yield*; rečíd- *cut away*:⁺číd- *cut*; reklúd- *shut away*:⁺klúd-:kiúd- *shut*; etc.

q. r⁺ (before vowels except /u/, opt., pop.), ri⁺ *re-, again, a second time, completely* . . ., intensive, as in:

i. Substantives, of types:

A. Adj/I–II: ridóppi- *twice double*:dóppi- *double*; ripiéno *wholly full, chock full*:pién- *full*; risácio *completely full*:sácio *full, satisfied*.

B. Nouns, of types:

I. f/Ia: ripróva *second trial, second proof*:próv- *trial, proof*.

II. m/IIb: ridóss- *something taller and in back*:dóss- *back*; riepílog- *résumé*:epílog- *epilogue*; rifrútto *interest on interest*:frútt- *interest, fruit*.

ii. Verbs, such as the following of types:

A. I/Reg/W: r(i)abbáss- *lower again*:abbáss- *lower*; rabbókk- *fill full*, riabbókk- *fill again*:abbókk- *fill*; rimánd- *put off, send away*:mánd- *send*; etc. etc. etc.

B. II/Reg or Irr: riápr- *reopen*:ápr- *open*; ripárt- *divide, depart again*:

párt- *divide, depart*; risént- *feel (deeply), resent*:sént- *feel*; rivɛn- *come again*: vɛn- *come*; etc.

C. II/ísK/W: rabbrivid- *shiver, shudder*:abbrivid- *id.*; rivɛr- *revere*: ⁺vɛr- *fear, worship*; etc.

D. IIa: ritɛn- *retain*:tɛn- *hold*; rivéd- *see again*:véd- *see*; rikád- *fall back*:kád- *fall;* etc.

E. IIIb: r(i)aččénd- *relight*:aččénd- *light*; rabbátt- *leave ajar*:abbátt- *beat down*; rikiéd- *request*:kiéd- *ask*; rifúlG- *be resplendent*:fúlG- *shine*; ristrínG- *restrict*:strínG- *squeeze*; etc. etc.

F. IV: ridúK- *reduce*:⁺dúK- *-duce, -duct*; rifáč- *re-do*:fáč- *do, make*; ripón- *replace*:pón- *place, put.*

G. Defective: riékko *here, there is . . . again*:ékko *here, there is . . . .*

r. ro⁺ *re-, thoroughly*, in rotóndo *round, rotund*:tónd- *round* adj/I–II; rovíst- *search thoroughly*:⁺víst- *search* I/Reg/W.

s. sub⁺ *sub-, under*, as in:

i. Adjectives, of types:

A. I–II: subáčido *subacid*:áčid- *acid*; subákkueo *subaqueous*:ákkue- *aqueous*; subkɔntrário *subcontrary*:kɔntrári- *contrary*; subočeániK- *suboceanic*: očeániK- *oceanic*; etc.

B. IIIb: subkoššénte *subconscious*:koššént- *conscious*; sublunáre *sublunary*:lunár- *lunar.*

ii. Nouns, of types:

A. f/Ia: subást- *auction*:ást- *pole.*

B. m/IIb: substrát- *substratum*:strát- *stratum*; subúrbi- *suburb*:⁺úrbi- (:úrb- *city* f/IIIb).

iii. Verbs I/Reg/W: subakkóll- *subcontract*:akkóll- *contract*; subaffítt- *sublet*:affítt- *let, rent out*; subləók- *sublet, subcontract*:ləók- *let out*; subodór- *smell faintly, whiff*:odór- *smell*; subórdin- *subordinate*:órdin- *order*; etc.

2. Substantives alone, with:

a. an⁺ (before vowels), a⁺ (before consonants) *a(n)- privative*, as in:

i. Adjectives, of types:

A. I–II: akataléttiK- *acatalectic*:kataléttiK- *catalectic*; akattóliK- *non-Catholic*:kattóliK- *Catholic*; akrɔmátiK- *achromatic*:krɔmátiK- *chromatic*; etc.

B. IIIb: amɔrále *amoral*:mɔrál- *moral.*

ii. Nouns f/Ia: anarkía *anarchy*:⁺arkí- *-archy*; anestesía *anaesthesia*: ⁺estesí- *-aesthesia.*

b. am⁺ *am-, around, both:*

i. Alone, in amplésso *embrace* m/IIb: ⁺pléss- *id.* (:pléss- *-plex[ed]* adj/ I–II).

ii. Followed by /ɛn/ in amɛndúe *both*:dú- *two* num/IIId.

c. arči⁺ *archi-, very . . ., extremely . . .*, as in:

i. Adjectives: e.g. arčibeáto *most happy*:beát- *blessed, happy* I–II; arčinót- *very well-known*:nót- *well-known* I–II; arčiríkk- *extremely rich*:ríkk- *rich*; etc.

ii. Nouns, of types:

A. m/Ib: arčidúka *archduke*:dúk- *duke.*

B. m/IIb: arčidiákɔno *archdeacon*:diákɔn- *deacon*; arčifánfano *arch-babbler*:fánfan- *babbler*; arčivéskovo *archbishop*:véskov- *bishop*.

C. m/IIIb: arčipréte *archpriest*:prét- *priest*; arčispedále *main hospital*: spedál- *hospital*.

d. ark⁺ *arch-*:

i. Alone, in arkánǧel- *archangel*:ánǧel- *angel* m/IIb; arkávɔlo (*distant*) *ancestor*:ávɔl- *ancestor*; etc.

ii. Followed by /i/, as in:

A. Adj/IIIb: arkiepiskopále *archiepiscopal*:episkopál- *episcopal*.

B. Nouns, of types:

I. m/Ib: arkimandríta *archimandrite*:mandrít- *mandrite*.

II. m/IIb: arkidiákɔno *archdeacon*:diákɔn- *deacon*.

III. f/IVd: arkidióčesi *archdiocese*:dióčes- *diocese*.

e. auto⁺, with the meanings:

i. In some derivatives, *self-*: e.g. autɔmóbile *self-moving*, *automobile*: móbil- *mobile* adj/IIIb; autodifésa *self-defense*:difés- *defense* f/Ia; autɔlesióne *self-injury*:lesión- *injury* f/IIIb.

ii. In others, *automotive* . . ., such as the following nouns of types:

A. m/IIb: autokárro *truck*, *lorry*:kárr- *car(t)*; autotréno *motor train*: trén- *train*; autoveíkɔlo *motor vehicle*:veíkɔl- *vehicle*.

B. f/IIIb: autɔmotríče *Diesel rail-car*:motríč- *motor-car*.

f. di(a)⁺ *di(a)-*, with the following distribution:

i. di⁺ in the following:

A. Adj/I–II: diɛléttriK- *dielectric*:eléttriK- *electric*; dióttriK- *dioptric*: óttriK- *optric*; diurétiK- *diuretic*:urétiK- *uretic*.

B. Nouns IVd: diosmósi *diosmosis*:osmóT- *osmosis*; diurési *diuresis*: uréT- *uresis*.

ii. dia⁺ elsewhere, as in:

A. Adj/I–II: diakrítiK- *diacritic(al)*:krítiK- *critic(al)*; diakróniK- *diachronic*:króniK- *chronic*; diamaɲɲétiK- *diamagnetic*:maɲɲétiK- *magnetic*; diatérmiK- *diathermic*:térmiK- *thermic*; diáfano *diaphanous*:⁺ʹfan- *-phanous*.

B. Nouns, of types:

I. f/Ia: diarréa *diarrhea*:⁺rré- *-rrhea, flow*.

II. m/Ib: diadéma *diadem*:⁺dém- *-dem*; diafrámma *diaphragm*: ⁺frámm- *phragm*; diagrámma *diagram*:⁺grámm- *-gram*.

III. m/IIb: diákɔno *deacon*:⁺ʹkɔn- *-con*; dialétto *dialect*:⁺létt- *-lect*; *diálogo* dialogue:⁺ʹlog- *word, -logue*; diámetro *diameter*:⁺ʹmetr- *-meter*.

IV. f/IIIb: diabéte *diabetes*:⁺bét- *-betes*.

V. f/IVd: diagnósi *diagnosis*:⁺gnós- *-gnosis*; diálisi *dialysis, sharp split*:⁺ʹliT- *-lysis, splitting*.

g. ɛn⁺ *en-, em-*, in:

i. Adj/I–II: ɛndémiK- *endemic*:⁺démiK- *of the people*.

ii. Nouns of types:

A. f/Ia: ɛnɛrǧía *energy*:⁺ɛrǧí- *-ergy*.

B. m/IIb: ɛnčéfalo *encephalus*:čéfal- *cephalus, head*.

c. f/IVd: énkliT- enklíT- *enclisis* (:+'kliT-):+klíT- *-clisis*; énfaT- *emphasis*:+'faT- *-phasis*.

h. etɛro+ *hetero-, varied*, in:

 i. Adjectives, of types:

   A. I–II: etɛróklito *heteroclyte, -ic*:+'kliT- *-clyte, -ic*; etɛrodósso *heterodox*:+dóss- *-dox*; etɛroğéneo *heterogeneous*:+ğéne- *of . . . kinds, -geneous*.

   B. IIIb: etɛrosessuále *heterosexual*:sessuál- *sexual*.

 ii. Nouns, in etɛrodína *heterodyne*:+dín- *-dyne, force*.

j. eu+ ev+ *eu-, good . . .*, in the following distribution:

 i. ev+ in evanğélo *evangel, gospel*:+anğél- *messenger* m/IIb.

 ii. eu+ elsewhere, as in:

   A. Adj/I–II: euğɛnétiK- *eugenetic*:ğɛnétiK- *genetic*.

   B. Nouns in +í- *-y, -ia* f/Ia: eufɛmía *euphemy*; eufɔnía *euphony*; eufɔría *euphoria*; eukarestía eukaristía *eucharist*; euritmía *eurhythmy*; eutanasía *euthanasia*.

k. ipɛr+ *hyper-*, as in:

 i. Adjectives of types:

   A. I–II: ipɛrkataléttiK- *hypercatalectic*:kataléttiK- *catalectic*; ipɛrkrítiK- *hypercritical*:krítiK- *critical*.

   B. IIIb: ipɛrsɛnsíbile *hypersensitive*:sɛnsíbil- *sensitive*.

 ii. Nouns of types:

   A. f/Ia: ipɛrkrítika *hypercriticism*:krítik- *criticism*.

   B. m/IIb: ipɛrspácio *hyperspace*:spáci- *space*.

   C. f/IIIb: ipɛrnutrícione *hypernutrition*:nutrición- *nutrition*; ipɛrtɛnsióne *hypertension*:tɛnsión- *tension*.

l. kak+ (before vowels), kako+ (before consonants) *kak(o)-, bad . . .*, in:

 i. Adj/I–II: kakéttiK- *cachectic*:éttiK- *hectic, feverish*.

 ii. Nouns in -í *-ia, -y* f/Ia: kakessía *cachexy*:ɛTT+ *fever*; kakofɔnía *cacophony*:+'fɔn- *sound*.

m. kat(a)+ *cat(a)-*, in the following distribution:

 i. kat+ in kátodo *cathode*:+'od- *road, way* m/IIb.

 ii. kata+ elsewhere, as in katarifranğénte *catarefrangent*:rifranğénte *refrangent* adj/IIIb; kataplásma *cataplasm*:plásm- *plasm* m/Ib; katakrési *catachresis*:krés- *chresis* f/IVd; and, with recessive stress, in katástrofe *catastrophe*:+'strof-:stróf- *strophe* f/IIIb.

n. kɔŋ+ (with following /n/ > /ɲ/) *cog-*, in kɔɲɲáto *cognate*:nát- *born* adj/I–II; kɔɲɲóme *family name, cognomen*:nóm- *name* m/IIIb.

o. meso+ *meso-*, in mesozóiK- *mesozoic*:+zóiK- *-zoic* adj/I–II; mesokárpo *mesocarp*:kárp- *carp* m/IIb.

p. met(a)+ *meta-*, with the following distribution:

 i. met+ in metɔnimía *metonymy*:+ɔnimí- *-onymy* f/Ia; metɛmpsikósi *metempsychosis*:+ɛmpsikós- *-empsychosis* f/IVd.

 ii. meta+ elsewhere, as in:

   A. Adj/I–II: metamórfiK- *metamorphic*:+mórfiK- *-morphic*; metafísiK- *metaphysic(al)*:físiK- *physical*.

B. Nouns, of types:

i. f/Ia: metáfora *metaphor*: +'fɔr- *-phor(a)*.

ii. m/IIb: metaplásmo *metaplasm*: +plásm- *plasm*; metabolísmo *metabolism*: +bɔlísm- *-bolism*; metakárpo *metacarpus*:kárp- *carp(us)*; meta-krɔnísmo *metachronism*: +krɔnísm- *-chronism*; metatárso *metatarsus*:társ- *tarsus*.

q. n(e[ss])+ *un-, not* . . ., in the following distribution:

i. n+ in nɛmíK- *enemy, hostile, unfriendly*: +ɛmíK-:amíK- *friendly* adj/I–II; nekuit+ *unfairness* (in nekuitóso *unfair* adj/I–II):ekuit+:ekuitáˣ *equity, fairness* f/VId.

ii. ne+ in neššiɛ́nte *ignorant*:šiɛ́nt- *knowing* adj/IIIb.

iii. ness+ in nessúno *no one, no* . . .:ún- *one* adj/I–II.

r. pan+ *pan-, all-*, as in:

i. Adjs/I–II: panǧermániK- *pan-Germanic*:ǧermániK- *Germanic*; pan-sláviK- *pan-Slavic*:sláviK- *Slavic*; etc.

iii. Nouns, of types:

A. m/Ib: panǧermanísta *pan-Germanist*:ǧermaníst- *Germanist*; pan-slavísta *pan-Slavist*:slavíst- *Slavist*; panteísta *pantheist*:teíst- *theist*; etc.

B. m/IIb: pandɛmónio *pandemonium*:dɛmóni- *demon(ium)*; panǧer-manísmo *pan-Germanism*:ǧermanísm- *Germanism*; panslavísmo *pan-Slavism*:slavísm- *Slavism*; panteísmo *pantheism*:teísm- *theism*.

s. par+ (before vowels), para+ (before consonants), as in:

i. Adjectives, of types:

A. I–II: parallélo *parallel*: +allél- *other*.

B. IIIb: parastatále *quasi-public*:statál- *of the state*.

ii. Nouns, of types:

A. f/Ia: parábola *parable, parabola*: +'bɔl- *-bola*; paraplɛǧía *paraplegia*: +pleǧí- *-plegia*; paranóia *paranoia*: +nói- *reason*; etc.

B. m/Ib: parɛnkíma *parenchyme*: +ɛnkím- *-enchyme*.

C. m/IIb: parélio *parhelion*:éli+ *sun*; parágrafo *paragraph*: +'graf- *-graph*; paratífo *paratyphus*:tíf- *typhus*.

D. m/IIIb: parasɛléne *paraselene*:sɛlén- *selene*.

E. f/IIIb: paragóǧe *paragoge*: +agóǧ- *-agoge*.

F. f/IVd: paráfrasi *paraphrase*: +'fras- *-phrasis*; parálisi *paralysis*: +'liT- *-lysis*.

t. pɛn+ *pen-, almost* . . ., in pɛnúltimo *penultimate*:últim- *ultimate* adj/I–II; pɛninsuláre *peninsular*:insulár- *insular* adj/IIIb; pɛnísola *peninsula*:ísol- *island* f/Ia; pɛnómbr- *penumbra*:ómbr- *shade, shadow* f/Ia.

u. seskui+ *sesqui-*, in seskuipláno *sesquiplane*:plán- *plane* adj/I–II: seskui-pedále *sesquipedal*:pedál- *pedal* adj/IIIb; seskuióssido *sesquioxide*:óssid- *oxide* m/IIb; seskuisɔlfúro *sesquisulphide*:sɔlfúr- *sulphide* m/IIb.

w. sɛmi+ *semi-, half* . . ., as in:

i. Adjectives, of types:

A. I–II: sɛmiapɛ́rto *half-open*:apɛ́rt- *open*; sɛmibárbaro *half-barbar-ous*:bárbar- *barbarous*; sɛmiintɛrráto *half-buried*:intɛrrát- *buried*; sɛmimórto *half-dead*:mórt- *dead*; sɛmisério *semi-serious*:séri- *serious*; etc.

B. IIIb: sɛmifinále *semi-final*:finál- *final*; sɛmilunáre *half-moon-shaped*:

lunár- *lunar, moon-shaped*; sɛmiresponsábile *half-responsible*:responsábil- *responsible*; sɛmitrasparénte *semi-transparent*:trasparént- *transparent*.

    ii. Nouns, of types:

      A. f/Ia: sɛmičirkonferénca *semi-circumference*:čirkonfɛrénca *circumference*; sɛmikróma *semi-chrome*:króm- *chrome*; sɛmimínima *semi-minim*:mínim- *minim*; etc.

      B. m/IIb: sɛmičírkolo *semi-circle*: čírkolo- *circle*; sɛmidiámetro *semi-diameter*:diámetr- *diameter*; sɛmirítmo *semi-rhythm*:rítm- *rhythm*; etc.

      c. f/IIIb: sɛmibréve *semi-breve*:brév- *breve*; sɛmikonsonánte *semi-consonant*:konsonánt *consonant*; sɛmivokále *semi-vowel*:vokál- *vowel*; etc.

    y. tris⁺ *three times* . . ., in trisáǧo *thrice holy*:⁺áǧ- *holy* adj/I–II; trisávolo *great-great-grandfather*:ávol- *greatgrandfather*.

    z. ultra⁺ *ultra-*, in:

    i. Adjectives, of types:

      A. I–II: ultramontáno *ultra-montane*:montán- *montane*; ultraviolétto *ultra-violet*:violétt- *violet*.

      B. IIIb: ultrapoténte *ultra-powerful*:potént- *powerful*; ultrasɛnsíbile *ultra-sensitive*:sɛnsíbil- *sensitive*.

    ii. Noun: ultravírus *filterable virus*:vírus *virus* m/VId.

    aa. viče⁺ vis⁺ *vice-*, in the following distribution:

    i. vis⁺ in visdómino *vice-lord*:dómin- *lord* m/IIb; viskónte *viscount*:kónt- *count* m/IIIb.

    ii. viče⁺ elsewhere, as in:

      A. Adj/IIIb: vičekomitále *pertaining to a viscount*:komitál- *pertaining to a count*.

      B. Nouns, of types:

        I. m/IIb: vičeammiráʎʎo *vice-admiral*:ammiráʎʎo *ulmiral*; vičedómino *vice-lord*:⁺dómin- *lord*; vičeprefétto *vice-prefect*:prefétt- *prefect*; etc.

        II. m/IIIb: vičekónsole *vice-consul*:kónsol- *consul*; vičepádre *foster-father*:pádr- *father*; vičereáme *viceroyalty*:reám- *realm*.

        III. f/IIIb: vičemádre *foster-mother*:mádr- *mother*.

        IV. m/VId: vičepodestáˣ *vice-mayor*:podestáˣ *mayor*; viceréˣ *viceroy*:réˣ *king*.

    3. Adjectives and adverbs, with:

    a. altreˣ *just* . . ., in altrettánto *just as much*:tánt- *so much* adj/I–II; altrettále *just such*:tál- *such* adj/IIIb; altressíˣ *just so*[7]:síˣ *so* adv/VI.

    b. ku⁺ demonstrative, in:

    i. Adjs/I–II: kuésto *this*:ést- *this* (archaic); kuéllo *that*:⁺éll- *that*.

    ii. Advs/VI: kuáˣ *here*:⁺áˣ indicating location (farther away from the person spoken to); kuíˣ *here*:⁺íˣ indicating location (nearer the person spoken to).

    4. Adjectives, pronouns and adverbs, with ko⁺ (before consonants), kod⁺ kot⁺ (before vowels), demonstrative, in:

    a. Adjectives, of types:

[7] Spelled *altresì*.

i. I–II: kodésto kotésto *that*:ést- *this* (archaic); kotánto *so much*:tánt- *so much*.

ii. IIIb: kotále *such*:tál- *such*.

b. Pronouns: kɔlúi *that person* (m.sg.):lúi *him*; kɔléi *that person* (f.sg.): léi *her*; kɔlóro *those persons*:lóro *them*.

c. Advs/VI: kɔláˣ *over there*:láˣ *there*; kosíˣ *thus*:sí *so*.

5. Adjectives alone, with:

a. alk⁺ indefinite, in the following of I–II: alkuánto *some (quantity)*:kuánt- *how many*; alkúno *some, some one*:ún- *one*.

b. čis⁺ *cis-*, *this (usually the Roman) side of* . . ., as in the following of I–II: čisalpíno *cisalpine*:alpín- *Alpine*; čismɔntáno *cismontane*:mɔntán- *montane*; čispadáno *cispadane*:padán- *Padane, of the Po*.

c. kada⁺ *each*, in kadaúno *each one*:ún- *one* I–II.

d. spi⁺ excessively, in spilungóne *very tall* IIIb:spilúng⁺ *very long*:lúng- *long, tall* I–II.

e. tɛr⁺ *three times* . . ., in térǧémino *triplicate*:ǧémin- *geminate* I–II.

f. u⁽ˣ⁾⁺ intensive, in u(b)briáko *drunken*:briák- *drunk* I–II.

g. vɛr⁺ negative, in vɛrúno *not one*:ún- *one* I–II.

6. Nouns alone, with:

a. Reduplication of initial CV: babáu *bow-wow*:báu *bow-wow* m/Vd or mcl.

b. /m/ > /b/ in bilióne *billion*:milión- *million* m/IIIb.

c. af⁺ *aph-* in afélio *aphelion*:⁺éli- *sun* m/IIb.

d. ana⁺ *ana-* in anabattísta *anabaptist*:battíst- *baptist* m/Ib; **anagrámma** *anagram*:⁺'gramm- *-gram* m/Ib.

e. anfi⁺ *amphi-* in anfiteátro *amphitheater*:teátr- *theater* and **anfíbrak-** *amphibrach*:⁺'brak- *-brach*, both m/IIb.

f. ba⁺ *left*, in babórdo *lee* (naut.):bórd- *board* m/IIb.

g. čirkum⁺ *circum-*, in čirkumnavigacióne *circumnavigation*:navigación- *navigation* f/IIIb.

h. deči⁺ *deci-*, *the tenth part of* . . ., as in the following of m/IIb: dečigrámmo *lecigram*:grámm- *gram*; dečílitro *deciliter*:'litr- *liter*; dečímetro *decimeter*:'mɛtr- *meter*; dečimillímetro *decimillimeter*:millímetr- *millimeter*; dečistéro *decistere*:stér- *stere*.

j. dis⁺ diss⁺ *dys-*, *bad* . . ., with the following distribution:

i. diss⁺ in dissɛntɛría *dysentery*:⁺ɛntɛrí- *-entery* f/Ia.

ii. dis⁺ elsewhere, as in the following of f/Ia: dislalía *dyslalia*:⁺lalí- *speech*; dispepsía *dyspepsia*:⁺pepsí- *digestion*; distrofía *dystrophy*:⁺trofí- *-trophy*; disuría *dysuria, trouble in urinating*:⁺urí- *urination*.

k. ett⁺ (before vowel), etto⁺ (before consonant), in the following of m/IIb: éttaro *hectare*:⁺'ar- *are*; ettográmma *hectogram*:grámm- *gram*; ettólitro *hectoliter*:'litr- *liter*; ettómetro *hectometer*:'metr- *meter*.

l. ɛˣ⁺ *name of letter* prefixed to phoneme represented by letter, with suffix ⁺0- m or f/IIId, on the phonemes /f l m n r s/:éffe *F*, élle *L*, émme *M*, énne *N*, érre ·*R*, ésse *S*.

m. ɛmi⁺ *hemi-*, *semi-*, *half-*, in ɛmikranía *hemicrania, migraine*:⁺kraní-

-crania f/Ia; ɛmisféro *hemisphere*:sfér- *sphere* m/IIb; ɛmistíkio *hemistich*:
⁺stíki- *stich* m/IIb.

n. fli(s)⁺ in fli(s)kórn- *brass horn*:kórn- *horn* m/IIb, c.

o. i⁺ in letter name, prefixed to the phonemes represented by the letter:
iks *X*:/ks/.

p. ï˟⁺ intensive in iddío *God*:dí-:dé- *god* m/IIb.

q. ipo⁺ *hypo-*, as in ipókrita *hypocrite*:⁺′krit- *-crite* m/Ib; ipoklɔríto *hypo-chlorite*:klɔrít- *chlorite* m/IIb; iposɔlfíto *hyposulphite*:sɔlfít- *sulphite* m/IIb.

r. ma⁺ (before nouns of f/Ia, m/Ib or m/VId), mɔn⁺ (before nouns of
m/IIIb) *my, maha-, great . . .*, in the following of:

   i. f/Ia:madáma *madame*:dám- *lady*; madamiğélla *mademoiselle*:damiğéll-
damsel; madónna *my lady, madonna*:dónn- *lady, woman*.

   ii. m/Ib or m/VId: maráğa, marağá˟ *maharajah*:ráğ- rağá˟ *rajah*.

   iii. m/IIIb: mɔnsiɲɲóre *monsignore*:siɲɲór- *lord*.

s. palin⁺ *palin-, again, re-*, in palinodía *palinode*:⁺odí- *ode* f/Ia; palíndrɔmo
palindrome:⁺′drɔm- *-drome* m/IIb; palinsésto *palimpsest*:⁺sést- *something
scraped* m/IIb; palinğénesi *palingenesis*:ğénes- *genesis* f/IVd.

t. panto⁺ *panto-*, in pantógrafo *pantograph*:⁺′graf- *-graph* m/IIb; panto-
mímo *pantomimist*:mím- *mime* m/IIb.

u. pros⁺ *pros-* in próstesi *prosthesis*:⁺′tes-:tés- *thesis* f/IVd.

w. tɛle⁺ *tele-, from far off*, as in the following of:

   i. f/Ia: tɛlefotografía *telephotography*:fotografí- *photography*.

   ii. m/Ib: tɛlegrámma *telegram*:⁺grámm- *-gram*.

   iii. m/IIb: tɛléfɔno *telephone*:⁺′fɔn- *-phone, sound*; tɛlégrafo *telegraph*:
⁺′graf- *-graph*; tɛleobiettívo *teleobjective*:obiettív- *objective*; etc.

   iv. f/IIIb: tɛlevisióne *television*:visión- *vision*.

7. Verbs alone, with:

a. d⁺ di⁺ di˟⁺ *de-, un-, off*, in the following distribution:

   i. d⁺ in dór- *gild*:ór- *put gold on . . .* I/Reg/W.

   ii. di˟⁺ before /f/ (except in difénd- *defend* IIIb/Reg/S¹, ²): e.g. differ-
differ:fɛr- *-fer, strike* II/ísK/W; diffónd- *diffuse*:fónd- *fuse* IIIb/Reg/S¹, ².

   iii. di⁺ elsewhere, as in the following of types:

       A. I/Reg/W: diláv- *weaken*:láv- *wash*; dimén- *agitate*:mén- *lead*;
dinɛg- *deny*:nɛg- *deny*; dismált- *remove enamel*:smált- *enamel*; dispér- *despair*:
spér- *hope*; etc. etc.

       B. II/Reg/W: dipárt- *depart*:párt- *part*.

       C. II/ísK/W: diğɛr- *digest*:⁺ğɛR- *-gest*; dilu- *dilute*:⁺lu- *-lute*.

       D. IIIb: dibátt- *debate*:bátt- *beat*; difénd- *defend*:fénd- *-fend, split*;
dimétt- *dismiss, resign*:métt- *put*; dipénd- *depend*:pénd- *hang*; dipínG- *depict*:
pínG- *paint*; diríG- *direct*:⁺ríG-:réGG- *rule, guide*; dirómp- *break (up, to pieces)*:
rómp- *break*; etc.

       E. IV: díst- *be distand*:⁺′st-:stá- *stand*.

b. intro⁺ *intro-*, as in intrɔmétt- *introduce, put in*:métt- *put* IIIb/Reg/S¹, ²;
introdúK- *introduce*:⁺dúK- *-duce, -duct* IV/Reg/S¹, ².

c. so(d)dis⁺ *satis-*, so(d)disfáč- *satisfy*:fáč- *do* IV/Irr/S¹, ².

d. sɔr⁺ *sur-, over, above*, as in the following of types:

i. I/Reg/W: sɔrmónt- *surmount*:mónt- *mount*; sɔrpáss- *surpass, pass over*:páss- *pass*; sɔrvéʎʎ- *supervise, watch over*:véʎʎ- *watch*; sɔrvól- *fly over*:vól-*fly*.

ii. IIIb/Reg/S[1, 2]: sɔrprénd- *surprise*:prénd- *take*; sɔrr*éGG*- *support*: r*éGG*- *rule, guide*; sɔrríd- *smile*:ríd- *laugh*.

e. sus[+] sub(s)-, in suššít- *excite*:čít- *cite* I/Reg/W; suššɛtt[+] *suscept-* (alternant Non-Finite C, in suššettíbile *susceptible* adj/IIIb, suššettívo *susceptible* adj/I–II) :[+]čep- *-cept, take* II/ísK/W.

f. u[x+] *off*, in uččíd- *kill*:[+]číd- *cut, -cise* IIIb/Reg/S[1, 2].

3.132. EXOCENTRIC derivation (always with a specific suffix, in 'parasynthetic' formation, i.e. formation with both a prefix and a suffix at the same time), is accomplished for:

1. Substantives derived from nouns, with the prefixes:

a. dodeka[+] *dodeca-, twelve*, with the suffixes:

i. [+]0- *having* . . . adj/I–II, on nouns of:

A. f/Ia: dodekasíllabo *dodecasyllabic*:síllab- *syllable*.

B. Nominal base: dodekágɔno *dodecagonal*:[+']gon[+] *angle*.

ii. [+]0- *thing having* . . . m/IIb, in dodekaédro *dodecahedron*:[+]édr[+] *hedron, base*.

b. ɛndeka[+] *hendeca-, eleven*, with the suffix [+]0- *having* . . . adj/I–II, in ɛndekasíllabo *hendecasyllabic*:síllab- *syllable* f/Ia.

c. iso[+] *iso-, same*, with the suffixes:

i. [+]0- *having* . . . adj/I–II, as in isóbaro *isobaric*:'bar[+] *pressure, weight*; isokiméno *isochimenic*:[+]kimen[+] *summer*; isókrɔno *isochronic*:'krɔn[+] *time*; isómɛro *isomeric*: [+]mɛr[+] *part*; isótɛro *isoteric*:[+']tɛr[+] *summer*; isotérmo *isothermic*:tɛrm[+] *heat*; isótopo *isotopic*:'top[+] *place*.

ii. [+]0- *having* . . . adj/IIIb, in isóššele *isosceles*:[+']ššɛl[+] *leg, side*.

d. ka[+] pejorative, with suffix [+]0- *having* . . . adj/I–II, in kamúso *flatnosed*:mús- *nose, snout* m/IIb.

2. Indefinite pronouns, with suffix [+]0- adj/I–II, with čask(ed)[+] *each* . . ., in časkedúno časkúno *each one*:ún- *one* adj/I–II.

3. Verbs, with suffix [+]0- I/Reg/W, on nouns, with ann[+] *ad-, in-*, on annákku-*water*:ákku- *water* f/Ia; annásp- *wind on a reel, gesticulate*:ásp- *reel* m/IIb.

3.133. ENDOCENTRIC AND EXOCENTRIC derivation, i.e. with the same prefix occurring in both endocentric and exocentric (parasynthetic) formations, is accomplished for:

1. Substantives and verbs (endocentric), nouns from verbs and verbs from nouns (exocentric), with intɛr[+] *inter-, between*, in:

a. Endocentric formations on:

i. Substantives:

A. Adjectives, of types:

I. I–II: intɛralleáto *inter-Allied*:alleát- *Allied*; intɛrmédio *intermediate*:médi- *mediate, middle*; intɛrplanetário *interplanetary*:planetári- *planetary*; intɛrurbáno *interurban*:urbán- *urban*; etc.

II. IIIb: intɛrkɔmunikánte *inter-communicating*:kɔmunikánt- *com-*

municating; intɛrmuskɔláre *intermuscular*:muskɔlár- muscular; intɛrnaciɔnále *international*:naciɔnál- *national*; etc.

    B. Nouns, of types:

       I. f/Ia: intɛrdipɛndénca *interdependence*:dipɛndénca *dependence*; intɛrlínea *space between two lines*:líne- *line*; intɛrvísta *interview*:víst- *view*; etc.

       II. m/IIb: intɛrbinário *six-foot way*:binári- *track*; intɛrlúdi- *interlude*:lúdi- *-lude*; etc.

       III. f/IIIb: intɛrkapédine *interstice, hollow space*:kapédin- *-stice*.

       IV. m/VId: intɛrré^x *acting king*:ré^x *king*.

    ii. Verbs, such as the following of types:

       A. I/Reg/W: intɛrkál- *intercalate*:kál- *drop down*; intɛrróg- *interrogate*:róg- *rogate*.

       B. II/ísK/W: intɛrfɛr- *interfere*:fɛr- *-fer, strike*; intɛrloku- *be interlocutor*:⁺loku- *speak*; etc.

       C. IIIb: intɛrčéd- *intercede*:čéd- *cede*; intɛrčíd- *cut in two*:⁺číd- *cut*; intɛrklúd- *shut out*:⁺klúd-:kiúd- *shut*; intɛrkórr- *intervene*:kórr- *run*; etc.

       D. IV/Irr/S$^{1,\ 2}$: intɛrdíK- *forbid*:díK- *say*.

    b. Exocentric formations of:

       i. Noun (with suffix ⁺0- m/IIIb) on verb IIIb/Irr/S^1, in intɛrésse *interest*:éss- *be* IIIb/Irr/S^1.

       ii. Verb (with suffix ⁺0- *-ate* I/Reg/W), on noun m/IIb, in intɛrfɔʎʎ- *interfoliate*:fɔʎʎ- *leaf, page*.

  2. Substantives and verbs (endocentric), adjectives from nouns and verbs from substantives (exocentric), with dis⁺ (di^{x+} before fíd- *trusting, -worthy* adj/I–II; ⁺fíčil-:fáčil- *easy* adj/IIIb; fám- *fame* and fórm- *form* f/Ia; fɛr- *-fer, strike* II/ísK/W; and fónd- *fuse* IIIb/Reg/S$^{1,\ 2}$) *dis-, un-, away*, in:

    a. Endocentric formations, on:

       i. Adjectives, of types:

       A. I–II: disadátto *unsuited, unfitted*:adátt- *suited, fitted*; diskáro *displeasing*:kár- *dear, pleasing*; disɔnésto *dishonest*:ɔnést- *honest*; etc.

       B. IIIb: disavvɛnénte *unattractive*:avvɛnént- *attractive*; diskɔnvɛnévɔle *unsuited*:kɔnvɛnévɔl- *suited*; diskɔrtése *discourteous*:kɔrtés- *courteous*; dissímile *dissimilar*:símil- *similar*; dissɔlúbile *dissoluble*:sɔlúbil- *soluble*; diffícile *difficult*:⁺fíčil-:fáčil- *easy*.

       C. IVd: díspari *uneven, unequal, odd*:pár- *equal, even*.

    ii. Nouns, of types:

       A. f/Ia: disarmɔnía *disharmony*:armɔní- *harmony*; disgrácia *disgrace*:gráci- *grace*; diskɔrtesía *discourtesy*:kɔrtesí- *courtesy*; etc.

       B. m/IIb: disáǧ- *discomfort*:áǧ- *comfort*; disakkórdo *disagreement*:akkórd- *agreement*; disgústo *disgust, displeasure*:gúst- *pleasure, taste*; etc.

       C. m/IIIb: disamóre *lack of love*:amór- *love*; disɔnóre *dishonor*:ɔnór- *honor*.

       D. f/IIIb: disprɔpɔrcióne *disproportion*:prɔpɔrción- *proportion*; disunióne *disunion*:unión- *union*.

    iii. Verbs, of types:

       A. I/Reg/W: disabítu- *disaccustom*:abítu- *accustom*; disánim- *cause to lose courage*:ánim- *animate*; diskáčč- *chase away*:káčč- *chase*; dispréǧ- *contemn, disesteem*:préǧ- *esteem*; etc.

B. II/Reg or Irr: diskópr- *uncover*:kópr- *cover*; diskɔnvɛn- *be unfitting*: kɔnvɛn- *be fitting*; dispárt- *separate*:párt- *divide.*

C. III/ísK/W: differ- *differ*:fɛr- *-fer, strike.*

D. IIIa: distɛn- *hold back by force* (archaic):tɛn- *hold.*

E. IIIb: diskiúd- *disclose*:kiúd- *close,* diskɔnósK- *fail or refuse to recognize*:kɔnósK- *recognize*; diffónd- *diffuse*:fónd- *fuse,* etc.

F. IV: disfáč- *undo*:fáč- *do*; dispón- *dispose*:pón- *place, put*; distrá^x- *distract*:trá^x- *draw.*

b. Exocentric formations:

i. Adjectives, with suffix +0- IIIb, on nouns: diffórme disfórme *deformed*: fórm- *form* f/Ia.

ii. Verbs, with suffix +0- I/Reg/W, on nouns, e.g. of types:

A. f/Ia: diffám- *defame*:fám- *fame*; disnatúr- *denature*:natúr- *nature*; etc.

B. m/IIb: disartíkɔl- *disarticulate*:artíkɔl- *joint*; dissénn- *craze*:sénn- *mind*; etc.

C. m/IIIb: disárǧin- *overflow*:árǧin- *bank, dike*; disautór- *deprive of authority*:autór- *authority*; disfiór- *deflower*:fiór- *flower*; etc.

D. f/IIIb: dissét- *slake*:sét- *thirst.*

E. f/VId: dispodést- *deprive of power*:podest+:podestá^x*power.*

3. Substantives and verbs (endocentric) and adjectives from nouns, with de+ *de-, down, under-,* in:

a. Endocentric formations:

A. Adjs/I–II: dédit- *given over*:+'dit-:dát- *given*; denutríto *undernourished*:nutrít- *nourished.*

B. Noun f/VId: dɛnatalitá^x *drop in births*:natalitá^x *natality.*

C. Verbs, such as the following of types:

I. I/Reg/W: deámbul- *take a walk*:ámbul- *ambulate, walk*; deklám- *declaim*:klam+:kiám- *call*; detérmin- *determine*:términ- *terminate*; etc.

II. II/ísK/W: defɛr- *defer*:fɛr- *-fer, strike*; defin- *define*:fin- *finish*; etc.

III. IIIa: dekád- *decline, decay*:kád- *fall*; detɛn- *detain*:tɛn- *hold.*

IV. IIIb: dečéd- *decease*:čéd- *yield, cede*; dečíd- *decide*:+číd- *cut, -cide*; dekórr- *pass (of time)*:kórr- *run*; dekrésK- *decrease*:krésK *grow*; etc.

V. IV: dedúK- *deduce*:+dúK- *-duce, -duct*; depón- *depose, put down*: pón- *place, put*; detrá^x- *detract*:trá^x *draw, -tract.*

Recessive stress occurs in dérog- *derogate* I/Reg/W:róg- *rogate, draw up*; dédik- *dedicate*:+'dik- *-dicate* I/Reg/W (:díK- *say* IV/Irr/S[1, 2]).

b. Exocentric formation, with suffix +0- *having* . . . adj/IIIb, in deklíve *having a steep descent*:klív- *hill, steep descent* m/IIb.

4. Adjectives on adjectives (endocentric) and on verbs (exocentric), with ɔnni+ *omni-, all-*:

a. On adjs/IIIb: ɔnnipoténte *amnipotent*:potént- *potent, powerful*; ɔnnipresénte *omnipresent*:presént- *present*; ɔnniššiénte *omniscient*:šiént- *knowing*; ɔnniveǧǧénte *all-seeing*:veǧǧént- *seeing*.

b. On verb I/Reg/W, with recessive stress and suffix ⁺0- *-ous, -ing* adj/I–II: ɔnnívɔro *omnivorous*:⁺vór- *devour*.

5. Substantives, adverbs and/or verbs (endocentric) and verbs from substantives (exocentric), with:

a. e⁺ eˣ⁺ ek⁺ *e- ex- ec-*, *out, thoroughly, un-*, with the following distribution: 1) ek⁺ in ekléttiK- *eclectic* adj/I–II, eklampsía *eclampsia* f/Ia, ékloga *eclogue* f/Ia, ekʒéma *eczema* m/Ib, and eklíTT- *eclipse eclipt-* f/IV; 2) eˣ⁺ before /f/ and (opt.) in ɛ(l)líTT- *ellipse ellipt-* f/IVd; 3) e⁺ elsewhere. The prefix occurs in:

i. Endocentric formations of:

A. Adjs/I–II: édit- *published*:⁺ʹdit-:dát- *given*; edótt- *thoroughly versed*:dótt- *learned*; effrɛnáto *unbridled*:frɛnát- *bridled*; ɛmérito *emeritus*:mérit- *deserving*; etc.

B. Nouns, of types:

i. f/Ia: eklampsía *eclampsia*:⁺lampsí- *-lampsia*.

ii. m/Ib: ekʒéma *eczema*:⁺ʒém- *growth*.

iii. m/IIb: edítto *edict*:⁺ditt-:détt- *saying*; efflússo *outflow*:flúss- *flow*.

iv. f/IVd: eklíTT- *eclipse*, *eclipt-*:⁺líTT- *-lipse, -lipt-*; ellíTT- *ellipse, ellipt-*:⁺líTT- *-lipse, -lipt-*.

c. Verbs, of types:

i. I/Reg/W: éduk- *educate*:⁺ʹduk- (:⁺dúK- *-duce, -duct* IV/Reg/S¹, ²); élev- ɛlév- *elevate* (:⁺ʹlev-):lév- *raise*; emígr- *emigrate*:mígr- *migrate*.

ii. II/ísK/W: effɛr⁺ (in effɛrénte *efferent* adj/IIIb):fɛr- *-fer, strike*.

iii. IIIb: eččéll- *excel*:⁺čéll- *-cel*; eččéd- *exceed*:čéd- *cede*; effónd- *effuse*:fónd- *fuse*; ɛlɛGG- *elect*:léGG- *read, -lect*; etc.

ii. Exocentric formation, with ⁺0- I/Reg/W, in evír- *castrate*:⁺vír- *man* m/IIb.

b. iˣ⁺ inn⁺ in⁺ *in-* (negative, intensive, causative), in the following distribution: 1) iˣ before /l r/, before /sC/ only in spétt- *-spect* and spír- *breathe* I/Reg/W, ⁺stitu- *-stitute* and ⁺stru- *-struct* II/ísK/W, and stá- *stand* IV/Irr/S¹, and (with /n/ > /ɲ/) before the adjectives nót- *known* and núd- *nude* I–II and nóbil- *noble* IIIb; 2) inn⁺ before akku- *water* f/Ia, ésk- *bait* f/Ia, amór- *love* m/IIIb, álc- *raise* I/Reg/W and ánc- *before* adv/IV; and 3) in⁺ elsewhere; and occurring in:

i. Endocentric formations, on:

A. Adjectives, of types:

i. I–II: iɲɲóto *unknown*:nót- *known*; iɲɲúdo *naked*:núd- *nude*; illaudáto *not praised*:laudát- *praised*; innɔmináto *unnamed*:nɔminát- *named*; irrefrɛnáto *unbridled*:refrɛnát- *bridled*; inusitáto *unaccustomed*:usitát- *accustomed*; etc. etc.

ii. IIIb: iɲɲóbile *ignoble*:nóbil- *noble*; illegále *illegal*:legál- *legal*;

irriverénte *irreverent*:riverént- *reverent*; inkɔnčiliábile *irreconcilable*:kɔnčiliábil- *reconcilable*; inútile *useless*:útil- *useful*; etc.

   iii. IVd: impári *unequal*:pár- *equal*.

  B. Nouns: irrɛliǧóne *irreligion*:rɛliǧón- *religion* f/IIIb.

  c. Verbs, of types:

   i. I/Reg/W: iɲɲór- *be ignorant of*:⁺ɲór- *know*; innálc- *raise on high*: álc- *raise*; impórt- *import, be important*:pórt- *carry*; etc.

   ii. II/Reg/W: inségu- *pursue*:ségu- *follow*.

   iii. II/ísK/W: inib- *inhibit*:⁺ib- -*hibit*; infɛr- *infer*:fɛr- -*fer, strike*; insɛr- *insert*:⁺sɛr- -*sert*; etc.

   iv. IIIb: immérG- *immerse*:mérG- *merge*; inčénd- *light*:⁺čénd- *id.*; indispón- *indispose*:dispón- *dispose*; inténd- *intend, undertake*:ténd- *stretch*; etc.

   v. IV: impón- *impose*:pón- *put*; indúK- *induce*:⁺dúK- -*duce, -duct*; istá- *insist*:stá- *stand*.

  D. Adv/IV: innánci *before*:ánc- *rather, beforehand*.

  ii. Exocentric formations, with the suffixes:

   A. ⁺0- I/Reg/W, on:

   i. Adjs/I–II: imbiánk- *whiten*:biánk- *white*; impácc- *go crazy*:pácc- *crazy*; inkáv- *hollow out, excavate*:káv- *hollow*; innóv- *innovate*:nóv- *new*.

   ii. Nouns, e.g. of types:

    a. f/Ia: impérl- *adorn with pearls*:pérl- *pearl*; innákku- *water*: ákku- *water*; inésk- *load (e.g. gun)*:ésk- *bait, charge*; infarín- *cover with flour*: farín- *flour*; etc.

    β. m/IIb: irráǧǧ- *irradiate*:ráǧǧ- *ray*; imbród- *mess up with soup*: bród- *broth, soup*; impidókki- *louse up*:pidókki- *louse*; etc.

    γ. m/IIc: inǧinókki- *kneel*: ǧinókki- *knee*.

    δ. m/IIIb: imbaúl- *pack in a trunk*:baúl- *trunk*; illúmin- *illuminate*:lumin⁺:lúm- *light*; innamór- *make fall in love*:amór- *love*; etc.

   B. ⁺0- II/ísK/W, on:

   i. Adjectives, of types:

    a. I–II: illanguid- *make languid*:lánguid- *languid*; impovɛr- *impoverish*:póvɛr- *poor*; inaspr- *make harsh*:áspr- *harsh*; etc.

    β. IIIb: indebɔl- *weaken*:débɔl- *weak*; ingrand- *enlarge*:gránd- *large*; etc.

   ii. Nouns, as in impucc- *become stinking*:púcc- *stench* m/IIb; inčɛnɛr- *reduce to ashes*:čénɛr- *ashes* m/IIIb.

  c̣. ob⁺ (before /i l/) o⁺ (before /m/) oˣ⁺ (elsewhere) *ob-, against, away*, in:

   i. Endocentric formations, on:

   A. Adjs/I–II: oblúngo *oblong*:lúng- *long*; oskúro *obscure*:skúr- *dark*.

   B. Nouns, in okkáso *falling, setting*:kás- *case, fall* m/IIb; oččípite *occiput*:⁺čípit- *head* m/IIIb (:káp- *head* m/IIb).

   c. Verbs, e.g. of types:

   i. I/Reg/W: obiétt- *object*:⁺iétt-:ǧétt- *throw*; ossérv- *observe*:⁺sérv- *(pre)serve*; ottémpɛr- *obey*:témpɛr- *temper*; ottúr- *block up*:túr- *stop up*.

II. II/Reg/W: osseku⁺ *be obsequient* (in ossekuénte *obsequient* adj/
IIIb, pres. part.):seku⁺:ségu- *follow*.

III. II/ísK/W: offɛr- *offer*:fɛr- *-fer, strike*; ostru- *obstruct*:⁺stru-
-struct.

IV. IIIa/Irr/S¹: ottɛn- *obtain*:tɛn- *hold*.

V. IIIb: ɔmétt- *omit*:métt- *put*; okklúd- *occlude*:⁺klúd-:kiúd- *close*;
okkórr- *be necessary*:kórr- *run*; oččíd⁺ *set* (in oččidénte *occident* m/IIIb, on
Non-Finite A²); offénd- *offend*:fénd- *fend*; opprím- *oppress*:⁺prím-:prém-
press; ottúnd- *blunt*:⁺túnd- *render blunt*.

VI. IV/Irr/S¹' ²: oppón- *oppose*:pón- *put*.

VII. Verbal bases: oblat⁺ *bring as an oblation* (in oblatóre *oblator*
m/IIIb; obláto *oblate* adj/I–II; oblacióne *oblation* f/IIIb):lat⁺*bring, bear*.

  ii. Exocentric formations, with ⁺0- I/Reg/W, in the following based on:

    A. Adj/I–II: offúsk- *obfuscate*:fusk⁺:fósk- *dark*.

    B. Nouns, of types:

      I. f/Ia: oblítɛr- *obliterate*:litɛr⁺:léttɛr- *letter*; otténebr- *darken*:
ténebr- (pl.) *darkness*.

      II. m/IIb: oppúɲɲ- *assault*:púɲɲ- *fist, attack*.

      III. Nominal base: oppíl- *obstruct*:pil⁺ *obstruction*.

  d. po⁺ pos⁺ post⁺ *post-, after*, in the following distribution: 1) po⁺ before
meridián- *meridian* adj/I–II, mɛríǧǧ- *noon* m/IIb; 2) pos⁺ before /s/ and before
dɔmán- *tomorrow* m/IVd, and pón- *put* IV/Irr/S¹' ²; 3) post⁺ elsewhere; and
occurring in:

  i. Endocentric formations on:

    A. Adjectives, of types:

      I. I–II: pɔmɛridiáno *post-meridian, of the afternoon*:mɛridián- *merid-
ian*; postbélliK- *of the post-war period*:bélliK- *pertaining to war*.

      II. IIIb: postmilitáre *postmilitary*:militár- *military*.

    B. Nouns, of types:

      I. m/IIb: poskrítt- *post-script*:skrítt- *something written*; postkɔmúnio
post-communion sermon:kɔmúni- *communion*.

      II. m/IVd: posdɔmáni *day after tomorrow*:dɔmán- *tomorrow*.

    c. Verbs, in possɛd- *possess*:sɛd- *sit* IIIa/Reg/W; pospón- *postpone*:
pón- *put, place* IV/Irr/S¹' ².

  ii. Exocentric formation, with ⁺0- I/Reg/W, in postérg- *put behind
one's back, despise*:térg- *back* m/IIb.

  e. pre⁺ *pre-, previous(ly), outstanding(ly)*, in:

  i. Endocentric formations, on:

    A. Adjectives, of types:

      I. I–II: prebélliK- *pre-war*:bélliK- *pertaining to war*; prečitáto *pre-
viously cited*:čitát- *cited*; prɛmatúro *premature*:matúr- *ripe*; etc. etc.

      II. IIIb: prɛlimin** áre *preliminary*:⁺liminár- *-liminary*; prɛmilitáre
pre-military:militár- *military*; pr(e)ɛminénte *pre-eminent*:ɛminénte *eminent*;
etc.

    B. Nouns, e.g. of types:

      I. f/Ia: preistória *pre-history*:(i)stóri- *history*.

ii. m/IIb: preavvíso *previous notice*:avvís- *notice*; predɔmínio *pre-dominion*:dɔmíni- *dominion*; preǧudício *prejudice*:ǧudíci- *judgment*; etc.

iii. m/IIIb: prɛnóm- *Christian name*:nóm- *name*.

iv. f/IIIb: prekauzióne *precaution*:kauzión- *caution*.

c. Verbs, e.g. of types:

i. I/Reg/W: preaččénn- *indicate beforehand*:aččénn- *indicate*; predómin- *predominate*:dómin- *dominate*; prefigúr- *prefigure, represent beforehand*:figúr- *represent*; prɛmédit- *premeditate*:médit- *meditate*; etc.

ii. II/Irr/W: prɛmɔr- *predecease*:mɔr- *die*.

iii. II/ísK/W: prefɛr- *prefer*:fɛr- *-fer, strike*; prɛmun- *forearm, forewarn*:mun- *arm*; etc.

iv. IIIb: prečínG- *surround, gird (near outside)*:činG- *gird*; prekórr- *be precursor to . . .*:kórr- *run*; prefíGG- *prefix*:fíGG- *fix*; prɛnásK- *be born before . . .*:násK- *come into being*; etc.

v. IV: predíK- *foretell*:díK- *say*; prepón- *put before*:pón- *put, place*.

ii. Exocentric formation, with [+]0- I/Reg/W, in prečípit- *precipitate*:[+]čípit- m/IIIb:káp- *head* m/IIb.

f. pro[+] *pro-* (followed by /ˣ/ only before véd- vid[+] *see*), in:

i. Endocentric formations, on:

A. Nouns, e.g. of types:

i. m/IIb: proávo *great-grandparent*:áv- *grandparent*; pročínto *readiness*:čínt- *something girded*; proémio *proem*:[+]émi- *-em*; etc.

ii. m/IIIb: prokónsɔle *proconsul*:kónsɔl- *consul*; prodittatóre *vice-dictator*:dittatór- *dictator*; etc.

B. Verbs, e.g. of types:

i. I/Reg/W: prokáčč- *procure*:káčč- *hunt*; proklám- *proclaim*:[+]klám-:kiám- *call*; prokré- *procreate*:kré- *create*; etc.

ii. II/ísK/W: profɛr- *utter*:fɛr- *-fer, strike*; proib- *prohibit*:[+]ib--hibit*.

iii. IIIa: provvéd- *provide*:véd- *see*; provvid[+] (in provvidénte *provident* adj/IIIb, pres. part.):vid[+]:véd- *see*.

iv. IIIb: pročéd- *proceed*:čéd- *cede*; prokómb- *fall forward*:[+]kómb- *fall*; prɔmétt- *promise*:métt- *put*; etc.

v. IV: prodúK- *produce*:[+]dúK- *-duce, -duct*; propón- *propose*:pón- *put*.

ii. Exocentric formations, with [+]0- I/Reg/W, in prɔlúng- *prolong*:lúng-long* adj/I–II; propál- *publish*:pal[+] *public, open to view*.

g. s[+] privative, negative, intensive, in:

i. Endocentric formations, on:

A. Adjectives, of types:

i. I–II: skónč- *dirty, messy*:kónč- *in good shape*; skɔmpléto *incomplete*:kɔmplét- *complete*; skɔrrétto *incorrect*:kɔrrétt- *correct*; etc.

ii. IIIb: skɔnkórde *in disagreement*:kɔnkórd- *in agreement*; skɔrtése *discourteous*:kɔrtés- *courteous*; sleále *disloyal*:leál- *loyal*; etc.

B. Nouns, as in sfidúča *distrust*:fidúč- *trust* f/Ia; sfɔrtúna *misfortune*:fɔrtún- *fortune* f/Ia; svɛntúra *misfortune*:vɛntúra *fortune, luck* f/Ia; etc.

c. Verbs, e.g. of types:

I. I/Reg/W: sbattéẕẕ- *debaptize*:battéẕẕ- *baptize*; skáčč- *chase off*: káčč- *chase*; skámbi- *exchange*:kambi- *change*; etc. etc.

II. II/Reg or Irr: sbóll- *cease to boil*:bóll- *boil*; spárt- *divide*:párt- *divide, part*; svεn- *faint*:vεn- *come*; etc.

III. II/ísK/W: sfin- *lose force, vigor*:fin- *finish*; sminu- *diminish*: +minu- *id.*; spul- *polish off, make opaque*:pul- *polish, clean*; erc.

IV. IIIa/Reg/S[1]: skád- *decline, fall due*:kád- *fall*.

V. IIIb: sbátt- *beat against*:bátt- *beat*; šérn- *discern*:čérn- *see clearly* (archaic); šínG- *ungird*:čínG- *gird*; etc.

VI. IV: sdíK- *deny, belie, admit a falsehood*:díK- *say*; sfáč- *undo*: fač- *do*.

ii. Exocentric formations, with suffixes:

A. +0- I/Reg/W, on:

I. Adjectives, of types:

α. I–II: sbiánk- *turn pale*:biánk- *pale, white*; skáv- *excavate*:káv- *hollow*; spián- *smooth off*:pián- *level, smooth*; etc.

β. IIIb: smóll- *soften up*:móll- *soft*.

II. Nouns of types:

α. f/Ia: sbánd- *disband*:bánd- *band*; sbárb- *remove the beard of* . . .:bárb- *beard*; sgrammátik- *make mistakes in grammar*:grammátik- *grammar*; spátri- *exile*:pátri- *fatherland*; etc.

β. m/IIb: sbakkán- *raise an uproar*:bakkán- *uproar*; skitárr- *play the guitar badly*:kitárr- *guitar*; smónak- *unfrock (a monk)*:mónak- *monk*.

γ. m/IIc: slábbr- *break the edge of* . . .:lábbr- *lip, edge*.

δ. m/IIIb: sdént- *remove, break the teeth of* . . .:dént- *tooth*; svéntr- degut:véntr- *belly*; sfɔlgór- *be resplendent*:fɔlgór- *flash (of lightning)*; etc.

ε. f/IIIb: srádik- *uproot*:rádik+:radíč- *root*; spriǧón- *free from prison*:priǧón- *prison*; svérǧin- *devirginate*:vérǧin- *virgin*; etc.

B. +0- II/ísK/W, on:

I. Adjectives, of types:

α. I–II: sbalɔrd- *daze*:balórd- *dull, dazed*; sdur- *become less hard*: dúr- *hard*; skiar- *clear up*:kiár- *clear*; etc.

β. IIIb: svεrd- *lose green color*:vérd- *green*.

II. Nouns, e.g. of types:

α. f/Ia: sbiẕẕ- *work off one's irritation*:bíẕẕ- *irritation*.

β. m/IIb: svεlen- *deprive of poison*:vεlén- *poison*.

γ. m/IIIb: sfavɔr- *disfavor*:favór- *favor*; sfiɔr- *lose flower, beauty*: fiór- *flower*; svigɔr- *lose force*:vigór- *vigor, force*; etc.

δ. f/IIIb: svest- *unclothe*:vést- *clothing*.

h. š+ *dis-*, negative, in:

i. Endocentric formations, on adjs/I–II: šátto *sloppy*:átt- *apt, fit, in good condition*; šálbo *pale*:álb- *white*.

ii. Exocentric formations, with suffix 0- I/Reg/W, on nouns f/Ia: šákku- *rinse*:ákku- *water*; šánk- *lame*:ánk- *haunch*; šérb- *remove the grass from*:érb- *grass*; šópεr- *cease work*:ópεr- *work*.

j. se⁺ *away from*, in verbs, in:

i. Endocentric formations: sepár- (also, with recessive stress, sépar-) *separate*:pár- *prepare* I/Reg/W; sečérn- *separate, distinguish*:čérn- *distinguish, see clearly* IIIb/Reg; sedúK- *seduce*:⁺dúK- *-duce, -duct* IV/Reg/S[1, 2]; and in the verbal bases sečéd⁺ *secede* (in sečésso *remote place* m/IIb; sečessióne *secession* f/IIIb:sečɛss⁺ Non-Finite C, alternant):čéd- *cede* IIIb/Reg/W; and sɛléGG⁺ *select* (in sɛlétto *select* adj/I–II, on Non-Finite C):léGG- *read, pick out* IIIb/ Reg/S[1, 2].

ii. Exocentric formation with 0- I/Reg/W, in segrég- *segregate*:greg⁺: gréǧǧ- *herd* f/IIIb.

k. sos⁺ so˟⁺ *sus- sub-, lightly* . . ., in the following distribution: 1) sos⁺ before the verbal roots pénd- *hang*, pínG- *push* and tɛn- *hold*; 2) so˟⁺ elsewhere; and occurring in:

i. Endocentric formations, on:

A. Nouns m/IIb: sobbórgo *suburb*:bórg- *burgh*; soppánno *lining*:pánn-*cloth*; sostráto *substratum*:strát- *stratum*.

B. Verbs, e.g. of types:

i. I/Reg/W: sobbálc- *bounce lightly*:bálc- *bounce*; sofférm- *stop briefly*:férm- *stop*; sogguárd- *look at sidewise and on the sly*:guárd- *look at*; sop-piánt- *supplant*:piánt- *plant*; etc.

ii. II/Reg or Irr: sobbóll- *boil lightly*: bóll- *boil*; sovvɛn- *subvent, help*:vɛn- *come*.

iii. IIIa: sostɛn- *sustain*:tɛn- *hold*.

iv. IIIb: sokkórr- *succor*:kórr- *run*; soffríGG- *fry lightly*:fríGG-*fry*; soǧǧúnG- *add*:ǧúnG- *join*; sɔmmɔv- *agitate, instigate*:mɔv- *move*; sopprím-*suppress*:prím⁺:prém- *press*; etc.

ii. Exocentric formations with suffixes:

A. ⁺0- m/IIb, on noun f/Ia: soggólo *neckband*:gól- *throat* f/Ia; sok-kóšo *upper part of thigh*:kóšš- *thigh*.

B. ⁺0- I/Reg/W, on nouns m/IIb: soǧǧórn- *sojourn*:ǧórn- *day*; soǧǧóǧ-*subjugate*:ǧóg- *yoke*.

l. stra⁺ *extra-, excessively, very, over-, par excellence*, in:[8]

i. Endocentric formations, on:

A. Nouns, of types:

i. f/Ia: stravittória *excessive victory*:vittóri- *victory*.

ii. m/IIb: strafaššísmo *fascism à outrance*:faššísm- *fascism*; strapúnt-*pallet*, strapontin:púnt- *point*; straripóso *complete rest*:ripós *rest*; stratémp-*bad weather*:témp- *weather*; stravício *abuse (of food or drink)*:víti- *vice*; etc.

iii. m/IIIb: strapaése *country par excellence*:paés- *country*.

v. f/VId: stračittá˟ *city par excellence*:čittá˟ *city*.

iv. m/VId: strakafféˣ *extrafine coffee*:kafféˣ *coffee*.

B. Adjectives, of types:

i. I–II: stradóppio *more than ouble*:dóppi- *double*; stragónfio *over-inflated*:gónfi- *inflated*; strakáro *excessively dear*:kár- *dear*; strakɔnténto *more*

---

[8] Cf. B. Migliorini, Saggî sulla Lingua del Novecento² 81–83 (Firenze, 1942).

than glad:kɔntént- *glad*; strapiéno *chock full*:pién- *full*; stravékkio *very old*: vékki- *old*; etc. etc.

    ii. IIIb: stradotále *outside the dowry*:dotál- *pertaining to a dowry*; stragránde *over-large*:gránd- *large*; strapoténte *very powerful*:potént- *powerful*; stravagánte *extravagant*:vagánt- *wandering*; etc.

    c. Verbs, e.g. of types:

      i. I/Reg/W: strafálč- *pull a boner*:fálč- *cut with a scythe*; stralód- *praise to excess*:lód- *praise*; strapág- *pay too much*:pág- *pay*; strapárl- *talk too much*:párl- *talk*; etc.

      ii. IIIa: stragód- *enjoy beyond measure*:gód- *enjoy*; stravéd- *see very well, 'see things'*:véd- *see*; stravɔl- *want too much*:vɔl- *want, wish*.

      iii. IIIb: strabév- *drink to excess*:bév- *drink;* strakɔč- *overcook*:kɔč- *cook*; strapérd- *lose excessively*:pérd- *lose*; stravólG- *distort*:vólG- *turn*.

      iv. IV: strabɛnedíK- *bless beyond measure*:bɛnedíK- *bless;* strafáč- *overdo*:fáč- *do*; stramaledíK- *curse with all one's heart*:maledíK- *curse*.

    ii. Exocentric formations, with suffix +0- I/Reg/W, on substantives:

    A. Adj/I–II: strapácc- *maltreat*:pácc- *crazy*.

    B. Nouns of types:

      i. f/Ia: stralún- *roll the eyes, stare (like a lunatic)*:lún- *moon*; straríp- *overflow the banks*:ríp- *bank*.

      ii. m/IIb: strafór- *pierce*:fór- *hole*; stravás- *extravasate*:vás- *vessel*.

      iii. m/IIIb: strakán- *work like a dog* (refl.):kán- *dog*.

  m. suˣ+ *sub-, suc-, under*, in:

    i. Endocentric formations, on:

    A. Nouns, of types:

      i. m/IIb: suddekáno *sub-deacon*:dekán- *deacon*; súkkubo *succubus*: +'kub- *-cubus*; summúltiplo *sub-multiple*:múltipl- *multiple*; sussídio *subsidy*: +sídi- *-sidy*.

      ii. m/IIIb: sukkursále *branch*:+kursál- *-cursal*.

    B. Verbs, of types:

      i. I/Reg/W: suddéleg- *subdelegate*:déleg- *delegate*; suffúmik- *fumigate*:fúmik- *id.*; súpplik- *supplicate*:+'plik-:piég- *fold*; surróg- *surrogate*:róg- *-rogate, draw up*; sussúlt- *jerk*:+súlt-:sált- *jump*.

      ii. II/Reg/W: susségu- *follow immediately*:ségu- *follow*.

      iii. II/ísK/W: suǧǧer- *suggest*:+ǧer- *-gest*; suppl- *supply*:+pl- *fill*.

      iv. IIIb: suččéd- *succeed*:čéd- *cede*; suččíd- *cut at the base*:+číd- *cut*; suččínG+ (in suččínto *succinct* adj/I–II, past part.):čínG- *gird*; suddistíngu- *sub-distinguish*:distíngu- *distinguish*; suddivíd- *subdivide*:divíd- *divide*; sussíst- *subsist*:+síst- *-sist*.

      v. IV: suppón- *suppose*:pón- *place, put*.

    ii. Exocentric formations, with the suffix +0- I/Reg/W, in suppúr- *suppurate*:pur+:pús *pus* m/VId.

  n. tra+ *trans-, over, off* (followed by /ˣ/ only before tɛn- *hold*), in:

    i. Endocentric formations, on:

    A. Adj/I–II, in travérs- *transverse*:+vɛrs- *turned* (:vért- *turn* IIIb/ Reg).

B. Verbs, e.g. of types:

ɪ. I/Reg/W: trabáll- *waver, wobble*:báll- *dance*; trabálc- *jolt, jerk*: bálc- *bounce*; tralášš- *leave off*:lášš- *leave*; trapiánt- *transplant*:piánt- *plant*; etc.

ɪɪ. II/Irr/W: trasál- *start, jump*:sál- *jump*.

ɪɪɪ. IIIa: trattɛn- *entertain*:tɛn- *hold*; travéd- *see wrongly*:véd- *see*.

ɪᴠ. IIIb: trafí*GG*- *transfix*:fí*GG*- *fix*; tralú*K*- *shine through*:lú*K*- *shine*; trašŝéʎʎ- *choose carefully*:šéʎʎ- *choose*; traskrív- *transcribe*:skrív- *write*; etc.

ᴠ. IV: tradú*K*- *translate*:⁺dú*K*- *-duce, -duct*.

ii. Exocentric formations, with suffix ⁺0- I/Reg/W, e.g. on nouns of types:

ᴀ. f/Ia: trabókk- *spill over, out*:bókk- *mouth*; trakánn- *swallow*:kánn- *throat, reed*; tralíɲɲ- *get away from the line, degenerate*:liɲɲ⁺:líne- *line*; traví- *get off the road, go astray*:ví- *road, way*.

ʙ. m/IIb: travás- *pour*:vás- *vessel*; travís- *change appearance*:vís- *face, appearance*.

o. trans⁺ *trans-*, in:

i. Endocentric formations, on:

ᴀ. Adjs/I–II: transalpíno *trans-Alpine*:alpín- *Alpine*; transatlántiK- *transatlantic*:atlántiK- *Atlantic*; transočeániK- *transoceanic*:očeániK- *oceanic*; transiberiáno *trans-Siberian*:siberián- *Siberian*; etc.

ʙ. Nouns, of types:

ɪ. m/IIb: transúnto *résumé*:súnt- *id.*

ɪɪ. f/IIIb: transacióne *transaction*:ación- *action.*

c. Verbs, in transí*G*- *come to terms* IIIb/Reg/W: ⁺í*G*- *act.*

ii. Exocentric formation, with suffix ⁺0- I/Reg/W, in transustánci- *transsubstantiate*:sustánci- *substance* f/Ia.

p. tras⁺ *trans-, across, through*, in:

i. Endocentric formations, on:

ᴀ. Adjs/I–II: traslúčido *translucid*:lúčid- *lucid*; traspadáno *trans-Padane*:padán- *Padane, of the Po.*

ʙ. Verbs, e.g. of types:

ɪ. I/Reg/W: traskúr- *neglect*:kúr- *care for*; trasmígr- *transmigrate*: mígr- *migrate*; trasmút- *transmute*:mút- *change*; etc.

ɪɪ. II/ís*K*/W: trasfer- *transfer*:fɛr- *-fer, strike*; trasgred- *transgress*: ⁺gred- *tread*; traspar- *appear through*:⁺par- *appear.*

ɪɪɪ. IIIb: trasfónd- *transfuse*:fónd- *fuse*; traskórr- *pass*:kórr- *run*; trasmétt- *transmit*:métt- *place, put.*

ɪᴠ. IV: traspón- *transpose*:pón- *put, place.*

ii. Exocentric formations, with suffix ⁺0- I/Reg/W, on:

ᴀ. Nouns of types:

ɪ. f/Ia: trasfigúr- *transfigure*:figúr- *figure*; trasfórm- *transform*:fórm- *form.*

ii. m/IIb: trasmɔ́d- *be excessive*:mɔ́d- *manner*.

iii. m/IIIb: traskɔlór- *change color*:kɔlór- *color*.

B. Verb I/Irr/W, in trasánd- *neglect*:and- *go*.

6. Substantives and verbs (endocentric) and adjectives on nouns (exocentric), with ab⁺ aˣ⁺ as⁺ *ab-, vice, last*, in the following distribution: 1) ab⁺ or aˣ⁺ before sént- *-sent*; 2) as⁺ before /p t/; 3) ab⁺ elsewhere; occurring in:

a. Endocentric formations, on:

i. Nouns m/IIb, in ablegáto *vice-legate*:legát- *legate*; abɔmás- *abómas-abomasus*:ɔmás- ómas- *omasus*.

ii. Adj/IIIb: absénte assénte *absent*:⁺sént- *-sent, being*.

iii. Verbs, of types:

A. I/Reg/W: abérr- *be aberrant*:érr- *err, wander*; abiúr- *abjure*:⁺iúr-: ğúr-*swear*; abnég- abnég- *abnegate*:nég-nég-*deny*; abús-*abuse*:ús-*use*; aspórt-*carry away*:pórt- *carry*; and, with recessive stress, ábdik- *abdicate*:⁺'dik- *-dicate* (:díK-say IV/Irr/S¹, ²) and ábrog- *abrogate*:róg- *-rogate, draw up*.

B. IIIa: astɛn- *keep away from, abstain*:tɛn- *hold*.

c. IIIb: abrád- *abrade*, scrape off:rád- *shave, scrape*.

b. Exocentric formations, with ⁺0 *-al* adj/IIIb, in abnórme *abnormal*: nórm- *norm* f/Ia.

7. Substantives (endocentric) and adjectives or nouns on nouns (exocentric), with:

a. allo⁺ *allo-*, in:

i. Endocentric formations, in nouns f/Ia: allopatía *allopathic treatment*: ⁺patí- *-pathy*; allotropía *allotropy*:⁺tropí- *-tropy*.

ii. Exocentric formations, with the suffix ⁺0- *-ic, -ous* adj/I–II, in alloglótt- *alloglottic*:glɔtt⁺ *throat, speech*; allóğeno *allogenous*:⁺'ğen⁺ *origin*.

b. ambi⁺ *ambi-*, in:

i. Endocentric formation, in ambidéstro *ambidextrous*:déstr- *dexterous* adj/I–II.

ii. Exocentric formation, with the suffix ⁺0- *having . . .* adj/IIIb, in ambiğénɛre *having both genders*:ğénɛr- *gender* m/IIIb.

c. apo⁺ *apo-*, in:

i. Endocentric formations, in:

A. Adj/I–II: apodíttiK- *apodeictic*:díttiK- *deictic*.

B. Nouns, of types:

I. m/Ib: apoftégma *apophthegm*:⁺ftégm- *-phythegm, saying*; apotéma *apotheme*:tém- *theme*; apóstaT- *apostate*:⁺'staT- *one who stands*.

II. m/IIb: apoğéo *apogee*:⁺ğé- (*thing above the*) *earth*; apólog- *apologue* :⁺'log- *-logue*; apóstɔlo *apostle*:⁺'stɔl- *one sent*.

III. f/IIIb: apókop- *apocope*:⁺'kop- *cutting*; apóstrof- *apostrophe* (*rhetorical*):⁺'strof-:stróf- *strophe*.

IV. f/IVd: apoteósi *apotheosis*:⁺teóT- *making into a god*; apɔnevrósi apɔneurósi *aponeurosis*:nevróT- neuróT- *neurosis*; apódosi *apodosis*:⁺'dos- *giving*; apófisi *apophysis*:⁺'fis- *-physis*.

ii. Exocentric formation, with suffix ⁺0- *having* . . . adj/I–II, in apógrafo *copied*:⁺′graf- *writing* f/IIIb.

d. di⁺ *di-, having two* . . ., in:

    i. Endocentric formations, on nouns of types:

      A. m/Ib: digrámma *digraph*:⁺grámm- *writing, graph*.

      B. m/IIb: digámbo *diiamb*:gámb- *iamb*; dístiko *distich*:⁺′stik- *stich*.

    ii. Exocentric formations, with suffixes:

      A. ⁺0- *-ic, having* . . . adj/I–II, on nouns of types:

        I. f/Ia: disíllabo *disyllabic*:síllab- *syllable*.

        II. Nominal base: diédro *dihedrous, -on*:⁺édr⁺ *hedron, base*; dítter- *dipterous*:⁺′ttɛr⁺ *-pteryx*.

      B. ⁺0- *having* . . . adj/IIIb, in dikotilédone *having two cotyledons*: kotilédon- *cotyledon* m/IIIb.

      C. ⁺0- *thing having* . . . m/IIb, in díttik- *diptych*:⁺′ttik⁺ *-ptych*; dittóngo *diphthong*:⁺′ttɔng⁺ *-phthong, sound*.

e. deka⁺ *deca-, ten times, having ten* . . ., in:

    i. Endocentric formations, based on nouns m/IIb: dekagrámm- *decagram*; grámm- *gram*; dekálitr- *decaliter*:′litr- *liter*; dekálog- *decalogue*:⁺′log- *-logue*; dekámetro *decameter*:′mɛtr- *meter*; dekastéro *decastere*:stér- *stere*.

    ii. Exocentric formations, with suffixes:

      A. ⁺0- *having* . . . adj/I–II, in dekasíllabo *decasyllabic*:síllab- *syllable* f/Ia; dekágono *decagon(al)*:⁺′gon⁺ *angle*.

      B. ⁺0- *thing having* . . . m/IIb, in dekaédr- *decahedron*:⁺édr⁺ *hedron*.

f. epi⁺ (ep⁺ before /o ɔ/) *ep(i)-*, in:

    i. Endocentric formations, based on:

      A. Adjs/I–II: epidémiK- *epidemic*:⁺démiK- *-demic*; epizoótiK- *epizootic*:⁺zoótiK- *-zootic*.

      B. Nouns, of types:

        I. m/Ib: epigrámma *epigram*:⁺grámm- *-gram*.

        II. m/IIb: epičéntr- *epicenter*:čéntr- *center*; epičíklo *epicycle*:číkl- *cycle*; epígono *epigone*:⁺′gɔn- *one coming after*; epílogo *epilogue*:⁺′log- *-logue*; epódo *epode*:⁺ód- *ode*; etc.

        III. f/IIIb: epidérmide *epidermis*:⁺dérmid- *dermis* (:dérm- *skin* m/Ib); epiglóttid- *epiglottis*:glóttid- *glottis*; epítome *epitome*:⁺′tɔm- *-tome*.

    ii. Exocentric formations, with suffix ⁺0- *having* . . . adj/I–II, in epónimo *eponymous*:⁺ónim- *name* m/IIb.

g. eso⁺ *exo-*, in:

    i. Endocentric formations, based on:

      A. Adjs/I–II: esočéntriK- *exocentric*:čéntriK- *of the center*; esotérmiK- *exothermic*:térmiK- *thermic*.

      B. Noun f/IVd: esosmósi *exosmosis*:osmóT- *osmosis*.

    ii. Exocentric formations, with suffix ⁺0- *having* . . . adj/I–II, in esógɛno *exogenous*:⁺′gɛn⁺ *origin*.

h. ɛndo⁺ *endo-*, in:

    i. Endocentric formations, based on:

A. Adjs/I–II: εndocéntriK- *endocentric*:čéntriK- *of the center*; εndo-térmiK- *endothermic*:térmiK- *thermic*; εndovεnóso *endovenous*:vεnós- *venous*.

B. Noun f/IVd: εndosmósi *endosmosis*:osmóT- *osmosis*.

ii. Exocentric formation, with suffix ⁺0- *having* . . . adj/I–II, in εndógεno *endogenous*:⁺'ǧεn⁺ *origin*.

j. esa⁺ *hexa-*, in:

i. Endocentric formation, in esavalénte *hexavalent*:valént- *valent* adj/IIIb.

ii. Exocentric formations, with suffixes:

A. ⁺0- *having* . . . adj/I–II, in eságɔno *hexagonal*:⁺'gɔn⁺ *angle*.

B. ⁺0- *thing having* . . . m/IIb, in esaédro *hexahedron*:⁺édr⁺ *hedron*, *base*.

k. etta⁺ *hepta-*, in:

i. Endocentric formation, in ettavalénte *heptavalent*:valént- *valent* adj/IIIb.

ii. Exocentric formations, with suffixes:

A. ⁺0- *having* . . . adj/I–II, in ettágɔno *heptagonal*:⁺'gɔn⁺ *angle*.

l. makro⁺ *macro-*, *great*, in:

i. Endocentric formations, in makroskópiK- *macroscopic*:⁺skópiK- *-scopic* adj/I–II; makrokósmo *macrocosm*:kósm- *cosmos* m/IIb.

ii. Exocentric formations, with suffix ⁺0- *having* . . . adj/I–II, in makro-čéfalo *macrocephalous*:čéfal- *cephalus, head* m/IIb.

m. mikro⁺ *micro-*, *small*, in:

i. Endocentric formations, on nouns of:

A. f/Ia: mikrografía *micrography*:grafí- *-graphy, writing*.

B. m/IIb: mikróbi- *microbe*:⁺'bi- *living thing, life*; mikrófɔno *micro-phone*:⁺'fɔn- *sound*; mikrográmmo *microgram*:grámm- *gram*; mikrokókko *micrococcus*:kókk- *coccus*; mikrɔrganísmo *microorganism*:ɔrganísm- *organism*; etc.

C. m/VId: mikrofárad *microfarad*:fárad *farad*.

ii. Exocentric formation, with suffix ⁺0- *having* . . . adj/I–II, in mikro-čéfalo *microcephalous*:čéfal- *cephalus, head* m/IIb.

n. miria⁺ *myria-*, *10000*, in:

i. Endocentric formations on nouns m/IIb: miriagrámmo *myriagram*:grámm- *gram*; mirialítro *myrialiter*:lítr- *liter*; miriámetro *myriameter*:⁺'mεtr- *meter*.

ii. Exocentric formation, with suffix ⁺0- *having* . . . adj/I–II, in miriá-podo *myriapod*:⁺'pod- *foot*.

o. mɔn⁺ (before /a o/), mɔno⁺ (elsewhere), *mon*(*o*)-, *one*, in:

i. Endocentric formations, e.g. on:

A. Adjectives, of types:

I. I–II: mɔnófago *monophagous*:⁺'fag- *-eating, -phagous*; mɔnoǧené-tiK- *monogenetic*:ǧenétiK- *genetic*; mɔnɔmaníaK- *monomaniac*(*al*):maníaK- *maniac*(*al*.

II. IIIb: mɔnovalénte *monovalent*:valént- *valent*.

B. Nouns, of types:

I. f/Ia: mɔnografía *monograph*:grafí- *writing*, *-graph(y)*; mɔnɔmanía *monomania*:maní- *mania*; mɔnodía *monody*:⁺odí- *-ody*; etc.

II. m/Ib: mɔnárka *monarch*:⁺árk- *ruler*; mɔnográmma *monogram*:⁺grámm- *-gram*.

III. m/IIb: mɔnólogo *monologue*:⁺′log- *-logue*; mɔnoteísmo *monotheism*:teísm- *theism*; etc.

IV. f/IVd: mɔnŏĝénesi *monogenesis*:ĝéneT̂- *genesis*.

ii. Exocentric formations, with suffixes:

A. ⁺0- *having* . . . adj/I–II, based on nouns of types:

I. f/Ia: mɔnosíllab- *monosyllabic*:síllab- *syllable*.

II. m/IIb: mɔnókɔlo *one-eyed*:⁺ɔkɔl⁺:ókki- *eye*; mɔnótɔno *monotonous*:tón- *tone*.

B. ⁺0- *having* . . . adj/IIIb, in mɔnokotilédɔne *monocotyledonous*:kotilédɔn- *cotyledon* m/IIIb.

C. ⁺0- *thing having* . . . m/IIb, based on nouns of types:

I. f/Ia: mɔnokórdo *monochord*:kórd- *chord*; mɔnɔrímo *poem with only one rhyme*:rím- *rhyme*.

II. m/IIb: mɔnɔrítmo *poem with only one rhythm*:rítm- *rhythm*; mɔnovérbo *puzzle with one word as its solution*:vérb- *verb, word*.

p. ɔmo⁺ *homo-* (*same*), in:

i. Endocentric formations, in ɔmoĝéneo *homogeneous*:⁺ĝéne- *-geneous*, *of a kind* adj/I–II; ɔmosessuále *homosexual*:sessuál- *sexual* adj/IIIb.

ii. Exocentric formations, with the suffix ⁺0- *having* . . . adj/I–II, on nouns m/IIb, in ɔmófɔno *homophonous*:⁺′fɔn⁺ *sound*; ɔmólogo *homologous*:⁺′log- *-logue*; ɔmónimo *homonymous*:⁺ónim- *name*.

q. ɔrto⁺ *ortho-*, *correct* . . ., in:

i. Endocentric formations, in:

A. Adjectives, of types:

I. I–II: ɔrtodósso *orthodox*:⁺dóss- *-dox, thinking*.

II. IIIb: ɔrtogɔnále *orthogonal, right-angled, perpendicular*:⁺gɔnál- *-angled*.

B. Nouns f/Ia: ɔrtoepía *orthoepy*:⁺epí- *pronunciation*; ɔrtofɔnía *correct pronunciation*:⁺fɔní- *-phony, sounding*; ɔrtografía *orthography*:grafí- *writing, -graphy*; etc.

ii. Exocentric formation, in ɔrtóttero *orthopterical*:⁺′ttɛr⁺ *-pteryx, wing*.

r. pɛnt⁺ (before vowel), pɛnta⁺ (before consonant) *penta-*, *five*, in:

i. Endocentric formations, in nouns of types:

A. m/Ib: pɛntárka *pentarch*:⁺árk- *-arch, ruler*; pɛntagrámma *pentagram*:⁺grámm- *-gram*.

B. m/IIb: pɛntátlo *pentathlon*:⁺átl⁺ *-athlon, contest*.

C. f/IVd: pɛntápɔli *pentapolis, five cities*:⁺′pɔl- *city*.

ii. Exocentric formations, with the suffixes:

A. ⁺0- *having* . . . adj/I–II, on nouns of:

I. f/Ia: pɛntasíllabo *pentasyllabic*:síllab- *syllable*.

II. Nominal base: pɛntágɔno *pentagonal*:⁺′gɔn⁺ *angle*.

B. +0- *thing having* . . . m/IIb, based on nouns of:

I. f/Ia: pɛntakɔ́rdo *pentachord*:kɔ́rd- *chord*.

II. Nominal base: pɛntatéuko *Pentateuch*:+téuk+ *book*.

s. pɛri+ *peri-, around*, in:

i. Endocentric formations, on nouns of:

A. m/Ib: pɛrizɔ́ma *loincloth*:+zɔ́m- *girding*.

B. m/IIb: pɛriánto *perianthum*:+ánt- *flower*; pɛrímetro *perimeter*: +'metr- *meter*; pɛríodo *period*:+'od- *road*.

C. f/IVd: pɛrífrasi *periphrasis*:+'fras- *phrasis*; pɛristálsi *peristalsis*: +stálT- *-stalsis -stalt-*.

ii. Exocentric formation, in pɛríptɛro pɛríttɛro *peripterical*:+'pter+ +'ttɛr+ *-pteryx, wing*.

t. pɔli+ *poly-*, in:

i. Endocentric formations, on:

A. Adjs/I–II: pɔligráfiK- *polygraphic*:gráfiK- *graphic*; pɔlisintétiK- *polysynthetic*:sintétiK- *synthetic*; pɔlitékniK- *polytechnic*:tékniK- *technic(al)*; etc.

B. Nouns, e.g. of types:

I. f/Ia: pɔliarkía *polyarchy*:+arkí- *-archy, rule*; pɔlifɔnía *polyphony*: +fɔní- *-phony*; pɔligrafía *varied literature*:grafí- *writing*; etc.

II. m/Ib: pɔliteáma *polytheama, theater for varied spectacles*:+teám- *spectacle*.

III. m/IIb: pɔlígrafo *polygraph*:+'graf- *writer*; pɔlisíndeto *polysyndeton*:síndet- *syndeton*; pɔliteísmo *polytheism*:teísm- *theism*; etc.

IV. f/IVd: pɔližénesi *polygenesis*:žéneT- *genesis*.

ii. Exocentric formations, with suffixes:

A. +0- *having* . . . adj/I–II, e.g. on nouns of types:

I. f/Ia: pɔlisíllabo *polysyllabic*:síllab- *syllable*.

II. m/IIb: pɔlikrɔ́mo *polychrome*:krɔ́m- *color, chrome*; pɔlisénso *having many senses*:séns- *sense*.

III. Nominal bases: pɔlígɔno *polygonal*:+'gɔn+ *angle*; pɔlígamo *polygamous*:+'gam+ *mate*; pɔlimɔ́rfo *polymorphous*:mɔ́rf+ *morph,- form*.

B. +0- *thing having* . . . m/IIb, as in pɔliédro *polyhedron*:+édr+ *hedron*, *base*.

u. pseudo+ *pseudo-*, in:

i. Endocentric formations, on:

A. Adjectives, as in pseudokattóliK- *pseudo-Catholic*:kattóliK- *Catholic* adj/I–II; pseudoklássiK- *pseudo-classical*:klássiK- *classical* adj/I–II.

B. Nouns, e.g. of types:

I. m/IIb: pseudofilɔ́sofo *pseudo-philosopher*:filɔ́sof- *philosopher*; pseudolettɛráto *fake man of letters*:lettɛrát- *man of letters*; pseudónimo *pseudonym*: +ɔ́nim- *name*; etc.

II. m/IIIb: pseudodottóre *quack*:dottór- *doctor*; etc.

ii. Exocentric formation, with suffix +0- *having* . . . adj/I–II, in pseudomɔ́rfo *pseudomorphic*:mɔ́rf+ *morph, form*.

w. si^{x+} (before /l m/), sin$^+$ (elsewhere) *syl- sym- syn-*, as in:

    i. Endocentric formations, as on nouns of:

      A. f/Ia: simmetría *symmetry*:$^+$metrí- *measure*; simpatía *sympathy*: $^+$patí- *-pathy, suffering*; sinfonía *symphony*:$^+$fɔní- *-phony*.

      B. m/Ib: síntɔma *symptom*:$^{+'}$tɔm- *-ptom*.

      C. m/IIb: sindrómo *syndrome*:$^+$dróm- *-drome*; sínodo *synod*:$^{+'}$od- *road*; etc.

      D. f/IIIb: sílloǧe *sylloge*:$^{+'}$loǧ- *gathering*; sínkope *syncope*:$^{+'}$kop- *-cope, cutting*; etc.

      E. f/IVd: silléssi *syllepsis*:$^+$léTT- *-lepsis, -lept-*; simbióso *symbiosis*: bióT- *life*; sintássi *syntax*:$^+$táTT- *-taxis, putting*; etc.

    ii. Exocentric formations, with suffix $^+$0- *having* . . . adj/I–II, in sínkrɔno *synchronous*:'krɔn$^+$ *time*; sinónimo *synonymous*:$^{+'}$ɔnim- *name* m/IIb.

    y. tetra$^+$ *tetra-, four*, in:

    i. Endocentric formations, on nouns of:

      A. f/Ia: tetraloǧía *tetralogy*:$^+$loǧi- *-logy*.

      B. m/Ib: tetrárka *tetrarch*:$^+$árk- *-arch, ruler*.

    ii. Exocentric formations, with suffixes:

      A. $^+$0- *having* . . . adj/I–II, on nouns of:

        I. m/IIb: tetrástilo *tetrastyle, having four columns*:$^{+'}$stil-:stíl- *column, style*.

        II. Nominal base: tetrágono *tetragonal*:$^{+'}$gɔn$^+$ *angle*.

      B. $^+$0- *thing having* . . . m/IIb, in tetrakórdo *tetrachord*:kórd- *chord* f/Ia; tetraédro *tetrahedron*:$^+$édr$^+$ *hedron, base*.

    z. tri$^+$ *tri, three*, in:

    i. Endocentric formations, on:

      A. Adjectives, of types:

        I. I–II: trifɔrkúto *three-pointed, -pronged*:fɔrkút- *pointed, pronged*; triǧémino *triplet*:ǧémin- *twin*; trikɔrpóreo *having three bodies*:kɔrpóre- *corporeal*; etc.

        II. IIIb: trilatɛrále *trilateral*:latɛrál- *lateral*; trivalénte *trivalent*: valént- *valent*.

      B. Nouns, e.g. of types:

        I. f/Ia: trikrɔmía *three-color reproduction*:$^+$krɔmí- *-chromy*; triloǧía *trilogy*:$^+$loǧí- *-logy, discourse*; etc.

        II. m/IIb: triklínio *dining-room*:$^+$klíni- *couch*.

        III. m/IIIb: trinipóte *third nephew*:nipót- *nephew*.

        IV. f/IIIb: triparticióne *tripartition*:partición- *partition*; trisecióne *trisection*:sেción- *section*.

    ii. Exocentric formations, with the suffixes:

      A. $^+$0- *having* . . . adj/I–II, e.g. on nouns of types:

        I. f/Ia: trisíllabo *trisyllabic*:síllab- *syllable*.

        II. m/IIb: tripétalo *tripetaled*:pétal- *petal*; trítono *three-toned*:$^{+'}$tɔn-: tón- *tone*.

        III. Nominal base: trígono *triangular*:$^{+'}$gɔn$^+$ *angle*.

      B. $^+$0- *having* . . . adj/IIIb, e.g. on nouns of types:

i. f/Ia: trikórme *three-formed*:fórm- *form*; trikórde *three-stringed*: kórd- *string*; trilíngue *trilingual*:língu- *language*.

ii. m/IIb: triénne *triennial*:⁺énn-:ánn- *year*; trilústre *of three five-year periods*:lústr- *five-year period*.

iii. m/IIc: trikórne *three-horned*:kórn- *horn*; trimémbre *three-membered*:mémbr- *member*.

iv. m/IIIb: tričípite *three-headed*:⁺čípit- *head* (:káp- *head* m/IIb); trikɔlóre *three-colored, tricolor*:kɔlór- *color*; trimotóre *three-motored*:motór- *motor*.

v. f/IIIb: trifáse *triphase*:fás- *phase*; trifáuče *having three throats*: fáuK- (pl.) *throat*; trikúspide *tricuspid*:kúspid- *cusp*.

c. ⁺0- *thing having* . . . m/IIb, e.g. on nouns of types:

i. f/Ia: trifɔʎʎo *trifolium, trefoil*:fɔʎʎ- *leaf*; trívio *trivium, crossroads*: ⁺′vi-:ví- *way*.

ii. m/IIb: triángɔlo *triangle*:ángɔl- *angle*; tríglif- *triglyph*:⁺′glif-*glyph*; trímetro *trimeter*:′mɛtr- *meter*; tripláno *triplane*:plán- *plane*.

iii. Nominal bases: tríduo *period of three days*:⁺′du⁺ *day*; triédro *trihedron*:⁺édr⁺ *hedron, base*; tríttiko *triptych*:⁺′ttik⁺ *-ptych*; trittóngo *triphthong*:⁺ttóng⁺ *-phthong, sound*.

d. ⁺0- *thing having* . . . m/IIIb, e.g. on nouns of:

i. m/IIb: triréme *trireme*:rém- (*bank of*) *oar*(*s*).

ii. m/IIIb: tridénte *trident*:dént- *tooth*; triméstre *trimester, quarter*: mɛstr⁺:més- *month*.

iii. Nominal bases: trípode *tripode*:⁺′pod⁺ *foot*.

3.2. Composition. Compounds are either endocentric or exocentric; the former belong to the same form-class as their head, whereas the latter are formed with a suffix which places them in a form-class different from that of the head. Where a subordinate (attribute) element of more than one syllable has a full stress in its independent form, the full stress is replaced in a compound by intermediate stress, unless otherwise stated.

3.21. Endocentric Compounds are of the following types:

3.211. Substantives. Compounds with the structure: adverbial attribute + head, occur with both adjectives and nouns as the head. The first element is either an adjective, an adverb, or a preposition.

1. The adjective súper- *super* (*heightened*) occurs prefixed to a great many substantives of all types,[9] as in:

a. Adjectives, of types:

i. I–II: sùperastúto *super-astute*:astút- *astute*; sùpermodérno *super-modern*:modérn- *modern*; sùperrápido *super-rapid*:rápid- *rapid*; sùperumano *superhuman*:umán- *human*; etc.

ii. IIIb: sùperarbitrále *super-arbitral*:arbitrál- *arbitral*; sùperdissetánte *super-quenching*:dissetánt- (*thirst-*) *quenching*; sùperfíne *super-fine*:fín- *fine*; sùperpopɔláre *super-popular*:popɔlár- *popular*; sùperútile *super-useful*:útil- *useful*; etc.

b. Nouns, e.g. of types:

---

[9] For an extensive collection of material, cf. B. Migliorini, Saggî sulla Lingua del Novecento² 70–79 (Firenze, 1942).

i. f/Ia: sùperfémmina *super-woman*:fémmin- *woman*; sùperlínea *super-line*:líne- *line*; sùpermárka *super-brand*:márk- *brand*; sùperpásta *super-paste*: pást- *paste*; etc., and even, with double prefix, sùpersùperoperétta *super-super-operetta*:operétt- *operetta*. *supermercado*

ii. m/Ib: sùperfaššísta *super-fascist*:faššíst- *fascist*; sùperimpressionísta *super-impressionist*:impressioníst- *impressionist*; sùperpatrióta *super-patriot*: patriót- *patriot*; sùperpoéta *super-poet*:poét- *poet*; etc.

iii. m/Id: superčínema *super-cinema*:čínema *movie*.

iv. m/IIb: sùperaliménto *super-food*:alimént- *food*; sùperбállo *super-dance*:báll- *dance*; sùperčírko *super-circus*:čírk- *circus*; sùperkolósso *super-colossus*:kolóss- *colossus*; sùperpaʎʎáččo *super-clown*:paʎʎáččo *clown*; sùperuómo *superman*:uóm- *man*; etc.

v. m/IId: sùperío *super-ego*:ío *ego* (:ío *I* pron.).

vi. m/IIIb: sùpersapóne *super-soap*:sapón- *soap*.

vii. f/IIIb: sùperautomóbile *super-automobile*:automóbil- *automobile*; sùperaviacióne *super-aviation*:aviación- *aviation*; sùpermòtonáve *super-motorship*: mòtonáv- *motor-ship*; sùperpopolacióne *over-population*:popolación- *population*; etc.

viii. f/IIId: superfíče *surface*:fíč- -*face*.

ix. m/VId: sùperbár *super-bar*:bár *bar*; sùperkaffé[x] *super-coffee*:kaffé[x] *coffee*; sùperfilm *superfilm*:fílm *film*; etc.

x. f/VId: sùperčiviltá[x] *super-civilization*:čiviltá[x] *civilization*; sùpernacionalitá[x] *super-nationality*:nacionalitá[x] *nationality*:nacionalitá[x] *nationality*; sùperuniversitá[x] *super-university*:universitá[x] *university*.

2. Adverbs, including the following:

a. éstra *extra*, in:

i. Adjectives, of type:

A. I–II: èstrauteríno *extra-uterine*:uterín- *uterine*.

B. IIIb: èstradotále *in addition to the dowry*:dotále *pertaining to a dowry*; èstrafíne *extrafine*:fín- *fine*; èstrağudiciále *extra-judicial*:ğudiciál- *judicial*; èstralegále *extra-legal*:legál- *legal*; èstraterritoriále *extra-territorial*:territoriál- *territorial*.

ii. Noun, in èstradósso *outside curve* (archit.):dóss- *back* m/IIb.

b. kóntro *against, counter-, a second time, in turn*, in nouns, e.g. of types:

i. f/Ia: kòntrodáta *counter-date*:dát- *date*; kòntrofigúra *counter-figure*: figúr- *figure*; kòntrokaténa *counter-chain*:katén- *chain*; kòntromína *counter-mine*: mín- *mine*; kòntrorifórma *Counter-Reformation*:rifórm- *Reformation*; etc.

ii. m/IIb: kòntrobiʎʎétto *countermanding note*:biʎʎétto *note*; kòntrosénso *nonsense*:séns- *sense*; kòntrospionáğğo *counter-espionage*:spionáğğ- *espionage*; etc.

iii. f/IIIb: kòntroacióne *counteraction*:ación- *action*; kòntrokorrénte *current in opposite direction*:korrént- *current*; kòntrolúče *contrasting light*:lúč- *light*; kòntrorivolucióne *counter-revolution*:rivolución- *revolution*; etc.

c. nón *not*, in nonkuránte *not caring*:kuránt- *caring* adj/IIIb; nonsénso *nonsense*:séns- *sense* m/IIb.

d. rétro *back (of)*, *thing behind* . . ., in:

　　i. Adjectives, of types:

　　　　A. I–II: retroattívo *retroactive*:attív- *active*; rètroskrítto *written on reverse of page*:skrítt- *written*; rètrovisívo *retrovisive*:visív- *visive*.

　　　　B. IIIb: rètrostánte *standing behind*:stánt- *standing*.

　　ii. Nouns, mostly of f/Ia: rètrobókka *post-buccal cavity*:bókk- *mouth*; rètrobottéga *room behind shop*:bottég- *shop*; rètroššéna *backstage*:šén- *stage, scene*; rètrotérra *hinterland*:térr- *land*; rètrovíe (pl.) *rear communications*:víway, communication.

e. sópra^x (before consonant or vowel other than /a u/), sòpr^+ (before /a u/) *sur-, supra-, over-, extra-* mostly(*surpassing*), in:

　　i. Adjectives, of types:

　　　　A. I–II: sòpraindikáto *indicated above*:indikát- *indicated*; sòprammɔdáno *of the other world*:mɔndán- *of the world*; soprumáno *super-human*:umán- *human*.

　　　　B. IIIb: sòpraɛminénte *outstanding*:ɛminént- *eminent*; sòpraffíne *super-fine*:fín- *fine*.

　　ii. Nouns, of types:

　　　　A. f/Ia: sòpraffáššа *outer bandage*:fášš- *bandage*; sòprakkálca *outer stocking*:kálc- *stocking*; sòpraskárpa *overshoe*:skárp- *shoe*.

　　　　B. m/IIb: sòprappéso *overweight, excess weight*:pés- *weight*; sòprapprécco *extra charge*:précco *price*; soprúso *abuse*:ús- *use*.

　　　　C. f/IIIb: sòpraddóte *gift in addition to dowry*:dót- *dowry*.

f. sótto (with loss of final vowel before following vowel) *under, sub-*, as in:

　　i. Adjs/I–II: sòttokutáneo *subcutaneous*:kutáne- *cutaneous*; sòttɔmaríno *submarine*:marín- *marine*; sòttomúltiplo *submultiple*:múltipl- *multiple*; sòttɔnotáto *noted below*:nɔtát- *noted*.

　　ii. Nouns, e.g. of types:

　　　　A. f/Ia: sòttokálca *understocking*:kálc- *stocking*; sòttománika *undersleeve*:mánik- *sleeve*; sòttoprefettúra *subprefecture*:prefettúra *prefecture*; etc.

　　　　B. m/IIb: sòttobósko *underbrush*:bósk- *wood, forest*; sòttokápo *subchief*:káp- *chief*; sòttokuóko *sub-cook*:kuók- *cook*; sòttopassáǧǧo *underpass*:passáǧǧ- *passage*; etc.

　　　　C. m/IIIb: sòttobikkiére *soucoupe, coaster*:bikkiére- *tumbler*; sòttofrútiče *sub-frutex*:frútič- *frutex*; sòttórdine *sub-order, subordinate position*:órdin- *order*; sòttotɛnénte *second lieutenant*:tɛnént- *lieutenant*; etc.

　　　　D. f/IIIb: sòttobáse *sub-base*:bás- *base*; sòttopositióne *sub-position*:positión- *position*; sòttovéste *undergarment*:vést- *garment*; etc.

　　　　E. f/IIId: sòttospéče *sub-species*:spéč- *species*.

g. sovr^+ (before vowels), sóvra (followed by /^x/ except before /r/) *above, over-, super-* (*surpassing*), as in:

　　i. Adjectives, of types:

　　　　A. I–II: sòvrakkáriko *overloaded*:kárik- *loaded*; sòvrumáno *super-human*:umán- *human*.

　　　　B. IIIb: sòvrɛminénte *outstanding*:ɛminént- *eminent*; sòvrintɛlligíbile *surpassing human intelligence*:intɛlliǧíbil- *intelligible*; sòvrannaturále *supernatural*:naturál- *natural*; sòvraraciɔnále *superrational*:raciɔnál- *rational*.

ii. Noun, in sòvrastámpa *overprint*:stámp- *print, press* f/Ia.

h. súˣ *above, over*, in adjectives of types:

i. I–II: sùaččɛnnáto *above-indicated*:aččɛnnát- *indicated*; sùddétto *above-said*:détt- *said*; sùespósto *previously expounded*:espóst- *expounded*; sùnnɔmináto *above-named*:nɔminát- *nominated, named*.

ii. IIIb: sùrrɛnále *superrenal*:rɛnál- *renal*.

3. Prepositions, including:

a. fraˣ *between, among*, in frattémpo *meantime*:témp- *time* m/IIb.

b. pɛr *through, completely*, per-, in:

i. Adjs/I–II: pérfido *perfidious*:⁺′fid-:fíd- *faithful*; pɛrfétto *perfect*:⁺fétt-:fátt- *done*.

ii. Nouns, e.g. of types:

A. m/IIb: pɛrfosfáto *perphosphate*:fosfát- *phosphate*; pɛrklɔrúro *perchloride*:klɔrúr- *chloride*; pɛrmanganáto *permanganate*:manganát- *manganate*; pɛrossído *peroxide*:ossíd- *oxide*; etc.

B. f/IIIb: pɛrtósse *horse-cough*:tóss- *cough*.

3.212. ADJECTIVES occur with bases of the following structure:

1. Coordinate, with neither element subordinate to the other, and having the form-class of the second element; the initial element has SV:

a. Zero, in pòstɛlefóniK- *postal and telephonic*, pòstɛlegráfiK- *postal and telegraphic*, adjs/I–II = póst- *mail* f/Ia + tɛlefóniK- *telephonic*, tɛlegráfiK- *telegraphic* adjs/I–II.

b. /o/, in kiàroskúro *chiaroscuro* adj/I–II = kiár- *clear* adj/I–II + skúr- *dark* adj/I–II; sòrdomúto *deaf and dumb* adj/I–II = sórd- *deaf* adj/I–II + mút- *dumb* adj/I–II; àgrodólče *bitter-sweet* adj/IIIb = ágr- *bitter* adj/I–II + dólč- *sweet* adj/IIIb.

2. Attribute + head, the attribute having its normal SV or being apocopated, and being a:

a. Noun or pronoun, indicating a direct object or other type of complement, as in fèdedéɲɲo *trustworthy* adj/I–II = féd- *faith* f/IIIb + déɲɲ- *worthy* adj/I–II; sèddičénte *soi-disant* = séˣ *oneself* + dičént- *saying* adj/IIIb; sèmmovénte *self-moving* = séˣ *oneself* + movént- *moving* adj/IIIb.

b. Adverb, e.g. in adjectives of types:

i. I–II: áltolokáto *high-placed* = ált- *high* adv/II + lokát- *placed*; àncidétto *afore-said* = ánc- *before* adv/IV + détt- *said*; bènkreáto *well-bred* = bén- *well* adv/III + kreát- *brought up*; màlkáuto *incautious* = mál- *badly* adv/III + káut- *cautious*; etc.

ii. IIIb: bènestánte *well-to-do* = bén- *well* adv/III + stánt- *standing*; bènevɔlénte *benevolent* = bén- *well* adv/III + vɔlént- *wishing*; etc.

3.213. NUMERALS occur in:

1. Coordinate compounds, with the form-class of the second element, and primary stress on:

a. The first element (which has SV zero) and the second element being unstressed, in the numerals from *11* to *16* inclusive, with ⁺diči (:diɛč- *ten*) num/IVd as their second element: undiči *eleven* (:ún- *one* adj/I–II); dóciči *twelve* (:dó⁺: dú- *two* num/IIId); trédiči *thirteen* (:tré⁺:tréˣ *three* num/VId); kuattórdiči *fourteen* (:kuattór⁺:kuáttr- *four* num/IVd); kuíndiči *fifteen* (:kuín⁺:čínku- *five* num/IIId); sédiči *sixteen* (:sé⁺:sé- *six* num/IVd).

   b. The second element, with the first element having as its SV:

   i. /aˣ/, in the numerals dičassétte *seventeen* and dičannóve *nineteen*, each with the element dič⁺ (:diéč- *ten* num/IVd) + sétt- *seven* or nóv- *nine* nums/IIId.

   ii. Zero before vowels and normal SV before consonants in dičótto *eighteen* (= dič⁺ *ten* + ótt- *eight* num/IId) and all compound numerals above 21: e.g. vɛntúno *twenty-one* (= vént- *twenty* num/IVd + ún- *one* adj/I–II); vèntidúe *twenty-two* (= vént- *twenty* num/IVd + dú- *two* num/IIId); trèntótto *thirty-eight* (= trént- *thirty* num/Id + ótt- *eight* num/IId); trèntanóve *thirty-nine* (= trént- *thirty* num/Id + nóv- *nine* num/IIId); etc.

   2. Subordinate, with adjectival attribute preceding head, and the first (attributive) element having as its SV:

   a. Zero, in čɛrtúni *some, certain* . . . (pl.) = čért- *certain* adj/I–II + ún- *one* I–II; talúni *some* (pl.) = tál- *such* adj/IIIb + ún- *one* I–II.

   b. /e/, in àmbedúe *both* = ámb- *both* adj/IId + dú- *two* num/IIId.
   3.214. Nouns show the following types of compounds:

   1. Coordinate, with:

   a. Complete elements of:

   i. Different words: àbbìččíˣ *ABC* m/VId = áˣ *A* + bíˣ *B* + číˣ *C*, all m/VId; a(b)be(č)čed⁺ *ABC* = áˣ *A* + bé⁽ˣ⁾ *B* + čé⁽ˣ⁾ *C*, all m/VId; kàffɛllátte *coffee and milk* m/IIIb = kafféˣ *coffee* m/VId + látt- *milk* m/IIIb; kòmpravéndita *buying and selling* f/Ia = kómpr- *buying* f/Ia + véndit- *selling* f/Ia.

   ii. The same word repeated, with its own stem-vowel in the first part of the compound, and:

   A. No alteration: kìnakína *quinine*:kín- *id.* f/Ia.

   B. Vocalic alternation, /i/ in the first part and /a/ in the second, in nìnnanánna *lullaby*:nínn- *id.* f/Ia; trìkketrákke *tric-trac*:tríkk- *id.* m/IIIb.

   b. Abbreviated elements, with the initial few phonemes of the words concerned, with suffix ⁺0-, gender and number formation being:

   A. m/VId: akmónital akmɔnitál *acmonital, ersatz alloy for coins* = ak⁺ (spelling pronunciation of the first syllable of *acciaio* = aččáio *steel*) + mɔn⁺ (for mɔnetári- *monetary* adj/I–II) + ital⁺ (for italián- *Italian* adj/I–II).

   B. f/IIIb: aldéid- *aldehyde* = al (for álkɔl- alkoól *alcohol* m/IIIb or VId) + deid⁺ (for deidrát- *dehydrated* adj/I–II).

   2. Subordinate, with the structure:

   a. Attribute + head, the former being:

   i. An adjective:

   A. With unvarying stem-vowel, the latter being:

   1. Zero, as in ǧɛntìldónna *gentlewoman* = ǧɛntíl- *gentle, noble* adj/IIIb + dónn- *woman* f/Ia; gràndúka *grand duke* = gránd- *great* adj/IIIb +

dúk- *duke* m/Ib; dùrallumínio *duraluminum* = dúr- *hard* adj/I–II + allumíni-
aluminum m/IIb; galàntuómo *gentleman* = galánt- *gallant* adj/IIIb + uóm-
man m/IIb; màlgústo *bad taste* = mál- *bad* adj/I–II + gúst- *taste* m/IIb; etc.

    II. The proper stem-vowel for an attribute in the singular modifying
the head of a phrase (§4.111.1): e.g. fàlsaríga *line (for copying)* = fálsa *false*
adj/I–II + ríg- *line* f/Ia; piàttafórma *platform* = piátta *flat* adj/I–II + fórm-
form f/Ia; àltopiáno *plateau* = álto *high* adj/I–II + pián- *plain* m/IIb; frànko-
bóllo *postage-stamp* = fránko *free* adj/I–II + bóll- *stamp* m/IIb; mèdioévo
middle ages = médi- *middle* adj/I–II + év- *age* m/IIb; màlaféde *bad faith*
= mála *bad* adj/I–II + féd- *faith* f/IIIb; etc.

    B. With stem-vowel varying from singular to plural, as for an attribute
modifying the head in a phrase (§4.111.1): e.g. àltofórno *smelting furnace*, pl.
àltifórni = alt- *high* adj/I–II + fórn- *furnace, oven* m/IIb; bàssofóndo *slum*,
pl. bàssifóndi = báss- *low, base* adj/I–II + fónd- *depth* m/IIb; etc.

    ii. A substantive, indicating:

    A. Possessor, in the names of days of the week formed with dí^x *day*
m/VId as second element; the first element has the stem-vowel:

    I. Zero, in vènɛrdí^x *Friday*:vénɛr- *Venus* f/IIIb.

    II. /e/ in the other names: lunedí^x *Monday*:lún- *moon* f/Ia; ǧovedí^x
Thursday:ǧóv- *Jove* m/IIIb; màrtedí^x *Tuesday*:márt- *Mars* m/IIIb; mèrkɔledí^x
Wednesday:mérkɔl^+:mɛrkúri- *Mercury* m/IIb.

    B. Apposition, as in bàrbaǧánni *owl, blockhead* = bárb- *beard,* (*uncle*
NIt.) f/Ib + ǧánn- *Johnny* m/IVd.

    C. Object connected with an action performed (mostly direct object),
with stem-vowel:

    I. The normal stem-vowel: e.g. àkkuapláno *aquaplane* = ákkua
water f/Ia + plán- *plane* m/IIb; àrtefátto *artifact* = árte *art* f/IIIb + fátt-
fact m/IIb; nùllatɛnénte *proletarian* = núlla *nothing* + tɛnént- *owner, holder*
m/IIIb; luɔgotɛnénte *lieutenant* = luɔ́go *place* + tɛnént- *holder* m/IIIb.

    II. /e/, as in àkkuedótto *aqueduct* = ákku- *water* + dótt- -*duct*
m/IIb; aèrɛmóto *windstorm* = aér- *air* m/IIIb + mót- *motion* m/IIb; terrɛmóto
earthquake = térr- *earth* f/Ia + mót- *motion* m/IIb.

    III. /i/, in many compounds, such as àkkuivénto *wind-and-rain-
storm* = ákku- *water* f/Ia + vént- *wind* m/IIb; àgrifóʎʎo *acrifolium* = ágr-
bitter adj/I–II + fɔ́ʎʎ- *leaf, folio* m/IIb; àgrimɛnsúra *agrimensure* = ágr-
field + mɛnsúr- *measuring* f/Ia; etc. etc.

    IV. /o/, in very many compounds,[10] such as àkrokɔ́ro *acrocore,*
plateau surrounded by mountains = ákr^+ *summit* + kɔ́r- *region* m/IIb; tɛrmosi-
fóne *central heating system* = térm^+ *heat* + sifón- *syphon* m/IIb. But when the
second element has recessive stress, the first element loses its stress entirely:
e.g. akrókɔro *acrocore* = ákr^+ summit + ^+'kɔr-:^+kɔ́r- *region* m/IIb; aǧógrafo
hagiographer = ^+áǧ- *holy, saint* adj/I–II + 'graf- -*grapher* m/IIb; tɛrmómetro
thermometer = térm^+ *heat* + 'mɛtr- *meter* m/IIb; etc. etc.

---

[10] Extensive material in Migliorini, 'I prefissoidi', in Saggî sulla Lingua del Novecento²
7–54 (Firenze, 1942).

v. /is/, in certain compounds with the first element ğúr⁺ *jur-,
law:* e.g. ğùrisdicióne *jurisdiction*:⁺dición- *-diction* f/IIIb; ğùrispérito *legal
expert*:périt- *expert* m/IIb; ğùrisprudénte *legal expert, jurisprudent*:prudént-
prudent (person) m/IIIb.

iii. An adverb, with the second element an infinitive: e.g. bènestáre *wel-
fare* = bén- *well* + stár- *to stand* m/IIIb; bènéssere *well-being* = bén- *well* +
ésser- *to be* m/IIIb.

b. Head + attribute, the attribute being:

i. An adjective, agreeing in gender with the head and inflected according
to its form-class, and the head being:

A. Variable, as in àkkuafórte *nitric acid,* pl. àkkuefórti = ákku- *water*
f/Ia + fórt- *strong* adj/IIIb.

B. Invariable, with stem-vowel:

I. Zero, as in fièngréko *fenugreek* m/IIb = fién- *hay* m/IIb + grék-
Greek adj/I–II.

II. The usual stem-vowel: e.g. àssafétida *assafoetida* f/Ia = áss-
assa f/Ia + fétid- *fetid* adj/I–II; bànkarótta *bankruptcy* f/Ia = bánk f/Ia +
rótt- *broken* adj/I–II; kàmposánto *cemetery* m/IIb = kámp- *field* m/IIb +
sánt- *holy* adj/I–II; pàlkoššéniK- *stage* m/IIb = pálk- *board* m/IIb + šéniK-
scenic adj/I–II; etc.

ii. A noun, indicating possessor or thing related to what is referred to by
the head. This type of compound has three sub-types of inflection, with the
form-class determined by:

A. The last element, which has stem-vowel:

I. Normal, the head having its normal stem-vowel and being:

α. Variable: e.g. kàpobrigánte *chief brigand,* pl. kàpibrigánti
m/IIIb = káp- *head* m/IIb + brigánt- *brigand* m/IIIb; kàpokómiK- *head
comedian* (sg. kàpokómiko, pl. kàpikómiči) m/IIb = káp- *head* m/IIb + kómiK-
comedian m/IIb.

β. Invariable: e.g. bàɲɲomaría *double boiler* (lit. *bath of Mary*)
f/Ia = báɲɲo *bath* m/IIb + marí- *Mary* f/Ia; àkkuavíta *aqua vitae* f/Ia =
ákku- *water* f/Ia + vít- *life* f/Ia; kàpomakkiníssta *chief machinist* m/Ib = káp-
head m/IIb + makkiníst- *machinist* m/Ib. Some compounds have both this
type of inflection and that mentioned in the preceding paragraph: e.g.
kàpokómiK- *chief comedian* (pl. kàpikómiči or kàpokómiči) m/IIb; kàpokuóko
chief cook m/IIb; kàpoluógo *provincial capital* m/IIb; etc.

II. /e/, with gender and number f/IIIb, the head having its normal
stem-vowel and being invariable, in àkkuavíte *aqua vitae* + ákku- *water* f/Ia
+ vít- *life* f/Ia.

B. The first element, with the second element invariable and having its
normal stem-vowel: e.g. kàpobánda *ring-leader,* pl. kàpibánda m/IIb = káp-
head m/IIb + bánd- *band* f/Ia; kàpokáčča *leader of the chase* m/IIb = káp-
head m/IIb + káčč- *chase* f/Ia; kàpolíssta *person at the head of the list* m/IIb =
káp- *head* m/IIb + líst- *list* f/Ia.

3.215. PRONOUNS show, in additions to the formations enumerated in §2.2,
the following combinations of indefinite pronouns:

1. Repetition, with primary stress on second element only: kekké[x] *whatever* = ké[x] *what?* repeated.

2. Pronoun + relative phrase containing Timeless A 3.sg. of éss- *be* IIIb/Irr/S[1], in kèkkessía *whatever* (lit. *what it may be*).

3.216. VERBS occur in compounds with the structure: complement + head, the complement belonging to one of the following form-classes:

1. Substantive, normally a direct object or indicating means or result of the action, with stem-vowel:

a. The normal stem-vowel: e.g. bàrkamén- *beat around the bush* = bárk-boat f/Ia + mén- *lead* I/Reg/W; ǧìróvag- *wander aimlessly* = ǧír- *turn* m/IIb + [+']vag-:vág- *wander* I/Reg/W; kàpovólG- *turn upside down* IIIb/Reg/S[1, 2] and kàpovólt- *id.* I/Reg/W = káp- *head* + vólG- *turn* IIIb/Reg/S[1, 2] or vólt- *id.* I/Reg/W; partéčip- *participate* = párt- part f/IIIb + [+']čip- -*cipate* I/Reg/W; ràdiotrasmétt- *broadcast* = rádio *radio* f/IId + trasmétt- IIIb/Reg/[1, 2].

b. Zero, with an alternant form of the noun (unstressed): saláss- *let blood* = sa[+] (:sángu- *blood* m/IIIb) + láss- *let* (archaic):lášš- *id.* I/Reg/W.

c. /e/, as in putreféč- *putrefy* = putr[+] *rotten* + féč- *make* IV/Irr/S[1, 2].

d. /i/, as in èkuidíst- *be equidistant* = éku- *equal* adj/I–II + díst- *be distant* I/Reg/W; èkuilíbr- *equilibrate* = éku- *equal* + líbr- *balance* I/Reg/W; tèrǧivérs- *tergiversate* = térG[+] (:térg- *back* m/IIb) + vérs- *turn* I/Reg/W; èkuivál- *be equivalent* = éku- *equal* adj/I–II + vál- *be worth* IIIa/Irr/S[1, 2]; and many compounds based on [+']fik- -*fy* I/Reg/W (:féč- *make* IV/Irr/S[1, 2]): e.g. àčidífik- *acidify*:áčid- *acid* adj/I–II; čèrtífik- *certify*:čért- *certain* adj/I–II; kiarífik- *clarify*:kiár- *clear* adj/I–II; barbífik- *put forth roots, grow a beard* (humorous):bárb- *beard* f/Ia; etc. etc.

2. Verb, with stem-vowel /e/, in tùmeféč- *tumefy* = tum[+] *swell up* + féč- *make* IV/Irr/S[1, 2].

3. Preposition, including the following:

a. ad, (before vowels), a[x], (before consonants) *to*, *ad-*, intensive, as in the following compounds of types:

i. I/Reg/W: abbáʎʎ- *dazzle*:báʎʎ- *id.*; abbást- *be enough*:bást- *be sufficient*; adór- *adore*:ór- *pray*; ammír- *admire*:mír- *id.*; etc. etc.

ii. II/Reg/W: assál- *assail*:sál- *go up*; assént- *assent*:sént- *feel*; etc.

iii. II/Irr/S[1]: avvƐn- *happen*:vƐn- *come*.

iv. IIIa: akkád- *happen*:kád- *fall*; attƐn- *grasp*:tƐn- *hold*; etc.

v. IIIb: abbátt- *beat down*:bátt- *beat*; atténd- *attend*:ténd- *tend, stretch*; attínG- *get, obtain*:tínG- *touch*; etc.

vi. IV: addíK- *dedicate, assign*:díK- *say*; appón- *place at, to*:pón- *place, put*; astá[+] (in astánte *spectator, person present* m/IIIb, pres. part.):stá- *stand*.

b. fra[x], *between, among; wrongly, mis-*, as in the following of types:

i. I/Reg/W: framméskɔl- *intermix*:méskɔl- *mix*; frastáʎʎ- *cut at random*:stáʎʎ- *cut up*; frastórn- *disturb, upset*:stórn- *turn aside*; frastuón[+] (as base for frastuóno *din* m/IIb):stuón- *make an unpleasant noise*.

ii. IIIb: frainténd- *misunderstood*:inténd- *understand*; frammétt- *put among*:métt- *put*.

iii. IV: frappón- *put between, interpose*:pón- *put, place*.

c. pɛr, *through, by, for, per-*, as in the following of types:

    i. I/Reg/W: pɛrdón- *pardon*:dón- *donate*; pɛrdúr- *last a long time*: dúr-last; pérme- *permeate*:⁺'me- *wander, pass*; pérɔr- pɛrór- *perorate* (:⁺'ɔr-): ór- *orate*; pɛrtrátt- *treat thoroughly*:trátt- *treat*; etc.

    ii. II/Reg/W: pɛrségu- *persecute*:ségu- *follow*.

    iii. II/Irr/S[1]: pɛrvɛn- *get through, succeed*:vɛn- *come*.

    iv. II/ísK/W: pɛrčep- *perceive*:⁺čep- *-ceive*; pɛrvɛrt- *pervert*:⁺vɛrt- *turn*.

    v. IIIa: pɛrmán- *remain*:⁺mán- *(re)main*; pɛrsuád- *persuade*:⁺suád- -suade.

    vi. IIIb: pɛrkórr- *run through*:kórr- *run*; pɛrkuót- *strike*:⁺kuót- *hit*; pɛrmétt- *permit*:métt- *put, send*; pɛrsíst- *persist*:⁺síst- -sist; pɛrvád- *pervade*: ⁺vád- -vade.

4. Adverbs, including:

    a. béne *well*, in bɛnedíK- *bless*:díK- *say* IV/Irr/S[1, 2].

    b. kóntro *against, counter-, again, in turn*, as in the following of types:

    i. I/Reg/W: kòntrobilánč- *counter-balance*:bilánč- *balance*; kòntrofírm- *countersign*:fírm- *sign*; kòntroíndik- *counter-indicate*:índik- *indicate*; kòntrórdin- *counter-order*:órdin- *order*.

    ii. IIIb/Reg/W: kòntrobátt- *hit back, fight against*:bátt- *beat, hit*.

    c. mále *evil, badly*, in màledíK- *curse*:díK- *say* IV/Irr/S[1, 2].

    d. rétro *back(wards)*, in rètrodát- *postdate*:dát- *date* I/Reg/W; rètročéd- *retrocede*:čéd- *cede* IIIb/Reg/W.

    e. sópr⁺ (before vowels[11]), sópra^x (before consonants) *sur-, super-, over-*, as in the following of types:

    i. I/Reg/W: sòprinnálc- *raise over*:innálc- *raise*; sòprakkárik- *overload*: kárik- *load*; sòprallód- *overpraise*:lód- *praise*; etc.

    ii. II/Irr/W: sòpravvɛn- *come unexpectedly*:vɛn- *come*.

    iii. IIIa/Reg/W: sòprassɛd- *put off, adjourn*: sɛd- *sit*.

    iv. IIIb: sòprečéd- *surpass*:ečéd- *exceed*; sòpraǧǧúnG- *arrive unexpectedly*:ǧúnG- *arrive*; sòpr(a)inténd- *superintend*:inténd- *intend*; sòprakkórr- *come to aid, help*:kórr- *run*; sòprammétt- *put above*:métt- *put*; sòpravvív- *survive*:vív- *live*.

    v. IV: sòprespón- *expound above*:espón- *expound*; sòpraffáč- *oppress*:fáč- *do*.

    f. sótt⁺ (before vowels), sótto (before consonants) *under-, sub-*, as in the following of types:

    i. I/Reg/W: sòtténtr- *subenter*:éntr- *enter*.

    ii. IIIa/Irr/S[1]: sòttáč- *keep (wrongly) silent*:táč- *keep silent*.

    iii. IIIb/Reg/S[1, 2]: sòttodivíd- *subdivide*:divíd- *divide*; sòttinténd- *understand from context*:inténd- *understand*; sòttométt- *submit*:métt- *put*; sòtténd- *subtend*:ténd- *tend, stretch*; sòttoskrív- *subscribe*:skrív- *write*.

    iv. IV/Irr/S: sòttopón- *subject*:pón- *put, place*; sòttostá- *be subject*: stá- *stand*; and (with SV zero in adverb) sottrá^x- *subtract*:trá^x- *draw*.

    g. sóvr⁺ (before vowels), sóvra^x (before consonants), as in the following of types:

---

[11] Except optionally in sòpr(a)inténd- *superintend* IIIb/Reg/S[1, 2].

i. I/Reg/W: sòvrabbónd- *be superabundant*:abbónd- *be abundant, abound*; sòvrakkárik- *overload*:kárik- *load*; sòvrastámp- *overprint*:stámp- *print*.

ii. IV/Irr/S: sòvrimpón- *superimpose*:impón- *impose*; sòvrappón- *superpose*:pón- *put*; sòvrastá- *be imminent, threaten*:stá- *stand*.

3.217. Adverbs occur in the type attribute + head, the attribute being:

1. The adjective áltr- *other, else* I–II, in àltrónde *from elsewhere*:ónd- *whence* adv/III, and àltróve *elsewhere*:óv- *where* adv/III.

2. An adverb, as in bènsí˟ *indeed* = bén- *well* adv/III + sí˟ *so* adv/VI; sìbbéne *indeed* = sí˟ *so* adv/VI + bén- *well* adv/III; ğàmmái *never* = ğá˟ *already* adv/VI + mái (*n*)*ever* adv/IV; làğğú˟ *down there* and làssú˟ *up there* = lá˟ *there* adv/VI + ğú˟ *down* and sú˟ *up*, both advs/VI; etc.

3. A preposition, such as one of the following:

a. d⁺ (before vowels), di (before consonants) *of, from*, as in davánti *before*: avánt- *before* adv/IV; dimólto *much, greatly*:mólt- *much, very* adv/II; dónde *whence*:ónd- *whence* adv/III; dóve *where*:óv- *where* adv/III.

b. da˟ *from*, in dappríma *at first*:prím- *first* adv/I.

c. in *in*, in indiétro *backwards*:diétr- *back* adv/II; inkóntro *towards, to meet*:kóntr- *against* adv/II.

d. pɛr *through, by*, in pɛrfíno *as far (as), even*:fín- *as far* adv/II; pɛrkóme˟ *how*:kóme˟ *how* adv/VI.

4. The conjunction ne˟ *nor*, in neánke nemmánko nemméno neppúre *not even*:ánke *also* adv/III; mánko méno *less* advs/II; púre *also* adv/III, respectively.

3.218. Prepositions show compounds of the type head (unstressed) + attribute, the latter being:

1. The adjective éss- *this*, in the m.sg. form ésso, in the archaic forms kɔnésso *with*:kɔn *with* prep/VI; lungésso *along*:lung- *along* prep/II; sottésso *under*: sótt- *under* prep/II; sovrésso *over*:sóvr- *over* prep/I.

2. The adverb ánke *also*, in finánke *even including* . . . prep/III:fín- *as far as* prep/II.

3.219. Conjunctions show only the compound sebbéne *even if* = se˟ *if* conj/VI + béne *well* adv/III.

3.22. Exocentric Compounds.

3.221. Adjectives occur with the following form-classes as base:

1. Noun, followed by suffix:

a. ⁺0- *having* . . . I–II, and preceded by:

i. One of the prefixes enumerated in §3.132–3: dodekasíllabo *dodecasyllabic*:síllab- *syllable* f/Ia; etc.

ii. A preposition: adúnk- *hooked* adj/I–II = ad *to* + ⁺únK⁺ *hook*.

iii. An adjective, with stem-vowel:

A. Zero, as in àkutángɔlo *acute-angled* = akút- *acute* I–II + ángɔl- *angle* m/IIb.

B. /i/, as in kuàdrisíllabo *quadrisyllabic* = kuadr⁺ (:kuáttr- *four* num/IId) + síllab- *syllable* f/Ia.

iv. A noun, with stem-novel /o/, as in àntropɔmórfo *anthropomorphic* = ántrop⁺ *anthrop-, man* + mórf⁺ *morph-, form*.

b. 0- *having* . . . IIIb, and preceded by:

i. One of the prefixes mentioned in §3.132–3: e.g. deklíve *having a steep descent*:klív- *steep descent* m/IIb; diffórme disfórme *deformed*:fórm- *form* f/Ia; imbérbe *beardless*:bɛrb⁺:bárb- *beard* f/Ia; etc.

ii. A numeral, without stem-vowel, before ⁺énn- (:ánn- *year* m/IIb): e.g. činkuanténne *fifty years old*:činkuánt- *fifty* num/I; kuaranténne *forty years old*:kuaránt- *forty* num/I; millénne *a thousand years old*:míll- 1000 num/IIIc.

iii. A substantive, with stem-vowel:

A. /i/, as in aɛrifórme *aeriform*:aér- *air* m/IIIb + fórm- *form* f/Ia; unifórme *uniform* = ún- *one* adj/I–II + fórm- *form* f/Ia.

B. /u/, with recessive stress, in kuadrúmane *four-handed* and kuadrúpede *quadruped(al)* = kuadr⁺ (:kuáttr- *four* num/IId) + mán- *hand* f/IIb and ped⁺:piéd- *foot* m/IIIb, respectively.

c. ⁺0- m/d, but with normal stem-vowel of the noun, and preceded by the prefix anti⁺ *against*: e.g. in antikárro *anti-tank*:kárr- *tank, car* m/IIb; antigás *anti-gas*:gás *gas* m/VId.

2. Pronoun (interrogative, unstressed), with suffix 0- adj/VId and preceded by an interrogative adjective, forming the indefinite adjective kuálkeˣ *some* = kwál- *which* adj/IIIb + kéˣ *what?*.

3. Verb root with suffix ⁺0- adj/I–II (before which /K/ > /K/) and preceded by a noun (direct object) with stem-vowel /í/:e.g. agríkɔlo *agricultural* = ágr- *field* m/IIb + kɔl- *cultivate* IIIb/Reg; armíǧero *armed*, alíǧero *winged* = árm- *weapon* and ál- *wing*, respectively, both f/Ib + ǧɛr⁺ *bear, carry*; fatídiK- *prophetic* = ʃát- *fate* m/IIb + díK- *say* IV/Irr/S¹' ²; etc.

3.222. Nouns occur with the following types of base:

1. Adjective (without stem-vowel) followed by noun (with meaning of complement) + ⁺0- with gender and plural formation of the noun: sìmilóro *an alloy of brass and zinc* m/IIb = símil- *similar* adj/IIIb + ór- *gold* m/IIb.

2. Noun:

a. Preceded by:

i. Noun, in a coordinate construction, with suffix ⁺0- f/Ia: tèrramára *terramara* = térr- *land* f/Ia + már- *sea* m/IIIb.

ii. Numeral (with SV /i/) and followed by ⁺0- *period of* . . . f/Ia: sèttimána *week* = sétt- *seven* num/IIId + ⁺mán- *morrow* m/IVd.

b. With stem-vowel /i/ and followed by an adjective (attributive) + ⁺0- *person or thing having* . . . m/IIb, especially in bird-names: e.g. kàpinéro *sparrow* = káp- *head* m/IIb + nér- *black* adj/I–II; kòdirósso *red-tail* = kód- *tail* f/Ia + róss- *red* adj/I–II; pèttirósso *red-breast* = pétt- *breast* m/IIb + róss- *red* adj/I–II; etc.

3. Verb, in:

a. Stem A (rhyzotonic, with TV /e/ or 0 > /i/),¹² followed by:

i. Noun (direct object), with its normal stem-vowel, and suffix ⁺0- *place, means or performer of action indicated* m/d, as in the following based on verbs of:

---

¹² These compounds are often analyzed as consisting of a 2.sg. imperative + noun, or of a Pres. A 3.sg. + noun. Cf. the author's note 'Ancora i composti del tipo *portabandiera, facidanno*', Lingua Nostra 9.22–23 (1948).

A. I/Reg/W: akkàttapáne *beggar* = akkátt- *beg* + páne *bread* m/IIIb; akkiàppakáni *dog-catcher* = akkiápp- *catch* + káni *dogs* m/IIIb; ammàccasétte *seven-at-a-blow*, *boaster* = ammácc- *slaughter* + sétt- *seven* num/IIId; pàrapétto *parapet* = pár- *protect* + pétt- *chest* m/IIb; etc. etc.

B. II/Reg/W: spàrtiákkue *watershed* = spárt- *divide* + ákkue *waters* f/Ia.

C. II/ísK/W: pulìššiorékki *ear-cleaner* = pulíšš- *clean* + orékki *ears* m/IIb; pulìššipiédi *doormat* = pulíšš- *clean* + piédi *feet* m/IIIb; etc.

D. IIIb: bàttipánni *clothes-beater* = bátt- *beat* + pánni *clothes* m/IIb; mèttimále *trouble-maker* = métt- *put* + mále *evil* m/IIIb; etc.

E. IV: fàčidánno *harm-doer* = fáč- *do* + dánno *harm* m/IIb; fàčimále *evil-doer* = fáč- *do* + mál- *evil* m/IIIb.

In most of these compounds, the noun stands alone; in a few, it is preceded by the definite article, as in bàttilóro *gold-beater* = bátt- *beat* IIIb/Reg/W + lóro *the gold* m/IIb; bèkkaláʎʎo *blind-man's buff* = békk- *peck* I/Reg/W + láʎʎo *the garlic* m/IIb.

ii. Adverbial complement or exocentric phrase, as in pìššallétto *bed-wetter* = píšš- *pee* I/Reg/W + allétto *in bed* exocentric phr.

iii. Noun (direct object), with suffix +0- *action indicated or means thereto*, with gender and plural formation of the noun, as in the following of types:

A. f/Ia: àlcabandiéra *flag-raising* = álc- *raise* I/Reg/W + bandiér- *banner*; etc.

B. m/IIb: bàttipétto *breast-beating* = bátt- *beat* IIIb/Reg/W + pétt- *breast*; pàssapórto *passport* = páss- *pass* I/Reg/W + pórt- *port*; pàssatémpo *pastime* = páss- *pass* I/Reg/W + témp- *time*.

C. m/IIIb: bàttikuóre *heart-beating* = bátt- *beat* + kuór- *heart*.

But the gender of the compound is masculine in bàčamáno *hand-kissing* m/IIb = báč- *kiss* I/Reg/W + mán- *hand* f/IIb.

iv. Adverb, with suffix +0- *action indicated or performer thereof* m/d and normal stem-vowel of adverb: bàčabásso *low bow* = báč- *kiss* I/Reg/W + báss- *low* adv/II; bùttafuóri *cue-man, prompter* = bútt- *throw* I/Reg/W + fuór- *out* adv/IV.

v. Verb, in root form, with suffix +0- *action indicated* f/Ia: bàttisóffia *breath-taking fear* = bátt- *beat* IIIb/Reg/W + sóffi- *puff* I/Reg/W; ǧìravólta *complete turn, spin* = ǧír- *turn* + vólt- *turn*, both I/Reg/W; pàrapíʎʎa *hubbub, confusion* = pár- *stop* + píʎʎ- *take*, both I/Reg/W; tòkkasána *infallible remedy* = tókk- *touch* + sán- *heal*, both I/Reg/W.

b. Stem A (rhyz.), followed by another verb in Stem A (rhyz.) (with TV > /i/ in each), with suffix +0- *action indicated* m/d: àndiriviéni *coming-and-going* = and- *go* I/Irr/W + rivɛn- *come back* II/Irr/S[1, 2]; sàliššéndi *coming-and-going* = sál- *go up* II/Irr/W + šénd- *go down* IIIb/Reg/[1, 2].

4. Phrase:

a. Endocentric:

i. Noun phrase of type:

A. Attribute (adjective) + head, with suffix +0- *person or thing having or characterized by* ... m/d, with SV of head: e.g. bèllumore *jolly fellow*:béllumóre *fine humor*; bónavóʎʎa *volunteer physician*:bónavóʎʎa *good will*; čĕntofóʎʎe *Achillea*:čéntofóʎʎe *100 leaves*; mìllepiédi *millipede*:míllepiédi *1000 feet*; trèálbɛri *three-master*:tréálbɛri *three masts*; etc.

B. Head + attribute (adjective or exocentric phrase), with inflection of:

I. Last element only, with suffix ⁺0- *person or thing having or characterized by* . . . and gender and plural formation of last element: e.g. bòkkadóro *golden-mouthed, sententious person* m/IIb:bókkadóro *mouth of gold*; kùlbiánko *a kind of bird* m/IIb:kúl(o)biánko *white arse*; pàlafítta *palafitta* f/Ia:pálafítta *a stake thrust (into the earth)*; pòmodóro *tomato* m/IIb:pómodóro *apple of gold*; etc.

II. Both elements, with suffix ⁺0- person *or thing having or characterized by* . . . masculine, with SV of normal inflection (singular and plural): pèllɛróssa *redskin, American Indian*:péllɛróssa *red skin*; pòmodóro *tomato*, pl. pòmidóri:pómodóro *apple of gold*.

ii. Verb phrase, with bound or free elements as complements, and suffix:

A. ⁺0- *thing saying* . . . m/d, with the normal final vowel as SV: misirícci *roly-poly doll* = misirícci *stand me up!* (lit. *let one stand me up*); làššapassáre *pass* = lášsapassáre *allow to pass!*.

B. ⁺0- *that which* . . . m/IIb: fàbbisóɲɲo *what is necessary*:fábbisóɲɲo *it makes need, it is necessary*.

b. Exocentric, with suffix ⁺0- *thing which is* . . . masculine, with singular SV = normal final vowel of phrase, and plural formation of type:

i. b: e.g. in the following of types:

A. m/IIb: akkónto *instalment* = akkónto *on account*; affrésko *fresco* = affrésko *freshly* (= aˣ *to, on* + frésko *fresh* adj/I–II); assólo *solo* = assólo *as a single (performer)*; dintórno *surroundings* = dintórno *around* (= dₗ *of* + intórno *around*); dòpopránzo *after-lunch period* = dópopránzo *after lunch*; lùngárno *Arno embankment* = lúngárno *along (the) Arno*; pɛrčénto *percent* = pɛrčénto *per 100*; etc.

B. m/IIIb: affáre *affair* = affáre *to do*; daffáre *to-do* = daffáre *to do*; lùngofiúme *river embankment* = lúngofiúme *along (the) river*; lùngotévɛre *Tiber embankment* = lúngotévɛre *along (the) Tiber*; pɛrmále *evil, harm* = pɛrmále *for evil*.

ii. d: e.g. dòpoguérra *post-war period* = dópoguérra *after war*; dòpolavóro (*Fascist*) *recreation organization* = dópolavóro *after work*; dòposkuóla *after-school program* = dóposkuóla *after school*.

5. Clause, with suffix ⁺0- *person to whom might be said* . . . m/d, with SV = normal final vowel of clause: tùmmistúfi *obnoxious, boresome person* = túmmistúfi *you gripe, bore me*.

3.223. PRONOUNS show only the type: indefinite pronoun = interrogative or indefinite adjective + noun + ⁺0- m/I (no plural):kuàlkósa kuàlkekkósa *something* = kuál- *which* adj/IIIb or kuálkeˣ *some* pron/VId, respectively + kós- *thing* f/Ia.

3.224. VERBS show only the type: preposition (aˣ *to*) + verb (in root form) + suffix (all I/Reg/W), with causative force:

1. ⁺i-: assédi- *besiege*:séd-:sɛd- *sit* IIIa/Reg/W.

2. ⁺ɛr-: abbévɛr- *water (animals)*:bév- *drink* IIIb(x)/Reg/S[1].

3. ⁺ént-: addɔrmént- *put to sleep*:dɔ́rm- *sleep* II/Reg/W.

3.225. INDECLINABLES all form exocentric compounds with the suffix ⁺0-, with SV = the normal final vowel of the last element of the compound.

1. Prepositions show only the type noun-phrase + ⁺0- *even with the . . . of . . .*: màlgrádo *in spite of . . .*: málgrádo *ill will, unwillingness.*

2. Adverbs show the types:

     a. Noun phrase, with suffix:

         i. ⁺0- *in the manner of . . .*: kàporovéššo *backwards*:káporovéššo *head reversed.*

         ii. ⁺0- *ly*, with the noun ménte *mind, manner* preceded by an adjective:

         A. In root form, in compounds of adjectives of IIIb ending in /Vl Vr/: e.g. àbilménte *cleverly, skillfully*:ábil- *clever, skillful*; spečàlménte *specially*: spečál- *special*; estɛriòrménte *exteriorly*:estɛriór- *exterior*; etc.

         B. In f.sg., in compounds of all other adjectives, as in the following based on adjectives of types:

         I. I: idiòtaménte *idiotically*:idiót- *idiot(ic)*.

         II. I–II: abbandɔnàtaménte *abandonedly*:abbandɔnát- *abandoned*; àltraménte *otherwise* (rare):áltr- *other*; bràvaménte *bravely*:bráv- *brave*; furiòsaménte *furiously*:furiós- *furious*; kàldaménte *hotly*:káld- *hot*; stùpidaménte *stupidly*:stúpid- *stupid*; etc. etc. etc.

         III. IIIb: àkrɛménte *sharply*:aKr- *sharp, bitter*; brèvɛménte *briefly*: bréve *brief*; dòlčɛménte *sweetly*:dólč- *sweet*; etc. etc.

         IV. IVd: pàriménte *equally*:pár- *equal*.

Compounds of this type are extremely frequent, being formed on almost all adjectives in the language.

     b. Exocentric phrase, of the types:

         i. Pronoun + preposition (alternant), with loss of final /ˣ/ of the pronoun and final /i/ thereof > /s/, all formed with the preposition alternant ko *with*, in méko *with me*:méˣ *me*; téko *with thee*:téˣ *thee*; séko *with himself (herself, itself)*:séˣ *himself (herself, itself)*; nósko *with us*:nói *us*; vósko *with you*:vói *you*. Outside of Tuscany, these forms are archaic or dialectal.

         ii. Preposition and:

         A. Adjective (m.sg.): abbásso *down* = aˣ *to* + básso *low* I–II; appiéno *fully* = aˣ *to* + pién- *full* I–II; àncitútto *before all* = ánci *before* (archaic) + tútt- *all* I–II; frattánto *meanwhile* = fraˣ *between* + tánt- *so much* I–II; invéro *in truth* = in *in* + vér- *true* I–II; etc.

         B. Noun (sg.), preceded by:

         I. Definite article (m.sg.), in alfíne *finally* = al *at the* + fín- *end* f/IIIb; alméno *at least* = al *at the* + mén- *least* m/IId.

         II. No intervening element: e.g. abbastánca *enough* = aˣ *to* + bastánc- *sufficiency* f/Ia; alláto *beside* = aˣ *at* + lát- *side* m/IIb; dakkápo *from the beginning* = daˣ *from* + káp- *head, beginning* m/IIb; infátti *in fact* =in *in* + fátti *facts*; etc. etc.

c. Pronoun, in pɛrkéˣ *why?* and pɛrčóˣ *therefore* = pɛr *for* + kéˣ *what?* and čóˣ *this*, respectively.

D. Adverb: addéntro *far in* = aˣ *to* + déntro *inside* adv/II; addiétro *backwards* and indiétro *in back, backwards* = aˣ *to* and in *in*, respectively + diétro *back(wards)* adv/II.

E. Another exocentric phrase: dappɛrtútto *everywhere* = daˣ *from* + pɛrtútto *through all, throughout*.

c. Adverb (nón *not*) + exocentric phrase: nòndiméno *nonetheless* = nón *not* + diméno *by less*; nònpɛrtánto *and yet* = nón *not* + pɛrtánto *for so much*.

3. Conjunctions are all formed with a relative pronoun or adverb as their last element, and with the first element (in root form, except when ending in consonant cluster, in which case SV is the normal one):

a. An adverb: e.g. allòrkéˣ *when* = allór- *then* adv/Ia + kéˣ *that*; allòrkuándo *when* = allór- *then* adv/Ia + kuándo *when*; àncikéˣ *before* = ánci *before, rather* adv/IV + kéˣ *that*; bènkéˣ *although* = bén- *well* adv/III + kéˣ *that*; ğàkkéˣ *since* = ğáˣ *already* adv/VI + kéˣ *that*; etc.

b. A preposition: dakkéˣ *since* = daˣ *from* prep/VI + kéˣ *that*.

c. An exocentric phrase: affìnkéˣ *so that* = affín(e) *for (the) purpose* + kéˣ *that*.

CHAPTER IV. PHRASE-STRUCTURE

4.0. Phrases in Italian are combinations of linguistic forms larger than a single free morpheme and taking the place of a single morpheme of a given form-class in an utterance. A phrase whose function in the utterance is determined by the form-class of one of its constituents is ENDOCENTRIC, and the element which determines its function is its HEAD; the other elements are SUBORDINATE to the head and are termed COMPLEMENTS (in verbal phrases) or ATTRIBUTES (in other types of phrases). Thus, in English, *good boy* is an endocentric noun phrase, with the noun *boy* as its head and the adjective *good* as attribute. A phrase whose function is not the same as that of any of its elements is EXOCENTRIC; among exocentric phrases are included preposition-plus-object phrases (e.g. Eng. *to the man*) and clauses serving as attributes or complements in other phrases (e.g. Eng. the man *who is coming*, he left *as I came in*). In addition to these main types of phrases, there are other combinations which are universal for all types of phrases and clauses.

4.01. ALTERNATIONS OF PHONEMES occur as follows in phrasal combinations:

1. Elision (§1.613) occurs:

a. In a substantival (head) phrase (§4.111), before a singular head after a determinant (§4.111.5.b.iv), buón- *good* adj/I–II, béll- *beautiful* adj/I–II and sánt- *holy, Saint* used as a title: e.g. luómo *the man*:uómo *man*; unuómo *a man*; umbélluómo *a handsome man*; lánima *the soul*:ánima *soul*; unánima *a soul*; buónánima *good soul*; sántantónio *St. Anthony*; sántágata *St. Agatha*.

b. In a verbal phrase (§4.13):

i. Optionally, of the conjunctive pronouns mi *me*, ti *thee*, si *him- her-itself* or *themselves*, vi *you*, lo *him* or *it*, la *her* or *it* (§2.21) and of the conjunctive adverbs vi *there* and ne *of it, etc.* (§2.41): e.g. m(i)áma *he loves me*; t(i)aspétto *I wait for you*; l(a)óvvísta *I've seen her*; n(e)ómmólte *I have a lot of them*.

ii. Automatically (with unstressed /i/ before following vowel normally absorbed in the preceding palatal sound, §1.41.3) of ʎi *to him* and či *to us, there*; e.g. ʎinséɲɲa *he teaches him*; čindúče *he induces us*.

c. In an exocentric (preposition-plus-object) phrase:

i. Of the preposition di₁ *of*, optionally (very frequent): e.g. d(i)ánime *of souls*; d(i)élɛna *Helen's*.

ii. Of the preposition da˟₁ *from*, only in certain set phrases: e.g. dáltra-párte *on the other hand*; dórainnánci *from now on*; dallóraimpói *from then on, thenceforth*.

iii. Of other prepositions ending in vowels, occasionally, especially in set phrases: e.g. séncáltro *of course* (lit. *without other*).

d. In other types of phrases, primarily in certain set phrases: e.g. nɛm-ménío *me neither*.

2. Apocope (§1.612) occurs only before 'pure' consonants (§2.123.2.a):

a. In substantival (head) phrases:

i. Of elements preceding the head:

A. When the head is m.sg., of:

I. A determinant ending in /n l/: e.g. unsérvo *a servant*; illíbro *the book*; kuélpósto *that place*.

II. The adjectives buón- *good*, béll- *beautiful* and sánt- *holy, Saint* (all I–II) and the nouns dónn- *lord, Don* (m/IIb) and frát- *Brother* m/IIIb (> frá^x): e.g. umbuónsérvo *a good servant*; ilbéllíbro *the beautiful book*; sáñgovánni *St. John*; dóñgovánni *Don Giovanni*; frákkristóforo *Brother Christopher*.

III. Often, the adjectives tál- *such* and kuál- *which*: e.g. kuállíbroᴈ *Which book?*; untálmóndo *such a world*.

B. When the head is f.sg., only after suór- *sister* used as a title: e.g. suórterésa *Sister Teresa*; and in the set phrases lúnáltra *the one* (f.sg.) . . . *the other* and unasólvólta *one time only*.

C. When the head is m. or f., sg. or pl., optionally of grand- *big* (with consequent simplification of /ndC/ > /nC/, §1.411.7): e.g. ungrán(dε)líbro *a big book*; unagrán(de)karriéra *a great career*; unagrámbrúttas ɔrprésa *a helluva nasty surprise*; gránkóse *great things*.

ii. Of the head, only with such as end in /m n l r/ before a following attribute; in modern speech, only after siɲɲór- *Mr.* in the singular and in set phrases (sg.): e.g. ilsiɲɲórmónti *Mr. Monti*; amórpróprio *amour propre, self-esteem*; umórnéro *black mood*; ildólčestílnuóvo *the Dolce Stil Nuovo*.

b. In substantival (attribute) phrases (§4.112), after a preceding adverbial attribute with stem ending in /n l/: e.g. bénfátto *well done*.

c. In verbal cores (§4.131):

i. Of an infinitive:

A. When immediately followed by a conjunctive pronominal or adverbial element (§§2.21, 2.41): e.g. trovárne *to find some*:trováre *to find*; parlárvi *to talk to you*:parláre *to talk*; vedérmi *to see me*:vedére *to see*; léǧǧerlo *to read it*:léǧǧere *to read*; dárʎelo *to give it to him*:dáre *to give*.

B. Elsewhere, optionally and only before close juncture (§1.61), especially after fáre *to cause to* . . .: e.g. parlártróppo *to talk too much*; andárfuóri *to go out*; durárfatíka *to work hard* (lit. *to endure fatigue*); fárpɔrtáre *to cause to be brought*, i.e. *to have brought*.[1]

ii. Of other verbal forms, only where the resultant verbal form would end in /r m n/ before close juncture, and rarely: e.g. faččámprésto *let's hurry* (lit. *let's make quickly*); párlantróppo *they talk too much*.

d. In adverbial and other phrases, only in certain set locutions: e.g. óróra *just now*:óra *now*; imménkɛnnónsidíče *in less time than it takes to tell it*:méno *less*.

4.02. AGREEMENT. This term refers to the concordance of number, gender or person between two or more elements of a phrase or clause; elements are said to be IN AGREEMENT when their number, gender or person is the same. The concordance of substantives and pronouns of feminine gender is exclusively feminine; a substantive or pronoun or combination thereof not exclusively feminine calls for masculine (i.e. non-feminine) gender agreement: e.g. buónepersóne

---

[1] Cf. H. S. Noce, Italica 18.197–201 (1941).

good persons (f.pl.), buóniragácci *good boys* (m.pl.), but buónifratélliessɔrélle *good* (m.pl.) *brothers* (m.pl.) *and sisters* (f.pl.). With the 2.pl. verb used to a single person (§2.01.5), pronouns and verbs referring to that person are 2.pl., and in other elements agreement is sg. and gender indicates the sex of the person spoken to: e.g. vóisiétebuóno *you* (m.sg.) *are good*; visiétevestíta? *Have you* (f.sg.) *dressed yourself?*. With the 3.sg. feminine pronouns léi (free oblique form), la, (conjunctive accusative) and le, (conjunctive dative) used in the meaning of *you* (cf. §2.21), agreement in gender may be either with the grammatical form of the pronoun or with the sex of the person referred to: e.g. léi émmóltobuóno *you* (m.sg.) *are very good*; léi émmóltobuóna *you* (f.sg.) *are very good*.

Other aspects of agreement and the requirements in specific phrase- and clause-types will be dealt with under the appropriate headings (§§4.111, 4.12, 4.132, 5.121).

4.03. UNIVERSAL COMBINATION-TYPES. Any free form (§2), phrase (§4) or clause (§5) may occur alone or preceded by a connective (§2.43) such as nón, *not*, ánke *also*, eˣ, *and*, oˣ, *or*, máˣ, *but*. Combinations of phrases or clauses (either alone or preceded by a connective), normally of equivalent function in the utterance, may then occur:

1. With no connective preceding any of the elements in the combination:

   a. When the elements are different, with the meaning of a list or enumeration: unčibreíno dipɛrníči, dikɔníʎʎi, diranókkie, dilučértɔle *a little fricassee of partridges, of rabbits, of frogs, of lizards* (Pinocchio VIII); uómini, dónne, ragácci, ragácce *men, women, boys, girls*.

   b. When the elements are the same form, phrase, or clause repeated, with a meaning of emphasis: unlíbrográndegránde *a very big* (lit. *big big*) *book*; unavočínasottílesottíle *a very thin little voice*; sólosólosólo *all, all alone*; líllíˣ *right then and there* (lit. *there there*):líˣ *there*. (Cf. §4.23.2 for the special use of a 2.sg. imperative repeated, with the meaning of an exocentric adverbial phrase: e.g. kammínakammína *after much walking*).

2. With a connective before:

   a. All elements; used in this way, the connective eˣ . . . eˣ . . . has the meaning *both . . . and . . .*; oˣ . . . oˣ means *either . . . or . . .*; and néˣ . . . néˣ . . . *neither . . . nor . . .*: e.g. ɛllúiɛlléi *both him and her*; oaskuóla, oassɛntíreipíffɛri *either to school or to hear the fifes* (Pinocchio V); néssínnénnóˣ *neither yes nor no*.

   b. The last element; this is the normal type of coordinate combination: e.g. ʎabbraččaménti, ʎistriccónidikóllo, ipiccikóttidɛllamičícia ɛllɛʒukkátedɛlla-véraessinčérafratɛllánca *the embraces, the close hugs, the friendly pinches and the clonks with the noodle of true and sincere brotherhood* (Pinocchio VI); kɔnlebráčča, kɔlpétto, kɔnlegámbe ekkoipiédi *with his arms, with his chest, with his legs and with his feet* (ibid. XVIII); guardárɔnodikuá, guardárɔnodiláˣ, ɛnnónvídɛrones-súno *they looked this way, they looked that way, and they didn't see anybody* (ibid. XX); etc. etc. etc. But a coordinate phrase of this type normally does not occur as the object in an exocentric preposition-plus-object phrase, its place being taken by a coordinate series of phrases each introduced by the same preposition; cf. the second example in the preceding sentence. When a clause containing piúˣ *more* is followed by one introduced by eppiúˣ *and more*, the resultant coordinate series has the meaning *the more . . . the more . . .*: e.g. máppiú lɔrita𝄢𝄢áva ɛlloskɔrčíva, eppiú kuélnásoimpɛrtinénte divɛntávalúngo *the more he cut it off and shortened it, the longer that impertinent nose became* (Pinocchio II).

4.1. ENDOCENTRIC PHRASES occur in the function of all types of free morphemes.

4.11. SUBSTANTIVAL phrases have a substantive (adjective or noun) as the head, and are of two types according to the function of the substantive in the utterance: that of head, or that of attribute in some further phrasal construction.

4.111. SUBSTANTIVAL (HEAD) phrases. All attributes and other constituents of a substantival (head) phrase agree with the head in number and gender: e.g. ilprímofióre *the first flower* (m.sg.); iprímifióri *the first flowers* (m.pl.); laprímavióla *the first violet* (f.sg.); leprímevióle *the first violets* (f.pl.). With a head consisting of a coordinate phrase (§4.03), the agreement is that shown in Table IX. Examples: A: unlíbroeunǧɔrnáletedésko *a German book and newspaper*; língua-

TABLE IX
AGREEMENT OF ATTRIBUTE WITH COMPOUND SUBSTANTIVE HEAD

	Heads	Attribute
A	Sg. or pl., same gender	Same no. and gender
B	One or both sg., different gender	a) m.pl., or b) agreeing with nearest head
C	Pl., different gender	Agreeing with nearest head

ɛllɛttɛratúraitaliána *Italian language and literature*; língueɛllɛttɛratúremodérne *modern languages and literatures*. B: lakraváttaɛllábitoskúro (or skúri) *the dark tie and suit*; unlíbroeunarivístatedéski (or tedéska) *a German book and magazine*; unlíbroeddɛllɛrivístetedéske *a German book and some German magazines*. C: ǧardíniekkásevastíssime *very extensive gardens and houses*; lɛmánieipiédilegáti *hands and feet bound*; ipiédiɛllɛmánilegáte *feet and hands bound*.

The elements preceding and following the head of a substantival (head) phrase occur in the order shown in Table X.

TABLE X
ORDER OF ELEMENTS IN SUBSTANTIVAL (HEAD) PHRASE

I. (Num.) + (Poss.)⎫
II. (Attr.) + (Det.) + (Poss.) + (Ord. Adj.) + (Num.)⎭

$$+ \text{(Attrib.)} + \text{HEAD} + \begin{cases} \text{(Poss.)} \\ \text{(Subst.)} \\ \text{(Adv.)} \end{cases} + \text{(Exoc. Phr.)} + \text{(Clause)}$$

Special Abbreviations: Attr. = attribute; Det. = determinant; Exoc. Phr. = exocentric (preposition - plus - object) phrase.

1. A substantival attribute immediately preceding the head is always an unrepeated, unmodified adjective: e.g. unvékkiofàllɛɲɲáme *an old carpenter*;

umbélburattíno *a fine marionette*. This order of adjective + head indicates emphasis, transferred meaning, or generic, habitual or essential quality: e.g. kattívɔragácco *bad boy!*; ivéripóvɛri *the real poor*; unapíkkɔlabúka *a little hole*; umbuónlétto *a fine bed*; labiánkanéve *the white snow*; ʎinútilikɔmpliménti *useless compliments*. Exceptionally, the adverb ǧáˣ *already* also may precede a substantive head, in the meaning *former*: e.g. ilǧáppaláccofalkɔniéri *the former Falconieri palace*.

2. A possessive adjective or the pronoun altrúi *others', someone else's* may immediately follow the head; this order indicates emotional stress or emphasis: e.g. bábbɔmío *my daddy*; fatínamía *my little Fairy* (Pinocchio XI); lamíkɔmío *my friend*; iparérialtrúi *other people's opinions*.

3. A substantival attribute following the head may be an adjective, a noun, a substantival (attribute) phrase:

a. This is the normal order for most adjectives, including verbal participles: e.g. umburattínomaraviʎʎóso *a marvelous marionette*; lɛnɛrǧíaɛléttrika *electric energy*; ilpaeséllovičíno *the nearby village*; ilgrílloparlánte *the talking cricket*; láššaarrotáta *the sharpened axe*; unnasónespropositáto *an enormous huge nose*; etc. etc. With an adjective as head: e.g. ilbúrbɛrobɛnéfiko *the beneficent boor, le Bourru Bienfaisant*; ilsántoprotettóre *the patron saint*; stánkɔmórto *dead tired*.

An attributive numeral follows its head only in poetry or in arithmetical or commercial discourse: e.g. ánnivɛntúno *twenty-one years*; lírekuíndiči eččɛntésimikuaránta *fifteen lire and forty centesimi*. A numeral following a noun in the singular indicates order in a sequence: e.g. páǧinasèssantótto *page sixty-eight*.

b. A noun modifying a substantival head indicates:

i. Apposition: e.g. ilpoétavirǧílio *the poet Virgil*; ilprofessórɛróssi *Professor Rossi*; mástrantónio *master Antonio*; róma, lačittáetérna *Rome, the Eternal City*; tɔrkuátotásso, autóredɛllaǧerusalémmɛlibɛráta *Torquato Tasso, author of the Gerusalemme Liberata*. Of this type are personal names cited with such titles as siɲɲóre *Mr.* m/IIIb, siɲɲóra *Mrs.* f/Ia, siɲɲorína *Miss* f/Ia, dottóre *Dr.* m/IIIb, etc.; such appositions are normally preceded by the definite article (§4.111.5.b.iv.ᴀ), except when used as vocatives (§5.22): e.g. ilsiɲɲórmɛnótti *Mr. Menotti*; łasiɲɲóraklɛménti *Mrs. Clementi*; ildottórdiǧovánni *Dr. Di Giovanni*; but siɲɲorínamónti *Miss Monti!*.

ii. Thing or person characterizing what is referred to by the head; the characterization may refer to purpose, description, type or something connected with what is referred to: e.g. skálomérči *goods station*; depósitobagáʎʎi *baggage checkroom*; unautɔmóbilefíat *a Fiat automobile*; trénɔlámpo *express train* (i.e. *train [as fast as] lightning*); péššespáda *swordfish*; péššeburattíno *marionette-fish* (Pinocchio); víakavúr *Cavour Street*; ilgovérnosalándra *the Salandra government*; salsíččetípoviénna *Vienna-type sausages*. This is the type of specification used to indicate the sex of animals for which Italian has nouns of only one gender, by using an apposition consisting of máskio *male* or fémmina *female*: e.g. ungɔríllafémmina *a female gorilla*; unapantéramáskio *a male panther*.

iii. With the adjective prímo *first* or with numerals from dúe *two* to trèntúno *thirty-one* used as heads in the m.sg. and preceded by the definite article, a month-name used as a following noun attribute indicates the month whose day the adjective or numeral refers to: e.g. ilprímomáǧǧo *the first of May*; ilkuáttrosettémbre *the fourth of September*; ilvèntičínkuedičémbre *December 25th*. The archaic m.pl. article li, *the* (§2.123.2.a) is also used with numerals in this type of phrase: e.g. likuáttrosettémbre *September 4*.

c. All substantival (attribute) phrases follow the head they modify, including those built around adjectives which, when unmodified, normally precede the head (§4.111.1): e.g. unléttopókobuóno *a not very good bed*; unfàllεɲɲámemóltovékkio *a very old carpenter*; unavočínasottílesottíle *a very thin little voice*; unálberokárikodiᴢekkíninuóvi *a tree laden with new sequins*.

4. Further attributes following the head may be non-substantival elements: adverbs, exocentric (preposition-plus-object) phrases (§4.21) or relative clauses.

a. Adverbs: e.g. unuómokosí˟ *such a man* (lit. *a man so*); lánnodópo *the year after*; ilpaesáǧǧodintórno *the countryside around*. This type of attribute occurs especially with the adverbs kuí˟ and kuá˟ *here*, lí˟ and lá˟ *there*, after heads preceded by demonstratives: e.g. kuéstuómokuí˟ *this man here*; kuéllafinéstralí˟ *that window there*.

b. Exocentric (preposition-plus-object) phrases used as attributes are extremely frequent, indicating:

i. Possession, purpose, origin, characteristics, etc.: e.g. labókkadεlburattíno *the marionette's mouth*; unabóttedivíno *a cask of wine*; unvásoinalabástro *an alabaster vase* (lit. *a vase in alabaster*); ǧovánnidaudíne *John of* (lit. *from*) *Udine*; unamákkinaavvapóre *a steam engine*; róbadammátti *nonsense* (lit. *stuff for madmen*); lasúasɔrεllínadaikapélliturkíni *his little sister with the blue hair* (Pinocchio XIII).

ii. Apposition, with the preposition di, *of*: e.g. lačittáddimiláno *the city of Milan*; ilréɲɲoditália *the Kingdom of Italy*; bírbadumburattíno *rascal of a marionette!*. In some instances, an appositive element may optionally stand alone or form part of a preposition-plus-object phrase: e.g. piácca(dεl)plebiššíto *Plebiscite Square*; ilnóme(di)frančésko *the name (of) Francis*. An apposition of this phrasal type is normal after an adjective head preceded by a demonstrative: kuélbirikínodipinókkio *that rascally Pinocchio*; kuéllinútiledimíofratéllo *that good-for-nothing brother of mine*; kuélbuónvékkiodimástročiliéǧa *that good old Master Cherry* (Pinocchio I).

c. Clauses, normally introduced by relative elements (pronouns, adjectives, adverbs), are also very frequent, with the meaning of:

i. Descriptive or qualificative attributes: e.g. ǧénte keurlávaeǧǧestikuláva *people who were yelling and gesticulating*; ipeskatóri keéranorakkóltisullaspiáǧǧa *the fishermen who were gathered on the beach* (Pinocchio XIII).

ii. Appositions: e.g. lidéa kessúamádre laiutεrébbe *the idea that his mother would help him*; kébbéllakósa, potéssiavérεletúeáli *what a beautiful thing, could I but have your wings!* (Pinocchio XIII).

In relative clauses serving as attributes of this kind, a relative adjective pronoun agrees in number and gender with the head the clause modifies (often shown only by the further agreement of elements in the relative clause): e.g. ilragácco keévvεnúto *the boy who came* (ke˟ *who* and vεnúto *came* agreeing with ragácco *boy* m.sg.); laragácca keévvεnúta *the girl who came* (ke˟ *who*, vεnúta *came* and ragácca *girl* all f.sg.); iragácci kessónovɛnúti *the boys who came* (m.pl.); leragácce kessónovɛnúte *the girls who come* (f.pl.); ʎiuómini deikuálisiparláva *the men about whom people were talking* (ikuáli *the which* and ʎiuómini *the men* m.pl.); etc.

In a relative clause of this type, functioning as attribute, use of a present or past tense of a verb indicates pure description and reference to actuality: e.g. ilfattɔríno keévvɛnútoiéri *the postman who came yesterday*; éumburattínɔmaraviʎʎóso kessábballáre *it's a marvelous marionette that knows how to dance*. Use of a timeless tense indicates exclusion of all possibilities but what has certain specified or desired characteristics: vóʎʎofabbrikármiumburattínɔmaraviʎʎóso kessáppiaballáre *I want to make for myself a marvelous marionette that should know how to dance*.

A relative clause or other attribute following a substantival head with limitative meaning has no change in pitch-contour between head and attribute: e.g. ilfattɔrínokeévvɛnútoiéri *the postman who came yesterday* (i.e. that postman and no other). One with explanatory, parenthetical meaning has a separate pitch-contour, the head being uttered with rising intonation and followed by comma disjuncture (§1.61.1): e.g. ilfattɔríno, keévvɛnútoiéri *the postman, who came yesterday*.

5. A substantival (head) phrase constituted with one or more of the types of attributes enumerated in §§4.111.1–4, may further be preceded by a sequence of one or more elements in either of the orders indicated as I or II in Table X; except that a phrase may not have a possessive both preceding and following the head.

    a. Order I (Numeral + Possessive + further elements) is a closed construction, which may not be preceded by other modifiers in the phrase; it is the order used when a numeral and a possessive are present and not limited by a determinant: e.g. čínkuɛmiéifratélli *five brothers of mine*; dúɛnóstriamíči *two friends of ours*.

    b. Order II contains the following elements, here enumerated in the order of their closeness to the head of the phrase:

    i. A numeral or other quantitative expression or equivalent phrase: e.g. dúeuómini *two men*; čínkuàntadúesettimáne *fifty-two weeks*; diéčibrávisɔldáti *ten brave soldiers*; móltibuónilíbri *many good books*; dúɛmílamɔnétedóro *two thousand gold coins*; tántepɛrsóneintɛlliǧénti *so many intelligent persons*. The quantitative adjective kuálke[x] *some, a few* is always followed by a head in the singular: e.g. kuálkeǧǧórno *some day*; kuálkekkósa *something*; kuálkeóra *a few hours*.

With all numerals except ún- *one* and its compounds, number agreement is always in the plural, as in the examples above. With ún- *one*, the head is in the singular: úngórno *one day*; with compound numerals ending in [+]ún- *-one*, the head is normally in the plural and the numeral invariable in the m.sg. (with apocope where permissible): e.g. vɛntúnlíbri *twenty-one books*; settàntúnléttɛre *seventy-one letters*; trèntúmbéllɛmɔnétedarǧénto *thirty-one fine silver coins*. This type of agreement is obligatory when a definite article precedes: ivɛntúnoskɔlári *the twenty-one students*; itrèntúnǧórnidikuéstɔmése *the thirty-one days of* *this month.* The head may, however, subject to the restriction mentioned in the preceding sentence, be in the singular, with the compound numeral in ⁺ún- -*one* agreeing in gender and number, a type of agreement somewhat preferred by purists: e.g. vèntúnlíbro *twenty-one books*; sessàntúnaléttɛra *sixty-one letters.*

A phrase containing a numeral modifier and plural head, if preceded by the indefinite article un- *a* (§4.111.5.b.iv.ʙ) has the meaning *about . . .*: e.g. untréntánni *about thirty years*; unsettántamétri *about sixty meters.*

    ii. An ordinal adjective: e.g. iprímióttoğórni *the first eight days* (i.e. *the first week*); isekóndičéntoánni *the second hundred years.*

    iii. A possessive or the pronominal forms kúi *whose, of which* (rel.) or altrúi *of others, someone else's.* The possessive is not further preceded by a definite article when modifying one of the following in its simplex form, in the singular and with no other attributive elements (numerals, adjectives) preceding it:

ẓía *aunt*			ğénɛro *son-in-law*		
fíʎʎa *daughter*			kɔɲɲáto *brother-in-law*		
kɔɲɲáta *sister-in-law*			kuğíno *cousin*		m/IIb
kuğína *cousin*	f/Ia		maríto *husband*		
nuóra *daughter-in-law*			suóčɛro *father-in-law*		
sɔrélla *sister*			pádre *father* m/IIIb		
suóčɛra *mother-in-law*			nipóte *nephew, grandson, niece, grand-*		
ẓío *uncle*			*daughter* mf/IIIb		
fíʎʎo *son*	m/IIb		mádre *mother*	f/IIIb	
fratéllo *brother*			móʎʎe *wife*		

or a title of respect such as altécca *Highness*, eččɛllénca *Excellency*, ɛminénca *Eminence*, siɲɲɔría *Lordship* (all f/Ia) or maestáˣ *Majesty* or santitáˣ *Holiness* (f/VId). Thus: míofratéllo *my brother*; míamóʎʎe *my wife*; vóstropádre *your father*; súɔmaríto *her husband*; nóstrafíʎʎa *our daughter*; vóstrasiɲɲɔría *your Lordship*; súasantitáˣ *His Holiness.*

Under other circumstances, the possessive attribute is preceded, if by no other determinant, then by the definite article: e.g. levóstresɔrélle *your sisters*; ituóifratɛllíni *your little brothers*; latúabuónasɔrellína *your good little sister*; lasúavékkiamádre *his old mother.* Examples with other words as heads: ilmíobábbo *my daddy*; latúabéllabɔrsétta *your pretty little purse*; isuóitrèntačínkuefi ríni *his thirty-five florins*; lasúabárbabiánka *his white beard*; ikúipiédi *whose feet*; ʎ(i)altrúiparéri *other people's opinions.*

Use of an exocentric phrase consisting of the preposition di, *of* + a free personal pronoun (§2.21), taking the place of a possessive adjective attribute, occurs occasionally, but is used only for extreme clarity or in bureaucratic style: e.g. ildiléimaríto *her husband* (instead of súomaríto).

    iv. A determinant, i.e. one of the following elements: the definite article L- *the* (§2.123.2); the indefinite article = un- (unstressed) *a, an*; a demonstrative adjective = kuést- *this*, kodést- *that*, kuéll- *that*; an interrogative adjective, including the interrogative or exclamatory kéˣ *what.*

A. The definite article gives the meaning of a specific thing already referred to, or of something referred to in the abstract: e.g. ilkɔ́nto *the bill*; lapáǧina *the page*; ʎ(i)assassíni *the assassins*; leguέrre *the wars*; lalibertáˣ *liberty*. Used with names of the days of the week in the singular, the definite article indicates periodicity: ilmɛrkɔledíˣ *every Wednesday*; ilsábato (*on*) *Saturdays*.

The definite article often precedes family names used alone: e.g. ilmakiavέlli *Machiavelli*; ilfogaccáro *Fogazzaro*; ilvέrga *Verga*; ladɛlέdda *Deledda*. In nineteenth-century Italian, this usage was widespread and normal; at present, it is chiefly humorous or sarcastic, as opposed to the use of the family name without definite article: e.g. mɔntanári *Montanari*; dannúncio *d'Annunzio*; mussɔlíni *Mussolini*.[2] With given names, the definite article occurs in familiar use with feminine names: laǧannέtta *our Jenny*; lamaría *our Mary*; its use with masculine names (e.g. ilrénco *Renzo*; lɛnríko *Henry*) is characteristic of Northern Italy and is condemned by purists.

The definite article appears in the m.sg. form lo, before piúˣ *more* and méno *less* used as heads in the set phrases lopiúˣ *the more* (*most*) and lɔméno *the less* (*least*); and in the pl. form e, in the set phrases constructed with tútti tútte *all* + e *the* + numeral: e.g. tútt(i)edúe *both* (lit. *all the two*); cf. below, §4.111.6.

B. The numeral un- used unstressed in this position has approximately the meaning of an indefinite article = *a, an*, and occurs only with singular heads: e.g. ungɔ́rno *a day*; unatávɔla *a table*; ungrɔ́ssofálko *a huge falcon*; unastɔ́rialúnga *a long story*; unamέʣʣaǧɔrnáta *a half day, half a day*; unsúoamíko *a friend of his*. It does not occur followed by a numeral or quantitative elements, except in phrases of the type discussed above in §4.111.5.b.i: untréntánni *about thirty years*.

C. The demonstrative adjectives kuést- *this*, kodést- and kuέll- *that* (all I–II): e.g. kuéstɔmóndo *this world*; kuéstɛmɔnétedɔ́ro *these golden coins*; kuéllɛčinkuɛlíre *those five lire*; kuéstɔmíofratέllo *this brother of mine*; kodéstevɔ́streidée *those ideas of yours*. •

D. The element kéˣ *what* in this position, preceding a noun head, has interrogative or exclamatory meaning = *what? what a . . . !*: e.g. kéllíbro *what book?* or *what a book!*; kéččínkuɛlíreɔ́ *What five lire?*; késtupidáǧǧine *what stupidity!*; képpekkáto *what a pity!*; kébbrúttaidéa *what an unpleasant idea!*. This element also occurs before adjective heads, but its use in such position is condemned by purists: e.g. kébbέllo *how beautiful!*.

E. The adjective ɔ́ɲɲi *every, each* IVd (always followed by a head in the singular) or the adjective tál- *such* IIIb (preceded by the indefinite article): e.g. ɔ́ɲɲimíolíbro *every book of mine*; ɔ́ɲɲipersónaraǧɔnévɔle *every reasonable person*; untálepíkkɔlosɔmáro *such a little donkey*.

6. Before a substantival (head) phrase containing any of the elements listed in the preceding subsections 1–4 and 5.a, b.i–iv. A–c, only a few further preceding modificatory elements may occur: the adjectives tútt- *all* I–II, ámbo *both* IId and àmbedúe *both* IIId; the numeral phrases of the type tútt(i)edúe *both*, tútt(i)etréˣ *all three* (§4.111.5.b.iv.A, §4.113.2); and, very rarely, with emphatic

---

[2] Cf. Language 17.33–39 (1941).

or emotional overtones, other adjectives: e.g. túttoilpúbbliko *all the public*; tútt(i)imiéiamíči *all my friends*; túttelevóstredɔmánde *all your questions*; károilmíoamíko *my dear friend*. The adjective áltro occurs before a phrase consisting of numeral + head: e.g. áltrevéntipersóne *twenty other persons*.

4.112. SUBSTANTIVAL (ATTRIBUTE) phrases usually have adjectives as their heads, and the structure of either ATTRIBUTE + HEAD or HEAD + ATTRIBUTE.

1. A preceding attribute in such a phrase is usually an adverb or equivalent phrase: móltostánko (m.sg.), móltostánka (f.sg.), móltostánki (m.pl.), móltostánke (f.pl.) *very tired*; bénfátto *well done*; pókobuóno *not very* (lit. *little*) *good*; tróppostúpido *too stupid*; abbastántabéllo *beautiful enough*; própriosikúro *really*; vèraméntekɔnténto *truly happy*; gràvɛméntɛmaláto *seriously ill*; etc. etc.

2. A following attribute is normally:

a. An adverb, with emphatic or demonstrative meaning: e.g. kiároabbastánca *quite clear*; malátogràvɛménte *seriously ill*; piččínokosí[x] *so little*; áltotánto *so high* (with accompanying gestures).

b. A noun or equivalent phrase, indicating:

i. Object partaking of the quality referred to by the adjective: méstailvólto *sad of countenance*; pállidoilvólto *pale of face*; túttosúdičolafáččaɛllemáni *all dirty as to the face and the hands*, i.e. *with hands and face all dirty*; piénɔlafantasía *with the imagination full* (lit. *full as to the imagination*).

ii. Measure: e.g. lúngodúekilómetri *two kilometers long*; áltočínkuepiédi *five feet high*; distántetrémmíʎʎa *three miles distant*.

iii. Object exemplifying the quality referred to by the adjective, especially in phrases referring to types of colors: e.g. vérdeɔlíva *olive green*; ǧállokanaríno *canary yellow*; biánkoavório *ivory white*.

c. An exocentric (preposition-plus-object) phrase: e.g. biánkokómeunimmáǧinedičéra *white as a waxen image*; piénodiǧóia *full of joy*; kɔnténtodivedérvi *glad to see you*; nečessárioallasalúte *necessary to health*; dispóstoappartíre *ready to leave*; aliénodallinvídia *free from envy*. The use of certain prepositions is determined by the adjective on which the exocentric phrase depends, as follows:

i. The preposition a[x]ₗ *to* is used after such adjectives as:

dispósto *disposed*, ready		sgradíto *displeasing*	I–II
gradíto *pleasing*		vičíno *near*	
káro *dear*	I–II	kɔnfórme *conforming*	
kɔntrário *contrary*		sgradévɔle *displeasing*	IIIb
nečessário *necessary*		útile *useful*	
nočívo *harmful*			

ii. The preposition da[x]ₗ *from* is used after such adjectives as:

aliéno *alien, free*		assénte *absent*	
líbɛro *free*	I–II	immúne *immune*	IIIb
lɔntáno *far*		réduče *returned*	
prófugo *fleeing*			

iii. The preposition di, *of, to* is used after such adjectives as:

ávido *avid, eager*		piéno *full*	
dénno *worthy*		ríkko *rich*	I–II
desidɛróso *desirous*	I–II	sikúro *secure*	
diméntiko *forgetful*		fértile *fertile*	IIIb
kɔnténto *glad*		mémɔre *mindful*	
liéto *glad, happy*			

d. An exocentric (preposition-plus-object) phrase or a clause, indicating term of comparison, after such adjectives of comparative meaning as méʎʎo *better* and péǧǧo *worse* (both IId) or miʎʎóre *better* and peǧǧóre *worse* (both IIIb). The distribution of these modifiers is parallel to their distribution after comparative adverbs (§4.14.2.b, c): e.g. miʎʎóredimé[x] *better than me*; peǧǧóre-disúamóʎʎe *worse than his wife*.

4.113. NUMERAL phrases are of the following types:

1. Additive, in which a series of numerals indicates a total sum: e.g. čénto-činkuánta *150*; míllɛnòvečéntokuattórdiči *1914*. In phrases of this type, numerals and numeral expressions under 100 are preceded by the hundreds, these in their turn by the thousands, and these by the millions, billions, trillions etc.: e.g. trémmilióni činkuečéntonovàntakuáttromíla, óttočéntosettàntasétte *3,594,877*.

2. Inclusive, in which a numeral is preceded by tútt- *all* adj/I–II in the plural + e, def. article: e.g. tútt(i)edúe *both* (lit. *all the two*); tútt(i)ečínkue *all five*; etc. (Cf. §4.111.5.b.iv.A).

4.12. PRONOMINAL phrases are of the types:

1. Attribute (adjective, normally tútt- *all* I–II) + head, implying emphasis: túttinói *all of us*.

2. Head + attribute (adjective or numeral): e.g. íostésso *I myself*; léistéssa *she herself*; lúisólo *he alone*; vóidúe *you two*. A combination of plural pronoun + the adjective áltr- *other* I–II in this use serves as an emphatic phrase: e.g. nóiáltri *we* (lit. *we others*); vóiáltre *you* (lit. *you others*) f.pl. The attribute may also be a relative clause: e.g. ío, kessónosúofíʎʎo *I, who am his son*.

3. Head + apposition (substantive): e.g. nóiuómini *we men*; vóiáltredónne *you women*; vóiitaliáni *you Italians*; lórosinnóri *you gentlemen*.

Agreement in pronominal phrases is required, where possible, in number and gender.

4.13. VERBAL phrases. In certain phrases a conjunctive pronoun is present, of the same person and number (where possible) as the verb form, and referring to the agent; such phrases are termed REFLEXIVE: e.g. mivédo *I see myself*; léisévvísta *she saw herself*; andársɛne *to go away* (lit. *to go oneself hence*). Phrases not having this characteristic are NON-REFLEXIVE.

4.131. THE PERFECT PHRASE consists of two verbal forms: an AUXILIARY, inflected as a verb + a PAST PARTICIPLE, inflected as an adjective.

1. As auxiliaries are used éss- *be* IIIb/Irr/S[1] and av- *have* IIIa/Irr/S[1]. The choice of auxiliary is determined as follows:

a. The auxiliary éss- is used with all reflexive verbal phrases and with certain simple verbs (mostly with meanings implying motion or change of condition) not taking a direct object, such as:

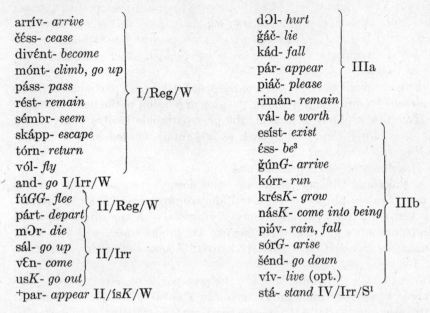

arrív- *arrive* ⎫
čéss- *cease* ⎪
divént- *become* ⎪
mónt- *climb, go up* ⎪
páss- *pass* ⎬ I/Reg/W
rést- *remain* ⎪
sémbr- *seem* ⎪
skápp- *escape* ⎪
tórn- *return* ⎪
vól- *fly* ⎭

and- *go* I/Irr/W

fúGG- *flee* ⎫ II/Reg/W
párt- *depart* ⎭

mɔr- *die* ⎫
sál- *go up* ⎪ II/Irr
vɛn- *come* ⎬
usK- *go out* ⎭

⁺par- *appear* II/ísK/W

dɔl- *hurt* ⎫
ǧáč- *lie* ⎪
kád- *fall* ⎪
pár- *appear* ⎬ IIIa
piáč- *please* ⎪
rimán- *remain* ⎪
vál- *be worth* ⎭

esíst- *exist* ⎫
éss- *be*[3] ⎪
ǧúnG- *arrive* ⎪
kórr- *run* ⎪
krésK- *grow* ⎪
násK- *come into being* ⎬ IIIb
pióv- *rain, fall* ⎪
sórG- *arise* ⎪
šénd- *go down* ⎪
vív- *live* (opt.) ⎭

stá- *stand* IV/Irr/S¹

b. Other verbs have as their auxiliary in the perfect phrase the verb av- *have*.

c. For the choice of auxiliary with the modal verbs dov- *ought* etc. when followed by an infinitive complement, cf. §4.133.2.a.

2. The meaning of the perfect phrase is, where the auxiliary is in Present or Timeless A, that of a present perfect or of a simple past, interchangeably; when it is in other tenses or non-finite forms, that of a perfect. Examples of simple verbs with auxiliary éss-: sónoarriváto *I* (*have*) *arrived*; séidivɛntáto *you have become, you became*; éandáto *he went, he had gone*; siámopartíti *we* (*have*) *departed*; siétevɛnúti *you came, you have come*; sónokadúti *they fell, they have fallen*; síaǧúnto (*that*) *I, you, he* (*have*) *arrived*; érovissúto *I had lived*; sarákkórso *he shall have run*; fúrrimásto *he had remained*; fóssɛrokreššúti (*that*) *they had grown*; esséndostáto *having been*. Examples of reflexive verbs with auxiliary éss-: misónovísto *I have seen myself, I saw myself*; siérakredúto *he had believed himself*; čisarémmouččísi *we should have killed ourselves*; etc. Examples of verbs with auxiliary av-: óppréso *I have taken, I took*; áikɔrrétto *you* (*have*) *corrected*; áffátto *he did, he has done*; abbiámɔlétto *we* (*have*) *read*; avétedimɛntikáto *you forgot, you have forgotten*; ánnovɔlúto *they* (*have*) *wished*; ábbianodétto (*that*) *they* (*have*) *said*; avévokɔminčáto *I had begun*; avrétedáto *you will have given*;

---

[3] The regular past participle essúto *been* is archaic and not in regular use; instead, státo (: stá- *stand*) is regularly used in the sense of *been*, e.g. éstáto *he has been*; ɛravátestáti *you* (m.pl.) *had been*.

ébbesostituíto *he had substituted*; avéssemanğáto *he had eaten*. The perfect phrase formed with Past C of the auxiliary (e.g. fúipartíto *I had left*; ébbepósto *he had put*, etc.) is used only in dependent clauses introduced by temporal conjunctions such as kuándo *when* (§4.24); otherwise, normal past perfect phrases are formed with Past A of the auxiliary: e.g. εravámouššíti *we had gone out*; viεravátedivεrtíti *you had amused yourselves*; avévibevúto *you had drunk*.

3. The past participle in a perfect phrase agrees with other elements of the utterance as follows:

a. Where the auxiliary is av-, the agreement of the past participle depends on the presence of a direct object and its position in relation to the perfect phrase:

i. If no direct object is present, the past participle is invariable, in the m.sg.: e.g. ókkapíto *I (have) understood*; avévakantáto *he had sung*; avránnomanğáto *they will have eaten*.

ii. If a direct object is present, and if it is:

A. Preceding the perfect phrase (the normal position for a relative pronoun or equivalent phrase, or for a conjunctive pronoun with a non-imperative finite verb), the past participle normally agrees with the direct object in gender and number: e.g. lekóse keavétevíste *the things which you have seen*; leavevátemanğáte *you had eaten them*; lókkantáta *I have sung it* (sc. lakancóne *the song*).

B. Following the perfect phrase, the past participle either agrees with the direct object in gender and number, or (more often) is invariable in the m.sg.: e.g. óllétto (also óllétta) latúaléttεra *I (have) read your letter*; avrébbekapíto (or kapíte) levóstreidée *he would have understood your ideas*.

b. Where the auxiliary is éss-:

i. With reflexive verbs, the agreement of the past participle is the same as with the auxiliary av-: e.g. misónotrováto (m.sg.), misónotrováta (f.sg.) *I found myself, I was*; siémmutáta *she changed herself*; kuéllavočina mεlasónfigurátaío *that little voice, I imagined it to myself* (Pinocchio I); nónčisarémmomáiimmağináto (or immağináta) unatálekatástrofe *we would never have imagined to ourselves such a catastrophe*. Agreement of the past participle with a preceding indirect object occasionally occurs: čisiámokompráti unakása *we (have) bought ourselves a house*.

ii. With simple verbs, the past participle has the agreement of a predicate complement (§4.133.1.a), i.e. it specifies the number and gender of the agent, agreeing with the subject if there be one: e.g. ledónne sónopartíte *the women have left*; éinkominčáta lakommédia *the comedy has started*; lastráda éradivεntátaunpantáno *the road had become a mud-puddle* (Pinocchio XIII); čisónoandáto (m.sg.), čisónoandáta (f.sg.) *I have gone there, I went there*.

4. The auxiliary and participle in a perfect phrase may be separated only by an adverb or adverbial phrase: e.g. óğğápparláto *I've already spoken*; nónlómmáidétto *I never said it*.

4.132. THE VERBAL CORE, or center of every verbal phrase, consists of a verb, either in simple form or in a perfect phrase, and alone or accompanied by not more than two conjunctive personal pronouns and/or adverbs. The conjunctive pronouns thus used are the bound forms listed in §2.21; the element si₁ has the meaning of either a third person reflexive (*him- her- itself, themselves*) or an indefinite agent (*one, they, people,* the English passive etc.). The conjunctive adverbs used in a verbal core are či₁ and vi₁ *here, there* (replacing any exocentric preposition-plus-object phrase introduced by aˣ₁ *to*) and ne *of him, her, it, them* (replacing any exocentric phrase introduced by di₁ of or daˣ₁ from). Before /l ʎ n/ of a following conjunctive element, the final /i/ of mi₁ ti₁ si₁ či₁ vi₁ > /ɛ/, and ʎi₁ *to him* and le₁ *to her* both > ʎɛ₁: e.g. mi₁ *to me* + ne₁ *of it* > mɛne₁; ʎi₁ *to him* + lo *him, it* > ʎɛlo₁; le₁ *to her* + la₁ *her, it* > ʎɛla₁.

1. When two conjunctive elements occur together in a verbal core, they occur in the following order: (indirect object) before (1.–2. person direct object) before (či₁ or vi₁ conjunctive adverbs) before (3. person non-reflexive direct object) before (si₁ reflexive direct object or indefinite agent) before (ne₁ conjunctive adverb). Examples: mɛlo₁ *it to me*; čɛli₁ *them to us*; vɛne₁ *to you of it*; ʎɛne₁ *to him of it, to her of it*; miči₁ *me there*; vɛlo₁ *him there*; čɛle₁ *them here*; losi *one . . . it*; two successive conjunctive elements do not normally begin with the same phoneme: thus, viči₁ *you there*, but čivi₁ *us there* (not vivi₁ or čiči₁).

2. The conjunctive element(s) of a verbal core always immediately precede or follow the simple verb form or, in a perfect phrase, the auxiliary, as follows:

a. They follow a non-finite form (except an infinitive in a negative imperative minor clause, §5.21.1) or an Imperative (including ɛ́kko *behold, here is, there is*) not accompanied by a negative element: e.g. basándosi *basing himself*; trovátosi *having found himself*; vestírmi *to dress me* (*myself*); spiɛ́gati *explain yourself*; váttɛne *get out of here!* (lit. *go thyself hence!*); sediámoči *let's seat ourselves!*; kalmátevi *calm yourself!*; parlátɛmɛne *tell me about it!* (lit. *speak to me out of it!*); ɛ́kkɔla *here she is* (lit. *behold her!*).

b. They precede other finite forms, except in archaizing or telegraphic style:[4] e.g. mitróvo *I find myself*; sibása *he bases himself*; lovédi *you see it*; čɛneandiámo *we go away* (lit. *we go ourselves hence*); tɛnedaráˣ *he will give you some*; losivéde *one sees it*; misónosedúto *I seated myself*; čɛravámovísti (m.pl.) *we had seen ourselves*; nónʎɛneparláte *don't speak to him about it!*; etc. etc.

4.133. COMPLEMENTS are further, modifying elements in the verbal phrase, either verbal infinitives or gerunds or forms of non-verbal classes. They normally follow a verbal core, but not infrequently precede with emphatic meaning, as outlined in §5.132. The various types of complements are:

1. Substantive or pronoun, or equivalent head phrase. Personal pronouns used as complements in verbal phrases outside of the verbal core (§4.132) are always in the stressed free oblique form (§2.21), with emphatic meaning: e.g. védeméˣ *he sees* ME; ɛ́llúi *it's him*. Substantives or pronouns used as verbal complements have the following meanings and types of agreement:

a. Predicate complement, specifying the number and gender of the agent

---

[4] To save money in telegrams charged for by number of written words, since conjunctive elements following a verbal form are written together as one word, whereas preceding it they are written as separate words (cf. Appendix, Chapter 6).

and agreeing with the subject if there is one, after such verbs (termed COPULA-
TIVE verbs) as the following:

arrív- *arrive*
divént- *become*
páss- *pass* $\Big\}$ I/Reg/W
sémbr- *seem*
són- *sound*
tórn- *return*
divɛn- *become*
mɔr- *die* $\Big\}$ II/Irr
riusK- *turn out*

pár- *appear*
rimán- *remain* $\Big\}$ IIIa
ğúnG- *arrive*
krésK- *grow* $\Big\}$ IIIb
násK- *come into being*
stá- *stand, be* IV/Irr/S[1]

and also other verbs, especially and- I/Irr/W in the meaning of *should be, ought
to be*; fáč- IV/Irr/S[1, 2] in the reflexive with the meaning *become*; and tróv- I/
Reg/W, reflexive, meaning *find oneself, be*; also occasionally others of the verbs
listed in §4.131.1.a. Examples: pinɔ́kkio siféčetristo *Pinocchio became sad*
(Pinocchio V); nónéraunléɲɲodilússo *it wasn't a de luxe piece* (ibid. I); sitrovɔ́s-
sedútopɛrtérra *he was seated on the ground* (ibid.); lapúntadɛlnáso ʎ(i)éradi-
vɛntátaturkína *the point of his nose had become blue* (ibid.); míamóʎʎe nɛrimáse-
mɛraviʎʎáta *my wife was* (lit. *remained*) *amazed at it*; leopinióni vánnorispettáte
opinions should be respected.

Of this type are the phrases with passive meaning constructed with the verbs
éss- *be*, vɛn- *come, be* (indicating becoming) and and- *go, be, get* (indicating
change of condition): e.g. míofratéllo éstatouččísodaitedéski *my brother was
killed by the Germans*; ilfɔrtíno fuddifésostrènuaménte *the pillbox was defended
vigorously*; appɔ́koappɔ́ko, vɛnívatrasfɔrmátoinunpíkkɔlosɔmáro *he gradually
became transformed into a little donkey* (Pinocchio XVII); ilíbri andárɔnopɛrdúti
the books got lost. With passive phrases, the agent is indicated by an exocentric
(preposition-plus-object) phrase introduced by da[x], *by* (cf. §4.133.4), as in the
first example given in this paragraph.

A second predicate complement is found in passive phrases based on such
verbs as kiám- *call*, ɛléGG- *elect* etc. (§4.133.1.b): e.g. érakiamátoilgríso *he was
called Il Griso*; isuɔ́ipɔrtaménti fúrɔnoğudikátilodévɔli *his behavior was judged
praiseworthy*.

On occasion, a predicate complement does not agree with the subject, especially in case complement or subject or both are substantives with collective
meaning: e.g. túttokuélgrúppodiğénte éranoarrivátiinsvíccɛra *all that group of
people had arrived in Switzerland* (subj. m.sg., pred. m.pl.); gránpártedeičittadíni
fúrɔnoammaccáti *a large part of the citizens were slaughtered* (subj. f.sg., pred.
m.pl.).

b. Direct object, not agreeing with any other element in the sentence (except as specified for past participles in perfect phrases, §3.131.3.a.ii.в): e.g.
ɔ́imitátoiltúoesémpio *I imitated your example*; ilburattíno distéseisuɔ́ipánni *the
marionette spread out his clothes* (Pinocchio XIV); silevɔ́ilbɛrrétto *he took off his*

cap; lavólpe siaššugóunalágrima *the fox wiped off a tear* (Pinocchio XI); ékko ilnóstrokáropinókkio *here is our dear Pinocchio* (ibid.); etc. etc. etc.

Two direct objects (of which one may be a conjunctive personal pronoun) occur with certain verbs (of the basic meanings of *call, choose, deem*), including:

dikiár- *declare*	soprannómin- *nickname*	
ǧúdik- *judge*	stím- *esteem, deem*	I/Reg/W
kiám- *call*	tróv- *find, consider*	
nómin- *name*	kréd- *believe* IIIb/Reg/W	
proklám- *proclaim*	rénd- *render* IIIb/Reg/S[1,2]	
ripút- *consider*		

(left group braced as I/Reg/W)

The first direct object indicates the recipient of the action, and the second indicates the result or condition in which the recipient is placed by the action: e.g. stímoǧúlioungalàntuómo *I consider Julius a gentleman*; lokiamárɔnoilgríso *they called him Il Griso*; litróvomóltobuóni *I find them very good*.

c. Adverbial meaning, indicating:

i. Point of time or duration, with expressions referring to time: e.g. óppotútokampáredúeánni *I was able to live two years*; són rimástoináfrikaóttɔmési *I remained eight months* in Africa; nuotóttúttakuántalanótte *he swam the whole night*; laséra arrivómmíopádre *in the evening my father arrived*; vɔlárɔno túttoilǧórno ettúttalanótte *they flew the whole day and the whole night* (Pinocchio XIII).

ii. Distance: e.g. lanáve distávaankóratrédičimíʎʎa dalpórto *the ship was still thirteen miles away from the port.*

iii. Extent or intensity (e.g. weight, price, worth): pésadúekilográmmi *it weighs two kilograms*; kóstadúelíre *it costs two lire*; kóstakáro *it costs dear*; nónmipikkiártántofórte *don't hit me so hard!* (Pinocchio I).

2. Verb, in the infinitive, which has:

a. Active meaning, after certain verbs (termed MODAL verbs), such as:

desídɛr- *desire*	pɔt- *be able*	
ós- *dare*	sap- *know how*	IIIa
ús- *be accustomed*	sɔl- *be accustomed*	
dov- *be to, shall, ought, should* IIIa	vɔl- *wish, want*	

(desídɛr-/ós-/ús- braced as I/Reg/W)

Examples: desídɛrovedérlo *I desire to see him*; nónosávaparláre *he didn't dare to speak*; dévoandármene *I have to go away*; nómpotévaaprírlapórta *he couldn't open the door*; nonsapévainténdere daddóvekuélvéntouššísse *he couldn't* (lit. *didn't know how to*) *understand where that wind came from* (Pinocchio XVIII); nónvóʎʎɔmoríre *I don't want to die.*

A perfect phrase based on a modal verb takes av- as its auxiliary when the modal verb is not followed by a dependent infinitive: e.g. nónáppotúto *he hasn't been able, he wasn't able.* When the modal verb is followed by a dependent infinitive, the auxiliary may be av- in all instances, or (more often) may be éss- when the latter is the normal auxiliary of the verb in the infinitive. In either instance, the agreement of the past participle is that which is normal with the given auxiliary (§4.131.3). Examples:

Dependent verb takes auxiliary av-:	Dependent verb takes auxiliary éss-:
nónɔ́ppotútostudiáre *I haven't been able to study*	nónsónopotútoveníre (or nónɔ́ppotútoveníre) *I've not been able to come*
nónabbiámovɔlútoaiutárlo *we didn't want to help him*	nónsiámovɔlútirestáre (or nónabbiámovɔlútorestáre) *we didn't want to stay*
avévadovútočédere *she had had to yield*	éradovútapartíreinfrétta (or avévadovútopartíreinfrétta) *she had had to leave in a hurry*

When the dependent infinitive is in the reflexive and the modal auxiliary is in a perfect phrase, the modal verb and conjunctive reflexive pronoun may be treated in one of two ways:

    i. The reflexive pronoun forms part of the verbal core of the perfect phrase, which is then treated as a reflexive phrase with auxiliary éss- (§4.131.1.a), the past participle agreeing with the preceding reflexive pronoun and the dependent infinitive following without affixed pronoun: e.g. misónodovútovestíre *I had to dress myself*; séravɔlútaassikuráre *she had wanted to assure herself*; nónsiéranosapútiliberáre *they hadn't known how to free themselves*.

    ii. The reflexive pronoun forms part of the verbal core of the dependent infinitive and is suffixed thereto, the modal verb having the auxiliary av- with past participle invariable in the m.sg. (§4.131.1.b). The same sentences as those given at the end of the preceding paragraph: ɔ́ddovútovestírmi; avévavɔlútoassikurármi; nónavévanosapútoliberársi.

    b. Active or passive meaning, after certain verbs with the basic meanings of *perceive, cause, allow*, such as:

láš̌š- *let* I/Reg/W	véd- *see* IIIa/Reg/S[1,2]
sént- *feel, hear* II/Reg/W	fáč- *make, cause to, have* IV/Irr/S[1,2]
ud- *hear* II/Irr/W	

and also the defective imperative verb ékko *behold, here is, there is*. Examples: lafáta avévafáttopreparáre dugéntotáccedikaffé(ε)llátte *the Fairy had had prepared* (i.e. *caused to be prepared*) *two hundred cups of café-au-lait* (Pinocchio XV); láš̌šalagridáre *let her scold* (or *be scolded*); víderɔmuóversiunlumičíno *they saw a little light moving*; vídeapparíre umburattínovívo *he saw a live marionette appear* (Pinocchio XVII); ékkoušš̌írfuɔ́ridellákkua unɔrríbiletéstadimóstrɔmaríno *here was a horrible marine monster's head coming out of the water* (ibid.); sentívabáttersinelvíso alkúnegrándibuffátedivénto *he felt some big gusts of wind strike on his face* (lit. *strike for him in the face*) (ibid.).

    A following substantival phrase may indicate either the agent or the direct object of the activity referred to by the infinitive: e.g. fáčč̌okantárelakantánte

I have the singer sing, i.e. *I cause her to sing*; but fáččokantárɛlakancóne *I have the song sung*, i.e. *I cause it to be sung*. A conjunctive object pronoun replacing such a substantival phrase is affixed to the first verb, and is likewise ambiguous in its meaning: lafáččokantáre *I cause her to sing* (sc. lakantánte *the singer*) or *I have it sung* (sc. lakancóne *the song*).

With a dependent infinitive of this type with passive meaning, accompanied by a conjunctive pronoun or direct object, the agent is indicated by an exocentric (preposition-plus-object) phrase introduced by a^x, or da^x, *by*: e.g. fáččokantárlakancóne (d)alla kantánte *I have the singer sing the song* (lit. *I cause the song to be sung by the singer*); lafáččokantáre allakantánte *I have it sung by the singer*. Such an exocentric phrase indicating the agent may be replaced by a dative conjunctive pronoun: e.g. ʎɛlafáččokantáre *I have it sung by her*. On occasion the preposition da^x, *by* is also found introducing a phrase referring to the agent.

A construction of this type with verbs such as dikiár- *declare* I/Reg/W or díK- *say* IV/Irr/S[1, 2] + substantive phrase + infinitive indicating what is said, on the model of the Latin infinitive or indirect discourse, is archaic, literary or bureaucratic: e.g. dikiárokuéstoéssɛrvéro *I declare that this is true*.

3. Adverb or equivalent phrase (§4.14), which may be:

a. A verbal gerund, after the verbs and- *go* I/Irr/W, vɛn- *come* II/Irr/S[1, 2] and (most frequently) stá- *be* IV/Irr/S[1], forming a phrase with durative or progressive aspect meaning: e.g. stóllavɔrándo *I'm working*; éstátostudiándo *he's been studying*; vádomeditándo *I'm meditating*; vɛniámoskrivéndo *we're writing*.

b. Other adverbs, including a verbal gerund after other verbs than those mentioned in the preceding paragraph: e.g. sónokuí[x] *I'm here*; bɔllívaallɛgraménte *it was boiling cheerfully*; kantóbbéne *she sang well*; dárʎisúbito unabuónatiratínadɔrékki *to give him immediately a good ear-pulling*; ʎidísse, tɛntɛnnándominaččòsaménteilkápo *he said to him, shaking his head threateningly*; lofáččovɔlentiéri *I do it gladly*. In this same category of complements fall interrogative and relative adverbs: e.g. pɛrkénnómpuόiɛ́ pɛrkémmiánnomanɡátoipiédi. *Why can't you? Because they've eaten my feet.* (Pinocchio IV); dóvɛláivedútoɛ́ *Where did you see him?*; kuándébbɛročɛnáto *when they had eaten*.

4. Exocentric (preposition-plus-object) phrase: e.g. rimástosɛ́ncapiédi *having remained without feet*; stávaimpɛríkɔlodivíta *he was in danger of his life*; kɔrrévakɔnúnagámbasóla *he ran with only one leg* (Pinocchio IX); kɔminčɔabbručáre *it began to burn*; sirikiúsesɛ́ncafárrumóre *it closed without making any noise*. An exocentric phrase introduced by da^x, *by* accompanying a past participle or passive phrase (§4.133.1) indicates the performer of the action: e.g. fúuččísodaitedéski *he was killed by the Germans*; éingoiáto daltɛrríbilepéššekáne *he is swallowed by the terrible Dog-fish* (Pinocchio XVIII); pɛrkéttiséifáttoingiottíredalmóstroɛ́ *Why did you get yourself swallowed by the monster?* (ibid.). An exocentric phrase introduced by di, *of* and containing the minor-clause forms sí[x] *yes* or nó[x] *no* is found after such verbs as diK- *say*, kréd- *believe*: díssedisí[x] *he said yes, he said he would* (*did*, etc.); krédodinó[x] *I believe not*.

The choice of the preposition introducing an exocentric phrase containing an infinitive is in some instances determined by the following verb:

a. When the main verb and the infinitive refer to the same agent, certain verbs are followed by:

i. The preposition di, *of*, *to*, primarily with such verbs as:

dikiár- *declare* ⎫
ğúr- *swear*   ⎪
médit- *meditate*⎬ I/Reg/W
péns- *think*   ⎪
tént- *try*   ⎭
stabil- *decide* II/ísK/W

ottɛn- *obtain* IIIa/Irr/S[1,2]
dečid- *decide* ⎫
kréd- *believe* ⎬ IIIb
prɔmétt- *promise*⎭
díK- *say* IV/Irr/S[1,2]

Examples: dečísediandársɛne *he decided to go away*; díssediéssɛrmóltostánko *he said he was very tired*; krédodavérfáttobéne *I believe I have done well*.

ii. The preposition a[x], *to*, chiefly after such verbs as:

arrív- *arrive* ⎫
impár- *learn* ⎬ I/Reg/W
límit- *limit* (refl.)⎭

riusK- *succeed* II/Irr/W
ğúnG- *succeed* IIIb/Reg/S[1,2]
stá- *stand* IV/Irr/S[1]

Examples: imparóaskrívɛre *he learned to write*; séiğúntoakkapírefinàlménte *you've finally succeeded in understanding*. This construction after the verb stá- *stand* indicates intensity or length of action: stáassɛntíre *just listen!*; stáumpóavvedére *just look a little!*.

iii. The preposition da[x], *from*, after guárd- *keep* I/Reg/W and astɛn- *abstain, refrain* IIIa/Irr/S[1], both reflexive: e.g. misónoastɛnútodalrispóndɛre *I refrained from answering*; and after av- *have* IIIa/Irr/S[1], with meaning of future or obligatory action: e.g. nónónnúllaaddíre *I have nothing to say*, avévanodaskrívɛre *they had to write*.

iv. The preposition pɛr, *for*, with éss- *be* IIIb/Irr/S[1] or stá- *be* IV/Irr/S[1], forming phrases meaning *be about to* . . .: e.g. stávapɛrpiánğe re *she was about to cry*; and pɛr, *by* or kɔn, *with* after fin- *finish* II/ísK, with meaning *end up by* . . . *-ing*: e.g. finípperandáre or finíkkɔllandáre *he ended up by going, he finally went*; finíkkɔldáre unaskrɔllatínadikápo *he finally gave a little shake of his head* (Pinocchio X).

Phrases of this type, especially those introduced by di, (see sub-section i above) are in complementary distribution with direct object clauses (§4.133.5) introduced by ke[x] *that*, referring to a different agent than that referred to by the main verb, and having the verb of the dependent clause in a Timeless tense: e.g. krédo keábbiafáttobéne *I think he has done well*; stabilírɔno keiğókikɔminčássɛro *they decided that the games should start*.

b. When the main verb and the infinitive refer to different agents:

i. The preposition di, *of*, *to* is used after such verbs as:

kɔmánd- *command*⎫
órdin- *order*   ⎪
prég- *pray, beg*   ⎬ I/Reg/W
skɔnğúr- *beg*   ⎪
viét- *forbid*   ⎭

imped- *impede*⎫
proib- *prohibit*⎬ II/ísK/W
kiéd- *ask, beg*⎫
kɔnčéd- *grant*⎬ IIIb/Reg/S[1,2]

Examples: lopregɔ́ddiandársɛne *he begged him to go away*; leɔrdináronoditačére *they ordered her to be silent.*

ii. The preposition aˣ, *to* is used after such verbs as invít- *invite* and insépɲ- *teach*, both I/Reg/W, and pɛrsuád- *persuade* IIIa/Reg/S[1, 2]: e.g. minvitáronoaččɛnáre *they invited me to dine*; ʎipɛrsuásɛroappartíre *they persuaded him to depart.* After métt- *put, send* IIIb/Reg/S[1, 2] and dá- *give* IV/Irr/S[1], an infinitive introduced by aˣ *to* has passive meaning: darɔ́allaváreipánni *I'll give* (i.e. *send*) *the clothes to be washed.*

iii. The preposition daˣ, *from* is used after dissuád- *dissuade* IIIa/Reg/S[1, 2] and distɔ́ʎʎ- *dissuade* IIIb/Irr/S[1, 2]: e.g. lodissuásɛrodalluččídɛrsi *they dissuaded him from killing himself.*

5. Clause, with the meanings of:

a. Direct object, normally (but not always) introduced by keˣ⁀ *that*, seˣ⁀ *if* or another conjunction, or an interrogative element: e.g. víde kennónkomparívanessúno *he saw that no one appeared*; sivéde kekkuéllavočina mɛlasónfigurátaɪo *you can see that I imagined that little voice* (Pinocchio I); pɛrsɛntíre seččérakuálkevvočina *to hear if there was some little voice* (ibid.); dímmi kíséi *tell me who you are.*

Use of a Timeless tense in a direct object clause indicates doubt or uncertainty, or non-assurance of authenticity, and is very widespread after verbs or expressions meaning *say, think, believe, know*, etc., particularly in the negative or in interrogative sentences: e.g. nónsɔkkómeandásse *I don't know how it went* (*happened*); móltiitaliáni krédono kettúttiʎamɛrikáni síanoríkki *many Italians think all Americans are rich*; sipuóddíre keppartísseattastóni *you might say that he left gropingly* (Pinocchio IX); pɛrvedére kekkósačifóssedéntro *to see what there was inside*; kredéva sitrattássedunragácco *he thought it was a question of a boy*; paréva vɛníssedalláltromóndo *it seemed (that) it came from the other world.* It is obligatory after such verbs as desíder- *desire* I/Reg/W and vɔl- *wish* IIIa/Irr/S[1] and expressions of similar meaning: e.g. voléva keʎʎinsepɲássilitaliáno *he wanted me to teach him Italian.*

b. Adverbial complement, always introduced by a conjunction or relative element: e.g. kuándofuarrivátoaunčértopúnto, sifɛrmɔ́ˣ *when he had gotten to a certain point, he stopped* (Pinocchio XI); méntrekamminával, ilkuórɛʎʎibattévafórte *while he walked, his heart was beating violently*; sɛnnónlavórano, tántopéǧǧopɛrlóro *if they don't work, so much the worse for them*; loammonírono kɛnnómparlásse *they admonished him not to speak* (lit. *that he not speak*). After seˣ⁀ *if* and kuándo⁀ *when* referring to future time, the verb in the dependent clause is in Present B: lofarɔ́kkuándopotrɔ́ˣ *I'll do it when I'm* (lit. *when I'll be*) *able.* After kuándo⁀ *when* and other conjunctions or equivalent phrases referring to past time, the Past C tense of an auxiliary verb in a perfect phrase is used: e.g. kuándoébbɛročɛnáto *when they had dined.*

The use of a Timeless tense of the verb in the dependent clause is:

i. Obligatory, after certain conjunctions or conjunctional phrases, including:

ačč`ɔ`kkéˣ⁀ *in order that*   kuándo⁀ *if*
affìnkéˣ⁀ *in order that*   kuàlóra⁀ *if*
ankòrkéˣ⁀ *even though*   kuantúnkue⁀ *however much*
appàttokéˣ⁀ *on condition that*   nònkéˣ⁀ *not that*
bénkéˣ⁀ *although*   nónostántekéˣ⁀ *notwithstanding that*
dovúnkue⁀ *wherever*   ónde⁀ *so that* (purpose)
eččèttokéˣ⁀ *except that*   pùrkéˣ⁀ *provided that*
fuórkeˣ⁀ *except that*   sebbéne⁀ *although*
kásɔmái⁀ *in case*   seppúre⁀ *even if*

Examples: sebbénefóssemóltolɔntánodallaspiáǧǧa *although he was very far from the shore* (Pinocchio XIII); pùrkéllofáčča *provided that he do it*; affìnképpóssanokapíre *so that they can understand.*

    ii. Optional, use of the Timeless indicating anticipation or purpose, after such conjunctions or conjunctional phrases as:

asséɲɲokéˣ⁀ *so that*   kosìkkéˣ⁀ *so that*
attálpúntokéˣ⁀ *to such an extent that* pɛrkéˣ⁀ *so that, in order that*
avántikéˣ⁀ *before*   prìmakéˣ *before*
dimaniérakéˣ⁀ ⎫   sìkkéˣ⁀ *so that*
            ⎬ *in such a way that* tàlméntekéˣ⁀ ⎫
dimódokéˣ⁀ ⎭   ⎬ *so much that*
kéˣ⁀ *(so) that*   tántokéˣ⁀ ⎭

Examples: aspettándo keilčukíno avéssetúttoiltémpodimɔríreaffogáto *waiting for the little donkey to have* (lit. *so that the little donkey should have*) *all the time to die by drowning* (Pinocchio XVIII); spiególlakósa dimódokettúttipotésseɛrokapíre *he explained the matter in such a way that all might understand*; pɛrkéččandásse *so that he might go there*; prìmakéllamíkoarrivásse *before his friend arrived*.

    The dependent clause is in the negative after certain verbs, such as bád- *take care* and sospétt- *suspect* (both I/Reg/W) and tém- *fear* IIIa/Reg/W; after certain verbal phrases such as nóndúbit- *not to doubt* I/Reg/W and nónéss-dúbbio *not to be doubtful* IIIb/Irr/S[1]; and after certain conjunctions, such as fìnkéˣ⁀ and fíntántokéˣ⁀ *until*: e.g. témo kɛnnónsíaimpossíbile *I'm afraid it's impossible*; nóndúbito kɛnnónsíapossíbile *I don't doubt it's possible*; aspettóffìnkénnónarrivásse ilsúamíko *he waited until his friend arrived*.

    After the conjunction seˣ⁀ *if*, the use of a verb in Timeless C refers to a condition contrary to fact: e.g. seilmíobábbo fóssekuíˣ *if my daddy were only here!*; seavéssikapíto *if I had only understood!*. Such a clause usually depends on a verb in Past B: e.g. seilmíobabbo fóssekuíˣ, nónmɔriréidifáme *if my daddy were here, I wouldn't be dying of hunger*; sevvɔlésti, potrésti *if you wanted, you could* (lit. *would be able*).

    6. A minor clause, consisting of conjunction + infinitive, referring to the same agent as the main verb: nónsapévo settɔrnáreindiétro *I didn't know whether to turn back*; éroinčérto dóvetrovárlo *I was uncertain where to find him*.

    4.14. ADVERBIAL phrases have the following types of structure:

    1. Attribute + Head, the attribute being:

a. An adverb or equivalent phrase: e.g. móltobéne *very well*; tróppogràvɛménte *too gravely*; ɔrrìbilméntɛmále *horribly badly*.

b. A noun or equivalent phrase, in expressions of time: e.g. dúemésipríma *two months before*; tréǧǧórnidópo *three days after*.

2. Head + Attribute, the latter being:

a. An adverb or equivalent phrase, this position implying emphasis in contrast to the order Attribute + Head: e.g. máledavvéro *really badly*.

b. An exocentric (preposition-plus-object) phrase, modifying the adverbs piú^x *more*, méno *less*, other adverbs or equivalent phrases indicating comparison (e.g. méʎʎo *better*, péǧǧo *worse*), and kosí^x *so, as*. The preposition introducing the phrase is:

i. After an expression denoting comparison in greater or less degree:

A. di, *than* (or, less often, ke^x, *than*) before a substantive (head) or pronoun or equivalent phrase: e.g. piúddɛllitália (or piúkkɛllitália) *more than Italy*; piúddimíllekilómetri *more than a thousand kilometers*; ménodité^x *less than you*; péǧǧodilóro *worse than they*.

B. ke^x, *than* before a form of another class: e.g. piúkkevvérde *more than green*; piúkkɛmmái *more than ever*.

ii. In an expression denoting comparison in an equal degree, kóme^x *as:* e.g. kosíkkómevvói *just like you* (lit. *so as you*); or da^x, *so as to* before an infinitive: e.g. kosíddaofféndɛrvi *in such a way as to offend you*; or, either after tánto *so much* or alone, by kuánto (*as*) *much*: e.g. tántokuántovói *as much as you*.

c. A clause:

i. After expressions denoting comparison in greater or less degree, introduced by ke^x⌢ *than* and containing a finite verb in a Timeless tense, normally preceded by nón *not*: e.g. piúkkɛnnónsikredésse *more than people thought* (lit. *more than people didn't think*).

ii. After expressions denoting comparison in an equal degree, introduced by kóme^x *as*: e.g. kosíkkómeffáččoío *just as I do*; or, after tánto *so much*, introduced by kuánto *as much*: e.g. féčetántokuántopoté^x *he did as much as he was able*. In this type of attribute clause, the verb is normally in a non-Timeless tense.

Adverbial phrases of the types analyzed in subsections b and c immediately preceding are normally discontinuous when serving as attributes modifying substantives (usually adjectives) or adverbs, the adverb of comparison (piú^x *more*, méno *less*, kosí^x *as*, méʎʎo *better*, péǧǧo *worse* etc.) preceding the head it modifies, and the remainder of the adverbial phrase (the TERM OF COMPARISON) following: e.g. lafáme érapiúffórtedɛllapaúra *hunger was stronger than fear*; kínesáppiúddilóro *he who knows more about it than they*; unɔmínopiúllárgokɛllúngo *a little man more broad than tall*; kosískɔrtésedaofféndɛrla *so discourteous as to offend her*; éttántoššókkokuántosgarbáto *he is as foolish as* (*he is*) *awkward*; ékkosíintɛlliǧéntekómevvɔlɔntɛróso *he's as intelligent as* (*he is*) *willing*.

4.15. PREPOSITIONAL phrases consist of an adverb or exocentric (prepositionplus-object) phrase + a preposition (usually di, *of* or a^x, *at, to*): e.g. kóntrodi,

202 DESCRIPTIVE ITALIAN GRAMMAR

against; séncadi₁ *without*; déntrodi₁ *inside of*; kuántoaˣ₁ *as to, as for*; dappártedi₁ *on the part of*; pervíadi₁ and akkáusadi₁ *because of*; avvantáǧǧodi₁ *to the advantage of*; aɔnórdi *to the honor of*; frammézzoaˣ₁ *between*; etc.

4.16. Conjunctional phrases are constructed of adverb, preposition or exocentric (preposition-plus-object) phrase + conjunction (usually keˣ⌒ or kéˣ⌒ *that*): e.g. séncakéˣ⌒ *without that*; affínkéˣ *for the purpose that, so that*; pɛrkéˣ⌒ *so that*; sɛnnónké⌒ *except that* (lit. *if not that*); etc. Conjunctional phrases constructed of finite verbal form + conjunction (e.g. avvéɲɲakéˣ⌒ *although*, lit. *let it happen that*) are now archaic.

4.2. Exocentric Phrases are of the following types:

4.21. Preposition + Object, in which a preposition or equivalent phrase is followed by a substantive (head), a pronoun or a verbal infinitive, or an equivalent phrase (including all the complements that can accompany a verbal core, as outlined in §4.13): e.g. nɛllabottéga *in the shop*; diunvékkiofàllɛɲɲáme *of an old carpenter*; pɛrviadɛllapúnta *because of the tip*; dɛlsúonáso *of his nose*; kómeunačiliéǧamatúra *like a ripe cherry*; kómettúttiʎʎáltri *like all the others*; dallagrámpaúra *from the great fear*; dallɛparóle aifátti *from (the) words to (the) deeds*; pɛrméˣ *for me*; séncavói *without you*; kɔnnessúno *with nobody*; pɛraččéndɛreilfuóko *to light the fire*; kɔminčóaddíre *he started to say*; abbuttárlosulfuóko *on throwing it on the fire*; séncakapíre *without understanding*; etc. etc. etc. After in₁ *in* and kɔn₁ *with*, the definite article always precedes a verbal infinitive: e.g. kɔllandárdɛltémpo *with the passing of time*; nɛlfárečóˣ *in doing this*.

A phrase of this type consisting of di₁ *of* + the definite article + a substantive (head) or equivalent phrase has partitive meaning (some, any): e.g. dɛlpáne (*some*) *bread*; dɛllakárne (*some*) *meat*; dɛʎʎisbáʎʎi (*some*) *mistakes*; dɛllegrandíssimestupidáǧǧini (*some*) *enormous stupidites*.

A phrase consisting of in₁ *in* + a numeral or a substantive (head) phrase containing a numeral as attribute, indicates the number of persons or things involved as agents: e.g. siámointréˣ *there are three of us* (lit. *we are in three*); čandárɔnoinčínkue *five of them went there* (lit. *they went there in five*); nótoǧókodikárte, kessifáddɔrdinário inkuáttroǧokatóri *a well-known card-game, ordinarily played by* (lit. *in*) *four players* (Cappuccini-Migliorini, Vocabolario della Lingua Italiana 1694, sv. *tressette*).

A phrase introduced by aˣ₁ *on* or dópo *after* introducing a substantive head modified by a past participle attribute has the meaning of a temporal clause: e.g. abbattáʎʎafiníta *when the battle was finished*; dópoammaccátotéˣ *after you've been killed* (Pinocchio IX).

A preposition-plus-object phrase often has as the object of the preposition a substantive (head) further modified by a following adverb or equivalent phrase or exocentric (preposition-plus-object) phrase: e.g. kɔllalínguagiúččɔndɔlóni *with his tongue hanging dangling down* (Pinocchio I); kɔʎʎiókkifuóridɛlkápo *with his eyes out of his head* (ibid.). Less frequently the modifying adverb occurs between the preposition and its object: e.g. kɔndéntrounɔmínopiččínopiččíno *with a very little man inside* (Pinocchio XIII).

4.22. Substantival phrases with adverbial function have the structure: attribute (past participle) + head, in either this order or the reverse (the so-called 'nominative absolute', often in imitation of the Latin ablative absolute): e.g. eččettuátalasvíccera *except for Switzerland*; túttokonsideráto *all things considered*; čóffátto or fáttočóˣ *this having been done*; čóddétto *this having been said, when this had been said*; déttofátto *no sooner said than done*. A similar construction with a present participle is now literary or bureaucratic: e.g. vivéntemíamádre *while my mother was living*.

4.23. VERBAL phrases with adverbial function are of the following types:

1. The verbal forms sóno *they are* (often preceded by ór *now*) with a substantive (head) subject, or fáˣ preceded by a substantive (head) object, referring to time past, and equivalent in meaning to English . . . *ago*: e.g. piúddikuáttromésiórsóno *more than four months ago*; alkúniǧórnifáˣ *a few days ago*.

2. A 2.sg. imperative repeated two or three times, with durative adverbial meaning (*by* . . . *-ing, after much* . . . *-ing*): e.g. kréššikréšši *gradually* (lit. *by growing*); kammínakammínakammína *after much walking* (Pinocchio VIII); aspéttaaspéttaaspétta, vídekennónkomparívanessúno *after waiting a long time, he saw that no one appeared* (ibid. X); eskávaskávaskáva, féčeunabúkaprofónda *and by dint of much digging, he made a deep hole* (ibid. XII).

4.24. RELATIVE CLAUSES, normally (but not always) introduced by relative elements (adjectives, pronouns, adverbs) serve as exocentric phrases in that they take the place of substantival and adverbial attributes in substantive (head) phrases (§4.111.4.c), pronominal phrases (§4.12.2), verbal phrases (§4.133.5) and adverbial phrases (§4.14.2.c). For examples of these uses, cf. the sections cited.

5.0. TYPES OF CLAUSES. A MAJOR clause is one which contains a predicate (§5.11), with a finite verb as its center; a MINOR clause is one which does not contain a predicate, particularly a non-verbal form or phrase used as a complete utterance, or a special form such as čáo *hi!*, *good-bye!* or aimé˟ *woe is me!*.

5.1. MAJOR CLAUSES.

5.11. THE PREDICATE is the essential part of normal major-clause utterance, having as its center a finite verb form or equivalent phrase: e.g. kantáva *he was singing*; eppartírono *and they left*; ópperdúto *I have lost*; guárda *look!*; impikkiámolo *let's hang him!*; ékkoči *here we are*; kɔmínčaóra *let's start now*; lóvvɛndúta *I've sold it* (f.sg.); nónkapísko *I don't understand*; mispiegɛrómmέʎʎo *I'll explain myself better*; finíkkiedéndoğustícia *he ended up begging for justice*; ʎapríllepórtedɛllapriğóne *he opened for him the doors of the prison*; korrévaassálti kómeunkánlevriéro *he ran in leaps like a greyhound dog*; etc. etc.

Used in an independent predicate, a verb in Timeless A has a meaning of command or wish: e.g. véngapúre *just let him come*; víva *long may he live!*; of concession: e.g. síapúrvéro *even if it be true*; or of wonder or questioning: e.g. kekkósasíakuéstamúsikaↄ *What might this music be?* (Pinocchio VI). A verb in Timeless C used similarly indicates a wish contrary to present fact: kosíppotéssilevármilafáme *if I could only get rid of my hunger thus!* (Pinocchio XIV); fóssepúrvéro *if it were only true!*; lavéssisapútopríma *if I had only known it beforehand!*.

5.111. NEGATIVE PREDICATES have always a negative element—most often nón *not* or né˟ *neither*—preceding the predicate: e.g. nónkapísko *I don't understand*; nónlofaččo *I don't do it*; nónʎɛneóddáto *I haven't given him any of it*. Other negative elements, such as nessún- *no (one)* adj/I–II, núlla or niénte *nothing* prons., or mái *never* adv/IV, may either precede the verbal core, in which case no other negative element is present, or follow the verbal core, which is then preceded (as stated above) by nón *not* or né˟ *neither*: e.g. nessúnomivíde or nónmivídenessúno *no one saw me*; nónvédoniénte *I don't see anything* (lit. *I don't see nothing*).

The nouns míka (lit. *crumb*) and púnto (lit. *point*) are used as complements after negative verbal expressions, with emphatic meaning: nónlokrédomíka *I don't believe it at all*; nónóppúntofáme *I'm not at all hungry*.

5.112. SEQUENCE OF TENSES in subordinate clauses containing verbs in a Timeless tense and used as attributes in substantival phrases (§4.111.4.c), verbal phrases (§4.133.5) or adverbial phrases (§4.14.2c.), is determined by the tense of the verb in the predicate of the clause in which the subordinate clause is included (the MAIN clause). The presence of a verb in Past A or C, or of a perfect phrase containing a Past B, in the main clause calls for a Timeless C (alone or in a perfect phrase) in the subordinate clause; with a verb in the main clause in a tense other than those specified, the verb of the subordinate clause is in Timeless A. Examples: krédokɛllosáppia *I think he knows it* (Present A—Timeless A) ∼ kredévokɛllosapèsse *I thought he knew it* (Past A—Timeless C); témokeéʎʎinónsíaarriváto *I'm afraid he's arrived* (Present A—Timeless A in perfect phrase) ∼ tɛméikeéʎʎinónfóssearriváto *I was afraid he had arrived* (Past C—Timeless C in perfect phrase). Use of a verb in Timeless C in a subordinate clause with a non-past verb in the main clause indicates remoteness (including in time) or unlikelihood: e.g. nónsɔ́kkómeandásse *I don't know how it happened* (lit. went); nessúnosospettɛrá keilkɔlpévɔlefósselúi *nobody will suspect that the guilty one might be he.* Use of a verb in Timeless A in a subordinate clause with a past tense verb in the main clause indicates a generic situation (the 'aoristic present'): e.g. nónsapévomái kekkɔ́sasidébbafáreinkuélkáso *I never knew what ought to be done in that case.*

5.12. The Subject is a substantive (head)—including a verbal infinitive—or pronoun, or equivalent phrase, or a clause, optionally accompanying the predicate, and indicating the agent more specifically than does the person and number reference inherent in the finite verbal form of the predicate: e.g. kuéilíbri sónovérdi *those books are green* ∼ sónovérdi *they are green*; ilpovɛrétto émórto *the poor fellow's dead* ∼ émmórto *he's dead*; kiéʐ *Who is it?*; midispiáče kessíamaláto *I'm sorry* (lit. *it displeases me*) *that he's sick.* Personal pronouns occur as subjects only in the stressed nominative form, except that in current speech lúi *him, he* and léi *her, she, you* are normally used instead of éʎʎi *he* and élla *she, you*, which latter forms are now very formal or literary. Use of a simple personal pronoun subject indicates especial emphasis: e.g. díče *he says* ∼ lúidíče or éʎʎidíče *HE says*; siámovɔlútiandáre *we wanted to go* ∼ nóisiámovɔlútiandáre *WE wanted to go*; íotidóvvéntisóldi *I* (emphatic) *will give you twenty cents*; nɛmménɔlúiévvɛnúto *he didn't come either.* The pronoun kíˣ used without interrogative intonation (§1.53) means *he who* (definite) with a following non-Timeless verb, and *who(so)ever* (indefinite) with a following Timeless verb: e.g. kítróppovuóle, niénteáˣ *he who wants too much, gets nothing*; nóntifidáre dikítáofféso *don't trust him who has harmed you*; kíábbiaʃáttɔlaguérra sipuórréndɛrkóntodikuésto *whoever has fought* (lit. *made war*) *can realize this.*

5.121. Agreement of Subject and Predicate. The finite verbal form of a predicate agrees with the subject in:

1. Person, in that the predicate is in the lowest-numbered person contained in the subject (a substantive or equivalent phrase, and all non-personal pronouns, counting as third person): e.g. íotróvo *I find*; nóipɛnsiámo *we think*; túkrédi *you believe*; vóiandáte *you go*; lúidíče *he says*; kíloáddéttoʐ *Who said so?*; ilsópɲofiníˣ *the dream ended*; nóievvói čandrémo *you and we will go there*; vóiellóro čandréte *you and they will go there.*

2. Number, in that the verb of the predicate is in the highest number represented in the subject: e.g. kuéstɔragácco ébbuóno *this boy is good*; kuéstiragácci sónobuóni *these boys are good*; íoevvói lofarémo *you and I will do it.* With a compound subject, the verb of the predicate is normally plural: e.g. arlekkínoeppulčinélla esitárɔno *Harlequin and Punch hesitated*; pinɔ́kkio, lučípɲolo, ettúttiʎʎaltriragácci divɛntárɔnoʎʎamíčiditútti *Pinocchio, Lucignolo and all the other children became everybody's friends* (Pinocchio XVIII); leóre iǧórni lesettimáne passávanokómettántibaléni *the hours, the days, the weeks passed like so many lightning flashes* (ibid.). Occasionally, however, a predicate is in the singular, agreeing with the nearest element of the subject: e.g. unaparóla, unčénno, unindíciokualsíasi potévatradírlo *a word, a sign, any indication might betray him.*

In arithmetical formulas, an entire subject phrase may be treated as singular or plural: e.g. kuáttroettré fássétte (or fánnosétte) *four and three make seven*. On the other hand, a plural predicate is often found with a singular subject of collective meaning: e.g. túttokuélgrúppodiğénte éranoarrivátiinsvíccera *all that group of people had arrived in Switzerland* (subj. m.sg., pred. m.pl.).

5.122. TIMELESS TENSE IN SUBJECT CLAUSE occurs when a clause is subject of a predicate containing such verbs as:

$$\left.\begin{array}{l} \text{dispiáč- } \textit{displease} \\ \text{piáč- } \textit{please} \end{array}\right\} \text{IIIa/Irr/S}^1$$

rinkrésK- *cause sorrow* IIIb/Reg/S[1, 2]

Example: midispiáče (or mipiáče, or mirinkréšše) kessíamaláto *it displeases me* (or *it pleases me* or *it causes me sorrow*, i.e. *I'm sorry*) *that he is sick.*

5.13. ORDER OF ELEMENTS in a major clause is quite free, and subject to considerable variation.

5.131. THE SUBJECT may occur either preceding or following the verb; the position following the verb implies somewhat greater emphasis than that preceding the verb: e.g. ilkárroarrivóˣ or arrivóilkárro *the cart arrived*; íovádo or vádoío *I'll go*; lotirávano dódičiparíʎʎedičukíni *twelve pairs of little donkeys were pulling it*. The subject normally follows the verb in an intercalated clause (§5.134); cf. examples there given.

5.132. COMPLEMENTS of the verb, insofar as they are free forms not forming part of the verbal core (§4.132), normally follow it, most often in the order: adverb + direct object + other complements (first exocentric phrases and then clauses): e.g. vuóidármi kuáttrosóldi dikuéstabbečedárionuóvo? *Do you want to give me four cents for this new primer?* (Pinocchio V); nónkómpronúlla dairagácci *I don't buy anything from boys* (ibid.); illíbro fúvvendútolíˣ suddúepiédi *the book was sold there on the spot* (lit. *on two feet*) (ibid.); portárɔnopinókkiointriónfo ailúmidɛllaribálta *they carried Pinocchio in triumph to the footlights* (Pinocchio VI); dávaspessodeiregáli aifiʎʎuóli, kuándotɔrnávaakkása *he often used to give presents to his children, when he came back home.*

But a complement may precede the verb, under the following conditions:

1. In a relative or interrogative clause, the relative or interrogative element or the phrase containing it precedes the verb: e.g. eddóvɛmivɔlétekɔndúrreɖ *And where do you want to take me?*; kévvuóidammeˣɖ *What do you want from me?*; kuántéddistántedikuí ilkámpodeimirákɔliɖ *How far from here is the Field of Miracles?*; pɛrkívuóiillíbroɖ *Who do you want the book for?*; kuándoʎʎipárve keffóssɛlóra *when it seemed to him that it was time*; liníkuafróde dikúiérastátovíttima *the unfair deception of which he had been the victim.*

2. Other types of complements may precede the verb, with added emphasis accruing from this position: e.g. nɛllaparétedifóndo sivedévaunkaminétto *on the back wall was seen a fireplace* (Pinocchio II); allóra, dópoʎʎókki ʎiféčeilnáso *then, after the eyes he made his nose* (ibid.); allafíne, eppɛrbuónafɔrtúna, kapitóunkarabiniére *finally, and through good luck, there arrived a carabineer* (ibid.). When a subject is present, the complement(s) which precede the verb may precede the subject also, or may intervene between subject and verb: e.g. allóra labókka sméssedirídɛre *then the mouth stopped laughing* (Pinocchio II); appéna-

finítɛlɛmáni, ğeppétto sɛntíppɔrtársivíalaparrúkkadalkápo *scarcely had he finished the hands (than) Geppetto felt his wig snatched off his head* (ibid.); but also ğeppétto, pɛrnónguastáreifáttisuɔ́i, fínsedinónavvedérsɛne *Geppetto, so as not to spoil his work, pretended not to notice it* (ibid.); mállağénte keéraperlavía, vedéndokuéstoburattínodiléɲɲo kekɔrrévakómeunbarbéro, sifɛrmávainkantátaaguardárlo *but the people who were in the street, on seeing this wooden marionette which was running like a race-horse, stopped enchanted to watch him* (ibid.)

A special construction of this type is that of past participle + the conjunction keˣ⁀ in the meaning *when* + an auxiliary verb, the whole forming a subordinate clause containing a perfect phrase, with the meaning *when . . . had . . .*: e.g. sméssokeffúddipiɔ́vɛre *when it had stopped raining*; skríttakeébbilaléttɛra *when I had written the letter*.

5.133. Recapitulation of Complements. A conjunctive pronoun or adverb may occur affixed to the verb of a predicate with the same reference as an accompanying direct object complement or a phrase of the types substitutable by či, and vi, *here, there* or ne, *of it* (§2.41). This type of double reference is normal when the direct object (especially a clause) or phrasal complement precedes the verb: e.g. ibuğárdi nónlipɔ́ssosoffríre *I can't stand liars* (lit. *liars, I can't stand them*); ilgátto tɛlodɔ́ío *I'll give you the cat* (Pinocchio III); kuésto nónlopɔ́ssokrédɛre *I can't believe this*; kekkuéstosíavéro nónlokrédo *I don't think that this is true*; dikuattríni nónneɔ́mmólti *I don't have much money* (lit. *of coins I don't have many of them*). In current colloquial speech, this type of construction is widespread, even two complements being recapitulated in this fashion:[1] e.g. illíbro ammíopádre nónʎelɔ́ankóradáto *I haven't given my father the book yet* (lit. *the book to my father I haven't yet given it him*).

5.134. Intercalated Clauses occur in the middle of utterances, especially referring to the speaker and action of quotation, or vocative minor clauses (§5.22): e.g. viprɔmétto, dísseilburattíno, keddaɔ́ğğiinpɔ́i sarɔ́bbuɔ́no. *'I promise you,' said the marionette, 'that from today on I'll be good'* (Pinocchio V); túttiiragácci, replikɔ́ğğeppétto, kuándovɔ́ʎʎɔnoottɛnérekuàlkɔ́sa, díkɔnokosíˣ. *'All children,' replied Geppetto, 'when they want to get something, talk that way.'* (ibid.); allóra, ragáccomío, divértitiasbadiʎʎáre. *Then, my boy, amuse yourself by yawning* (Pinocchio XIV); etc.

5.2. Minor Clauses are all such clauses as do not contain a predicate, i.e. have no finite verbal core. Any minimum free form or phrase may occur as a minor clause utterance, and often, especially in animated conversation, minor clauses form the greater part of a series of successive utterances: e.g. the following dialogue (Pinocchio XIII), in which there are eight minor and four major clauses:

Pinocchio: kuántočé dikuíallaspiáğğa¿ *How far is it from here to the shore?* (Major)

Pigeon: piúddimíllekilɔ́metri. *More than a thousand kilometers.* (Minor)

Pinocchio: míllekilɔ́metri? A *thousand kilometers?* (Minor) ókkɔlómbomío, kébbéllakósa potéssiavérɛletúeáli. *Oh my Pigeon, how wonderful if I could have your wings!* (2 Minor)

[1] Cf. P. Meriggi, Volkstum und Kultur der Romanen 11.1–30 (1938).

Pigeon: sevvuɔívɛníre, tičipórtoío. *If you want to come, I'll carry you there.* (Major)

Pinocchio: kómeǰ *How?* (Minor)

Pigeon: akkavállo sullamíagróppa. *Astride of my back.* (Minor) sɛipésodi-mólto? *Are you very heavy?* (Major)

Pinocchio: péso? *Heavy?* (Minor) túttáltro. *Anything else but!* (Minor) sónleǧǧɛrokómeunafóʎʎa. *I'm as light as a leaf.* (Major)

The following types of minor clauses call for special mention:

5.21. INFINITIVAL minor clauses, i.e. those whose main element is a verbal infinitive, occur with the following meanings:

1. With a negative element (normally nón *not*), in complementary distribution with the 2.sg. imperative and having the meaning of a negative imperative: e.g. nónčibadáre *don't pay any attention to it!*; nónmipikkiártántofórte *don't hit me so hard!* (Pinocchio I); nómpratikárekuéllabírbadilučíɲɲɔlo *don't associate with that rascal Lucignolo* (Pinocchio XVII). Note that in this type of minor clause with negative imperative meaning, conjunctive elements are prefixed, not suffixed, to the infinitive (§4.132).

2. With or without accompanying subject, an exclamation or question indicating surprise, wonder, indignation etc.: e.g. eppɛnsáre keppotrébbɛrodivɛntáredɔmáni mílaoddúemíla *and to think that they might tomorrow become one thousand or two thousand!* (Pinocchio XI); burlármidivói? *Make fun of you?*; ío fáreunakósasímile? *I, do something like that?*.

3. Preceded by aˣ, *to* and always accompanied by a subject, the so-called 'infinitive of narration', indicating vivid action without reference to time: e.g. eilpóvɛroǧeppétto akkórrɛrʎidiétro *and poor Geppetto ran after him* (Pinocchio II); eppinókkio annuotárepiúlléstokɛmmái *and Pinocchio swam more quickly than ever* (ibid. XVIII).

4. Preceded by an interrogative element, with the meaning of a general question with no specific agent indicated: kéffáreǰ *what to do?*; kómespiegárʎeloǰ *How to explain it to him?*; pɛrképparláreǰ *Why talk?*; dóveandáreǰ *Where to go?*.

5.22. VOCATIVE use is made of substantives or pronouns, standing alone or coordinated with other clauses: ǧovǎnni *John!*; brŭno *Bruno!*; ǧúlia *Julia!*, faréste, galàntuómo, lakaritáddunsóldo aumpóvɛroragácco? *Would you, good man, give the alms of a penny to a poor boy?* (Pinocchio XIV); allóra, ragáccomío, divértitiasbadiʎʎáre *then, my boy, amuse yourself by yawning.* A substantive phrase with demonstrative adjective may also be used as a vocative: éi, kuélluómɔlaǧǧúˣ *Hey, that man there!* (i.e. *you there!*). Vocatives often occur coordinated with special minor-clause forms (§5.23.2): e.g. óppádre *O father!*; éitú *hey, you!*.

5.23. SPECIAL FORMS, used only as minor clauses, occur with such meanings as those of:

1. Affirmation and negation: e.g. síˣ *yes*; nóˣ *no*.

2. Calling attention: éi *hey!*; óˣ *O, oh*; ɔláˣ *hey there!*, etc.

3. Exclamation (surprise, pleasure, pain, disgust, hesitation, onomatopoeia, etc.): e.g. ái *ow!*; oibóˣ *golly!*; pú or puá *phew, phooey!*; urráˣ *hurray!*; pŝt *pst, sh!*; dín dón *ding dong*; etc.

APPENDICES

CHAPTER VI. ITALIAN ORTHOGRAPHY

Italian orthography is relatively simple, with generally consistent representation of Italian phonemes and morphemes. Most of its deficiencies are those of multiple representation of single phonemes and of inadequate or incomplete symbolization of stress, juncture and pitch contours.

6.1. VOWELS are represented by the five letters *a e i o u*: the open vowels /ɛ ɔ/ by *e* and *o* respectively, and the other vowel phonemes /i e a o u/ by the corresponding letters: e.g. víno *vino* 'wine'; púre *pure* 'yet'; bélla *bella* 'beautiful'; póko *poco* 'little'. Unstressed /ii/ at the end of a word is mostly written *i*, occasionally *î* or *j*, in the m.pl. ending of substantives: e.g. stúdii *studies* (m.pl.), spelled *studi(i)*, *studî* or *studj*.

6.2. CONSONANTS are represented by the sixteen letters *b c d f g l m n p q r s t v x z*. Irregularities in representation occur primarily in the guttural-palatal series.

1. Guttural-palatal consonants are represented as follows:

a. Triple representation is used for the phoneme /k/: before unstressed /u/ + V, by *q*; before the letters *e, i*, by *ch*; elsewhere, by *c*: e.g. kuíˣ *qui* 'here'; keˣ‿ *che* 'that'; kitárra *chitarra* 'guitar'; kokómɛro *cocomero* 'cucumber'; kúlo *culo* 'arse'. Exceptions: sokkuádro *soqquadro* 'confusion'; kuóre *cuore* 'heart'; kuóio *cuoio* 'leather'; kuóko *cuoco* 'cook'; kuóč- *cuoc-* 'cook' (vb.).

b. Double representation is used:

i. With different spellings before the letters *e, i* ~ elsewhere, for:

Phoneme	Spelling	
	Before *e, i*	Elsewhere
g	*gh*	*g*
č	*c*	*ci*
ǧ	*g*	*gi*
š	*sc*	*sci* (but *sc* at end of words)

Thus: gíro *ghiro* 'dormouse'; góla *gola* 'throat'; čénto *cento* '100'; čarláre *ciarlare* 'to chat(ter)'; ǧeláre *gelare* 'to freeze'; ǧardíno *giardino* 'garden'; šímmia *scimmia* 'ape'; šókko *sciocco* 'foolish'; marakéš *Marakesc* 'marrakesh:

In a few words, /č/ is optionally spelled *ci* and /š/ *sci* before the letter *e*, especially in substantive plural endings: e.g. kamíče *camic(i)e* 'shirts'; čéko *blind*, normally spelled *cieco* and thus distinguished from the homonymous čéko *ceco* 'Czechish'; šénca *scienza* 'science'. Such spellings occasionally give rise to spelling-pronunciations, e.g. čiéko for čéko *blind* or šiénca for šénca *science*.

ii. With different spellings before the letter *i* ~ elsewhere: the phoneme /ʎ/, spelled *gl* before *i* and *gli* elsewhere: e.g. ʎi, *gli* 'to him'; ʎɛne, *gliene* 'to him of it'; vóʎʎa *voglia* 'wish'; imbróʎʎo *imbroglio* 'mess'.

c. Single representation is used for /ɲ/, spelled *gn*: e.g. ɲókki *gnocchi*.

2. Other consonants all have single representation, as follows:

a. The phonemes /c/ and /z̨/ are both represented by z:[1] e.g. cámpa *zampa* 'paw'; z̨élo *zelo* 'zeal'.

b. The remaining phonemes are spelled with the same letters as those used in IPA and in our transcription, i.e. *p t b d f v m n l s² r:* e.g. páče *pace* 'peace'; tónno *tonno* 'tuna-fish'; bárba *barba* 'beard'; dólče *dolce* 'sweet'; fóndo *fondo* 'bottom'; váso *vaso* 'glass'; mólto *molto* 'much'; nóno *nono* 'ninth'; lána 'wool'; sálsa *salsa* 'sauce'; ráro *raro* 'rare'.

3. The consonant letter *h* stands for no separate phoneme; it is used in the graphs *ch* and *gh* (representing /k g/ before *e, i*; cf. above, §6.2.1.a, b.i), and elsewhere only in foreign words and in the spelling of the verbal forms ɔ̃ˣ *I have*, ái *thou hast*, áˣ *he has* and ánno *they have*, usually spelled respectively *ho, hai, ha, hanno*. (Cf. also §6.4.1.b.iv.)

The letters *k, w* and *y* are normally used only in the spelling of words borrowed from foreign languages; they are usually pronounced /k v i/, respectively: e.g. kódak *kodak*; váter *water* 'W.C., flush-toilet'; árri *Harry*. There is often confusion between *i, j* and *y*, between *v* and *w*, and between *h* and zero, in the spelling of foreign words and names: I have seen, in cinema posters in Rome, the spellings *Immj* (Jimmy) and *Arwej* (Harvey).

4. Double consonants are represented as follows:

a. In separate words:

i. The germinate clusters /ɲɲ ʎʎ šš/, occurring only intervocalically and always in that position, are represented by the same graphs as are the single phonemes, i.e. *gn, gl(i)* and *sc(i)*: e.g. báɲɲo *bagno* 'bath'; fóʎʎa *foglia* 'leaf'; ášša *ascia* 'axe'.

ii. Other geminate clusters are represented by the appropriate graph with its first letter doubled, except that the letter *q* is doubled as *cq*: e.g. bállo *ballo* 'dance'; mátto *matto* 'crazy'; sékki *secchi* 'dry'; máǧǧo *Maggio* 'May'; except in sokkuádro *soqquadro* 'confusion'.

b. Between morphemes in phrases, the doubling of an initial consonant represented by /ˣ/ in our transcription is written only in certain set phrases customarily spelled as one word: e.g. eppúre *eppure* 'and yet'; sebbéne *sebbene* 'although'; dakkápo *daccapo* 'again'. In other instances, it is not indicated: e.g. vábbéne *va bene* 'all right (lit. it goes well)'; éttróppo *è troppo* 'it's too much'; róbadammátti *roba da matti* 'nonsense (lit. stuff for crazy people)'.

5. Other consonant clusters are represented by the appropriate combinations of individual representations, except that /ks/, in the one base in which it occurs (uksor- *uxor-*), is represented by *x*: e.g. uksoričída *uxoricida* 'uxoricide'.

6.3. ELISION is represented by the use of an apostrophe (') after the elided form: e.g. unáltravólta *un' altra volta* 'another time'. But the apostrophe is

---

[1] In dictionaries and grammars, voiced /z̨/ is often represented by ž, z̨, ʒ or some similar special character: e.g. méžžo *half*, spelled *mèżżo, mèžžo, mèʒʒo*, etc. But this distinction is not customary in everyday spelling.

[2] In dictionaries and grammars, the voiced allophone [z] of the phoneme /s/ is often represented by ś, ş or ʃ: e.g. rósa *rose*, spelled *ròśa, ròşa, ròʃa*. This distinction, likewise, is not customary in ordinary writing.

not used in m.sg. forms in which a vowel precedes the final consonant: e.g. unáltroamíko *un altro amico* 'another friend'; umbéllamíko *un bell' amico* 'a fine friend'.

6.4. STRESS is represented as follows:

1. Full stress, when at all, is shown by the use of the acute accent (´) and of the grave accent (`) written over vowel letters. The acute is used only over the letters *e* and *o*, to represent the close vowels /e o/, and occasionally over *i* and *u*; the grave is used elsewhere: e.g. sé˟ *se* 'himself'; bótte *bótte* 'cask'; partí˟ *partì* or *partí* 'he departed'; tribú˟ *tribù* or *tribú* 'tribe'; etá˟ *età* 'age'. But in current usage,[3] consistent representation of full stress is given only on the last syllable of a written word, and only in:

a. Polysyllabic words ending in /˟/ and stressed on the final syllable: e.g. vɛrró˟ *verrò* 'I'll come'; kaffé˟ *caffè* 'coffee'.

b. Monosyllabic words:

i. Containing *i* or *u* followed by a stressed vowel: e.g. puɔ́˟ *può* 'he can'; ǧá˟ *già* 'already'.

ii. Certain monosyllables which are homonymous, except for the presence of stress, with others, and written with an accent mark to distinguish them:

Stressed	Unstressed
dá˟ *dà* gives'	da˟ˌ *da* 'from'
dí˟ *dì, dí* 'day'	diˌ *di* 'of'
é˟ *è* 'is'	e˟ *e* 'and'
ké˟⁀ *ché* 'for'	ke˟⁀ *che* 'that'
lí˟ *lì, lí* 'there'	liˌ *li* 'the'
sé˟ *sé* 'himself'	se˟⁀ *se* 'if'
sí˟ *sì, sí* 'yes'	siˌ *si* 'himself'

iii. Monosyllabic words used as the last elements of compounds: e.g. rifá˟ *rifà* 'he does again'; viǧɛré˟ *viceré* 'viceroy'; lassú˟ *lassù* or *lassú* 'up there'.

iv. In some usage, especially scientific writing, the grave accent is used instead of initial *h*- in the spelling of ɔ́˟ *ò* 'I have', ái *ài* 'thou hast', á˟ *à* 'he has', ánno *ànno* 'they have'.

2. Intermediate and weak stress are indicated by absence of accent mark: e.g. pɔ̀rtabagáʎʎi *portabagagli* 'porter', and the other examples cited heretofore.

3. Emphatic stress is represented by the writing of an exclamation mark after the utterance in which the emphatic stress occurs: e.g. ǧovǎnni *Giovanni!* 'John!'.

4. The circumflex accent mark (ˆ) is never used to indicate stress; it occurs occasionally over *i* at the end of a word standing for unstressed /ii/ (§6.1) of the m.pl.: e.g. desidérii *desiderî* 'desires'; and occasionally instead of the grave accent

---

[3] A complete and consistent system of stress indication has been proposed by G. Malagòli, L'accentazione italiana (Firenze, 1945), but this system has as yet not found general acceptance.

A thorough and complete discussion of Italian orthography is given by A. Camilli, Pronouncia e Grafia dell'Italiano² (Firenze, 1947)—not accessible to the writer until after this book was in press.

to distinguish a word from a homonym: e.g. vólto *vôlto* or *vòlto* 'turned' ~ vólto *volto* 'face'.

6.5. JUNCTURE. Close juncture is indicated, within morphemes, by absence of space in writing; cf. the examples given heretofore. Inflectional and derivational juncture is likewise symbolized by absence of space: e.g. andiámo *andiamo* 'we go'; dispɛràtaménte *disperatamente* 'desperately'. Open juncture and phrasal and clausal juncture are indicated by spaces between morphemes thus joined, except in the case of:

1. Conjunctive elements suffixed to verbal forms (§4.132.2.a), which are written together with the verbal forms: e.g. kɛllofačésse *che lo facesse* 'that he did it', but midíssedistudiárlo *mi disse di studiarlo* 'he told me to study it'.

2. Combinations of the prepositions:

aˣ₁ *to*	nɛˣ₁ (:in₁) *in*	pɛˣ₁ (:pɛr₁) *for, by*
daˣ₁ *from*	kɔˣ₁ (:kɔn₁) *with*	suˣ₁ *on*
dɛˣ₁ (:di₁) *of*		

with the definite article: e.g. aʎʎi₁ *agli* 'to the' (m.pl.); dal₁ *dal* 'from the' (m.sg.); dɛlla₁ *della* 'of the' (f.sg.); sulle₁ *sulle* 'on the' (f.pl.); etc.

3. Certain set phrases written as one word: e.g. dakkápo *daccapo* 'again'; dimólto *dimolto* 'greatly'.

Morphemes written separately in phrasal and clausal juncture are spelled in their basic forms, and consequently assimilations resulting from close juncture (§1.4) are, in such position, not represented in writing: e.g. umbuómbánko *un buon banco* 'a good bench'.

6.6. PITCH-CONTOURS are represented by the same symbols as used in our transcription: comma, period and question-mark; except that the falling intonation /ɛ̀/ is written *?*. Thus: dópodavérlouččíso, sɛneandóˣ *dopo d'averlo ucciso, se ne andò* 'after having killed him, she went away'; séikuíˣ? *sei qui?* 'Are you here?'; dóvevváiɛ̀ *dove vai?* 'Where are you going?'.

The use of other signs of punctuation (semi-colon, colon, quotation-marks etc.) and of capitalization is determined by non-linguistic factors, and will not be treated here.

6.7. THE ITALIAN ALPHABET in its customary order, with the intercalation (indented) of multiple graphs and accented letters, and their phonemic values, is here given for reference:

Letter or Graph	Phoneme(s) Represented
a	a
b	b
c	K (č before front vowels, k elsewhere)
ch	k before front vowels
ci + vowel letter	č before back vowels
d	d
e	e ɛ
é	é
è	ɛ̀

Letters and Graph	Phoneme(s) Represented
f	f
g	*G* (ǧ before front vowels, g elsewhere)
gh	g before front vowels
gi + vowel letter	ǧ before back vowels
gl(i) + vowel letter	ʎ (usually; sometimes gl)
gn	ɲ
h	No sound; cf. §§6.2.3, 6.4.2.d
i	i
î, j	ii (cf. §6.1)
l	l
m	m
n	n
o	o ɔ
ó	ó
ò	ɔ́
p	p
q	k before unstressed /u/ + V (but cf. §6.2.1.a)
r	r
s	s
sc	s*K* (š before front vowel, sk elsewhere)
sci	š before back vowel
t	t
u	u
v	v
x	ks
z	ʒ c

For the letters *k w y*, cf. §6.2.3.

CHAPTER VII. SAMPLE VERB PARADIGMS AND IRREGULAR FORMS

In this appendix will be given: 1) sample paradigms of verbs (regular and auxiliary); 2) a listing of verb roots in whose inflection there is irregularity in any of the forms, with citation of the irregular forms.

7.1. PARADIGMS.

7.11. REGULAR VERBS. As sample regular verbs will be chosen pórt- *carry* I/Reg/W; dórm- *sleep* II/Reg/W; fin- *finish* II/ísK/W; and bátt- *beat* IIIb/ Reg/W. (All verbs of Conjugation IV are irregular in some respect.) The forms based on Stems A, B and C will be given in the order mentioned, first the finite and then the non-finite forms based on each stem.

Present A ('Present Indicative')

1.sg.	pórto	dórmo	finísko	bátto
2.sg.	pórti	dórmi	finíšši	bátti
3.sg.	pórta	dórme	finíšše	bátte
1.pl.	portiámo	dormiámo	finiámo	battiámo
2.pl.	portáte	dormíte	finíte	battéte
3.pl.	pórtano	dórmɔno	finískɔno	báttɔno

Past A ('Imperfect')

1.sg.	pɔrtávo	dɔrmívo	finívo	battévo
2.sg.	pɔrtávi	dɔrmívi	finívi	battévi
3.sg.	pɔrtáva	dɔrmíva	finíva	battéva
1.pl.	pɔrtavámo	dɔrmivámo	finivámo	battevámo
2.pl.	pɔrtaváte	dɔrmiváte	finiváte	batteváte
3.pl.	pɔrtávano	dɔrmívano	finívano	battévano

Timeless A ('Present Subjunctive')

1.–3.sg.	pórti	dórma	finíska	bátta
1.pl.	pɔrtiámo	dɔrmiámo	finiámo	battiámo
2.pl.	pɔrtiáte	dɔrmiáte	finiáte	battiáte
3.pl.	pórtino	dórmano	finískano	báttano

Imperative

2.sg.	pórta	dórmi	finíšši	bátti
1.pl.	pɔrtiámo	dɔrmiámo	finiámo	battiámo
2.pl.	pɔrtáte	dɔrmíte	finíte	battéte

Non-Finite[1] A (Gerund)

Adv/II	pɔrtándo	dɔrméndo	finéndo	batténdo

214

Non-Finite[2] A (Present Participle)

Adj/IIIb	portánte	dərménte	finénte	batténte

Present B ('Future')

1.sg.	portɛró[x]	dərmiró[x]	finiró[x]	battɛró[x]
2.sg.	portɛrái	dərmirái	finirái	battɛrái
3.sg.	portɛrá[x]	dərmirá[x]	finirá[x]	battɛrá[x]
1.pl.	portɛrémo	dərmirémo	finirémo	battɛrémo
2.pl.	portɛréte	dərmiréte	finiréte	battɛréte
3.pl.	portɛránno	dərmiránno	finiránno	battɛránno

Past B ('Conditional')

1.sg.	portɛréi	dərmiréi	finiréi	battɛréi
2.sg.	portɛrésti	dərmirésti	finirésti	battɛrésti
3.sg.	portɛrébbe	dərmirébbe	finirébbe	battɛrébbe
1.pl.	portɛrémmo	dərmirémmo	finirémmo	battɛrémmo
2.pl.	portɛréste	dərmiréste	finiréste	battɛréste
3.pl.	portɛrébbero	dərmirébbero	finirébbero	battɛrébbero

Non-Finite B (Infinitive)

m/IIIb	portáre	dərmíre	finíre	báttere

Past C ('Preterite')

1.sg.	portái	dərmíi	finíi	battéi
2.sg.	portásti	dərmísti	finísti	battésti
3.sg.	portó[x]	dərmí[x]	finí[x]	batté[x]
1.pl.	portámmo	dərmímmo	finímmo	battémmo
2.pl.	portáste	dərmíste	finíste	battéste
3.pl.	portárəno	dərmírəno	finírəno	battérəno

Timeless C ('Past Subjunctive')

1.-2.sg.	portássi	dərmíssi	finíssi	battéssi
3.sg.	portásse	dərmísse	finísse	battésse
1.pl.	portássimo	dərmíssimo	finíssimo	battéssimo
2.pl.	portáste	dərmíste	finíste	battéste
3.pl.	portássero	dərmíssero	finíssero	battéssero

Non-Finite C (Past Participle)

Adj/I–II	portáto	dərmíto	finíto	battúto

7.12. Auxiliary Verbs (§4.131.1), i.e. av- *have* IIIa/Irr/S[1] and éss- *be* IIIb/Irr/S[1]:

	Present A		Past A	
1.sg.	ó[x]	sóno	avévo	éro
2.sg.	ái	séi	avévi	éri

3.sg.	áˣ	éˣ		avéva	éra
1.pl.	abbiámo	siámo		avevámo	ɛravámo
2.pl.	avéte	siéte		aveváte	ɛraváte
3.pl.	ánno	sóno		avévano	érano

Timeless A			Imperative		
1.–3.sg.	ábbia	sía	2.sg.	ábbi	síi
1.pl.	abbiámo	siámo	1.pl.	abbiámo	siámo
2.pl.	abbiáte	siáte	2.pl.	abbiáte	siáte
3.pl.	ábbiano	síano			

Present B			Past B		
1.sg.	avróˣ	saróˣ		avréi	saréi
2.sg.	avrái	sarái		avrésti	sarésti
3.sg.	avráˣ	saráˣ		avrébbe	sarébbe
1.pl.	avrémo	sarémo		avrémmo	sarémmo
2.pl.	avréte	saréte		avréste	saréste
3.pl.	avránno	saránno		avrébbɛro	sarébbɛro

Past C			Timeless C		
1.sg.	ébbi	fúi		avéssi	fóssi
2.sg.	avésti	fósti			
3.sg.	ébbe	fúˣ		avésse	fósse
1.pl.	avémmo	fúmmo		avéssimo	fóssimo
2.pl.	avéste	fóste		avéste	fóste
3.pl.	ébbɛro	fúrɔno		avéssɛro	fóssɛro

Non-Finite B			Non-Finite C	
avére	éssɛre		avúto	[(es)súto][1]

Non-Finite[1] A			Non-Finite[2] A	
avéndo	esséndo		avénte	[essénte][1]

7.2. IRREGULAR FORMS are listed in this section under the root to which they belong. Roots are given in alphabetical order,[2] with indication of their conjugation type. Forms not listed herein are understood to be regular; optional forms are enclosed in parentheses. Irregular Present B and Past B tenses are listed only in the 1.sg., and it is understood that the rest of the tenses follow, in their endings, the models given in §7.11; for 'strong' verbs with irregular rhyzotonic forms of Past C, only the 1.sg. is given and it is understood that the 3.sg. and 3.pl. have the endings indicated in §2.35.3, 6 and exemplified for av- *have* in §7.12.

aččénd- *light* IIIb/S[1, 2]: Past C 1.sg. aččési. Non-Finite C aččés-.
akkórG- *notice* IIIb/Reg/S[1, 2]: Past C 1.sg. akkórsi. Non-Finite C akkórt-.
and- *go* I(x)/Irr/W: Present A 1.sg. vádo (vóˣ), 2.sg. vái, 3.sg. váˣ, 3.pl. vánno.

[1] Archaic and not in present everyday use. The past participle essúto *been* is normally replaced by státo (:stá- stand IV/Irr/S[1]): e.g. sónostáto.
[2] Alphabetical order is that of the normal Roman alphabet, with special characters immediately following the normal characters which they most closely resemble, and capitals following small letters.
As the list given here is intended for reference purposes only, detailed cross-references to the sections in which the irregularities are discussed are not given; it is hoped to do this in a forthcoming Italian Lexicon.

Timeless A 1.–3.sg. váda, 3.pl. vádano. Imperative 2.sg. vá^x. Present B 1.sg. and(ε)rɔ́^{x}. Past B 1.sg. and(ε)réi.

ápr- *open* II/Reg/S$^{1,\,2}$: Past C 1.sg. apérsi. Non-Finite C apért-.

árd- *burn* IIIb/Reg/S$^{1,\,2}$: Past C 1.sg. ársi. Non-Finite C árs-.

assíd- *seat* IIIb/Reg/S$^{1,\,2}$: Past C 1.sg. assísi. Non-Finite C assís-.

attínG- *draw* IIIb/Reg/S$^{1,\,2}$: Past C 1.sg. attínsi. Non-Finite C attínt-.

bév- *drink* IIIb(x)/Reg/S^1: Present B 1.sg. (bɛrrɔ́^{x}). Past B 1.sg. (bɛrréi). Non-Finite B bé(vε)re. Past C 1.sg. bévvi.

$^+$čéd- *-cede* IIIb/Reg/S$^{1,\,2}$: Past C 1.sg. $^+$čéssi. Non-Finite C $^+$čésso.

$^+$číd- *-cide, -cise* IIIb/Reg/S$^{1,\,2}$: Past C 1.sg. $^+$čísi. Non-Finite C $^+$čís-.

čínG- *gird* IIIb/Reg/S$^{1,\,2}$: Past C 1.sg. čínsi. Non-Finite C čínt-.

dá- *give* IV/Irr/S^1: Present A 1.sg. dɔ́^{x}, 2.sg. dái, 3.sg. dá^x, 3.pl. dánno. Timeless A 1.–3.sg. día. Past C 1.sg. diédi, 2.sg. désti. Timeless C 1.sg. déssi.

díK- *say* IV/Irr/S$^{1,\,2}$: Present A 2.pl. díte. Imperative 2.sg. dí^x, 2.pl. díte. Non-Finite B díre. Past C 1.sg. díssi. Non-Finite C détt-.

dilíG- *love* IIIb/Reg/S$^{1,\,2}$: Past C 1.sg. diléssi. Non-Finite C dilétto.

divíd- *divide* IIIb/Reg/S$^{1,\,2}$: Past C 1.sg. divísi. Non-Finite C divís-.

dov- *owe* IIIax/Irr/W: Present A 1.sg. dévo (débbo), 2.sg. dévi, 3.sg. déve, 1.pl. dobbiámo, 3.pl. dévəno (débbəno). Timeless A 1.–3.sg. déva (débba), 1.pl. dobbiámo, 2.pl. dobbiáte, 3.pl. dévano (débbano). Present B 1.sg. dovrɔ́^{x}. Past B 1.sg. dovréi.

dɔl- *hurt* IIIax/Irr/S^1: Present A 1.sg. dɔ́lgo (dɔ́ʎʎo), 3.pl. dɔ́lgəno (dɔ́ʎʎəno). Timeless A 1.–3.sg. dɔ́lga (dɔ́ʎʎa), 3.pl. dɔ́lgano (dɔ́ʎʎano). Present B 1.sg. dərrɔ́^{x}. Past B 1.sg. dərréi. Past C 1.sg. dɔ́lsi.

$^+$dúK- *-duce, -duct* IV/Reg/S$^{1,\,2}$: Present B 1.sg. $^+$durrɔ́^{x}. Past B 1.sg. $^+$durréi. Non-Finite B $^+$dúrre. Past C 1.sg. $^+$dússi. Non-Finite C $^+$dótt-.

esíG- *exact* IIIb/Reg/S^2: Non-Finite C esátt-.

esplód- *explode* IIIb/Reg/S$^{1,\,2}$: Past C 1.sg. esplɔ́si. Non-Finite C esplɔ́s-.

fáč- *do*, make IV/Irr/S$^{1,\,2}$: Present A 1.sg. fáččo (fɔ́^{x}), 2.sg. fái, 3.sg. fá^x, 1.pl. faččámo, 2.pl. fáte, 3.pl. fánno. Timeless A 1.sg. fáčča, 1.pl. faččámo, 2.pl. faččáte, 3.pl. fáččano. Imperative 2.sg. fá^x, 1.pl. faččámo, 2.pl. fáte. Present B 1.sg. farɔ́^{x}. Past B 1.sg. faréi. Non-Finite B fáre. Past C 1.sg. féči. Non-Finite C fátto.

$^+$fénd- *-fend* IIIb/Reg/S$^{1,\,2}$: Past C 1.sg. $^+$fési. Non-Finite C $^+$fés-.

fíGG- *fix* IIIb/Reg/S$^{1,\,2}$: Past C 1.sg. físsi. Non-Finite C fítt-.

fínG- *feign* IIIb/Reg/S$^{1,\,2}$: Past C 1.sg. fínsi. Non-Finite C fínt-.

flétt- *bend* IIIb/Reg/S$^{1,\,2}$: Past C 1.sg. fléssi. Non-Finite C fléss-.

$^+$flíGG- *-flict* IIIb/Reg/S$^{1,\,2}$: Past C 1.sg. $^+$flíssi. Non-Finite C $^+$flítt-.

fónd- *melt* IIIb/Reg/S$^{1,\,2}$: Past C 1.sg. fúsi. Non-Finite C fús-.

fránG- *break* IIIb/Reg/S$^{1,\,2}$: Past C 1.sg. fránsi. Non-Finite C fránt-.

fríGG- *fry* IIIb/Reg/S$^{1,\,2}$: Past C 1.sg. fríssi. Non-Finite C frítt-.

$^+$fúlG- *shine* IIIb/Reg/S$^{1,\,2}$: Past C 1.sg. $^+$fúlsi. Non-Finite C $^+$fúlt-.

fúnG- *serve (as)* IIIb/Reg/S$^{1,\,2}$: Past C 1.sg. fúnsi. Non-Finite C fúnt-.

ǧáč- *lie* IIIa/Irr/S^1: Present A 1.sg. ǧáččo, 1.pl. ǧaččámo, 3.pl. ǧáččəno. Timeless A 1.–3.sg. ǧáčča, 1.pl. ǧaččámo, 2.pl. ǧaččáte, 3.pl. ǧáččano. Past C 1.sg. ǧákkui.

ğúnG- *join, arrive* IIIb/Reg/S$^{1, 2}$: Past C 1.sg. ğúnsi. Non-Finite C ğúnt-.

$^{+}$ím- -*eem, buy* IIIb/Reg/S^2: Non-Finite C $^{+}$ént-.

indúlG- *indulge* IIIb/Reg/S$^{1, 2}$: Past C 1.sg. indúlsi. Non-Finite C indúlt-.

intríd- *knead* IIIb/Reg/S$^{1, 2}$: Past C 1.sg. intrísi. Non-Finite C intrís-.

kád- *fall* IIIax/Reg/S^1: Present B 1.sg. kadró^{x}. Past B 1.sg. kadréi. Past C 1.sg. káddi.

kiéd- *ask* IIIb/Reg or Irr/S$^{1, 2}$: Present A 1.sg. (kiéggo), 3.pl. (kiéggono). Timeless A 1.sg. (kiégga), 3.pl. (kiéggano). Past C 1.sg. kiési. Non-Finite C 1.sg. kiést-.

kiúd- *close* IIIb/Reg/S$^{1, 2}$: Past C 1.sg. kiúsi. Non-Finite C kiús-.

$^{+}$klúd- -*clude* IIIb/Reg/S$^{1, 2}$: Past C 1.sg. $^{+}$klúsi. Non-Finite C $^{+}$klús-.

kórr- *run* IIIb/Reg/S$^{1, 2}$: Past C 1.sg. kórsi. Non-Finite C kórs-.

kóʎʎ- *gather* IIIb/Irr/S$^{1, 2}$: Present A 1.sg. kólgo, 3.pl. kólgono. Timeless A 1.–3.sg. kólga, 3.pl. kólgano. Past C 1.sg. kɔlsi. Non-Finite C kólt-.

kɔnósK- *know* IIIb/Reg/S^1: Past C 1.sg. kɔnóbbi.

kópr- kɔpr- *cover* II/Reg/S$^{1, 2}$: Past C 1.sg. kopérsi. Non-Finite C kopért-.

kɔč- *cook* IIIb/Reg/S$^{1, 2}$: Past C 1.sg. kóssi. Non-Finite C kótt-.

$^{+}$kɔt- *shake* IIIb/Reg/S$^{1, 2}$: Past C 1.sg. $^{+}$kóssi. Non-Finite C $^{+}$kóss-.

krésK- *grow* IIIb/Reg/S^1: Past C 1.sg. krébbi.

$^{+}$líd- -*lide* IIIb/Reg/S$^{1, 2}$: Past C 1.sg. $^{+}$lísi. Non-Finite C $^{+}$lís-.

léd- *injure* IIIb/Reg/S$^{1, 2}$: Past C 1.sg. lési. Non-Finite C lés-.

léGG- *read* IIIb/Reg/S$^{1, 2}$: Past C 1.sg. léssi. Non-Finite C létt-.

$^{+}$lúd- -*lude* IIIb/Reg/S$^{1, 2}$: Past C 1.sg. $^{+}$lúsi. Non-Finite C $^{+}$lús-.

mán- *remain* IIIax/Irr/S$^{1, 2}$: Present A 1.sg. $^{+}$mángo, 3.pl. $^{+}$mángono. Timeless A 1.–3.sg. $^{+}$mánga, 3.pl. $^{+}$mángano. Present B 1.sg. $^{+}$marró^{x}. Past B 1.sg. $^{+}$marréi. Past C 1.sg. $^{+}$mási. Non-Finite C $^{+}$mást-.

$^{+}$mérG- *merge* IIIb/Reg/S$^{1, 2}$: Past C 1.sg. $^{+}$mérsi. Non-Finite C $^{+}$mérs-.

mɔr- *die* II(x)/Irr/S^2: Present A 1.sg. muɔ́io, 1.pl. (moiámo), 3.pl. muɔ́iono. Timeless A 1.–3.sg. muɔ́ia, 1.pl. (moiámo), 2.pl. (moiáte), 3.pl. muɔ́iano. Present B 1.sg. mɔr(i)ró^{x}. Past B 1.sg. mɔr(i)réi. Non-Finite C mórt-.

mórd- *bite* IIIb/Reg/S$^{1, 2}$: Past C 1.sg. mórsi. Non-Finite C mórs-.

mɔv- *move* IIIb/Reg/S$^{1, 2}$: Past C 1.sg. móssi. Non-Finite C móss-.

múnG- *milk* IIIb/Reg/S$^{1, 2}$: Past C: 1.sg. múnsi. Non-Finite C múnt-.

naskónd- *hide* IIIb/Reg/S$^{1, 2}$: Past C: 1.sg. naskósi. Non-Finite C naskóst-.

násK- *come into being* IIIb/Reg/S$^{1, 2}$: Past C 1.sg. nákkui. Non-Finite C nát-.

neglíG- *neglect* IIIb/Reg/S$^{1, 2}$: Past C 1.sg. negléssi. Non-Finite C neglétt-.

$^{+}$nɛtt- -*nect, join* IIIb/Reg/S$^{1, 2}$: Past C 1.sg. $^{+}$néssi. Non-Finite C $^{+}$néss-.

nɔč- *harm* IIIb/Irr/S^1: Present A 1.sg. nóččo, 1.pl. noččámo, 3.pl. nóččono. Timeless A 1.–3.sg. nóčča, 1.pl. noččámo, 2.pl. noččáte, 3.pl. nóččano. Past C 1.sg. nókkui.

óffr- *offer* II/Reg/S$^{1, 2}$: Past C 1.sg. offérsi. Non-Finite C offért-.

pár- *appear* IIIax/Irr/S$^{1, 2}$: Present A 1.sg. páio, 1.pl. (paiámo), 3.pl. páiono. Timeless A 1.–3.sg. páia, 1.pl. (paiámo), 2.pl. (paiáte), 3.pl. páiano. Present B 1.sg. parró^{x}. Past B 1.sg. parréi. Past C 1.sg. pársi or párvi. Non-Finite C párs-.

$^{+}$pár- *appear* II/Irr/S$^{1, 2}$-W: as for pár- *appear* IIIax except for Present B and

Past B; for distribution of irregular Past and Non-Finite C, cf. §2.342.4.a.-
ii.D, G.

⁺péll- -pel IIIb/Reg/S¹, ²: Past C 1.sg. ⁺púlsi.   Non-Finite C ⁺púls-.

⁺pénd- -pend IIIb/Reg/S¹, ²: Past C 1.sg. ⁺pési.   Non-Finite C ⁺pés-.

— piáč- please IIIa/Irr/S¹: Present A 1.sg. piáččo, 1.pl. piaččámo, 3.pl. piácč, no.
Timeless A 1.-3.sg. piácča, 1.pl. piaččámo, 2.pl. piaččáte, 3.pl. piáččano.
Past C 1.sg. piákkui.

piánG- weep IIIb/Reg/S¹, ²: Past C 1.sg. piánsi.   Non-Finite C piánt-.

pínG- paint IIIb/Reg/S¹, ²: Past C 1.sg. pínsi.   Non-Finite C pínt-.

pióv- rain, fall IIIb/Reg/S¹: Past C 1.sg. pióvvi.

— pón- put IV/Irr/S¹, ²: Present A 1.sg. póngo, 3.pl. póngono.   Timeless A 1.-
3.sg. pónga, 3.pl. póngano.   Present B 1.sg. pɔrrɔˣ.   Past B 1.sg. pɔrréi.
Non-Finite B pórre.   Past C 1.sg. pósi.   Non-Finite C póst- póst-.

pórG- pórG- offer IIIb/Reg/S¹, ²: Past C 1.sg. pórsi pórsi.   Non-Finite C pórt-
pórt-.

— pɔt- be able IIIax/Irr/W: Present A 1.sg. pósso, 2.sg. puói, 3.sg. puóˣ, 1.pl.
possiámo, 3.pl. póssɔno.   Timeless A 1.-3.sg. póssa, 1.pl. possiámo, 2.pl.
possiáte, 3.pl. póssano.   Present B 1.sg. potróˣ.   Past B 1.sg. potréi.

prénd- take IIIb/Reg/S¹, ²: Past C 1.sg. prési.   Non-Finite C prés-.

⁺prím- -press IIIb/Reg/S¹, ²: Past C 1.sg. ⁺préssi.   Non-Finite C ⁺préss-.

protéGG- protect IIIb/Reg/S¹, ²: Past C 1.sg. protéssi.   Non-Finite C protétt-.

púnG- prick IIIb/Reg/S¹, ²: Past C 1.sg. púnsi.   Non-Finite C púnt-.

rád- shave IIIb/Reg/S¹, ²: Past C 1.sg. rási.   Non-Finite C rás-.

redíG- edit IIIb/Reg/S¹, ²: Past C 1.sg. redássi.   Non-Finite C redátt-.

réGG- rule IIIb/Reg/S¹, ²: Past C 1.sg. réssi.   Non-Finite C rétt-.

rénd- give back IIIb/Reg/S¹, ²: Past C 1.sg. rési.   Non-Finite C rés-.

⁺ríG- -rect IIIb/Reg/S¹, ²: Past C 1.sg. ⁺réssi.   Non-Finite C ⁺rétt-.

rispónd- answer IIIb/Reg/S¹, ²: Past C 1.sg. rispósi.   Non-Finite C rispóst-
rispóst-.

ród- gnaw IIIb/Reg/S¹, ²: Past C 1.sg. rósi.   Non-Finite C rós-.

rómp- break IIIb/Reg/S¹, ²: Past C 1.sg. rúppi.   Non-Finite C rótt-.

— sál- go up II/Irr/W: Present A 1.sg. sálgo, 3.pl. sálg, no.   Timeless A 1.-3.sg.
sálga, 3.pl. sálgano.

— sap- know IIIax/Irr/S¹: Present A 1.sg. sóˣ, 2.sg. sái, 3.sg. sáˣ, 1.pl. sappiámo,
3.pl. sánno.   Timeless A 1.-3.sg. sáppia, 1.pl. sappiámo, 2.pl. sappiáte, 3.pl.
sáppiano.   Present B 1.sg. sapróˣ.   Past B 1.sg. sapréi.   Past C 1.sg. séppi.

— sɛd- sit IIIa/Reg or Irr/W: Present A 1.sg. (séggo), 3.pl. (séggɔno).   Timeless
A 1.-3.sg. (ségga), 3.pl. (séggano).   *? W ?*

⁺síst- -sist IIIb/Reg/S²: Non-Finite C ⁺sistít-.   *— ? W ?*

skrív- write IIIb/Reg/S¹, ²: Past C 1.sg. skríssi.   Non-Finite C skrítt-.

sóffr- suffer II/Reg/S¹, ²: Past C 1.sg. sofférsi.   Non-Finite C soffért-.

sórG- rise IIIb/Reg/S¹, ²: Past C 1.sg. sórsi.   Non-Finite C sórt-.

— sɔl- be wont IIIax/Irr/S²: Present A 1.sg. sóʎʎo, 1.pl. sɔʎʎámo, 3.pl. sóʎʎono.
Timeless A 1.-3.sg. sóʎʎa, 1.pl. sɔʎʎámo, 2.pl. sɔʎʎáte, 3.pl. sóʎʎano.   Non-
Finite C sólit-.

spárG- scatter IIIb/Reg/S¹, ²: Past C 1.sg. spársi.   Non-Finite C spárt-.   *? also s*

perdere has p.p. perso or perduto

-solo
rid

spénG- spénG- *extinguish* IIIb/Reg/S[1, 2]: Past C 1.sg. spénsi spénsi. Non-Finite C spént- spént-.

— spéɲɲ- spéɲɲ- *extinguish* IIIb/Irr/S[1, 2]: Present A 1.sg. spéngo spéngo, 3.pl. spéngɔno spéngɔno. Timeless A 1.–3.sg. spénga spénga, 3.pl. spéngano spéngano.

[+]spérG- -*sperse* IIIb/Reg/S[1, 2]: Past C 1.sg. [+]spérsi. Non-Finite C [+]spérs-.

— stá- *stand* IV/Irr/S[1]: Present A 1.sg. stɔ́[x], 2.sg. stái, 3.sg. stá[x], 3.pl. stánno. Timeless A 1.–3.sg. stía, 1.pl. stiámo, 2.pl. stiáte, 3.pl. stíano. Past C 1.sg. stétti, 2.sg. stésti. Timeless C 1.sg. stéssi.

strínG- *press, squeeze* IIIb/Reg/S[1, 2]: Past C 1.sg. strínsi. Non-Finite C strétt-.

strúGG- *melt* IIIb/Reg/S[1, 2]: Past C 1.sg. strússi. Non-Finite C strútt-.

[+]suád- -*suade* IIIb/Reg/S[1, 2]: Past C 1.sg. [+]suási. Non-Finite C [+]suás-.

[+]súm- -*sume* IIIb/Reg/S[1, 2]: Past C 1.sg. [+]súnsi. Non-Finite C [+]súnt-.

— šéʎʎ- *choose* IIIb/Irr/S[1, 2]: Present A 1.sg. šélgo, 3.pl. šélg no. Timeless A 1.–3.sg. šélga, 3.pl. šélgano. Past C 1.sg. šélsi. Non-Finite C šélt-.

šénd- *descend* IIIb/Reg/S[1, 2]: Past C 1.sg. šesi. Non-Finite C šés-.

šínd- *split* IIIb/Reg/S[1, 2]: Past C 1.sg. šíssi. Non-Finite C šíss-.

— šóʎʎ- *undo* IIIb/Irr/S[1, 2]: Present A 1.sg. šólgo, 3.pl. šólgɔno. Timeless A 1.–3.sg. šólga, 3.pl. šólgano. Past C 1.sg. šólsi. Non-Finite C šólt-.

— táč- *be silent* IIIa/Irr/S[1]: Present A 1.sg. táččo, 1.pl. taččámo, 3.pl. táččɔno. Timeless A 1.–3.sg. táčča, 1.pl. taččámo, 2.pl. taččáte, 3.pl. táččano. Past C 1.sg. tákkui.

ténd- *stretch* IIIb/Reg/S[1, 2]: Past C 1.sg. tési. Non-Finite C tés-.

térG- *wipe* IIIb/Reg/S[1, 2]: Past C 1.sg. térsi. Non-Finite C térs-.

— tɛn- *hold* IIIax/Irr/S[1, 2]: Present A 1.sg. téngo, 3.pl. téngɔno. Timeless A 1.–3.sg. ténga, 3.pl. téngano. Present B 1.sg. tɛrrɔ́[x]. Past B 1.sg. tɛrréi. Past C 1.sg. ténni.

[+]tíngu- -*tinguish* IIIb/Reg/S[1, 2]: Past C 1.sg. [+]tínsi. Non-Finite C [+]tínt-.

tínG- *dye* IIIb/Reg/S[1, 2]: Past C 1.sg. tínsi. Non-Finite C tínt-.

— tóʎʎ- *take* IIIb(x)/Irr/S[1, 2]: Present A 1.sg. tólgo, 3.pl. tólgɔno. Timeless A 1.–3.sg. tólga, 3.pl. tólgano. Present B 1.sg. (tɔrrɔ́[x]). Past B 1.sg. (tɔrréi). Past C 1.sg. tólsi. Non-Finite C tólt-.

tórK- *twist* IIIb/Reg/S[1, 2]: Past C 1.sg. tórsi. Non-Finite C tórt-.

— trá[x]- *draw, pull* IV/Irr/S[1]: Present A 1.sg. trággo, 3.pl. trággono. Timeless A 1.–3.sg. trágga, 3 pl. trággano. Past C 1.sg. trássi.

[+]túnd- -*tude* IIIb/Reg/S[1, 2]: Past C 1.sg. [+]túsi. Non-Finite C [+]tús-.

— ud- *hear* II/Irr/W: Present A 1.sg. ɔ́do, 2.sg. ɔ́di, 3.sg. ɔ́de, 3.pl. ɔ́dɔno. Timeless A 1.–3.sg. ɔ́da, 3.pl. ɔ́dano.

únG- *smear* IIIb/Reg/S[1, 2]: Past C 1.sg. únsi. Non-Finite C únt-.

— usK- *go out* II/Irr/W: Present A 1.sg. ésko, 2.sg. éšši, 3.sg. éšše, 3.pl. éskɔno. Timeless A 1.–3.sg. éska, 3.pl. éskano.

[+]vád- -*vade* IIIb/Reg/S[1, 2]: Past C 1.sg. [+]vási. Non-Finite C [+]vás-.

— vál- *be worth* IIIax/Irr/S[1, 2]: Present A 1.sg. válgo, 3.pl. válg no. Timeless A 1.–3.sg. válga, 3.pl. válgano. Present B 1.sg. varrɔ́[x]. Past B 1.sg. varréi. Past C 1.sg. válsi. Non-Finite C váls-.

in)trudgere -si - ɔo

véd- *see* IIIax/Reg or Irr/S[1, 2]: Present A 1.sg. (véggo), 3.pl. (véggɔno). Timeless A 1.–3.sg. (végga), 3.pl. (véggano). Present B 1.sg. vedrɔ́ˣ. Past B 1.sg. vedréi. Past C 1.sg. vídi. Non-Finite C (víst-).

⁺véll- *pull off* IIIb/Irr/S[1, 2]: Present A 1.sg. ⁺vélgo, 3.pl. ⁺vélgɔno. Timeless A 1.–3.sg. ⁺vélga, 3.pl. ⁺vélgano. Past C 1.sg. ⁺vélsi. Non-Finite C ⁺vélt-.

vɛn- *come* III/Irr/S[1, 2]: Present A 1.sg. véngo, 3.pl. véngɔno. Timeless A 1.–3.sg. vénga, 3.pl. véngano. Present B 1.sg. vɛrrɔ́ˣ. Past B 1.sg. vɛrréi. Past C 1.sg. vénni. Non-Finite C vɛnút-.

vínK- *conquer* IIIb/Reg/S[1, 2]: Past C 1.sg. vínsi. Non-Finite C vínt-.

vív- *live* IIIbˣ/Reg/S[1, 2]: Present B 1.sg. vivrɔ́ˣ. Past B 1.sg. vivréi. Past C 1.sg. víssi. Non-Finite C vissút-, vitt⁺.

vɔl- *wish* IIIax/Irr/S[1]: Present A 1.sg. vóʎʎo, 1.pl. vɔʎʎámo, 3.pl. vóʎʎɔno. Timeless A 1.–3.sg. vóʎʎa, 1.pl. vɔʎʎámo, 2.pl. vɔʎʎáte, 3.pl. vóʎʎano. Present B 1.sg. vɔrrɔ́ˣ. Past B vɔrréi. Past C 1.sg. vólli.

vólG- *turn* IIIb/Reg/S[1, 2]: Past C 1.sg. vólsi. Non-Finite C vólt-.

⁺vólv- *-volve, turn* IIIb/Reg/S[2]: Non-Finite C ⁺vɔlút-.

CHAPTER VIII. THE TREATMENT OF LATIN LOAN-WORDS

8.0. LATIN LOAN-WORDS are borrowed into Italian with great freedom and with a minimum of adaptation to Italian phonology and form-classes, thus providing almost an entire second vocabulary for Italian to draw on, especially in learned discourse. Latin loan-words which are well established in Italian have been treated, for the purpose of this book, as a part of the Italian vocabulary, and their partial resemblances to Italian derivational bases have been discussed in Chapter III: e.g. ⁺klúd- -*clude*:kiúd- *close* or ⁺flor- *flor-*:fióre *flower*.[1] Other Latin words may be borrowed almost without limit; to aid in predicting the Italian form of such borrowings, it is our purpose to enumerate here the phonological and inflectional adaptations made in such words when taken into Italian.

8.1. PHONOLOGICAL ADAPTATION. In general, Latin borrowings are pronounced in accordance with the phonological correspondences of Italian orthography (§6.7).

8.11. STRESS is placed on the syllable on which stress falls automatically in Latin, in substantives in the accusative case: e.g. Lat. augusto- > augústo *Augustus*; but Lat. kaesar(e)- > čésare *Caesar*.

8.12. VOWELS AND DIPHTHONGS are reproduced as follows:

1. Stressed: quantity is disregarded, except in the case of Lat. /o·/, which > It. /ó/ in the next to the last syllable: e.g. čičeróne *Cicero* < Lat. kikero·n(e)-; fetóre *fetor* < Lat. feto·r(e)-. Otherwise, Lat. /o o·/ > It. /ɔ/, and Lat. /e e·/ > It. /ɛ/: e.g. gregório *Gregory* < Lat. grego·rio-; ménsa (*dining-*) *table* < Lat. me·nsa; lukrécia *Lucretia* < Lat. lukre·tia-. The vowels /i a u/ are taken over unchanged: e.g. číppo *cippus* < Lat. kíppo-; arvále *Arval* < Lat. arua·li-; úmbro *Umbrian* < Lat. umbro-. The Latin diphthong /au/ is kept as such: e.g. náuta *sailor* < Lat. nauta-; but Lat. /ae oe/ > /ɛ/: e.g. ménade *Maenad* < Lat. maenad(e)-; čésare *Caesar* < Lat. kaesar(e)-; féto *fetus* < Lat. foeto-.

2. Unstressed: quantity is disregarded, and Latin vowels are kept as such in Italian, with the automatic alternation of It. /e ɛ/ and /o ɔ/ in unstressed position (§1.411.1, 2) and with the replacement of stem-vowels indicated in §8.21: e.g. ekuiparáre *to equate* < Lat. aekuipara·re; lukúllo *Lucullus* < Lat. lukullo-; moníle *necklace* < Lat. moni·li-. Diphthongs are treated as when stressed (cf. preceding section); e.g. naufragáre *to shipwreck* < Lat. naufraga·re; ekuipara·re *to equate* < Lat. aekuipara·re. But unstressed /u/ before a vowel (spelled *v* in the modern writing of Latin) > It. /v/: e.g. varróne *Varro* < Lat. uarro·n(e); vésta *Vesta* < Lat. uesta-; and initial unstressed /i/ before a vowel > It. /ǧ/: e.g. ǧámbo *iamb* < Lat. iambo-; ǧúlio *Julius* < Lat. iu·lio-.

8.13. CONSONANTS:

1. Single consonants:

a. Lat. /k g/ > It. /K G/; /t k/ before /iV/ > /c/; e.g. čésare *Caesar* < Lat. kaesar(e).; veǧécio *Vegetius* < Lat. uegetio-.

---

[1] As a result, of course, many historical sound-changes are listed, in reverse order, in the replacements of phonemes enumerated in §3.0.

b. Lat. /h/ > It. 0: e.g. ɔrácio *Horace* < Lat. horatio-.

c. Other consonants are rendered by the same phonemes in Italian: e.g. brúto *Brutus* < Lat. bru·to-; katóne *Cato* < Lat. kato·n(e); mémmio *Memmius* < Lat. memmio-; etc.

2. Consonant clusters:

a. The Latin clusters /gn/ and /gl/ are kept in initial position but /gn/ in medial position > /ɲɲ/: e.g. gnáio *Cnaeus* < Lat. gnaio-; gličério *Glicerius* < Lat. glike·rio-; but íɲɲeo *igneous* < Lat. igneo-.

b. Lat. /sk/ > It. /sK/ and /ks/ > It. /ss/: e.g. šipióne *Scipio* < Lat. skipio·n(e); masséncio *Maxentius* < Lat. maksentio-. But /ks/ is often kept in eks⁺ *ex-* and uksɔr⁺ *uxor-*.

c. Other Latin clusters are kept or simplified as indicated in §1.221, 222: e.g. fragménto framménto *fragment* < Lat. fragmento-; plága *region* Lat. plaga-; etc.

8.2. INFLECTION.

8.21. SUBSTANTIVES (normally nouns) are transferred as follows:

1. Number formation:

a. Italian stem is based on Latin nominative in Lat. neuter stems ending in at-, and Italian form-class is Ib: e.g. dógma *dogma* m/Ib < Lat. dogma(t)-.

b. Italian stem is based on Latin stem in other Latin borrowings, and Italian form-classes are as follows:

Latin stem ends in:	Italian form-class:
-a	Ia (f.), Ib (m.)
-o-, -u	IIb
-i, 0²	IIIb
-e	IIId

Thus: vésta *Vesta* < Lat. uesta-; čínna *Cinna* < Lat. kínna; mário *Marius* < Lat. mario-; ído *Ide* < Lat. idu-; arvále *Arval* < Lat. arua·li-; effíǧe *effigy* < Lat. effigie-. But the Latin suffix ⁺ta·t- *-ty* is replaced by It. ⁺táˣ VId: e.g. idɔneitáˣ *idoneity, fitness* < Lat. idoneita·t-.

2. Gender normally remains the same in m. and f. nouns, with Lat. neuter gender > It. masculine: e.g. ǧúlia *Julia* f/Ia > Lat. iu·lia; čínna *Cinna* m/Ib < Lat. kínna; énnio *Ennius* m/IIb < Lat. ennio-; kástro *castle* < Lat. castro-neuter. But Latin feminines in -u- oscillate: e.g. ído *Ide* m or f/IIb > Lat. idu- f.

8.22. VERBS. In general, only verbs of the Latin 'first conjugation' with imperfective stem in -a·- are borrowed; these are transferred to the Italian conjugation I/Reg/W: e.g. ekuipar- *equate* I/Reg/W < Lat. aekuipara·-; náufrag- *shipwreck* I/Reg/W < Lat. naufraga·-. Verbs of other conjugations are usually adapted phonologically and morphologically to the Italian popular developments of their elements: e.g. manɔmétt- *manumit, set free* IIIb/Reg/S[1, 2] < Lat. manumitte-, adapted to It. máno *hand* f/IIb and métt- *put, send* IIIb/Reg/S[1, 2].

---

[2] That is, Latin 'consonant stems' are treated as if their stem-vowel were the /e/ appearing in acc. or abl. sing.; this /e/ has been given in parentheses in our examples, e.g. Lat. kaesar(e)- *Caesar*.

GLOSSARY OF TECHNICAL TERMS

1. THE PHONETIC TRANSCRIPTION used in Chapter I (enclosed in square brackets) is essentially that of the International Phonetic Association (IPA). The relevant IPA symbols, with brief descriptions in terms of physiological articulation and approximate English equivalents, are as follows:

[a]	Low central vowel, like 'General American' *a* in *father*.
[b]	Voiced bilabial plosive, like *b* in *bite*.
[d]	Voiced dental plosive, like *d* in *dental* (but not alveolar, as in English).
[e]	High-mid front unrounded vowel, like *e* in *they*.
[ɛ]	Low-mid front unrounded vowel, like *e* in *bed*.
[f]	Unvoiced labio-dental fricative, like *f* in *foot*.
[g]	Voiced velar plosive, like *g* in *goon*.
[ĝ]	Voiced pre-velar plosive, like *g* in *gear*.
[i]	High front unrounded vowel, like *i* in *machine*.
[i̯]	High front unrounded semi-vowel, like *y* in *they* or *boy*.
[j]	High front unrounded semi-consonant, like *y* in *yard*.
[k]	Unvoiced velar plosive, like *k* in *kodak*.
[k̂]	Unvoiced pre-velar plosive, like *k* in *keep*.
[l]	Voiced dental lateral, like *l* in *leave*.
[ʎ]	Voiced palatal lateral, somewhat like *lli* in *million*.
[m]	Voiced bilabial nasal, like *m* in *madame*.
[ɱ]	Voiced labio-dental nasal, like *m* pronounced with lips and teeth in position for *f*.
[n]	Voiced dental nasal, like *n* in *nasal* (but not alveolar, as in English).
[ɲ]	Voiced palatal nasal, somewhat like *ni* in *onion*.
[ŋ]	Voiced velar nasal, like *ng* in *singing*.
[o]	High-mid back rounded vowel, like *oa* in *boat*.
[ø]	High-mid front rounded vowel, like *eu* in French *peu*.
[ɔ]	Low-mid back rounded vowel, like *au* in *mauve*.
[p]	Unvoiced bilabial plosive, like *p* in *pope*.
[ɸ]	Unvoiced bilabial fricative, like *f* pronounced with lips in position for *p*.
[r]	Voiced dental trill, like Spanish *r*.
[s]	Unvoiced dental sibilant, like *s* in *sissy*.
[š]	Unvoiced palatal sibilant, like *sh* in *shush*.
[t]	Unvoiced dental plosive, like *t* in *tight* (but not alveolar, as in English).
[θ]	Unvoiced dental fricative, like *th* in *thick*.
[u]	High back rounded vowel, like *oo* in *boot*.
[u̯]	High back rounded semi-vowel, like *w* in *now*.
[v]	Voiced labio-dental fricative, like *v* in *vivacious*.
[w]	High back rounded semi-consonant, like *w* in *west*.
[x]	Unvoiced guttural fricative, like *ch* in German *Bach*.
[z]	Voiced dental sibilant, like *z* in *zebra*.
[ž]	Voiced palatal sibilant, like *s* in *measure*.
[']	Extra heavy stress.

[']   Full stress.

[ˌ]   Stress intermediate between full and weak.

[:]   Indicates that the preceding vowel letter stands for a long vowel sound.

2. THE PHONEMIC TRANSCRIPTION used throughout (enclosed in slant lines wherever necessary to set it off from the surrounding text, otherwise not) is a simplified version of the IPA phonetic transcription, with the omission of certain symbols that represent non-significant positional variants of phonemes, and with the substitution of certain other symbols for convenience and simplicity:

/c/   Unvoiced dental stop with sibilant release [t^s].

/č/   Unvoiced palatal stop with sibilant release [t^š].

/ǧ/   Voiced palatal stop with sibilant release [d^ž].

/ẓ/   Voiced dental stop with sibilant release [d^z].

$\left.\begin{array}{c} '' \\ ' \\ ` \end{array}\right\}$ written over vowel letter $= \left\{\begin{array}{l} \text{emphatic stress } [''] \\ \text{full stress } ['] \\ \text{intermediate stress } [ˌ] \end{array}\right.$

For special symbols representing alternations of phonemes, see §1.6.

3. TECHNICAL TERMS in alphabetical order, with brief definitions. Each term is followed by a symbol indicating which field of linguistics it is used in: P for phonetics and phonemics, M for morphology, and S for syntax.

Agreement (S).   Correspondence in some respect (e.g. gender, number, person) between elements of the same phrase or clause.

Allophone (P).   One of the one or more sounds subsumed under the same phoneme.

Alternant (P, M).   A sound or form which alternates with another sound or form in the same phoneme or morpheme.

Alveolar (P).   Pronounced with the tongue against the upper gum ridge.

Apical (P).   Pronounced with the tip of the tongue.

Assibilate (P).   A sound produced by complete stoppage of the breath and sibilant-like release.

Attribute (S).   An element in a phrase whose form and/or position is determined by another element (the *head*). Traditional term, 'modifier'.

Back (P).   Pronounced with the top of the tongue in the back of the mouth.

Bilabial (P).   Pronounced with both lips.

Bound (M, S).   Not occurring alone; opposite of *free*.

Breath-group (P).   The succession of sounds uttered on a single breath, between two pauses.

Checked (P).   Ending in one or more consonants.

Chest-impulse (P).   The impulse of expulsion of air from the lungs correlated with each syllable.

Clause (S).   The major unit of utterance in a language.

Concordance-class (S).   A class of forms determined by agreement (concordance) required between them and other forms.

Conjunctive (M).   Used only in connection with other forms, in Italian said of pronouns occurring only with verbs.

Consonant (P).   A sound produced by obstruction of the breath-stream and with audible friction.

Derivation (M). The process whereby forms of a given class are made on the basis of other forms of the same or a different form-class.

Dental (P). Pronounced with the tongue against the inside of the upper front teeth.

Disjunctive (M). Used apart from other forms, in Italian said of pronouns whose use is not restricted to accompaniment of verbs.

Dorsal (P). Pronounced with the top of the tongue.

Endocentric (M, S). Whose form-class or function is determined by that of one of the constituent elements (the *head*).

Exocentric (M, S). Whose form-class or function is not determined by that of any of the constituent elements.

Feminine (M). A gender, in Italian restricted in its agreement to other forms of the same gender.

Finite (M). Showing tense, person, and number in its inflectional form.

Flap (P). A sound produced with a single tap of the tongue (or other movable organ of speech).

Form-class (M). A class of forms, determined by criteria of form or syntax. Traditional term, 'part of speech'.

Fortis (P). Pronounced with relatively strong muscular tension.

Free (P). Not ending in a consonant.

Free (M, S). Occurring alone as well as together with other elements.

Fricative (P). A sound produced by channeling the breath through a narrow transverse slit.

Front (P). Pronounced with the tongue in the front of the mouth.

Frontal (P). Pronounced with the top of the tongue.

Gender (M). A category of inflection determined by concordance or agreement; in Italian, feminine or masculine.

Guttural (P). A sound produced with the tongue against the soft palate.

Head (S). The element in a phrase which determines the function of the phrase in larger combinations.

High (P). Pronounced with the top of the tongue raised high in the mouth.

High-mid (P). Pronounced with the top of the tongue raised in the middle of the mouth, but rather high than low.

Homorganic (P). Pronounced in the same position (with the same organs of speech).

Inflection (M). The relation to each other, or the sum total, of minimum forms with the same basic meaning and different grammatical functions.

Isogloss (General Linguistics). The geographical boundary between two areas showing divergent linguistic phenomena for corresponding sounds, phonemes, morphemes, constructions or meanings.

Juncture (P). The manner in which speech sounds are joined or separated.

Labial (P). Pronounced with the lips.

Labio-Dental (P). Pronounced with teeth and lip (usually upper teeth and lower lip).

Lateral (P). A sound produced by passage of the breath-stream over one or both sides of the tongue.

Lenis (P). Pronounced with relatively weak or lax muscular tension.

Low (P). Pronounced with the top of the tongue low in the mouth.

Low-mid (P). Pronounced with the top of the tongue raised toward the middle of the mouth, but rather low than high.

Major clause (S). A clause of the type most favored (occurring most frequently and consistently) in a language; in Italian, a clause containing a finite verb.

Manner (of articulation) (P). The way in which the stream of breath is obstructed in the production of a consonant.

Masculine (M). A grammatical gender; in Italian = non-feminine, not exclusively feminine.

Minor clause (S). Any clause not a major clause; in Italian, one not containing a finite verb.

Minor-clause form (M). A special form used only in minor clauses. Traditional term, 'interjection'.

Morpheme (M). A significant class of linguistic forms, comprising one or more alternants.

Nasal (P). A sound produced with the use of the nasal cavity as a resonance chamber.

Non-Finite (M). Not showing tense, person or number.

Number (M). A category determined by agreement and referring to the number of things; in Italian, singular and plural.

Palatal (P). Pronounced with the tongue against the hard palate.

Past (M). Referring to time restricted exclusively to the past.

Phoneme (P). A significant class of speech sounds, comprising one or more similar sounds (*allophones* or *positional variants*).

Phrase (S). A combination of forms taking the place of a single form in an utterance.

Pitch-contour (P). The pattern formed by the succession of pitches on the syllables of a breath-group.

Plosive (P). A sound produced by a complete stoppage of the breath-stream followed by an explosive release.

Plural (M). Referring to more than one.

Position (of articulation) (P). The place in the mouth where the breath-stream is obstructed in the production of a consonant.

Positional variant (P). Allophone.

Predicate (S). That part of a clause containing a verbal form.

Present (M). Non-past; referring to time not restricted to the past.

Pre-velar (P). Pronounced with the tongue in front of the soft palate.

Root (M). The part of a form remaining relatively constant in sound and meaning throughout its inflection and (in Italian) to which the stem-vowel is added.

Rounded (P). Pronounced with the lips puckered or rounded.

Semi-consonant (P). A sound produced in the position of a vowel (usually a high vowel), but consonantal in being produced by obstruction of the breath-stream and with audible friction.

Semi-vowel (P). A sound produced in the position of a vowel (usually a high vowel), like a vowel in being produced without audible friction, but not the most sonorous sound in the syllable as is a full vowel.

Sibilant (P). A sound produced by the stream of breath being channeled through a narrow depression or trough more or less in the center of the tongue.

Singular (M). Referring to only one.

Stem (M). Root plus stem-vowel.

Stem-vowel (M). A vowel added to the root.

Stress (P). The degree of force with which air is expelled from the lungs.

Subject (S). An element added to the predicate, indicating the actor.

Syllable (P). A segment of a breath-group comprised between two low points of sonority.

Tense (M). A set of verbal forms having the same basic meaning and referring to the same time of action, and differing from each other only in regard to the person and number of the actor.

Timeless (M). Not referring primarily and inherently to any time of the action, whether past or non-past ('present', cf. above s.v. *present*). Traditional term, 'subjunctive'.

Trill (P). A sound produced by repeated flaps or taps of the tongue or other movable organ of speech.

Unrounded (P). Pronounced with the lips not rounded or puckered.

Unvoiced (P). Pronounced without concomitant vibration of the vocal chords.

Velar (P). Guttural.

Verbal core (S). The complex of elements comprising a verbal form and such conjunctive pronouns and/or adverbs as are joined to it.

Voiced (P). Pronounced with concomitant vibration of the vocal chords.

Vowel (P). A sound produced without obstruction of the breath-stream or audible friction.

Zero (P, M). The absence of a significant feature of sound or form, as contrasted with its presence elsewhere.

For definitions of the names of form-classes ('parts of speech'), see the various sub-sections in Chapter 2.